W9-ARH-079

Freedom in My Heart

Freedom in My Heart

VOICES FROM THE UNITED STATES NATIONAL SLAVERY MUSEUM

UNITED STATES
NATIONAL SLAVERY MUSEUM
in association with
NATIONAL GEOGRAPHIC
Washington, D.C.

Contents

An African-American girl attending an elementary school affiliated with the Hampton Normal and Agricultural Institute in a 1905 photograph

Preceding pages: A 1914 photograph captures a family riding into town in Greene County, Georgia.

Contributor Information

AUTHORS

FORMER GOVERNOR L. DOUGLAS WILDER
Foreword

VONITA FOSTER, PH.D.
Introduction

JOHN HOPE FRANKLIN, PH.D.
Epilogue

GOVERNOR TIM KAINE
Afterword

GERALD A. FOSTER, PH.D.
Chapters 6, 7

HEATHER LINDQUIST
Chapters 1, 4, 5, 10

NATALIE ROBERTSON, PH.D.
Chapters 2, 3, 8, 9

CYNTHIA JACOBS CARTER, ED.D.
Sidebars, Galleries

DONNA WELLS
Sidebars

EDITOR

CYNTHIA JACOBS CARTER, ED.D.

ESSAYISTS

IRA BERLIN, PH.D.
Chapter 5

CHARLES BLOCKSON
Chapter 6

AMBASSADOR PAMELA E. BRIDGEWATER
Chapter 2

BILL COSBY, ED.D.
Chapter 4

GERALD A. FOSTER, PH.D.
Chapter 8

DOROTHY HEIGHT, PH.D.
Chapter 9

C. C. PEI
Chapter 10 (A Gallery)

NATALIE ROBERTSON, PH.D.
Chapter 3

PRESIDENT ELLEN JOHNSON-SIRLEAF
Chapter 1

BEN VEREEN
Chapter 7

JUAN WILLIAMS
Chapter 10

"Hallelujah" by sculptor Ken Smith, a celebration of the Emancipation Proclamation, in the U.S. National Slavery Museum's garden

Looking Back at Our History

L. DOUGLAS WILDER, FORMER GOVERNOR OF VIRGINIA

Various books have been written about the history of slavery and the African-American experience, and numerous occasions (mostly involving Black History Month in February) take place in which it forms a part, yet one finds little structured education on slavery and its effects. Notable is the lack of zeal among those in our public school systems to place any emphasis on slavery as a part of America's history or what has subsequently taken place in the U.S. as a result of slavery. This lack of knowledge or desire to become more educated about the history of slavery in the United States is amazing in and of itself, and such an omission of that part of our history affects us today.

GEOGRAPHY IS NO EXCUSE

I find it surprising when people say they know nothing about slavery because they live in a certain part of the country, thereby exempting themselves from needing to know about their history. This is especially surprising in view of fully documented instances of how the North "promoted, prolonged, and profited from slavery," in the words of the subtitle of *Complicity,* a study of the North's profit from and dependence on slavery.

The year in which *Freedom in My Heart* is being published is posing a new question for Americans: whether a person of African ancestry is going to be elected the next President of the United States. That question is pregnant with many underlying issues such as preparedness, qualification, and ability to represent all citizens fairly and whether, in fact, America is ready to elect a President of color.

One of the reasons that I fastened on to the idea to establish a museum dedicated solely to explaining slavery in the U.S. was to show how those enslaved people had come to reclaim their families, restructure their values, and rebuild their hopes. For the most part, all nations in the world have experienced slavery in some degree. Yet the story of American slavery is like none other; African Americans have held a desire for inclusiveness in a society that for so long rejected them.

When we consider our oppression in being kidnapped from our native Africa—where we lived as artisans and craftsmen—and brought to the U.S. in chains to be sold, why should we be any more ashamed of our history of persecution than the Jewish people who experienced Holocaust torment during World War II? Why should we be reluctant to want to learn more about our history, as victims at the hands of those more powerful than we were?

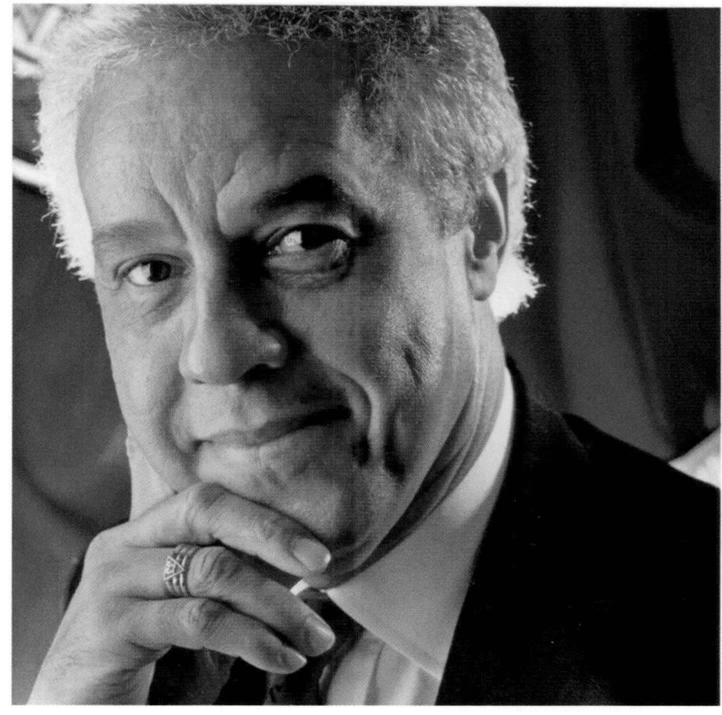

L. Douglas Wilder, the grandson of slaves, in 1989 became the first Black to be elected governor. He later spearheaded the effort to build a national slavery museum.

A DEFINITION OF CITIZENSHIP

When we consider that three of the first four U.S. Presidents owned slaves, it tells you that the American Constitution and the Declaration of Independence were, for the most part, hollow documents until the courts were called upon to make real determinations as to what constituted "citizenship" and what constituted the rights and privileges of all citizens.

I find it fascinating that no mention of citizenship is made anywhere in the U.S. Constitution until the 14th Amendment, following the Civil War, in which it states that all persons "born or naturalized" in the United States should be considered "citizens" thereof. In effect, the Civil War was required to bring about this definition of "citizenship" and an explanation of how it would be applied to all individuals.

A century later, I ran for office in a state that brought the first persons of color to its shores in vast numbers. In the "red-letter year" of 1619 in Virginia, a Dutch frigate landed at Jamestown with some 20 members of color aboard; they were primarily indentured servants yet subsequently were enslaved. Some 25 to 30 years later, slavery was declared legal in Virginia. From that point onward, the largest immigration of Africans and the largest concentration of a slave population occurred right there, in Virginia.

Reflective of our beginnings in the U.S. as slaves, it has long been held that most minorities or ethnic groups must gain entry-level positions to prove what I term as "proficiency in preceding degrees." That is what the Office of Lieutenant Governor allowed me to do. Even though I had once described that office as vacuous, it became a necessary step in terms of my later seeking election to the Office of Governor.

I was elected to lead Virginia in 1989, following my start in political life some 20 years earlier as the first African American to serve in the Virginia State Senate since Reconstruction. I remained in the senate for 16 years before deciding to move up in the governance of Virginia by seeking the Office of Lieutenant Governor in 1985, and later winning the highest office in Virginia—this time, as the first African American anywhere in the U.S. to be elected governor.

JOURNEY TO AFRICA

In 1992, while serving as governor, I led a trade mission to Africa, with Senegal being the first stop on a seven-nation tour. We went to Gorée Island, off the coast of Dakar, the capital of Senegal. There we listened to the griot tell the story of slavery and describe the ordeal of the slaves imprisoned there. We witnessed the slave cells, the auction blocks, and the holding pens. We toured the "room of no return," where slaves would pass through the last door out toward the ocean, before being chained on the waiting ships.

Standing there, a strange and almost surreal experience gripped me. I looked out beyond that room and could vividly imagine the thoughts and fears of those who had made that passage across the ocean, to a land they did not know or understand. Forebears of mine had made that journey, unwillingly, into the unknown. And here I stood centuries later, as the governor of that land where they were enslaved, leading a group of whites to the very place from which those slaves were chained and shipped. I could only think to myself, That's a long journey, and God only knows how many stories along the way there were that had never been told.

That's when the idea first came to me that the story of U.S. slavery must be told, reflecting both the history of the ultimate rise of those "citizens" as well as America's continuing efforts to grapple with the impact of slavery throughout our nation's history. The following year, at the Second African/African-American Summit held in Gabon, where I was asked by the late Leon Sullivan—a civil rights crusader and humanitarian, who established the event in 1991—to give the keynote address, I announced the need for establishing this U.S. slavery museum in Virginia.

OPENING A DIALOGUE

I never envisioned, nor do I now believe, that there was ever a need to affix guilt or blame or to cause people emotional pain for the actions of their forefathers. For most people, this did not even apply. Slave ownership depended on the wealth of an individual, and most Americans were not wealthy. Likewise, for those African Americans whose families had been subjected to the ravages of slavery, the only real need for retribution involved the ultimate expectation of receiving fair and equal treatment under the law.

Today, whether from the Black or white perspective, we see a mixed reaction from those on both sides who either find slavery too painful a subject to discuss or feign an awareness and claim a knowledge of slavery while, in reality, possessing little, if any, true understanding.

Yes, 2008 is a presidential election year in which race is an overriding issue. Yet in an odd way not easily explained, we as a nation have not readily seen the value of confronting our racial origins by looking back at the history of ourselves. Honest, open dialogue is educational. We owe to the present and future generations a true picture of what makes us Americans and how we came to be the great nation that exists today.

I am pleased that National Geographic has taken the initiative to develop a publication like *Freedom in My Heart* that in many ways will serve as a prelude to the rich resources that will be available in the United States National Slavery Museum.

L. Douglas Wilder
Former Governor of Virginia
2008

Introduction

VONITA FOSTER, EXECUTIVE DIRECTOR, U.S. NATIONAL SLAVERY MUSEUM

As you open this book and begin to read, listen to the voices. They are the voices of those who survived slavery, of those who endured its inhumanity, of those who kept freedom in their hearts every day of their lives. Listen to what they're saying as they bear witness to their lives, their experiences, and their contributions. These voices will tell you a story—one that has never been told in its entirety before now. The complete story of slavery in America has remained dormant for too long, and today we begin to reveal a chronicle of a people's struggles, successes, and contributions under the most heinous and cruel conditions imaginable.

THE MUSEUM'S BEGINNINGS

In 1992, then-governor of the Commonwealth of Virginia Lawrence Douglas Wilder announced the need for the creation of a national slavery museum. It would be constructed and located in Virginia, the birthplace of slavery in America. He led a state trade mission to the continent of Africa, and while there visited Gorée Island, located off the coast of Senegal in West Africa.

During the early transatlantic slave trade, this island was one of the several ports of departure for Africans on their way to North America. In 1993, while traveling to Gabon to deliver a keynote address at the Second African American Conference, Governor Wilder announced publicly his commitment to build a national slavery museum in the United States. He began working diligently toward creating the only museum in America that would focus exclusively on telling a more complete story about the institution of American slavery.

As founder and chairman of the board of directors of the museum he received in 2002, from a commercial developer and avid supporter, a gift of 38 acres overlooking the Rappahannock River in Fredericksburg, Virginia. This site would become home to the United States National Slavery Museum and be the birthplace of a new understanding about slavery itself.

THE MUSEUM'S MISSION

The United States National Slavery Museum will serve as the center of learning on slavery, focusing on facts and accurate information not often read about in history books or talked about in classrooms. Slavery is presented in a larger, more expansive and balanced context, revealing the complexity of the institution itself. The museum's exhibitions focus exclusively on repositioning slavery in the history of North America so that we are able to see more clearly slavery's political, economic, and social dimensions. Consequently, the issue of slavery will be a uniting phenomenon rather than a dividing one as visitors come to view and understand slavery in a different and more enlightening manner. Moreover, the temporary exhibits will reveal human rights issues affecting our world today.

The museum will provide the urgently needed common ground where people of all ethnicities and beliefs can discuss, learn, interact, refine, and implement positive changes in our nation. The museum will tell the complete story of the perseverance, contributions, hardships, and struggles of slaves and free Blacks in America. If we learn from our past, we will certainly have a rich future.

We as one people must listen, learn, and remember the truth, and with the creation of the USNSM, we will open the door that heretofore has been closed to most Americans on an important historical issue that will challenge people's thinking by providing knowledge, understanding, and a love for the *entire* American story never quite told in a balanced and accurate manner.

THE ULTIMATE FREEDOM

This wonderful book of the USNSM produced in conjunction with the National Geographic Society entitled *Freedom in my Heart: Voices From the United States National Slavery Museum* chronicles more than 230 years of unprovoked acts of dehumanization visited upon black men, women, and children on a daily basis.

"Freedom in My Heart" not only provides the title of this important book, it also celebrates the hope for slaves and free Blacks and how their true pursuit of liberation sustained them each day as they endured the absurdity of their involuntary servitude.

During the history of the world many people endured the pain of slavery. However, if we look closely and examine the institution of slavery in the Americas, we will observe the rare use of racial superiority as a foundation and justification for its existence. This is why slavery in America is unique when compared with global slavery from the beginning of time to the present day: It grew out of efforts to destroy and deny a culture, a heritage, and objectified Africans as property *for life*. Thus, the quest for freedom and the spirit of freedom in the hearts of many enslaved Africans sustained them and even bolstered their post-slavery travails. We will see that the ultimate freedom that was the exclusive province of the slaves was the indescribable freedom carried within their souls.

The voices, essays, images, and photographs to be found in this publication will become a staple in public and private libraries throughout the United States. The information contained within these covers is simply a prelude to the one-of-a-kind building and grounds overlooking the scenic Rappahannock River in Fredericksburg, Virginia.

But the themes and ideas covered in both this companion book and in the museum galleries are more universal in nature and apply to more than just slavery in the Americas. Slavery is nothing new to social orders. It existed during antiquity and still exists today. Denial of basic human rights remains as wrong in the past as it is in the present. Hopefully the lessons learned from American slavery can help the peoples of the world keep this kind of tragedy from ever happening again.

Vonita Foster, executive director of the U.S. National Slavery Museum, on the site selected for the museum, 38 acres of land overlooking the Rappahannock River in Fredericksburg, Virginia.

A middle-class African-American family dines in a turn-of-the-century photograph by Frances Benjamin Johnston.

CHAPTER ONE

We Are One People

CHAPTER ONE

3.5 mya – 1300s

We Are One People

Africa is where the story begins. Here humans first walked upright and complex civilizations gave birth to rich cultures and new advances. Vast and infinitely varied, Africa's lands and cultures defy easy description, yet both have frequently been oversimplified by myth and obscured by misinterpretation. In books, poems, and polemics, Africa has often been characterized as the Dark Continent, cloaked only by deep jungles and peopled by primitives, as though the great pageant of human evolution, the staggering wonders of Egypt and other ancient civilizations, and precursors to the enduring miracle of writing first existed elsewhere.

In fact, the list of African inventions and innovations is extensive, and ranges from the humble to the sublime, from the everyday practicality of clay cookware and woven basketry to the alchemy of steelmaking. For many years, scholars believed Asia and the Middle East to be the sole locus of most of civilization's key innovations, such as iron smelting, the domestication of livestock, the development of writing, and grain cultivation and storage. In this view, Africa received and adapted inventions rather than contributed its own to the world stage. Yet, more recent research indicates that many of these breakthroughs may have occurred simultaneously and independently in Africa as well.

As eminent paleontologist Mary Leakey once asserted, discovery is shaped by belief: "You only find what you are looking for, really, if the truth be known." Freed from the myth of the "Dark Continent," future generations of students and scholars will undoubtedly unearth further proof of Africa's contributions to the world stage.

This process of rediscovery has already begun in the past several decades. For example, some scholars now concur that the Iron Age probably began in the Anatolian plains of Turkey 6,000 years ago, with the likelihood of an independent origin in Africa. According to archaeological evidence identified during the 1970s, the Haya of northwestern Tanzania knew how to turn raw ore into carbon steel as early as 2,000 years ago. They used deceptively simple tools in combination with a sophisticated preheating process to attain the highest quality steel possible. From this cradle in East Africa, the knowledge of iron smelting quickly spread throughout ancient Africa. By 500 B.C., "the trade of the blacksmith was found all over Africa, from north to south and from east to west," noted anthropologist Franz Boas (1858-1942). "With his simple bellows and a charcoal fire he reduced the ore that is found in many parts of the continent and forged implements of great usefulness and beauty."

Once believed to have first occurred in Asia, the domestication of cattle may also have African origins, according to archaeological evidence from 9,000-year-old African sites in what is now Egypt, including Nabta Playa and Bir Kiseiba. In this same location, archaeologists have unearthed signs of sorghum grain storage and cultivation 8,000 years ago. Thus, when a person today eats grain cereal, drinks a glass of cow's milk, and secures her home with a little steel key before rushing off to work, Africa's legacy is echoed at each step.

Left: Footprints fossilized in the Laetoli beds of Tanzania's Great Rift Valley offer early evidence of bipedalism among Africa's hominids.

Previous pages: Morning clears over the grasslands of Oldonyorok, Tanzania. In the distance lies Mount Maru, one of Africa's highest mountains.

"No great civilization, be it African, Asian, or European developed in total isolation. Why should America then?"

— *Ivan Van Sertima, historian, linguist, anthropologist*

Above all, Africa is our bloodline, the ancestral homeland of all the world's peoples. If the modern human family tree is traced back far enough, approximately 60,000 years ago, it leads to one intrepid group of people who walked out of Africa to populate the globe. A worldwide research project (the Genographic Project) conducted by geneticist Spencer Wells and sponsored by the National Geographic Society has fully substantiated the speculation that Charles Darwin first put forth in *Descent of Man* in 1871: "It is somewhat more probable that our early progenitors lived on the African continent than elsewhere." While great mammals ranged the other continents, humans (hominids) first walked upright, formed societies, raised families, fought, loved, and worshipped on Africa's shores and savannas. As paleontologist Louis Leakey discovered from the abundant fossil record, "Africa was the birthplace of man himself, and . . . for many hundreds of centuries thereafter, Africa was in the forefront of all world progress."

To reclaim Africa's true place in history, it first needs to be understood that 400 years of the slave trade with Europe and the Americas fractured its diverse cultures, devastated its populations, weakened its governments, and destroyed the historic records that make a complete picture possible. Today, by seeing Africa as the birthplace of world civilization and humankind's ancestral homeland, the myth of the "Dark Continent"—and the shadow of racism it casts—can finally be dispelled.

MOTHER TO ALL PEOPLES

On a sunbaked plain in Tanzania a set of 54 footprints emerge from a layer of volcanic ash as if they were left yesterday. But these tracks were left by three upright hominids (generally identified as *Australopithecus afarensis*) walking north in the Great Rift Valley of East Africa approximately 3.5 million years ago. Discovered by Mary Leakey in 1978, these ancient tracks strongly indicate that bipedalism, the ability to walk upright, first evolved among the hominids of Africa. More recent discoveries in Ethiopia suggest that this trait may have evolved (among hominids) even earlier, perhaps six million to seven million years ago.

As to the great question that Darwin posed in 1871, "where was the birthplace of man"—not a distant branch of the family tree, but the one that clearly leads to "us"—the evidence

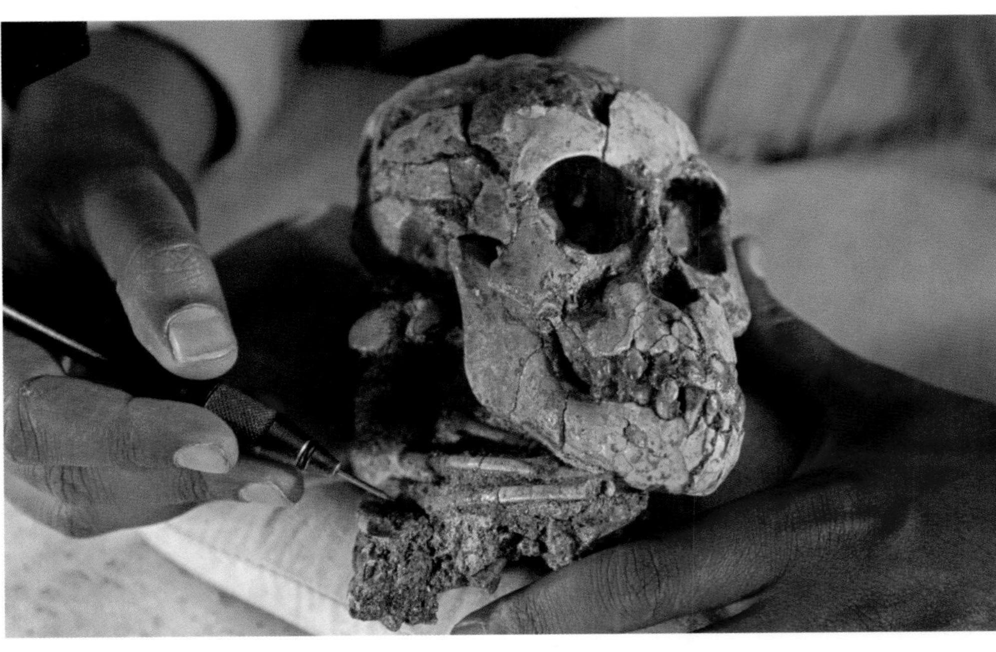

Right: Rare details, such as a full set of unerupted adult teeth, make this 3.3-million-year-old infant fossil the most complete on record.

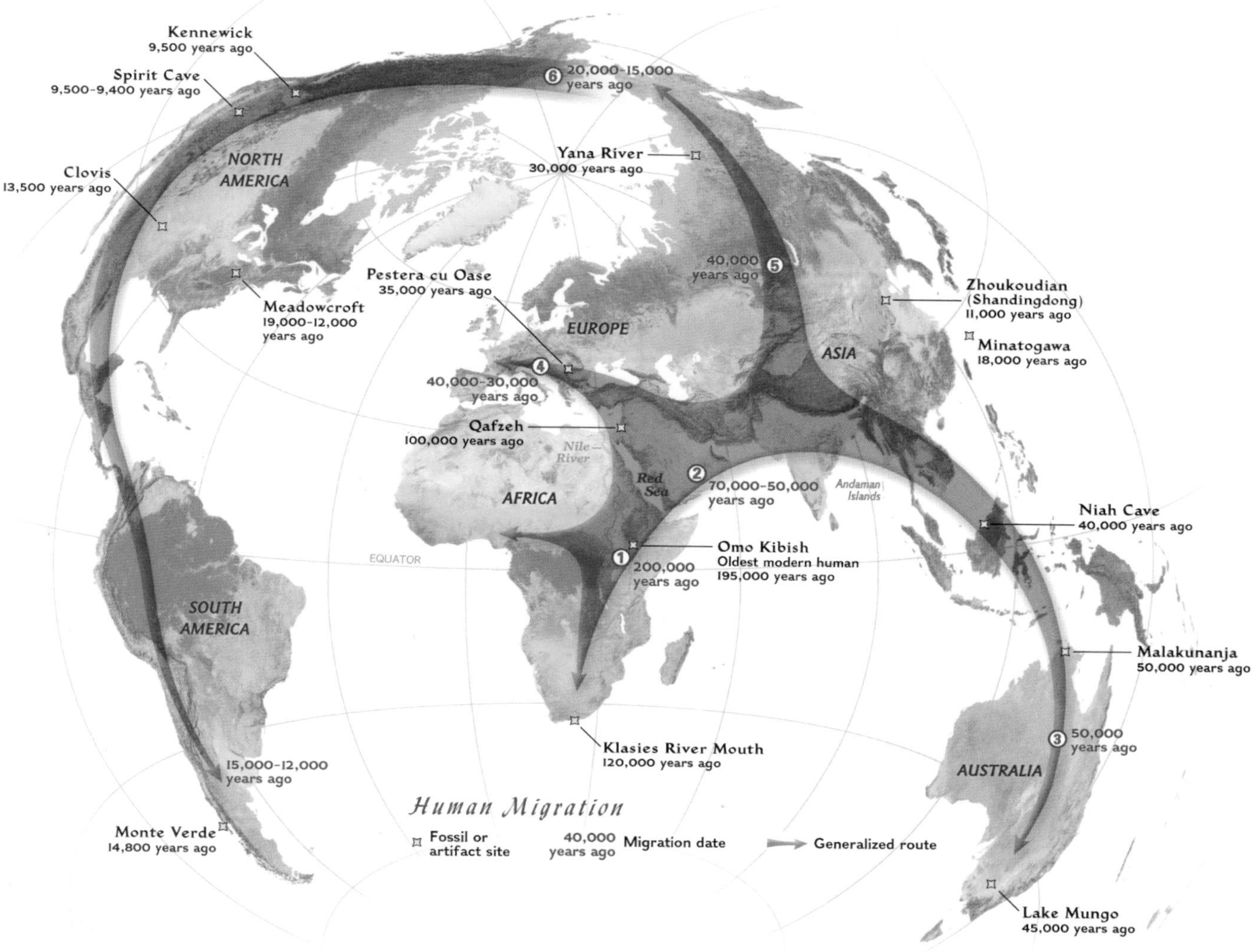

Above: Combining hard fossil evidence with genetic research, scientists can trace the migration patterns of modern humans from their origins in Africa.

continues to point to Africa, and with increasing clarity. Fossil skulls found in Ethiopia by a team from the University of California at Berkeley fill in what had previously been a gap in the fossil record (from between 300,000 and 100,000 years ago) and connect "earlier archaic African forms to later fully modern ones."

These 160,000-year-old skulls, in combination with recent genetic studies, suggest that Mother Africa is far more than metaphor. All modern humans, from the Sudan to Sweden, may well share a maternal ancestor, an African woman who lived around 170,000 years ago. As determined by genetic tests that rely on mitochondrial DNA (DNA that resides in a cell's mitochondria and remains largely unaltered through millennia), this "Mitochondrial Eve" (see page 21) is clearly African and clearly related to all humans living today, regardless of skin color or appearance.

Based on a worldwide genetic study (relying on unique DNA markers that show up only in the Y, or male, chromosome), Spencer Wells of the Genographic Project draws even more specific conclusions about where and when the earliest human ancestors lived. He believes that San Bushmen living in Africa today are direct descendants of a shared ancestral group, the San people who lived in the Rift Valley of East Africa 60,000 years ago.

We are indeed one people. We are all African.

"Watching our own DNA instruction book emerge letter by letter . . . provided a profound sense of awe unlike anything I could've imagined."

— Dr. Francis Collins, Former Head of the National Human Genome Research Institute

GREAT UNITY IN DIVERSITY

Africa is truly a vast place to call "home." While at first glance it may appear to be a monolith, it is in truth a spectacular mosaic. Its sheer size defies easy comprehension, though, and is not reflected by most traditional maps. At 11,668,545 square miles, it can easily hold the combined landmasses of China, the United States, Europe, India, Argentina, and New Zealand within its borders. Despite this immensity, it has a relatively short coastline, lacking numerous inlets and harbors. It also rests on an elevated plateau, making access to the interior difficult.

Africa is capped by coastal margins of Mediterranean-style ecosystems at the top and bottom. Long ago a lush savanna, the barren slash of Sahara now separates North from sub-Saharan Africa. Like a broad, green belt at Africa's waist, the tropical (equatorial) rain forest forms the continent's heart and center. Below the Equator, South Africa gradually transitions from rain forest to coastal climates, while the Great Rift Valley in East Africa (the one place all people may actually call home) reveals that the two tectonic plates on which the continent rests, the African plate and the Arabian plate, are gradually pulling apart.

As a contemporary Ethiopian saying goes, "We all fetch from the same river," meaning rivers connect people and cultures through time, space, and shared resources. Africa's three great rivers, the Nile, Niger, and Congo, also help connect chapters in its vast history. The world's longest river, the Nile, runs through the contemporary countries of Egypt, Sudan, and Uganda. Historically, it may well trace the primary path that human ancestors used to reach other lands, and its route indicates that there was once a fluid exchange between Egypt and the ancient black civilizations of Kush and Nubia to the south. The Niger curves like a scythe between Guinea and coastal Nigeria, thereby connecting sub-Saharan Africa with the equatorial region. Its waters once supported the emergence of the great kingdoms

Right: The ancient rock art of the San people, or Bushmen, in South Africa tells vivid stories of everyday life, from hunting to spiritual rituals.

Common Origins: Mitochondrial Eve

Most people think of their hometowns or where their grandparents lived when someone asks where they come from. But for centuries, scientists and scholars have been searching for a deeper, universal answer to that question, one that could serve for the whole human race. If we could follow our ancestors' footsteps back to the beginning, where would they lead us? Thanks to recent advances in genetic studies, scientists have conclusively pinpointed the location: Africa.

Until the late 20th century, paleoanthropology provided most of the answers about human evolution through the study of the skeletal remains of humans and their hominid ancestors, like *Australopithecus afarensis,* a species that lived 5.3 million to 1.8 million years ago. Perhaps the most the most famous *Australopithecus* is a 3.2-million-year-old female skeleton, nicknamed Lucy, who was discovered in 1974 at Hadar in the Afar Triangle of eastern Ethiopia. Many experts agree that she had a mixture of apelike and human features. She is believed to have had long, dangling arms, as well as a pelvis, spine, feet, and leg bones that assisted her in walking upright. But the fossil record has limitations in how much it can tell scientists about where *Homo sapiens* developed in the millions of years following Lucy's lifetime. Did humans evolve in Africa, or had other hominid ancestors left Africa and ventured into the Middle East, Asia, and Europe, where *Homo sapiens* might have evolved?

In the closing decades of the 20th century, advances in genetics gave scientists new ways to dig even deeper into human history by examining the information contained within our own bodies. Multigenerational lines of descent can be uncovered by analyzing the genetic contents of our cells: The Y chromosome (handed down from father to son) reveals paternal lineages, and mitochondrial DNA (or mtDNA, which is passed by mothers to their male and female offspring) shows maternal lineages. By following these genetic lines back in time, scientists have been able to identify common human ancestors and even know where they lived.

A man, nicknamed Adam, was found to have lived about 60,000 years ago. In 1987, Rebecca Cann and her colleagues at the University of California, Berkeley, identified an even older female ancestor, nicknamed Mitchondrial Eve, who lived in Africa. This woman's mtDNA was passed down to her descendants, who then migrated out of Africa and spread all over the world. They passed on their mtDNA to their offspring, and so on. Initially Cann estimated that this woman lived about 200,000 years ago, but later study put the date more firmly at 170,000 years ago, which, according to population geneticists, meant that Eve was African. Mitichondrial Eve's mtDNA is believed to be a part of the genetic makeup of all of humankind, no matter what race, and has helped identify where all humans come from: Africa.

C. J. C.

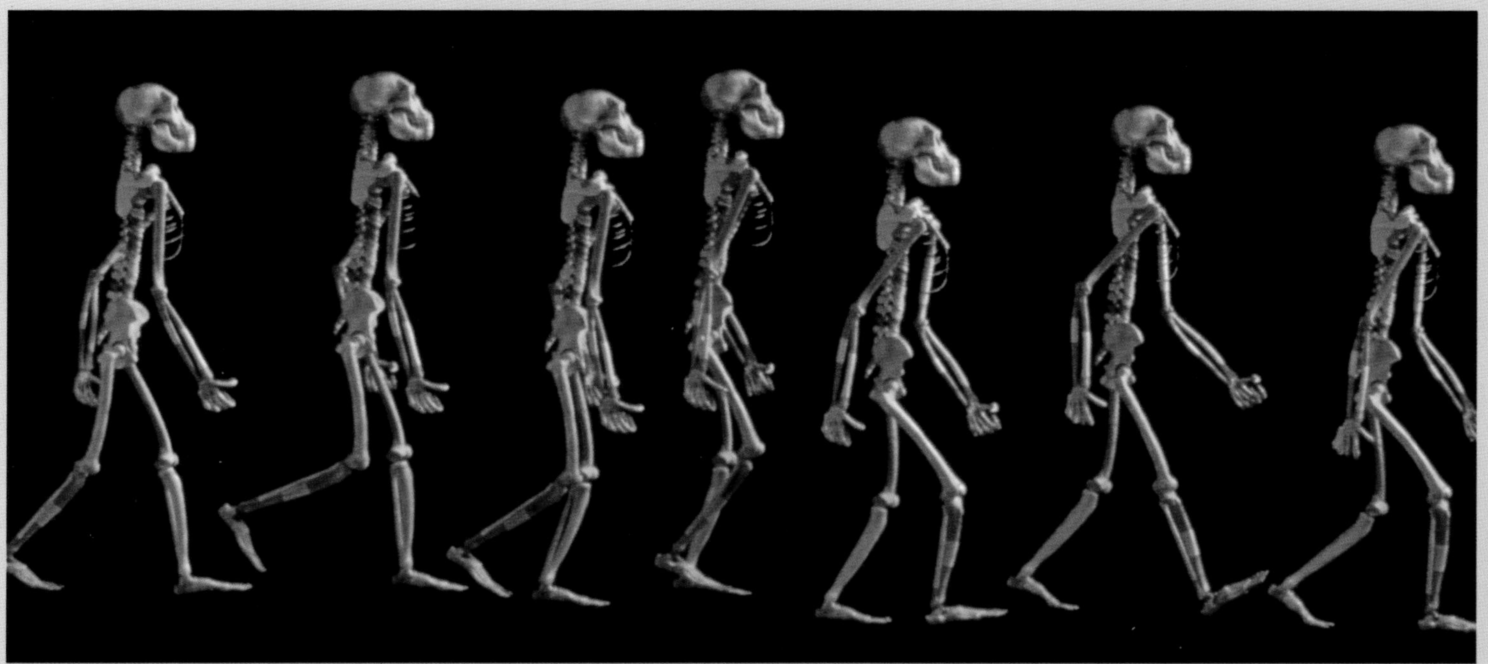

A plaster model of the fossil "Lucy" is positioned at various stages of her bipedal stride, illustrating how early humans may have adapted to walking upright. Owen Lovejoy of Kent State University reconstructed the skeleton with casts from the original, three-million-year-old fossil.

Right: Paleolithic arrowheads found in Tassili, Libya, provide early evidence of toolmaking on Africa's northern coast.

Below: A modern "raddle," constructed of brass and iron, is typical of the ancient tradition of metalworking in Africa.

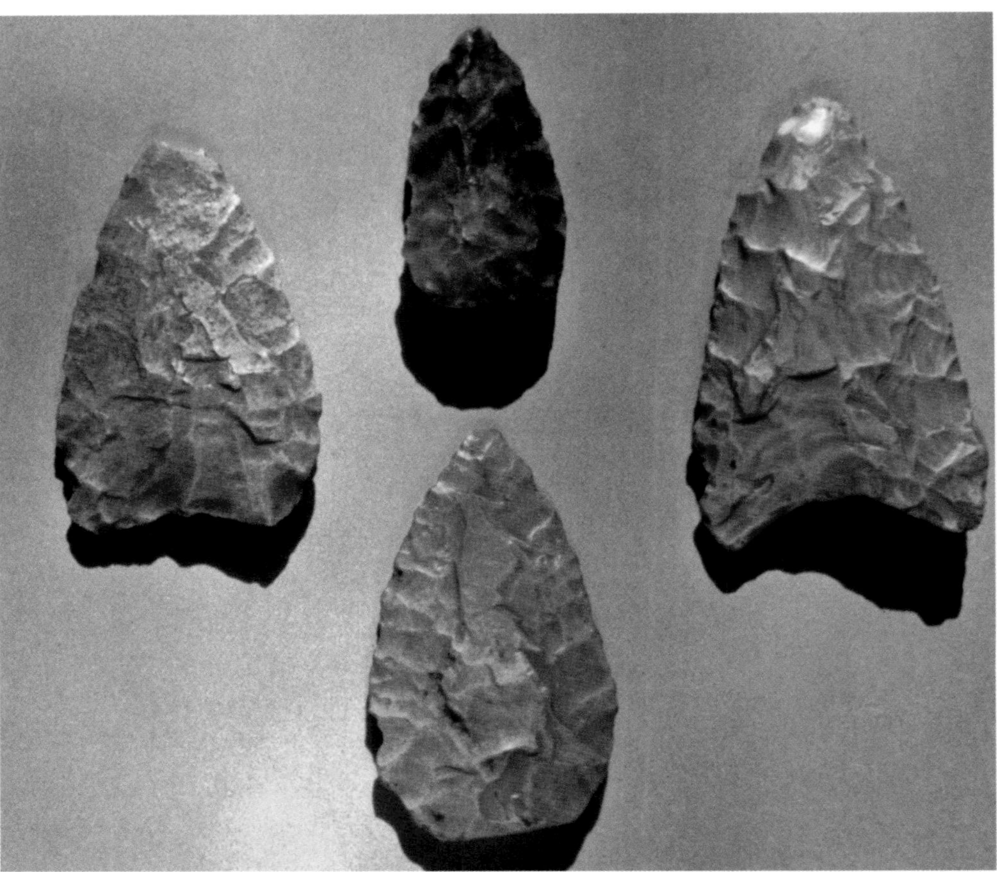

of West Africa in Mali and Ghana and acted as a conduit of the slave trade from the 15th to the 19th centuries. The Congo, also a conduit of human chattel throughout the slave trade with the Americas, connects the interior countries of the Democratic Republic of the Congo to Angola and the Atlantic Ocean.

As noted by eminent African-American historian Carter G. Woodson, Americans and Europeans exploring Africa during the 1800s appear to have been "on the outside looking at the continent through a glass darkly." This geographic remove may have supported myths and stereotypes of the Dark Continent, but in fact the vitality, variety, and diversity of Africa's cultures is immediately apparent to those who live or learn about them firsthand. Consider the following: Today the continent has 10 percent of the world's population, 54 nations, more than 1,000 different languages, and several thousand different ethnic groups. It remains a vibrant, diverse cultural landscape, as it has been throughout human history.

CULTURAL DIVERSITY

Africa's geographic (and genetic) diversity is matched only by its cultural complexity. Some historians speculate that the vastness of the continent also gave rise to its cultural subtlety and nuance. Thousands of years ago, as food and game became scarce in one region, a tribe or clan would simply subdivide, with one group moving to a less populatedarea, to carry on some traditions and invent others. As historian Basil Davidson concluded, "These traces of cultural interpenetration can be many times multiplied, and are fresh proofs of that great unity in diversity which gives so much of African culture its characteristic quality of resonance, complexity, and age."

Uncovering His Ancestry: Chris Tucker

In the 2006 PBS special *African American Lives*, nine famous African Americans hoped to trace their ancestry in the hope of identifying the African ethnic group or tribe from which they descended. Among them were television personality and philanthropist Oprah Winfrey; performer Whoopi Goldberg; musician Quincy Jones; physician and former astronaut Dr. Mae Jamison; Bishop T. D. Jakes; pediatric neurosurgeon Dr. Ben Carson; sociologist Sara Lawrence-Lightfoot; actor and comedian Chris Tucker; and the host and producer himself, educator and writer Henry Louis Gates, Jr.

Rather than relying solely on historical documents and archives, they used the data contained in their own cells—their DNA—to determine their heritage. DNA, a molecule found in the nucleus of a human cell, contains the genetic information handed down by parents to their children from generation to generation; tracking certain traits that are passed on via DNA can reveal much about a person's broad ethnic heritage and his or her ancestors. After the nine participants tested their DNA, the results were compared with the African Lineage Database, which contains DNA information of Africans from the regions exploited by the transatlantic slave trade.

Among the most complete results were those of Tucker, most famous for his roles in the *Rush Hour* series of movies. Before the DNA testing, researchers for the show had uncovered much about Tucker's family history in the U.S. They were able to trace his family back to the 1830s, a major achievement for an African American since vital records (such as birth, marriage, and death certificates) for enslaved African Americans were not always maintained and census records do not provide detailed information on family names and relations.

Tucker, born in Decatur, Georgia, in 1972 to Mary and Norris Tucker, learned that his pre–Civil War (1863-65) enslaved ancestors were part of a group of slaves who were divided up in a state lottery after the death of their owner. He also learned how his great-grandfather, Theodore A. Bryant, Sr., preserved the life of his vibrant Black community in the early 20th century (at the height of legal segregation) by acquiring 45 acres of land and selling it to neighbors and members of the Flat Rock United Methodist Church.

When the results from Tucker's DNA testing arrived, they proved to be the most revealing of the nine tested celebrities. His DNA link was within the last eight generations, which is rare, and was so strong that researchers were able to pinpoint the exact region and tribe where Tucker's ancestors came from.

His tests revealed that he was 83 percent sub-Saharan African, 10 percent Native American, and 7 percent European. Believing that his family ancestors were Ghanaian, he discovered that his mother's people were from Cameroon and that his father's people were linked to the Mbundu people who inhabit modern-day central Angola, an area where more than one in four Africans were captured and enslaved during the slave trade.

Tucker was no stranger to Africa before becoming involved with the *African American Lives* series. He had visited at least 13 different countries there to raise awareness of the economic issues facing several African nations. After receiving his DNA test results, Tucker, accompanied by Gates, traveled to an African village where his father's ancestors may once have lived. Villagers gave him a homecoming celebration, and one of the village elders told him stories that were handed down about the people who disappeared during the slave trade. Tucker also toured a local slave museum and was led to a region where many Mbundu people were captured and enslaved in the early 1700s. Clearly moved by the experience, Tucker said "I've seen the real Africa . . . I just fell in love with it. There's wisdom in knowing where you're from, and I know now. This is the greatest thing that has ever happened to me."

D. W.

Actor-comedian Chris Tucker (right) worked with Harvard professor Henry Louis Gates, Jr., to trace his ancestral roots on the 2006 PBS special African American Lives.

Recovering from the Slave Trade

PRESIDENT ELLEN JOHNSON-SIRLEAF WITH JOSEPH SAYE GUANNU

The year 2007 marked the 185th anniversary of the establishment in 1822 of Liberia as a country for emancipated slaves from the United States. An attempt to heal the wounds of slavery, colonization was seen as a way to restore former slaves to the lands of their ancestors. Slavery, as it existed during the transatlantic slave trade, was one of the worst demonstrations of man's inhumanity to man. Not only did it attempt to permanently deprive a people of their basic human rights and fundamental freedoms, but it also robbed the continent of Africa of its artisans and craftsmen, of its wisdom and technology, of its families and its heritage. It is a tragic legacy, one whose repercussions are still felt today and must be understood in order to be mended.

SLAVERY IN AFRICA

Slavery existed in Africa long before the transatlantic slave trade began. But in its African form, being a slave was never permanent. Slaves who were found to be talented or who were married to free persons might one day become free themselves. It is recorded in African history that a slave in the Mali empire named Sakura regained his liberty and went on to become the emperor as well (circa 1300). Similarly, oral Liberian history informs us that Zangba, a citizen of a landlocked polity, was sold into slavery in a neighboring coastal state, where he later became a man of power and influence. Because he was reduced to a slave, Zangba blockaded his original home up to the time of his death.

But the permanent nature of slavery associated with the transatlantic slave trade gave the institution more vicious and inhumane characteristics. The kidnapping of Africans to use as laborers in the Americas left behind a giant hole in the continent's population. It has been estimated that up to 50 million or more souls were forcibly removed from Africa during the centuries of slavery. This figure includes those killed during raids on towns and villages, those who died while trekking to waiting vessels, and those who died during the long passage to the Americas.

The Liberian shield conveys the significance of the country—established as an independent republic in 1847—as a home and refuge for emancipated slaves.

Africans sustained immense losses, material and intangible, during the transatlantic slave trade. These have been captured in the songs and stories of the breadwinners, successors to thrones, town criers, conveyors of glad tidings, and custodians of the heritage who were forcibly taken away and never returned. The theft of these peoples broke the fibers of African societies and shocked their spiritual, political, economic, and social foundations.

Slavery arrested the growth and development of institutions that transmitted knowledge and skills in West Africa for socioeconomic development. Given the instability created by slavery, knowledge of the production and distribution of goods and services declined and in some instances was forgotten, and so became nonexistent. Slavery took away herbalists and other professionals who, governed by tradition, passed their science down to select members of a family or clan.

These losses sustained by Africa made the continent an easy prey for the colonialists not long after the trade had been officially abolished. The great slave trade was a major factor in the destabilization and eventual disintegration of kingdoms and empires in precolonial Africa. The fall of the Bakongo empire illustrates how large and complex political societies in Africa crumbled in the face of slavery. Bakongo was founded by the Kongo (Congo) tribe under the leadership of Nimi Lukeni in the 15th century. At the height of its power Bakongo included parts of the Republic of the Congo, the Democratic Republic of Congo, and Angola. The empire retained diplomatic relations with Lisbon and the Vatican. The disintegration of Bakongo started with the introduction of slavery in 1506 during the reign of Manikongo, or Emperor of the Kongo, Nzinga Mbemba, who, being a Christian, bore the title/name of Dom Afonso I. By the 19th century the Manikongos had been reduced to puppets of Portuguese slavers and other adventurists.

Ellen Johnson-Sirleaf, Liberia's first elected female president and Africa's first elected female head of state, celebrated her country's 160th Independence Day on July 26, 2007. The festivities inspired reforms in education and health care.

Although slavery has been relegated to the pages of history, its vestiges still manifest themselves on both sides of the Atlantic. In Africa much remains to be desired of the relations between top management and the casual labor on plantations and concessions. Often laborers work under hazardous conditions, are paid meager wages, and have very limited opportunities for their personal growth and development and that of their families. In some quarters misconceptions about black Africans that Europeans used to legitimize their enslavement, and later their colonization, have not yet given way to science and reason. In some professional circles today the belief is expressed that the intelligent quotient of black Africans is far lower than that of whites.

WORKING TOGETHER

How can African Americans and Africans best help advance each other economically and emotionally? Despite their different allegiances, Africans and African Americans share cultural and spiritual ties that should be retained and strengthened. One way to achieve this goal is to accept and appreciate a cosanguinal relationship. A way forward in this regard is to invoke the spirit of Marcus Garvey, founder of the Back-to-Africa movement, one of whose objectives was the transfer of science and technology to Africa. Another way forward is education. Africans on both sides of the Atlantic should revisit African studies programs at American colleges and universities. In this way Africans in America in particular will come to understand and appreciate who they are, where they have come from, where they are today, and where they, along with their kin in the continent, should be going.

Additionally, the exchange of faculty and students between colleges and universities in the continent and traditional African-American colleges (or Black colleges) should be encouraged. Further still, institutions that are historically associated with African development, such as the Phelps Stokes Fund and the Booker T. Washington Foundation, and other educational programs should be empowered. The alleviation of poverty in Africa is critical to improving the economic and emotional lot of Africans in the homeland and in America. ■

Right: An ancient depiction of a papyrus plant suggests the literacy and complexity of early African culture.

Geographers and scholars often separate countries and cultures in Africa into one of five broad regions: North Africa, West Africa, Central Africa, East Africa, and southern Africa. Languages are also grouped into regional classifications, and include Afro-Asiatic, Niger-Congo, Nilo-Saharan, Khoisan. Yet within each of these geographic regions exist large linguistic groups; the extended family of dialects numbers in the hundreds. For example, in just one West African country, Benin—central to the story of slavery in the U.S.—54 distinct languages and dialects are still spoken today, according to research compiled by contemporary linguists:

Aguna
Aja
Anii
Anufo
Baatonum
Biali
Boko
Dendi
Ditammari
Ede Cabe
Ede Ica
Ede Idaca
Ede Ije
Ede Nago
Ede Nago, Kura
Ede Nago, Manigri-Kambolé
Fon
Foodo
French
Fulfulde, Borgu
Fulfulde, Gorgal
Gbe, Ayizo
Gbe, Ci
Gbe, Defi
Gbe, Eastern Xwla
Gbe, Gbesi
Gbe, Kotafon
Gbe, Maxi
Gbe, Saxwe
Gbe, Tofin
Gbe, Waci
Gbe, Weme
Gbe, Western Xwla
Gbe, Xwela
Gen
Gourmanchéma
Gun
Hausa
Ifè
Kabiyé
Kyenga
Lama
Lukpa
Mbelime
Miyobe
Mokole
Nateni
Ngangam
Notre
Tchumbuli
Tem
Waama
Yom
Yoruba

When the European slave trade arose in the 15th century, Africans from a multitude of villages and regions were enslaved. Given this cultural complexity, there was no typical enslaved African who made his or her way to the Americas. In fact, using the term "African" as an ethnic identifier is a by-product of slavery. Often, young men and women from one unique village could not speak the same language as those who shared their shackles in the holds of slave ships. Only once on America's shores did Ibo, Fon, and Mandinka peoples from Nigeria, Benin, and Senegambia become "African," and later, African American.

Lords of the Two Lands: Egypt's Black Pharaohs

During Egypt's Late Period (circa 715-332 B.C.), the nation's power had weakened as internal struggles among warlords threatened to tear apart the once great kingdom. But a series of new kings hailing from Nubia (called Kush by the Egyptians) would restore the land to its former greatness. In 730 B.C., the Nubian king Piye led his army northward into Egypt and waged a yearlong campaign to conquer it. After naming himself the Lord of the Two Lands, he returned to Nubia and ruled both kingdoms until his death in 715. Piye and his descendants have come to be called the 25th dynasty, the so-called black pharaohs, who ruled Egypt for more than three-quarters of a century and brought about a cultural rebirth.

Located mostly in present-day Sudan, Nubia had been a thriving kingdom for centuries—at times rivaling its neighbor Egypt in wealth, power, and cultural development. From Kerma, the first capital of Nubia (located just south of the Third Cataract of the Nile), Nubian kings grew wealthy through control of the trade routes that connected central Africa with Egypt. The Egyptians may have felt threatened by their prosperous neighbor and sent armies to conquer Nubia around 1500 B.C. Egypt controlled the land for roughly 400 years, during which time the Nubian people came to embrace Egyptian culture, from its language to its religion and burial practices to its architecture and pyramids. After Egypt's power began to decline around 770 B.C., Nubian leaders had come to see themselves as the rightful heirs and rulers of Egypt.

Although there were several great rulers during the time of the black pharaohs, one stands out: Taharqa, the son of Piye. Crowned in 690 B.C., Taharqa chose to rule Nubia and Egypt from Memphis. During his 26-year reign, he populated the landscape of both kingdoms with monumental architecture. In the Egyptian city of Thebes, he erected a giant kiosk at the Temple of Amun; today a 62-foot column still proudly stands tall as his legacy. In the Nubian city of Napata, he built two temples at the base of the holy mountain, Jebel Barkal. Atop the mountain, Taharqa had his name inscribed as an eternal tribute.

Militarily, Taharqa's primary foe was Assyria (located in modern Iraq), which sought to limit his control of valuable trade routes between the Levant and Egypt. After thwarting several invasion attempts, Taharqa eventually lost his hold on Memphis—and Egypt. He narrowly escaped to Napata, where he continued to rule Nubia until his death five years later. Built in the Egyptian style, his tomb in Nuri, Sudan, was excavated in 1917, its once rich contents stolen away centuries earlier by thieves. Despite the break-in, the tomb still contained many artifacts, including a large gold ring and more than 1,200 funerary objects called *shawabtis,* or helpers for the afterlife. The 25th dynasty's legacy can still be seen all across the Egyptian landscape—from the proud pyramids in Sudan to the monuments in Egypt, an eternal testament to the Lords of the Two Lands. *C. J. C.*

Statues of Egypt's Nubian kings, some reaching nearly ten feet high, were discovered in pieces at the Nubian capital of Kerma, in Sudan. Cracks in the stone show where the statues have recently been reassembled.

A colorful 19th-century German engraving depicts the reconstruction of a hall in the grand Alexandria Library in Egypt.

"Since, then, civilization depends upon scholarship and science, and these depend upon writing, civilization can only arise where the art of writing is known."

—Lord Raglan, soldier, anthropologist, author

"A DISTINCT AFRICAN NATION"

Centuries before Africa supplied the New World with enslaved laborers, it influenced Egypt, Greece, and the Middle East through cultural innovation and scholarship. Among the civilizations that arose in Africa, Egypt is the most famous. From its origins around 3100 B.C. to its conquest by Rome in A.D. 30, Egypt led the world in science, religion, architecture, art, geometry, astronomy, and math. The wonders of the Old Kingdom (2575 to 2150 B.C.) continue to astonish visitors to the Great Pyramids at Giza and Dahshûr, while the dazzling legacy of the New Kingdom (1530 to 1075 B.C.) reaches contemporary audiences through museum exhibits such as the treasures of King Tutankhamun's tomb.

Egypt's cultural connection to peoples of both the Middle East and Africa is indisputable during the 25th dynasty, when Nubians conquered and ruled Egypt during the late 700s B.C. Yet when European archaeologists Howard Carter, Georges Legrain, and others unearthed the Egyptian pyramid at Luxor in 1904, many observers shared the belief that Egypt was founded not on the legacy of more ancient African cultures, but by a race of "Hamites," light-skinned immigrants from the Middle East. Underlying this belief were two assumptions commonly held throughout the 19th and early 20th centuries: that Egypt evolved without any influence from the south or west of the Nile; and that Africans could not achieve the highest levels of civilization unless others (some say Europeans, Arabs, or Asians) first lit the way. More recent archaeological evidence about the origins of iron smelting, livestock domestication, and other hallmarks of civilization, paired with scientific insights that deconstruct myths about race, reveals Africa's true contributions to world history.

In order to fully appreciate Africa's contribution to world history, Egypt needs to be seen not as Middle Eastern, Asian, or European, but as a decidedly African country with deep roots in previous regional cultures. "African history is out of kilter," asserted historian John Henrik Clarke, "until ancient Egypt is looked upon as a distinct African nation."

Although the footprints left in the volcanic ash in the Great Rift Valley belonged to an ancient hominid rather than human *(Homo sapiens)* ancestor, these north-facing tracks point the way of much later patterns of migration as early people journeyed northward toward Egypt. Many archaeologists now believe that the Rift Valley area of Ethiopia and other areas south of Egypt was not just the cradle of humanity but also the cradle of civilization. Ancient sites in northwestern Tanzania indicate that iron smelting may have originated in sub-Saharan Africa. This controlled chemistry of ore, heat, and air made possible a series of tools that, in turn, made possible civilization building. From this region, asserted American anthropologist Lewis Henry Morgan (1818-1881), "came the metallic hammer and anvil, the axe and chisel, the plow with an iron point, the iron sword; in fine the basis of civilization, which may be said to rest upon his metal."

This lineage between ancient African cultures and Egypt was noted as early as Herodotus and Homer during the fifth and eighth centuries B.C. Herodotus, Greece's "Father of History," used the term "Ethiopian" (from the Greek for "burnt faces") to include the inhabitants of the Sudan, Egypt, Arabia, Palestine, western Asia, and India. For Herodotus, these Ethiopians were "the tallest, most beautiful and long-lived of the human races," while Homer praised them as "the most just of men, the favorites of the gods." Herodotus also

Detailed hieroglyphics on bone tags, dating from around 3200 B.C., offer evidence of early literacy in Africa.

> "The values and ethical decision making of today's medical practitioners . . . are rooted in principles and guidelines developed in antiquity. While it is impossible to date the beginnings of the practice of medicine, the need to 'heal' is universal, and the 'art' of medical practice was likely integral to all cultures. . . . While the science and art of medicine and medical practice have changed dramatically since the time of Imhotep, the values and ethics have remained relatively constant."
>
> *—Dr. Floyd J. Malveaux, former Dean, Howard University College of Medicine*

recorded that Egyptians used iron tools—a probable African invention—to build their great pyramids during the Old Kingdom, a claim borne out by subsequent archaeological evidence found at Giza in 1837 by Col. Howard Vyse. Thus, the exchange of ideas, technology, and cultural trends flowed all along the Nile, with and against its current. "The ancient Egyptians were Negroes," Senegalese historian Cheikh Anta Diop asserted unequivocally. "The moral fruit of their civilization is to be counted among the assets of the Black world."

Some scholars believe that precursors to the written word may also stem from Africa. According to this view, the hieroglyphics of Egypt (3100 B.C.) and the cuneiform of Sumeria (3200 B.C.) may both have sprung nearly simultaneously from common roots in a still more ancient African civilization. As Basil Davidson asserted, "Dynastic Egypt was not born into a void; it emerged from a Neolithic womb, and this womb was African."

Although little is known about individuals who lived in Africa long ago, other than Egypt's pharaohs and priests, the legacy of one remarkable man is unmistakable. Imhotep, a brilliant commoner who rose to the highest ranks of power in Egypt under King Djoser, was later immortalized as a god of medicine in both Egypt and Greece (as Asclepius). As a commoner, Imhotep may well have been of mixed ancestry, both African and Egyptian, since intermarriage between classes and races is indicated in murals of the period. A pioneering architect, he designed Egypt's first step pyramid (as opposed to earlier mud constructions) at Saqqara near Memphis in approximately 2630 B.C., an engineering feat that is as remarkable today as it was more than 7,000 years ago.

Other aspects of Imhotep's legacy did not weather the eons as successfully. Although he was worshipped as a deity long after his death, only fragments of his actual intellectual legacy survived the millennia. When Roman general Julius Caesar sacked the city of Alexandria (Egypt) in 48 B.C., his army burned most of what was then the world's greatest library, with extensive holdings in the same fields of philosophy, medicine, geometry, and astronomy that Imhotep once pioneered. This act of conquest also destroyed all traces of African contributions to the historic record. Although Romans rebuilt the library, much of this second Alexandrian Library was burned by Christian monks nearly 400 years later.

Yet during its heyday, the remarkable library, museum, and university at Alexandria enlightened and informed the ancient world's most brilliant minds. In its marble halls lined with papyrus scrolls, Euclid taught geometry, Apollonius wrote treatises on conic sections, Archimedes derived equations, Eratosthenes accurately calculated the Earth's circumference, and astronomers Ptolemy and Hipparchus described the cosmos.

"TOWARD THE SETTING SUN"

Several centuries later, and many hundreds of miles to the west, libraries at the University of Sankore in Timbuktu defined another great chapter in African scholarship and intellectual leadership. According to oral traditions recorded by historian John G. Jackson, the main pattern of migration in Africa was from east to west, out of the Nile valley and "toward the setting sun." The story of slavery in America matches this arc from east to west, with origins in West Africa and its great kingdoms of the golden age.

One of the great trading and cultural centers of West Africa, Ghana formed a crossroads between east and west, between sub-Saharan and Arab cultures, and between the rich salt mines of the north and the gold mines of the south. For nearly 1,000 years, from approximately A.D. 700 through the advent of the slave trade in the 1600s, a series of kingdoms constituted the golden age of West Africa. Well positioned for trade and commerce, cities at Djénné and Timbuktu in present-day Mali also became centers of learning. A visitor from Spain in 1513, Leo Africanus, marveled at Timbuktu's "many

Scientific Historian: Rick Kittles, Ph.D.

In 1977 television audiences sat spellbound watching Alex Haley's *Roots*. Haley's work fueled a generation of Americans to look for their ancestors. Now, 30 years later, a new generation of Americans, including Alex Haley's nephew Chris, are uncovering their family histories in greater detail through genetic genealogy, which tests a person's DNA to identify ethnic origins and inherited physical characteristics.

To support the finding that humans descended from a common African ancestor more than 60,000 years ago (see page 21) several projects have been undertaken to identify the genes in human DNA, to create tools for study, and to create databases to store and manipulate the collected data. The Human Genome Project (HGP), begun in 1990 through the coordinated efforts of the Department of Energy and the National Institutes of Health, remains one of the largest and most accurate efforts to support the idea of a common ancestor. Under the direction of Dr. Francis S. Collins, HGP laid the foundation for subsequent projects by allowing unrestricted use of all the data by the scientific community. It remains one of the largest and most accurate projects supporting a common ancestor among all humans. National Geographic's Genographic Project follows the migration history of that ancestor's descendants.

More recently, projects directed at African ancestry have begun to be developed. African Ancestry, co-founded by businesswoman Gina Paige and Rick Kittles, a molecular geneticist, applies the latest technologies in DNA testing. Kittles's work on the African Burial Ground Project in New York City (see pages 80-81) inspired him to compare his own DNA with the samples from an African DNA database; this work laid the groundwork for the formation of African Ancestry. Critics have pointed out the limitations of Kittles's work, and he admits that the genetic material used to trace ethnic lineage is only a minuscule part of a person's DNA makeup. Still, he considers it a starting point in showing that the African-American family history does not begin with slavery. *D. W.*

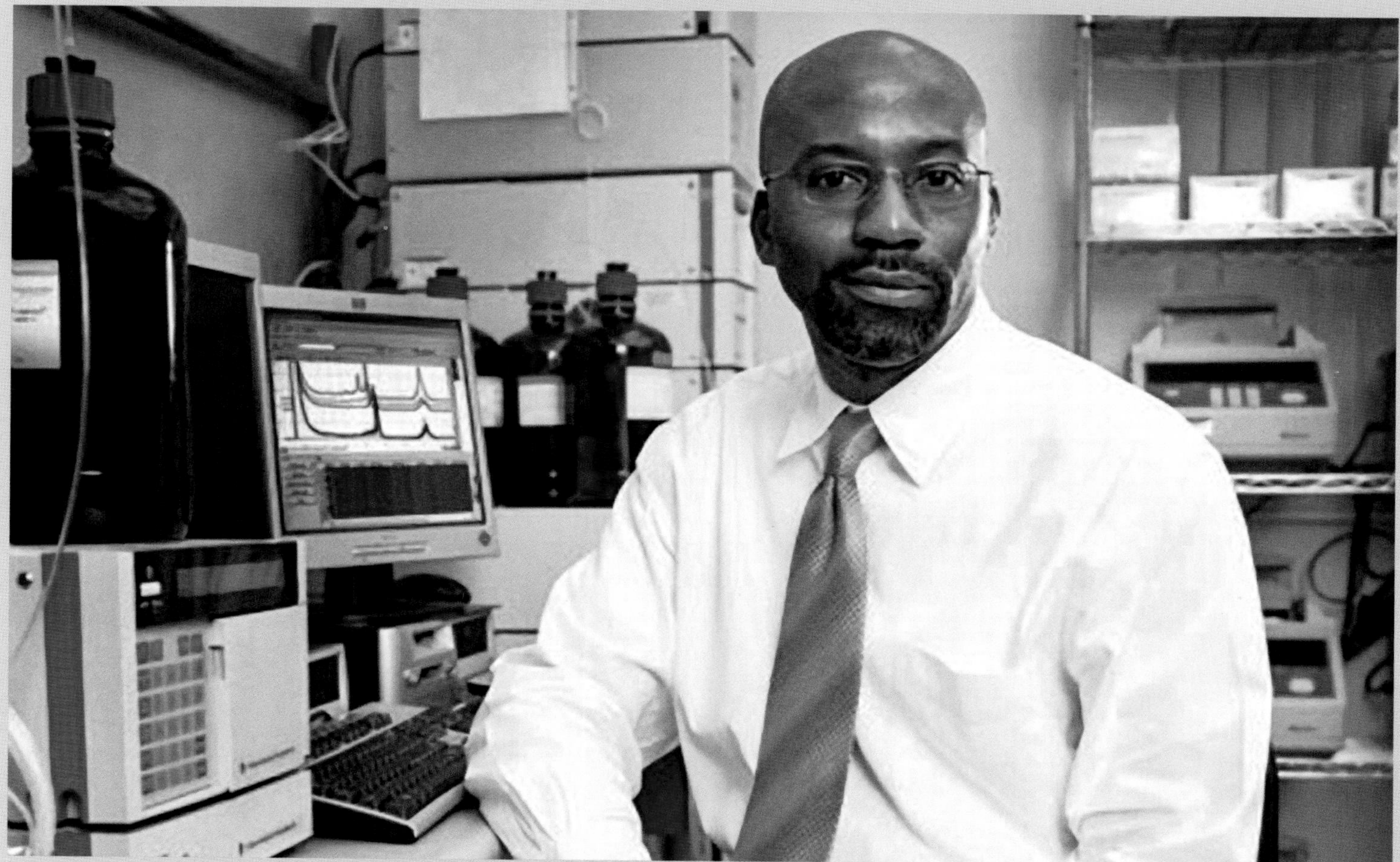

Many African Americans today rely on genetic evidence to discover and research their ancestral roots. Rick Kittles, co-founder of African Ancestry, is among those who use DNA to trace lineages to the time of slavery and beyond.

"The ancient Egyptians were Negroes. The moral fruit of their civilisation is to be counted among the assets of the Black world."

— Cheikh Anta Diop, historian, linguist, anthropologist, and Egyptologist

doctors, judges, priests and other learned men, that are well maintained at the king's cost." These "scholars of Timbuktu yielded in nothing, to the saints in their sojourns in the foreign universities of Fez, Tunis, and Cairo," according to 19th-century French journalist Felix Dubois. "They astounded the most learned men of Islam by their erudition."

As these medieval empires of West Africa looked to the east, they also faced west, across the Atlantic, toward the Americas. According to Mali's emperor, Mansa Musa, who led an epic pilgrimage to Mecca in 1324, he assumed the throne only after his predecessor, Mansa Abu Bakr II, set out to cross the Atlantic Ocean, and failed to return.

It may still be true that "Mali guards its secrets jealously," to quote a contemporary Malian *djeli,* or oral historian, "for the griots [West African storytellers], their depositories, will never betray them." Yet the secrets it has passed on are nevertheless wondrous to consider.

Even before the emperor of Mali set sail across the Atlantic in the early 1300s, earlier West African sailors may have caught the same prevailing trade winds and landed on America's shores around 500 B.C. or earlier.

The evidence that the first Africans to arrive in the Americas came not in chains but as free explorers and sailors doesn't appear in written manuscripts or carved on stone tablets. It can be seen in the sculptures, legends, eyewitness accounts, ancient maps, and scattered archaeological evidence they left behind in present-day Mexico. The reason for this is simple, asserted historian Ivan Van Sertima. "We cannot approach the study of shattered worlds like Africa and America the way we approach the study of Europe." Instead, "we are forced to venture into several disciplines . . . in order to grasp the true complexity of these vanished worlds."

And yet these vanished worlds have left more than a few traces. Some of these traces are in fact monumental, such as the massive Olmec (a Central American culture from 1200 to 400 B.C.) stone heads discovered at San Lorenzo, Mexico. These astonishing sculptures date to 500 B.C. and possess sculptural details that suggest West African origins. Other traces are almost whispers, such as Maya legends of long-ago forebears who came from the east, "from the other side of the water and the sea." (The Maya civilization, centered in Central America, endured from 2500 B.C. to A.D. 900.)

Norwegian explorer Thor Heyerdahl in 1970 sailed from Morocco to the island of Barbados on this papyrus craft, modeled after ancient Egyptian drawings.

A 1513 map, sketched by Turkish admiral Piri Reis, relied on maps from the fourth century B.C. to depict the known world.

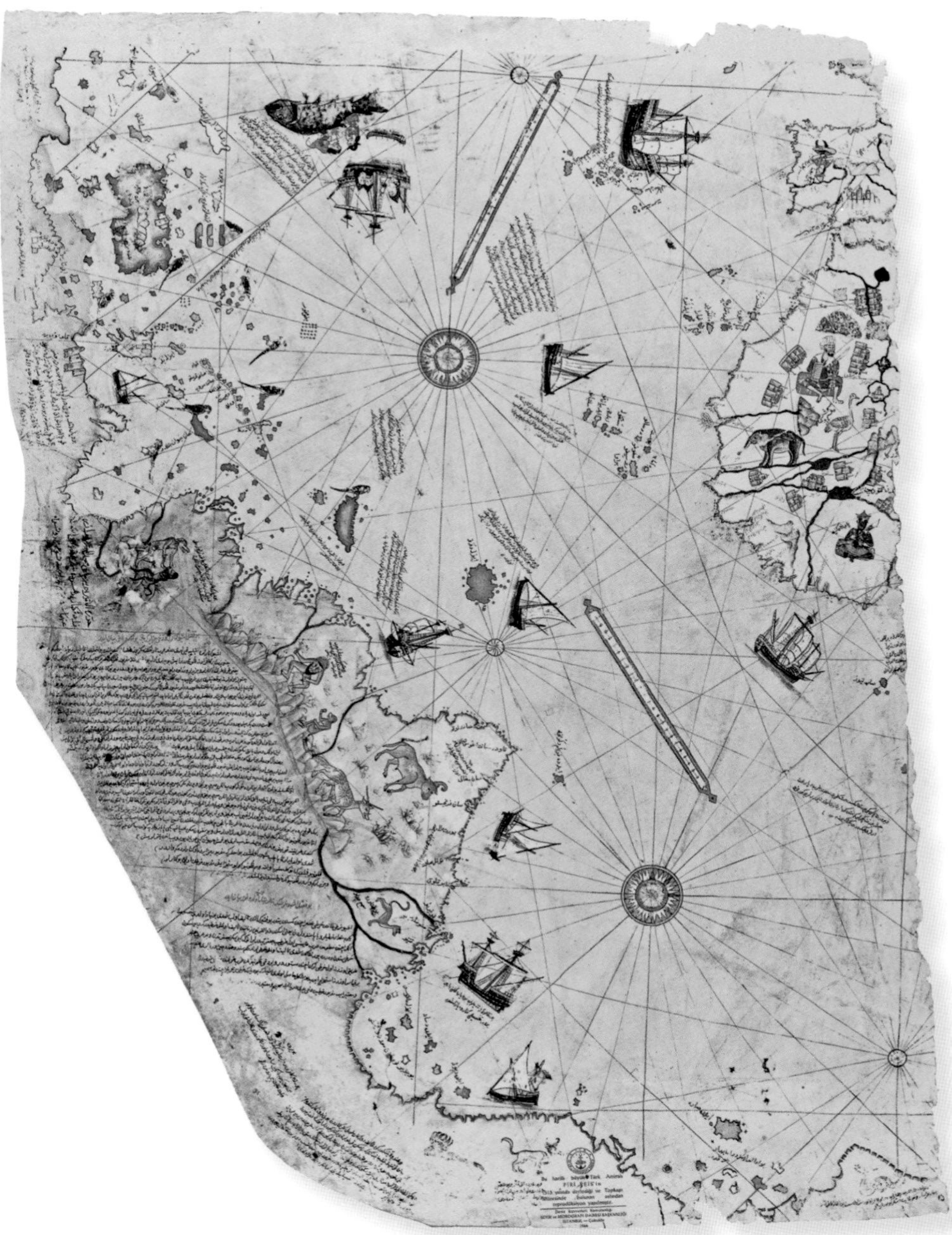

Some of the most convincing evidence, at least to western European minds, is from Ferdinand Columbus, the son of Christopher Columbus, who recorded that his father had seen blacks bearing gold-tipped spears when visiting Hispaniola (the location of Haiti and the Dominican Republic today). Columbus arranged for samples to be sent back to Spain, where the alloy was found to be identical in composition to the gold from Guinea.

One century after the U.S. finally abolished slavery in 1865, an intrepid sailor crossed the Atlantic in a reed boat made by craftsmen from Lake Chad. Thor Heyerdahl's journey demonstrated that sailors could indeed cross the Atlantic in vessels made from materials readily available to West African sailors of long ago.

Africa's legacy is nothing less than the origin, evolution, and civilization of humanity. Traces of its peoples and cultures are evident around the globe, from the microscopic realm of shared genetic material to the monumental civilizations it influenced.

Legacy of Imhotep

A GALLERY

During a 2005 graduation ceremony at the Howard University College of Medicine, a class of new physicians listened as their dean, Dr. Floyd Malveaux, spoke of the important innovators in the history of medicine. Recognizing a multitude of groundbreaking healers and scientists, his words stretched back to Egypt's Old Kingdom to proclaim the many great virtues of an ancient man of medicine, Imhotep.

Many ancient Egyptians wished to gain immortality, but Imhotep, an Egyptian whom many believe may be of African ancestry, is one of the few who actually achieved it through his contributions to medical science, his architectural innovations, and his reputation as a respected sage, scribe, and scientists. Not only was he highly respected during his lifetime, but he also continues to serve today as a figure that all peoples can look to as an example of the achievements and inventions to come out of ancient Africa.

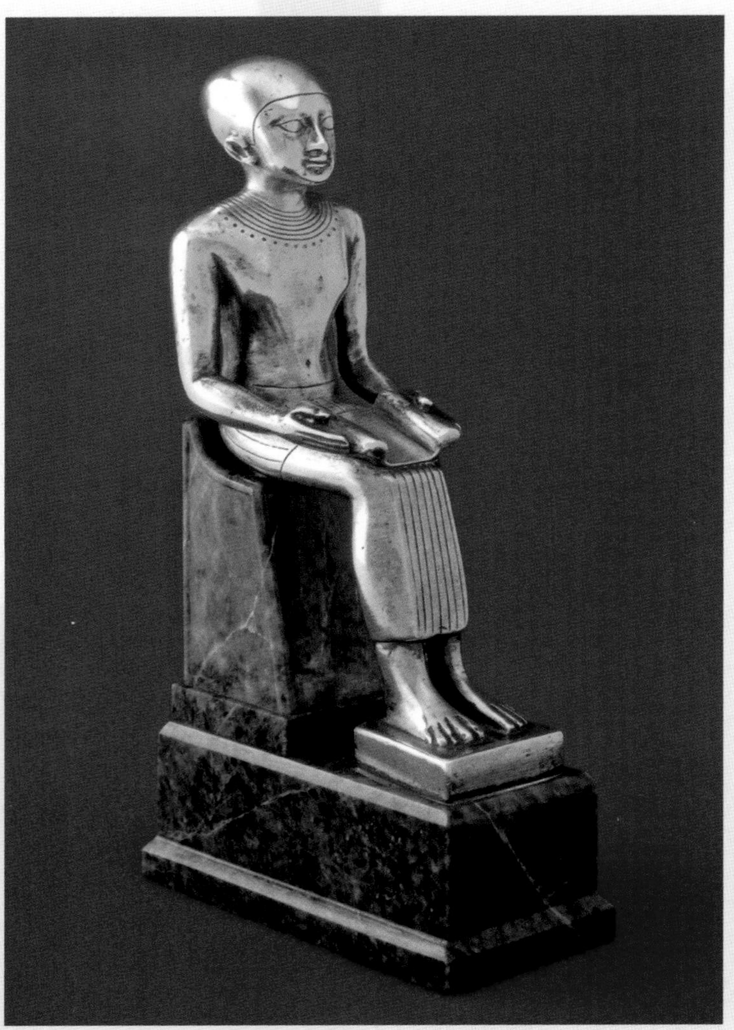

Revered through the ages as a physician and sage, Imhotep is still valued today for his contributions to medicine and science.

Born a commoner during Egypt's 3rd dynasty of the Old Kingdom (circa 2650-2575 B.C.), Imhotep used his many remarkable talents to advance both socially and politically. He ultimately served as vizier to Pharaoh Djoser and designed his massive funerary complex at Saqqara (located in the area that is now Memphis, Egypt), one of the world's first stone monumental structures. His impressive design pioneered the use of fluted columns, ornamental friezes, and galleries paved with marble and limestone—elements that would all appear centuries later in Greek and Roman architecture. The striking and magnificent step pyramid stands just about 180 feet tall and served as Djoser's tomb.

In addition to the Saqqara complex, perhaps Imhotep's most enduring legacy is related to his medical genius. Known also as the son of Ptah (an Egyptian god), Imhotep was credited with performing medical miracles in life and in death. Two thousand years after his death, he was deified as an Egyptian god and later as a Greek one. Today, Imhotep's medical legacy continues to garner him respect among modern medical professionals. At Morehouse College, in Atlanta, Georgia, one of the key undergraduate internship programs in public health is called Project Imhotep in his honor.

Much of Imhotep's life remains a mystery, but the high regard in which others held him has been passed down through the ages. He was revered after his death and eventually regarded as a deity. King Djoser inscribed his high opinion of Imhotep on the pedestal of a statue, which reads, in part:

> *The Chancellor of the King of Lower Egypt, the First after the King of Upper Egypt, Administrator of the Great Palace, Hereditary Lord, the High Priest of Heliopolis, Imhotep, the builder, the sculptor.*

Today, Imhotep's legacy endures in the minds of medical professionals, in the faces of visitors to the grand structures at Saqqara, and in the efforts of scholars who strive to learn more about this African man of many talents.

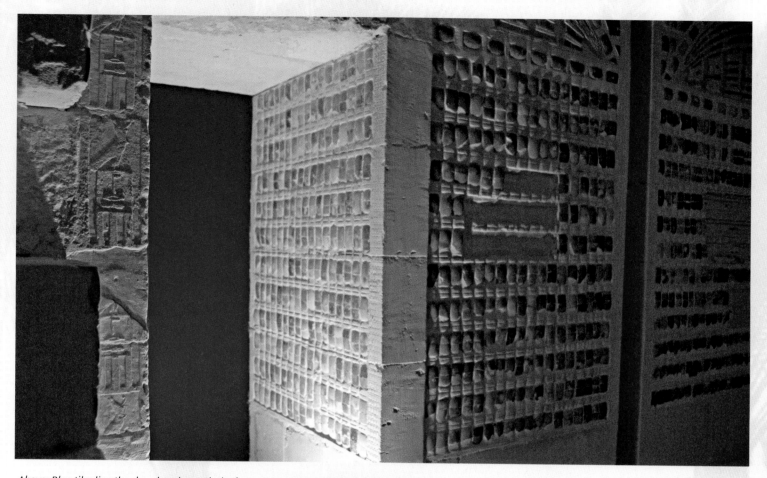

Above: Blue tiles line the chambers beneath the famous Step Pyramid at Saqqara. Designed by Imhotep, the monument is now recognized as Egypt's first pyramid. Below: A plinth from Egypt's 3rd dynasty shows the name Imhotep.

CHAPTER TWO

Homeland

Homeland

One hundred and eighty years before Christopher Columbus stumbled upon the Americas during his failed expedition to India, Abu Bakr II, the *mansa* ("emperor" in the Mandinka language) of the West African empire of Mali, dispatched a fleet of 2,400 vessels on exploratory expeditions to the Americas. Mali was one of three great West African empires that emerged as historical testaments to the fact that Africa, far from fitting the notion of a "dark continent" fictionalized in European explorers' narratives, was the genesis of major political, economic, intellectual, technical, and artistic developments before the arrival of European slave traders in the 15th century.

WEST AFRICAN EMPIRES

Like their ancient East African ancestors, West Africans have ruled well-organized, fortified, and prosperous empires for thousands of years beginning in A.D. 300. Ghana, Mali, Songhai, Dahomey, Nikki, Ndongo, Oyo, and Zazzau number among the prominent kingdoms and queendoms of West Africa. The extensive, complex history of kingship and queenship in West Africa contradicts the stereotype of Africans as uncivilized, savage peoples devoid of indigenous rule, guiding principles, and moral values.

Where a king or queen has been enthroned in West Africa, he or she has been divinely appointed. In the empire of Oyo, for example, the crown prince—or *aremo*, as he is called in the Yoruba language—will not ascend to the throne without the blessings of Shango, the Yoruba god of thunder, lightning, and fire. Because Shango metes out punishment to individuals who break moral and social codes, he administers justice. As a divine representative of the gods, and as the leader of the Oyo empire, the aremo is expected to rule judiciously when he becomes the *alafin* (king) of the Oyo peoples.

Another important principle that guides the selection of the king is that he should be chosen from among the ruling family. In matrilineal societies, power and wealth are transferred through the female line. Among the Asante peoples of Ghana, for example, the succeeding *asantehene* (as the king is called in the Akan language) is chosen from his own maternal brothers or from the male children of the sister of the reigning asantehene. Ideally, the crown prince would be the eldest son, provided he possesses the qualities requisite for kingship. The queen mother (the mother of the reigning asantehene) assesses if the eldest son is qualified and then nominates the successor, in consultation with the lineage elders.

In African societies, elders are shown deference because they are thought to possess wisdom gained from years of experience in matters of human relations. That wisdom is invoked during times of major decision-making, such as when a candidate is seeking the throne. The elders are also co-governors of African communities that are not managed solely based upon their expertise, but are governed by the wisdom of the ancestors who continue to influence the actions of living persons, according to indigenous religious

Left: A painting by Dutch artist Albert van der Eeckhout (1610-1666) depicts a regal and powerful African chief.

Previous pages: British troops join the King of the Asante for the first day of the Yam Custom, an important public ceremony, in this 1818 illustration.

Right: An 1853 German lithograph illustrates the unique architectural design of the village of the Songhay, a settlement along the route to Timbuktu.

belief systems. In Africa, there is no human endeavor, expression, or emotion that is not linked, directly or indirectly, to religion. Traditionally, indigenous African religions are polytheistic, their pantheons containing deities that symbolize, relate to, or address the gamut of human experiences, providing adherents with a broad range of concepts and philosophies that speak to, and that suggest solutions for, their worldly dilemmas.

Religion and family are the cornerstones of African cultures. Although family structures vary by culture, many of them extend to include grandparents, parents, children, aunts, uncles, and individuals who are not blood relatives but who are addressed, and respected, as "aunts" and "uncles." Some African families practice polygyny, allowing a man to have more than one wife. However, a man marries extra wives according to his financial means. In each case, he must demonstrate that he can adequately provide for her because in West African societies, dereliction of duty to family and divorce are considered abhorrent behaviors. Oftentimes, a man marries additional wives to help manage his estate in the city, in the village, or in both.

DIVERSE MODES OF LIVING AND TRADE

Contemporaneously, some West Africans enjoy a high standard of living that affords them the ability to maintain houses and land in various places. Africans do not live in huts. They live in houses whose architectural designs are as diverse as the cultures that created them. The architectural designs of houses, and the spatial layouts of villages or compounds, are often shaped by the topographies in which they are found. In some cases, their forms follow their functions. In the northwestern region of the Republic of Benin, in a community called Somba, Betammaribe hunter-warriors build a type of house referred to as a *tata*. It is a vertical structure made up of three tiers. The Betammaribe enter the house on the first tier, they sleep on the second tier, and they use the third tier as an observatory to view the approach of strangers. This architectural design was particularly useful during the transatlantic slave trade. When under siege by slave raiders, the Betammaribe sought safe haven in the upper tier of their houses. In comparison, the Takad peoples of Attakar, located in southern Kaduna (Nigeria), sought shelter on hilltops when under attack by slave raiders. They maintain their community on the hilltop, despite their supreme chief's requests that they return to

Above: Wood-carved fertility symbols, such as this pair from the Bambara of the Ivory Coast, are a long-held African tradition.

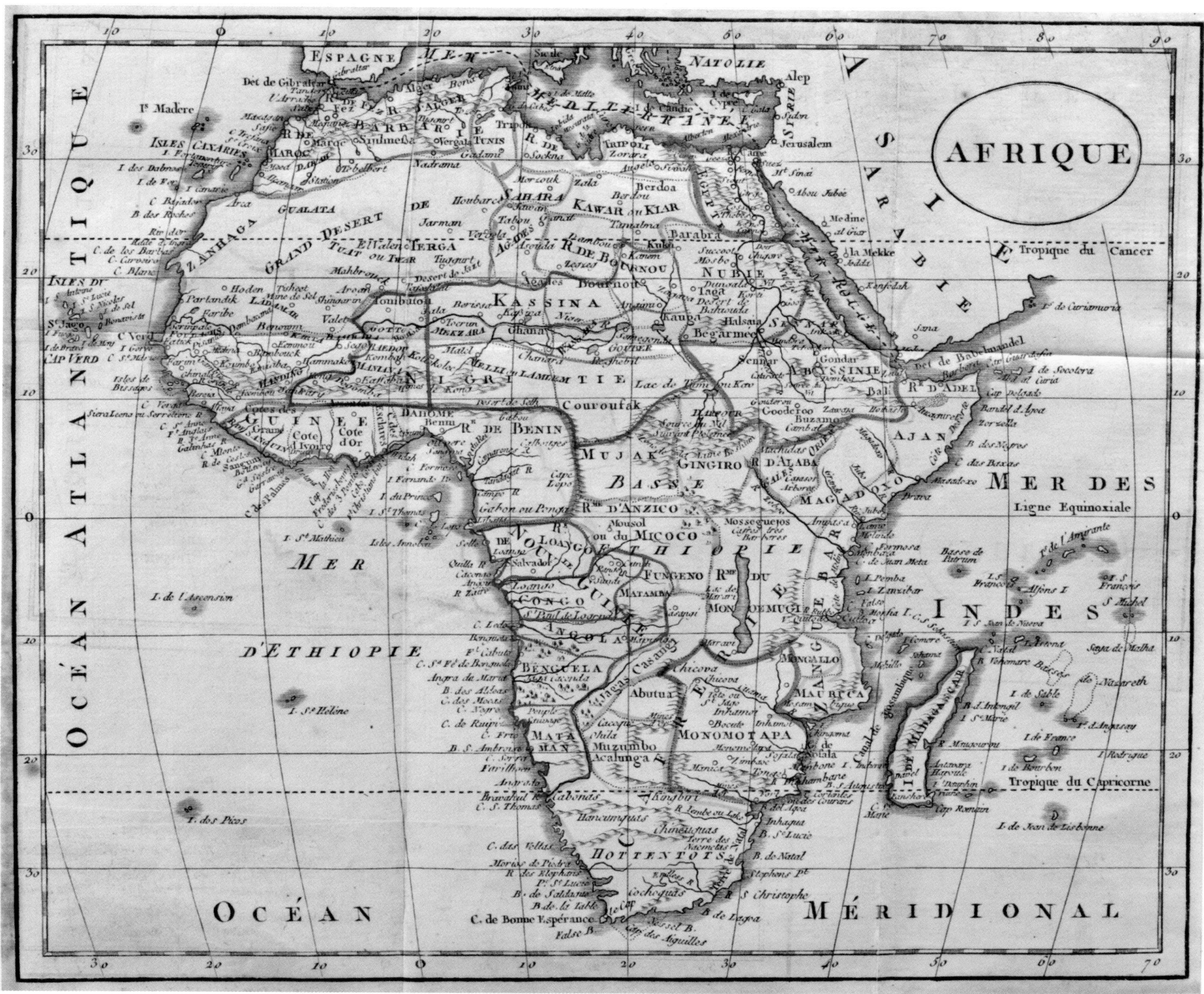

An early map of Africa shows roughly the boundaries of the continent's numerous kingdoms. Western colonization would disrupt these boundaries again and again, imposing artificial borders and instigating decades of internal strife.

the Takad villages on the plains. Thus, West Africans have made creative architectural use of various topographies, constructing their houses on hilltops and in the cliffs, as in the case of the Dogon peoples of Mali.

Cities and villages in the plains were fortified by extraordinary wall-rampart-ditch defense systems designed to repel and trap attackers. These systems contained several gates that permitted access to the city or village; that provided multiple modes of escape when under siege; and that facilitated the collection of tolls from traders. The gates were so important in the regulation of trade that they were manned by men whose primary responsibility included operating and maintaining them. For that reason, gatekeepers established their houses near the gates to which they were assigned. This also afforded them a strategic position from which they could gather intelligence about approaching enemies. Essentially, the gatekeepers served as sentinels and messengers for the king or supreme chief, who resided in the inner sanctum of the village or city. Major cities are often located

Right: A late 18th-century French engraving depicts an African craftsman with a sophisticated collection of tools.

Above: Masks, from Gabon (top) and the Ivory Coast, represent one of Africa's artistic traditions.

on the axis of lucrative trade routes, strategically positioned to gain access to important trade items and the revenues that they generate. A network of trade routes, some of which represent the major roads of today, radiate across the entire continent, connecting the north with the south and the east with the west. Before Columbus was born, Africans were trading in gold transported along a route that connected Ghana's commercial center of Kumbi Saleh in West Africa with that of Morocco in North Africa. The empires of Ghana, Mali, and Songhai controlled the gold fields of Wangara, and African traders from every corner of the continent traveled to those empires to acquire gold.

ARTISANS, SCIENTISTS, AND SCHOLARS

When Columbus questioned indigenes of the Caribbean regarding the origins of the gold in their possession, they replied that they acquired it from "black men who had come from

The Baule Queen: Aura Poku

According to the oral history of the Asante people, Aura Poku was destined to become queen of a new empire after the death of their leader, Osei Tutu, in 1717. Although known by some people as Awura and others as Alba, Aura Poku is believed by all to be the undisputed founder of the Baule people, a splinter Asante group that migrated to present-day Ivory Coast from the Gold Coast of Ghana.

Awura Poku was a beautiful girl who lived in the village of Sikasso. When she came of marrying age, she found that she could not conceive. She became known as Apaue, which means "the one through whom misfortune strikes." Poku lived with this stigma until she was 40 years old, when she became pregnant and bore a son that she named Kwaku. As Kwaku grew, Poku watched him with joy, protecting him because she had had him at an advanced age.

When Kwaku was ten years old, a man from the village named Kusi Obodum became king. He was cruel and would order the death of anyone who did not agree with him. Fearing Obodum and wanting to protect her son, Poku took the boy and several followers to search for another land that had been settled by an earlier group from her village.

When Obodum heard that Poku had fled, he sent troops to capture the group of runaways. As Poku and her group approached the Komoé River, which bordered Ghana and the Ivory Coast, they found that the banks were flooded. Desperate to cross the river and to save themselves from the quickly approaching troops, the group's high priest demanded that Poku make a sacrifice to the gods of the river of the purest object that could be found. After Poku made several suggestions, including choice cattle and goats, she learned from the high priest that only one thing would suffice: To save her people, Poku must sacrifice her son.

With time running out, Poku threw her son into the river, according to the oral tradition. Trees immediately formed a bridge that allowed the people to cross over to the other side. Poku stood on the original shore as the others looked back at her from across the river. The priest demanded that Poku join them on the other side. He declared that because of Poku's brave act, her son would forever be honored by the Baule people, whose name means "the son is dead." Poku was crowned queen of her people, and remnants of that original group remain in the village today. *C. J. C.*

As the Asante armies approached, Aura Poku saved her people from certain death by sacrificing her only child to the Komoé River. This bas-relief by sculptor Bekoin Kouame depicts the sacrificial act and the safe crossing of the Komoé.

Right: *An African craftsman demonstrates a traditional method of weaving in this late 18th-century French engraving.*

> "How can a proud and brave people like the Asante sit back and look while white men take away their king and chiefs. . . . If you, the chiefs of Asante, are going to behave like cowards and not fight, you should exchange your loincloths."
>
> — *Yaa Asantewaa, queen mother of the Asante Confederacy*

across the sea from the south and southeast." Thus, West African explorers and traders arrived in the Caribbean via the current of the South Atlantic Ocean that propels vessels in a south and southeastward direction. The economic genius of Africans within the contexts of transatlantic and trans-African trade is often overlooked in favor of stereotypical images of Africans as ignorant, backward peoples. Also overlooked are the more technical aspects of the gold trade such as metallurgy, one of the great hallmarks of civilization. Since ancient times, Africans have practiced metallurgy, the process by which gold, iron, and tin are extracted from the earth, purified, and forged (or die-cast) into utilitarian items such as agricultural tools, weapons, armor, and jewelry. Among the Asante peoples, gold objects are symbols of power that are traditionally reserved for the asantehene, the queen mother, and persons of high political status. In the presence of his constituents, the asantehene is adorned in gold jewelry. The finials atop his royal staffs are covered in gold leaf, and his royal stool is embellished with gold. Ghana is located in that section of the West African coast dubbed by Europeans as the Gold Coast, due to the large quantities of gold traded there. Historically, Africans have not merely "exchanged" gold for other trade items, but they did so using sophisticated systems of weights and measures. To ensure the best rate of exchange, Asante metallurgists created "gold weights" to be placed on a scale used to weigh gold dust or nuggets. Each gold weight was assigned a particular monetary value that corresponded to the value of the gold nuggets, or dust, on the opposite end of a balanced scale. The weights themselves were made of brass, and they were die-cast via a technological process called the lost-wax method. Essentially, the metallurgist superimposes a clay mold over a wax prototype

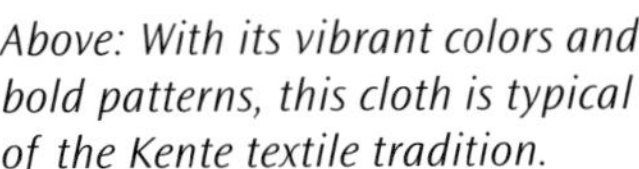

Above: With its vibrant colors and bold patterns, this cloth is typical of the Kente textile tradition.

Ethiopia's Last King: Haile Selassie

Emperor Haile Selassie of Ethiopia was one of the major forces behind the Pan-African movement of the 1960s and an influential world leader. He ruled Ethiopia for 60 years, as regent from 1916 to 1930 and as its emperor from 1930 to 1974. Selassie was immensely popular at home and abroad. He was known for his ability to adapt to change and is credited with modernizing the country's ancient civilization. Not only does the Ethiopian dynasty date back to the 13th century, his paternal grandmother was aunt to Emperor Menelik and claimed to be a direct descendant of Makeda (otherwise known as the Queen of Sheba) and King Solomon of ancient Israel.

He was born Lij Tafari Makonnen on July 23, 1892, in the village of Ejersa Goro to Yeshimebet Ali Abajifar and Ras Makonnen, a cousin and confidant of then Emperor Menelik II and Governor of Harar. He would not take the name Selassie until his appointment as king. He was educated in Harar, and as a child he spent much of his time at the imperial court in Addis Ababa, where he was exposed to the machinations of leadership. He was named a count in 1905 at the age of 13. His father died a year later, and Tafari's brother Yelma assumed the title of Governor of Harar. Emporer Menelik praised Tafari for his devotion to hard work and appointed him governor over part of the province of Sidamo in 1907. His brother died that same year, and three years later Tafari would assume the role of Governor of Harar. Later that year he married Menen Asfaw of Ambassel, who was the niece of Menelik's heir to the throne, Lij Iyasu.

Upon Emperor Menelik's death in 1913, Lij Iyasu succeeded to the throne, but his reign was marked by scandals and criticism. His interest in converting to Islam led to his being deposed in 1916, and Menelik's daughter, Zaudita, became empress. Tafari was appointed regent and heir to the throne. He remained regent until Zaudita's death in 1930. Tafari continued Menelik's initiative to modernize Ethiopia. Although this effort conflicted with Zaudita's conservative attention to tradition, Ethiopia underwent significant changes under the regency of Tafari. Amid the threat of economic imperialism, he inspected European schools, medical centers, churches, and other facilities as part of his plans to reform his country. He secured much support in his country, and when the empress died suddenly, he was crowned King of Kings in Ethiopia on November 2, 1930, and assumed the name Haile Selassie I, Power of the Trinity.

One of his first projects as emperor was to write a constitution that established a democratic practice but limited succession to the throne to Selassie descendants. Despite attempts to thwart European imperialism, Fascist Italy invaded Ethiopia in 1935, and the country was declared an Italian province the following year. Selassie and his family lived in exile until 1941 while seeking support in the overthrow of the Italian government. A number of African-American organizations supported his cause, and in appreciation for the American display of solidarity he told the American public: "So that the spirit of the cursed will not gain predominance over the human race whom Christ redeemed with his blood, all peace loving people should cooperate to stand firm in order to preserve and promote lawfulness and peace." In 1942, the Italian forces were defeated in a show of support from the United Kingdom, the Commonwealth of Nations, Free France, Free Belgium, and Ethiopian patriots.

A 1945 portrait of Haile Selassie depicts the Ethiopian emperor's triumph over Italian forces and his solidarity with Great Britain, as represented by their national flags.

Upon his return to power, he continued to travel to other countries to introduce Ethiopia as a peaceful country and to study modern methods. In 1963, he established the Organization of African Unity to promote solidarity and growth in the aftermath of African colonization. Selassie also maintained his pledge to modernize Ethiopia despite many protests and opposition. A sudden economic inflation in 1974 led to nationwide unrest. Selassie and his family were placed under house arrest and Selassie abdicated the throne. The following year, he died while still under house arrest. *D. W.*

Reflections on Slavery

AMBASSADOR PAMELA E. BRIDGEWATER

I have traveled to and lived and worked in many African countries over the course of 27 years in the Foreign Service of the United States. Several of those countries were major points of departure for my African ancestors who were ripped unwillingly from their countries, villages, and families on the West African coasts and later sold as slaves in countries in North America and other parts of the world. I must say that during each of my many visits to the slave forts in Ghana I experience a different reaction—sometimes anger, sometimes shame, sometimes sadness. Often forgotten, or purposefully omitted, is the fact that African traditional leaders or chiefs themselves were often complicit in this trade, selling human beings to traders for cowrie shells, alcohol, or other token commodities.

UNINTENDED CONSEQUENCES

The European traders recognized the potential value of cheap labor for southern plantations to spur their own economic development. They ignored the long-term impact this practice would have not only on the slaves but also on their owners and future generations. Some of the collaborating African chiefs could not have imagined the untold suffering and inhumanity slavery meted upon its victims and their progeny. I marvel at how Africans withstood the terrible journey, bondage, and innumerable examples of cruelty and contempt to build powerful societies far from their native shores that have prospered and developed far beyond the levels occurring in many their homelands.

Having served in Benin and Ghana as ambassador, I have had the chance to visit Ouidah, where our ancestors were taken from their homes to unknown shores, and seen the same at Senegal's Gorée Island. I have visited in Ghana many of the "castles" and forts erected by Europeans as staging places for their trade in human beings. These sites—Elmina, Cape Coast, and Christiansborg (Osu) Castles, to name a few—invoke a grim and terrible chapter in human history. The story of the tortuous journey of African men and women through the notorious Middle Passage is well documented. However, what may have been lost to most observers is the psychological impact of the slave trade and the impact on both African countries and those receiving slaves in North America and elsewhere.

Through her career in the U.S. Foreign Service, Ambassador Bridgewater has witnessed the vast repercussions of the slave trade in Africa.

I was particularly horrified by the manner in which our ancestors were separated—men and women in holding rooms, put through rituals designed to erase any thoughts or memory of home, culture, or tradition in their new environments. I think about pregnant slaves forced to give birth in indescribably harsh conditions and how both men and women were held in cold, dark rooms surrounded by human excrement and smells of their own sweat and blood. History records the "testing" of slaves to break their spirit and gauge their resolve and fortitude for the upcoming journey. We know all too well the fate of those who "passed" these trials and were taken from their native shores.

THE POWER OF CULTURE

What has been most interesting to me is the commonly held belief about the loss of culture that ensued as a result of the slave trade. I had the opportunity to talk with Ghana National Commission on Culture Chairman George Hagan about this. Professor Hagan noted that culture is key to life in Ghana and too powerful a force to be erased despite what slave traders and slave owners might have wished. We witness the legacy of this force in diasporic culture today through practices such as respect for the elderly, old superstitions like not sweeping out the back door because of possible bad luck, and preferences for certain foods (grits, okra, tomatoes) and in the outstanding and vibrant musical and artistic tradition of the Black aesthetic as embodied in the Negro spiritual, blues music, jazz, and many others. Such

European and American forts, like this one on Ghana's Cape Coast, still line African shores, a modern-day reminder of the centuries-old practice of slavery. Though the slave trade has long been eradicated, Africa has not forgotten the wounds it inflicted.

music sustained our ancestors and continues to provide outlets today for the trials and challenges experienced by the African diaspora. The cultural habits of dressing up on Sundays, of wearing head wraps that morphed into ornate hats, or "crowns," and colorful dress, all emanated from our ancestors. The cultural practice of caring for the extended family still resonates in many families of African descent, as does the ritual surrounding death and burial—grand occasions where many attend and funerals are delayed until friends, relatives, and family members gather from far and wide.

Although our slave ancestors did not forget the numerous cultural practices that defined us as a people, today, unfortunately, we see examples of modern slavery on the African continent. In reflecting on the transatlantic slave trade, I often say that we must never again allow such practices to occur. Yet women and children are trafficked and sold by their parents every day for promises of meager economic gain. They work as prostitutes or underage workers in dangerous environments where they are unable to go to school. Leaders of some African countries use the power of their offices and military might to suppress groups of their own people to protect their own selfish access to natural resources and control economic progress.

Consequently, as I visit and revisit slave forts and castles now thronged by international visitors from around the world, I often think that it is equally important that African men and women and their children witness these departure points for the sordid transatlantic slave trade. I am encouraged to see the increasing numbers from the African diaspora in the United States and other parts of the world visiting these sites, and believe it is imperative that this trend continue. Meanwhile, the United States National Slavery Museum currently under construction in my birthplace of Fredericksburg, Virginia, will be a modern monument and educational entity where people can go to learn, reflect, and, most important, act to make sure that never again will we have slavery in any form or fashion in Africa or anywhere else on Earth. ■

> "Do not presume
> to know the way
> to or around a garden
> better than the owner
> of the garden;
> always follow the person
> who brought you."
>
> — *Yoruba proverb from Nigeria, translated by Oyekan Owomoyela*

of the desired object; he pours molten metal into the clay mold, causing the wax to dissolve or become "lost." Once the metal has solidified, he opens the clay mold to reveal the metal product.

Knowledge of such processes as metallurgy is transferred generationally within a family or via guilds that are often composed of family members. Although metallurgy is the prerogative of men, both men and women engaged in cloth production. Cloth was heavily traded in trans-African and transatlantic trade networks, sometimes serving as a type of currency alongside cowrie shells and other items. Many West Africans have mastered the art and aesthetics of cloth production, creating richly textured and beautifully dyed textiles. The production of cloth involves several stages, including dying and weaving. Dying was, and continues to be, both a technique and an art. Yoruba women of Abeokuta, Nigeria, are internationally known for their *adire* textiles, beautifully patterned cloths resist-dyed in indigo that is indigenous to West Africa. In Africa, cloth, like jewelry, body art, and scarification, conveys considerable information about the wearer's identity, cultural affiliation, social status, or political rank. For example, the asantehene is entitled to wear a special pattern of *kente* cloth that, on the one hand, reflects his high rank and, on the other, distinguishes him from his constituents.

AGRICULTURE AND FARMING

While many Africans are highly skilled in the techniques of architecture, metallurgy, and cloth dying, they are, first and foremost, cultivators who have enjoyed a long relationship with plant material. Mandinka explorers brought a species of yam to the Americas, one that is indigenous to West Africa, contributing to the material evidence that confirms their arrival in the Americas before Columbus. Everywhere Africans traveled, they carried their agricultural knowledge with them. As enslaved peoples, Africans held tenaciously to their indigenous agricultural knowledge and religious beliefs. For most Africans, agriculture belongs to the spiritual realm where gods and nature are considered one force, indicated by the prevalence of special agricultural rites and festivals in Africa and in the African diaspora.

A 17th-century Nigerian plaque, once displayed in the palace of the Oba of Benin, depicts a servant collecting fruit.

East and West Africans have used the constellation as an almanac to analyze climatic changes and their effect on agriculture. The Dogon peoples of Mali and their Egyptian (the term "Egyptian" is a Greek reference to Nile Valley indigenes who defined themselves as Khemites or "black peoples") ancestors are credited with identifying the stars known as Sirius A and B. Egyptians delivered the first calendar to the world in 4236 B.C. After observing the movements and characteristics of the stars over long periods of time, Egyptians assigned names to specific stars. That body of names is known collectively and contemporaneously as the zodiac. Historically, it is known as the horoscope, reflecting the scope, vision, and intellect of the Egyptian deity Horus (known indigenously as Heru).

Consistent with their ancient meanings and functions, zodiac signs relate to, or help to explain, the relationships between astrological, agricultural, terrestrial, and human phenomena. For example, Taurus is represented by the bull, a symbol of power and dominance originally associated with Osiris (indigenously Ausar, the father of Heru). Because Osiris is credited with introducing the practice of agriculture, the bull also represents a beast of burden used to cultivate the soil. Aquarius, known indigenously as Menat (Water Bearer), is depicted as a human figure holding amphoras shedding water, symbolizing the inundation of the Nile (indigenously Hapi), overflowing its banks. A natural phenomenon influenced by stars,

Africans have traditionally possessed a deep kinship with the land, as illustrated in this 1797 drawing by the English explorer Mungo Park.

the inundation hydrated and nourished the Nile Valley with silt deposits that promoted the growth of crops.

AFRICAN CONTACT WITH EUROPE

As Olaudah Equiano, an Ibo captive from Isseke, West Africa, said about his peoples, "We are almost a nation of dancers, musicians and poets." To that list of artistic, creative, and expressive occupations one must add astrologists, mathematicians, architects, metallurgists, scholars, cultivators, healers, carvers, weavers, tanners, sculptors, dyers, traders, pre-Columbian explorers, and rulers of well-organized, prosperous empires. Such was the nature of West African life and culture before the arrival of European slave traders.

Europeans had been familiar with Africa and Africans since ancient times. North Africans, or Moors, ruled the Iberian Peninsula (the modern-day countries of Spain and Portugal) for more than 700 years, from A.D. 711 to 1492. The Romans were very familiar with Hannibal, the North African, who defeated them in key battles by using his innovative military strategies. Pythagoras and other Greeks learned their mathematical formulas and philosophies from African scholars in Egypt. Indeed, Egypt is geographically situated to the south of Greece, and the Greeks frequently traveled there to receive theoretical and practical training in the arts and sciences. In West Africa, Timbuktu and Gao were centers of learning that attracted students who came from around the world to receive training in medicine, law, history, and theology. When the Portuguese circumnavigated the continent of Africa in the 15th century, however, they were in search of commodities to monopolize for capital gain. They found

Armed with a matchlock, dog ready at his feet, a Portuguese soldier hunts leopards on African soil. The 16th-century brass plaque from Benin City, Nigeria, captures the significance of the sport to early European traders.

those commodities in the form of gold, ivory, and certain vulnerable, unsuspecting West Africans whom they kidnapped as evidence of their arrival in West Africa. Increasingly, the Portuguese sold those kidnapped Africans in various markets in Portugal.

Africans were not passive in the face of Portuguese aggression, however. From 1622 to 1659, Queen Nzinga (see page 51) and her brigades of archers fought a protracted war against Portuguese traders who were selling Umbundu peoples to European slave buyers. While African women have been mothers, wives, and artisans, they have also been queen mothers, administrators in the kings' courts, co-rulers of kingdoms, independent rulers of empires, military strategists, and warriors. Fierce and intelligent, Nzinga was simultaneously called the Queen of Ndongo and the Queen of the Matamba Mountains (located in eastern Ndongo in what is now Angola), which she used as a defensive stronghold against the Portuguese, some of whom she captured and held as prisoners. Although she signed a treaty with the Portuguese, her military prowess undermined Portuguese efforts to subdue the entire Umbundu nation. Because she valiantly defended the land, the culture, and the freedoms of the Umbundu peoples against the aggression of European enslavers, Queen Nzinga has been hailed as a "nationalist."

MYTH INVENTION

That Africa should be called the Dark Continent when it had well-organized, wealthy societies with intelligent, knowledgeable, highly skilled, and artistic peoples is ironic. Indeed, the contradiction is readily apparent to one who has read various histories of Africa that would allow the reader to develop a more accurate, comparative, and comprehensive knowledge of the African peoples. However, one has to understand the role of labeling as a necessary first step in any process of enslavement, genocide, or discrimination. In addition to being ideological, labeling is psychological and emotional. Ideologically, Europeans would find no justification or satisfaction in enslaving peoples considered civilized, spiritual, and talented. Instead, it seemed more logical and acceptable to enslave a people whom they considered inferior, primitive, and savage. Thus, with the support of racialist theories concocted by anthropologists and anchored in pseudoscience, European capitalists participated in a propagandistic campaign to redefine, discredit, and demonize the African peoples in the eyes of both Europeans and Africans. Once the Africans had been redefined as subhuman, the process of enslavement became more palatable to those who would reap enormous profits from it.

Europeans offered three key justifications for slavery. First, Europeans argued that the Africans possessed durable immune systems that could withstand diseases prevalent in the Americas and in the Caribbean. Although Africans were familiar with diseases like malaria and yellow fever, however, they possessed no immunological defenses against European-borne diseases such as tuberculosis, pneumonia, and various poxes. Consequently, many Africans perished when they contracted them. Second, the Europeans contended that slavery existed in Africa, and as a result, Africans would be familiar with systems of chattel slavery. There are some important differences, though, between African bondage and European slavery. In Africa, captives were forced to labor until their debts were satisfied, until they were sacrificed to the ancestors, or until they were sold to European and American slave buyers. In contrast, European systems of chattel slavery made bondage permanent and perpetual. In British North America, after 1662 the legal status of Africans born into European systems of chattel slavery was determined by the condition of the mother. Therefore, the children of enslaved mothers were slaves from birth and by law. In Africa, bondage was not based upon race. In European systems of chattel slavery, however,

Warrior Queen: Nzinga of Ndongo (Angola)

In the 1600s, the coastal nations of western African faced a growing threat from Portuguese slave traders. Growing demand for slave labor in colonial South America fueled an increasing Portuguese desire for a stronghold in Africa. Through occupation of African lands, the Portuguese could maintain a constant supply of slave captives for their sugar plantations in Brazil. This menace threatened the sovereignty of West African monarchs, but one fierce and intelligent ruler was able to defend her territory and deal with Portugal as an equal political power. Queen Nzinga of Ndongo and Matamba (located in modern Angola) stands out for her successful resistance to Portuguese occupation. Through a combination of military force, savvy diplomacy, and political manipulation, Nzinga maintained control of her lands and her people.

As part of a diplomatic effort to gain sovereignty for Ndongo lands, Queen Nzinga allowed the Portuguese to baptize her in the Jesuit faith.

In the early 1600s, custom prohibited Nzinga from taking the throne when her father, the king died. Instead her older brother, Mbandi, became king. Nzinga, however, believed herself to be the better monarch, more skilled in diplomacy and more intelligent. As king, Mbandi needed to decide how to thwart Portuguese attempts to kidnap the Mutumbu peoples into slavery. In recognition of his sister's prowess and savvy, Mbandi decided to enlist Nzinga as a negotiator and sent her to work out a peace agreement with the Portuguese fighters. Nzinga spoke their language, knew their ways, and was skilled at negotiating with the enemy.

By 1622, Nzinga traveled to Luanda, which had become the stronghold of the Portuguese. Her plan was to meet the new Portuguese governor, João Correia de Sousa. Nzinga realized the Ndongo needed to reposition itself in order to survive; the Portuguese needed to view the nation as an intermediary rather than a source of slave labor. She wisely brokered a settlement whereby the Ndongo kingdom would return Portuguese prisoners of war and assist the Portuguese in the slave trade in return for sovereign recognition. In addition, the Portuguese promised to withdraw their forces from Ndongo lands. Nzinga even accepted the Jesuit faith and was baptized, taking the name Anna de Sousa.

By 1624, Mbandi had died mysteriously; some believe he committed suicide, whereas others claim that Nzinga poisoned him. After his death, Nzinga took the throne, ignoring the custom that strictly forbade women from taking positions of power. Nzinga did not trust that the Portuguese would live up to their end of the agreement, and her suspicions were confirmed when the Portuguese refused to withdraw their army from the Ndongo lands and did not support her rule.

By 1626, Portugal had fully betrayed Ndongo and set upon a military invasion, forcing Nzinga and her people to flee farther west to the Matamba Mountains. There she built up her military forces by offering sanctuary to runaway slaves and Portuguese-trained African soldiers. From then until to 1659, Queen Nzinga and her brigades of archers fought a protracted war against Portuguese traders. She allied herself with the Netherlands in an attempt to reclaim all the lands of Ndongo, but their forces were not strong enough to totally defeat Portugal.

Despite the military difficulties, Nzinga was able to develop Matamba into a vital economic player and trading power, taking advantage of its position relative to the African interior. By the 1660s, Matamba had become a viable commercial state, capable of dealing with Portugal on equal footing.

Nzinga ruled for more than 40 years with the heart of a warrior rather than of a diplomat. She remained in power, doing battle up to the age of 60. Her people sometimes held mixed feelings toward her because she ignored Mbundu custom, but they also revered her for her courage, strength, and leadership. When she died in 1663 at the age of 82, Nzinga was celebrated as a queen. She was buried in a religious habit and draped in her pearls and her gold-accented royal robes.

Nzinga's legacy lives on among Angolans. Leaders like the Republic of Angola's ambassador to the United States, Josefina Pitra Diakité, a lawyer by training, consider Nzinga a great exemplar for women in leadership. The ambassador has on her Washington, D.C., office wall an artistic rendering of Nzinga, an example of how Nzinga's fortitude transcends the barrier of time, inspiring her Angolan descendants today.

C. J. C.

"The women of [Timbuktu] maintain the custom of veiling their faces, except for the slaves who sell all the foodstuffs. The inhabitants are very rich, especially the strangers who have settled in the country. . . . There are many wells containing sweet water in Timbuktu; and in addition, when the Niger is in flood canals deliver the water to the city. Grain and animals are abundant, so that the consumption of milk and butter is considerable."

— Leo Africanus (al-Hasan ibn Muhammad al-Wazzan al-Zaiyati), Arab traveler and geographer

dark skin was designated the badge of inferiority and permanent servitude, the legal proof of which is contained in the corpus of codes and statutes regulating race and slavery in the colonies and the States.

The Catholic Church provided the third, and the most powerful, justification for slavery. In the middle of the 15th century, the church issued a series of papal bulls (or edicts) that defined slavery as a Christian crusade, giving Portuguese and Spanish traders permission to invade Africa to "reduce all infidels to slavery." Within the process of enslavement, "infidel" is a convenient label that applied to all West African peoples who were not familiar with the Romanized Christianity that Europeans were introducing and using as an ideological and imperialistic instrument. Having received the support of the Catholic Church, Europeans were empowered to enslave Africans in the name of Romanized Christianity and in the names of their respective nations. In the enterprise of slavery, church and state were intimately linked in an effort to derive profits from the labor, knowledge, and skills of enslaved Africans. Moreover, a tax was placed on the head of each African man, woman, and child imported in the colonies. Because Africans were reduced to the status of commodities, they were bought, sold, and taxed like other merchandise. Revenue derived from such taxes not only enriched the royal coffers of Portugal, Spain, Holland, France, and Britain, but they filled the coffers of those in the United States engaged in the importation of Africans.

VALUED SKILLS IN THE COLONIES

Rather than reflecting the realities of African history and life, descriptions of Africa merely served as justifications for enslavement and colonization. These rationalizations signaled the transformation of the transatlantic slave trade from an unorganized endeavor characterized by indiscriminate kidnappings along the West African coast to a more organized one that would supply Europe's New World colonies with millions of African laborers who replaced Native Americans (and other indigenous populations in the Americas and the Caribbean) ravaged by European-borne diseases, arduous labor, and unspeakable atrocities committed against them by European traders arriving in the Americas and in the Caribbean. Initially, Native American and African slaves were used to transform the landscape of the colonies, in order to make those environments habitable for Europeans. After living in those environments for some time, European colonizers learned that their soils were capable of producing sugarcane, tobacco, rice, and cotton, and they would cultivate these crops for world consumption.

Since European climates and topographies did not lend themselves to the cultivation of such crops and staples, Europeans did not know how to grow them or possess the skills to cultivate them successfully. At first they relied exclusively on Native Americans and Africans and the knowledge and skills both groups possessed. Indeed, European and American plantation owners expressed preferences for particular African captives, according to the captives' knowledge and skills, which were valued and further exploited for capital gain.

Umbundu, Ibo, Yoruba, and Senegambian Africans were of considerable value to plantation owners in South Carolina and in Georgia, not only because they were excellent cultivators but also because they knew how to raise specific crops. For example, Ibo and Yoruba Africans specialized in indigo cultivation. Indigo became a cash crop, followed by rice, which was particularly well suited to the low-lying, marshy lands of coastal South Carolina and Georgia. In addition to agricultural knowledge, Africans brought their carving, smelting, and weaving skills, which allowed them to make the agricultural tools and rice

Modern Griots: Salif Keita and Sékou Diabaté

For centuries, griots, or oral historians, have been revered by the peoples of West Africa and West African ancestry. They hold the rank of musician in a caste system that dates back to the time of the great Malian empire, which flourished in West Africa from the 13th to the 16th century.

Historically, Griots have maintained the familial stories of their contemporaries. They act as living libraries, or in some cases, as the documents that detail historical events related to the men and women from their locale. In some cases, they can recount all of the stories, as handed down to them by many generations of their ancestors, of their tribespeople who were snatched by slave catchers.

These chroniclers are also considered to be culture carriers of family history. Griots, who today are found mostly in the West African countries of Mali, Guinea, Gambia, and Senegal, are praise singers and repositories of family records. Today, griots originate mostly from the Mandinka, Malinke, Bambara, Fula, Hausa, Tukuloor, Wolof, and Sere peoples. In addition to being poets, singers, and musicians, griots are revered by members of some African societies as the educators who remember and recite facts about the town or village and its inhabitants in the present and in the past.

One internationally renowned singer who considers himself a modern-day griot is Salif Keita. Born in 1949 in Mali, West Africa, Keita decided early in his life that he wanted to become a musician. Keita, who is not a traditional griot, came from a noble family; he is a descendant of a Mandinka warrior king who founded Mali, Sundiata Keita. This noble lineage almost excluded him from following this path, for tradition held that musicians should not be of the noble class—only from the djeli, or lower musician class. To further complicate matters, Keita was born an albino—lacking normal pigmentation in his skin, hair, and eyes—and nearly blind, which was a sign of bad luck in his culture. His mother hid him away from relatives and the community throughout his early childhood to keep him alive and safe. As Keita grew older, his father threatened to disown him upon learning of his desire to become a griot.

But Keita persevered and in 1967 moved from his village to the city of Bamako, where he got his start performing in nightclubs. He later joined a government-sponsored band, after playing in a band with his brother. As Keita's fame grew, he became known as a master of West African rhythms. Since then, he has carried on the griot tradition and has gained fame throughout much of the world. Like the historic griots, Keita uses his songs to tell the stories of the plight of his people who are living at home and abroad. His political songs recount the struggles and offer some solutions that might bring healing.

Another man from West Africa also carries on in the tradition of his ancestors. He is Sékou "Bambino" Diabaté of Guinea. Born in the small village of Siguiri, located on the Niger River in northeastern Guinea, Diabaté is descended from a long line of griots. When he was just 12 years old, the Guinean president, Ahmed Sékou Touré, heard him sing. Touré was so impressed by the boy's talent he urged him to join a state-sponsored jazz group called Bembeya. Diabaté heeded the president's call, and as the front man and the youngest member of that band, he earned the name Bambino.

A modern-day griot, Salife Keita of Mali performs during the 2006 Copenhagen Jazz Festival. His mix of music and storytelling has kept alive the centuries-old West African tradition.

Diabaté played with several groups and eventually formed his own band. This allowed him to hone his skills and carry on the griot traditions of recounting the history of his people through song. His work has brought him acclaim as he spreads Guinean music and the griot culture around the world. Carrying out his work on a global scale, Diabaté also serves as a Red Cross ambassador, charged with educating the world about the effects on children of war, poverty, suffering, and disease.

Keita and Diabaté join others, including West African women, who carry on the griot tradition. Some female griots, such as Amy Koita, are praise singers. Her traditions date back to her female ancestors, who sang about human nature and offered ways to live a good life. The family tradition goes back to the time of slavery, when the men would tell the stories and the women would sing.

Although these men and women are but a few of many modern-day musicians and griots, they believe that they have a great role to play in their own societies and on a global stage. By bringing the rhythms, the stories, the music, and the history of West Africa to the world, they carry on the same tradition on an international scale that others from their villages perform in a much smaller realm.

C. J. C.

"The drums of Africa still beat in my heart."

— *Mary McLeod Bethune, educator*

baskets that contributed to the material and technological success of colonial plantations.

GULLAH CULTURE

The South Carolina–Georgia region is also known as Gullah country, inhabited by descendants of Umbundu, Ibo, Yoruba, and Senegambian (Wolof, Serer, and Creole peoples of present-day Sierra Leone) Africans who have preserved various elements of their ancestors' West African heritages. The remoteness of Gullah country, comprising a chain of sea islands located off the coasts of South Carolina and Georgia, has allowed its inhabitants to live relatively uninfluenced by European culture. For example, Gullah peoples speak a dialect of English that is quite distinct, heavily influenced by the languages of West and Central Africa. Because Senegambian Africans brought the knowledge of rice cultivation to the Carolina-Georgia region, rice remains a staple in the diet of African Americans residing in that area. Gullah peoples continue to practice their African artistic traditions. Gullah men weave their own finishing nets, casting them over the rivers in the tradition of their Senegambian forefathers. Gullah women weave sweetgrass baskets that are expensive and highly sought after, because they embody artistic and technical skills that are indigenous to Senegambia.

The existence of a Gullah community that is distinctive and culturally diverse belies the notion of a monolithic African-American people. Instead, African Americans are as diverse as the many African cultures from which they descend. The presence of Africanisms (elements of African cultural heritages) in the Americas and in the Caribbean also dispels the myth that slavery and the transatlantic slave trade destroyed all vestiges of African culture in the New World. To the extent that Africans possessed artistic and technical knowledge and skills that contributed to the material and economic viability of plantations, and given that plantation owners expressed preferences for knowledgeable, skilled Africans over other groups, the myth that Africa was devoid of intelligent and industrious peoples is negated. Due to its lucrative nature, and despite protestations from humanitarians who were not empowered politically, or economically, to end the enslavement of African men, women, and children, the slave trade, which began in the 15th century, continued unabated for 400 years.

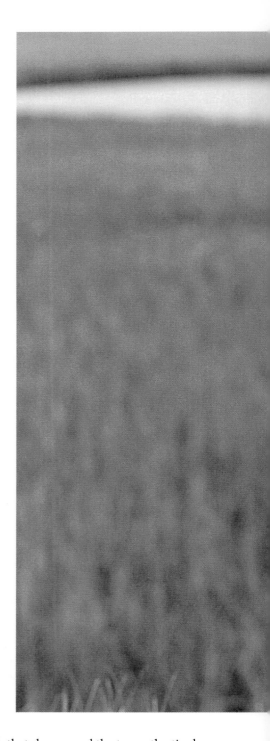

West African baskets made by coiling grass, a craft dating to the 1700s, are still made today by African-American weavers.

Faced with a rapidly modernizing world, African Americans throughout the U.S. have found many ways to keep their traditional culture from being forgotten. Marquetta L. Goodwine (above), known as Queen Quet of the Gullah nation, works today in South Carolina to promote awareness of the Gullah people and the need to maintain Gullah traditions. Similarly, Ida Wilson (inset), pictured in South Carolina in 1965, created woven baskets in Sierra Leone's shukublay *tradition. Baskets of this type are still sold today along Route 17, north of Charleston.*

Timbuktu's Treasures of Learning

A GALLERY

Contrary to a misconception popularized by European colonists, Africa was not a "dark continent," devoid of civilization and culture in the times before and after the slave trade began. This falsehood, invented by those seeking to justify their exploitation of the African peoples, took hold despite the robust centers of thought and culture established and maintained by the people of Africa for centuries. The extraordinary holdings of one of these great centers of learning, Timbuktu, recently have been rediscovered. An untold quantity of scholarly treasures from the great 15th-century libraries of the city bear witness to the overlooked intellectual centers of West Africa.

An early document on Islamic law, held today by the Mamma Haidara library in Timbuktu, evokes a rich African intellectual tradition.

Located in the modern-day nation of Mali, the magnificent kingdom of Timbuktu was founded more than 900 years ago. It stood as a great West African religious, commercial, and cultural center for more than 600 years. From far and wide, residents and travelers traversed north across the Sahara through Morocco and Algeria to lands that included Asia and Europe. In the 1800s, much of the great city eventually fell into ruins, becoming little more than a legend in the imaginations of some people. But in recent years, discoveries of ancient texts and historical documents are bearing witness to the vibrant cultural center that Timbuktu held in western Africa.

During its heyday in the 15th and 16th centuries, Timbuktu was one of the most robust centers of trade and learning in western Africa. It was a favorite place for merchants to exchange goods, but Timbuktu's lasting glory would be found in scholarship. Great thinkers, teachers, and students traveled there both to study and to teach. Great books were written, copied, and stored at the University of Timbuktu, making its literary holdings without equal in the region. Many books found in Timbuktu centuries ago were brought in from other parts of the world to be copied and stored, especially Islamic material. The works found in Mali covered a vast range of subjects, from Islam to topics regarding human behavior, history, and endeavor. When the city began to decline in the 1800s, many of these writings disappeared into private collections and were forgotten about by the world at large.

Today, there is a kind of renaissance occurring in Mali as these writings and texts have begun to resurface. Private collections formerly held by families have been made public, revealing scores of sacred manuscripts that date back over some 600 years. Some scholars estimate that there are more than 700,000 manuscripts housed throughout collections in Timbuktu. New centers of learning are springing up, reflecting the growing interest of scholars and the importance of historic preservation.

The discovery of many of these ancient manuscripts has caused great excitement over their literary content and a massive rush to preserve all that can be found. It is said that the storage conditions of some of these works has rendered them so frail that the written letters literally fall right off the paper as one turns the leaves of the manuscripts. To maintain this treasure trove of documents, the resdiscovered texts are now being preserved at Timbuktu's Ahmed Baba Center and in private family libraries, such as the Mamma Haidara Commemorative Library and the Library of Cheick Zayni Baye of Boujbeha, near Timbuktu.

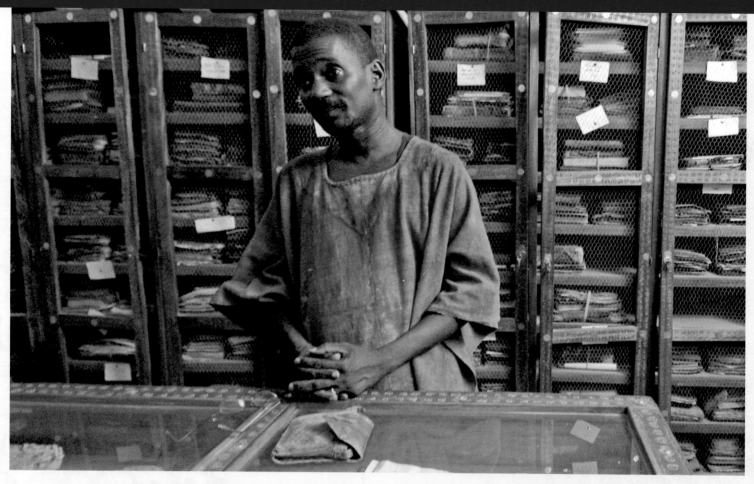

Ismaël Diadé Haïdara, a historian and philosopher and keeper of a collection of family manuscripts dating back centuries, says that Timbuktu has a "second chance" to become a great city again.

Through these manuscripts, centuries of history are being uncovered, honoring ancestors and giving witness to a marvelous history. Today Timbuktu has been designated a World Heritage site by the United Nations Educational, Scientific, and Cultural Organization (UNESCO). Forgotten for centuries to the sands of the Sahara, Timbuktu's rich legacy of sacred manuscripts could possess a treasure chest of African history.

Today much progress has been made, in large part because of the financial support that South Africa and several organizations have given, and continue to contribute, toward the restoration and housing of Timbuktu's ancient documents. This funding has enabled the repair and digitization of ancient documents. Some of these documents are available online now, and 300 of them will soon become available. In addition, the South African government is funding the building of an underground library that will house more than 30,000 books.

Sacred manuscripts have helped elevate Timbuktu's status as a city of rich cultural and historical significance.

So far, a great deal of light has been shed on the vast testaments to history that went undiscovered or forgotten for so long. People who once believed that they had no real written history now have a greater sense of pride. Until recently most Malians believed they had few choices in accessing their history. They thought that the only way to access their history and culture was through oral accounts of the griots, the musicians who mentally record and disperse the history and culture of their respective regions. But now they are celebrating, along with the rest of the world, a cadre of magnificent treasures.

CHAPTER THREE

Stolen Away

Stolen Away

The transatlantic slave trade began in the 15th century as a series of kidnappings of West African peoples by Portuguese traders circumnavigating the continent of Africa in search of gold and other valuable commodities. As the slave trade became more organized, African men, women, and children were objectified, assigned various values, traded, and ultimately taxed as commodities by European nations that would come to rely on enslaved Africans as the primary labor force for their colonies in the Americas and in the Caribbean. Known as black gold, African captives became so valuable as commodities that European nations fought each other for control of them. In pursuit of a monopoly over the slave trade, the Portuguese were quickly followed by the Spanish, the Dutch, and the British, who became the dominant suppliers of slaves to New World colonies, where slavery flourished for more than 400 years.

BEGINNINGS

In the 15th century, colonization of the Americas and the Caribbean created new demands for slave labor, derived originally from indigenous populations such as the Arawaks and the Caribs. Whenever and wherever Europeans made contact with indigenous peoples, however, it resulted in the disruption, displacement, and deaths of those peoples, who perished as a result of being subjected to arduous labor and exposed to European-borne diseases for which they possessed no biological defenses and as a result of gross abuses that were perpetrated against them. In his journal, Columbus recorded that he kidnapped 500 Arawaks and sent them to Spain to be sold for profit. The violence that Columbus perpetrated against indigenous peoples opened the way for their subsequent destruction by other European imperialists seeking to claim land, and riches, in the names of their respective nations. Violence was, in the opinion of Europeans, a necessary component of the colonization plan designed to subjugate and exploit indigenous populations. In many cases, Europeans used guns, swords, crossbows, and greyhounds to slaughter indigenous men, women (including pregnant women), and children simply for sport and amusement.

Father Bartolomé de Las Casas, who traveled with Columbus on his second voyage, played a major role in the enslavement of indigenous peoples in the Caribbean, and he used Christianity as an instrument for converting indigenes, thereby making them subservient and pliant for exploitation by Spanish colonizers. Las Casas and other officials of the Catholic Church owned Arawaks and Caribs as slaves. It was Las Casas who proposed increasing the enslavement of Africans to replace indigenes who were perishing in Spanish colonies. Before Africans were imported in massive numbers, however, European convicts were forced to labor in the colonies. But European convicts did not constitute a viable labor force, because they were not plentiful, and they lacked the agricultural knowledge and skills possessed by Africans. Thus, Africans were more attractive as laborers. Equally

Left: A weathered archway on Ghana's coast marks the entrance to Elmina Castle, where slaves were imprisoned before being shipped to the Caribbean.

Previous pages: A 19th-century English painting illustrates the crowded slave deck of the H.M.S. Albanez, *carrying cargo from the Guinea coast to the Caribbean.*

"The slave trade was not a statistic, however astronomical. The slave trade was people living, lying, stealing, murdering, dying. . . . The slave trade was a greedy king raiding his own villages to get slaves to buy brandy. . . . The slave trade was deserted villages, bleached bones on slave trails and people with no last names."

—Lerone Bennett, Jr., writer and social historian

important is the fact that slavery in the Caribbean, and in the Americas, was race based. Africans were reduced to a state of permanent slavery, based on their dark skin and all of the negative attributes assigned to it. Africans constituted a cheap, plentiful, and talented source of labor, a huge asset to European systems of enslavement that worked laborers to death. Arduous labor, nutrient-deficient diets, and poor health were factors that caused high mortality rates among Africans enslaved on plantations in the Caribbean and in the Americas. Consequently, plantation owners needed to rigorously and consistently replenish their labor supply. In 1518, the Spanish government issued the asiento, a license that granted Genoese merchants permission to import 4,000 Africans into Spanish colonies in the West Indies. The asiento was not given to the Genoese merchants; it was sold to them. Thus, the Catholic crown of Spain began to reap its first profits from the enslavement of African peoples. Moreover, a tax was placed on the head of each African man, woman, and child imported into Spanish colonies in the West Indies. African slaves were also taxed in North America. In fact, Article I, Section 9 of the U.S. Constitution provided for the taxation of Africans imported into the United States. The words "slave" and "slavery" were not included in the Constitution at the behest of James Madison, the Constitution's master architect and a slave owner. Instead, the language of Article I, Section 9 was left open for slave states to interpret according to their need to regulate imports. Moreover, most states in the Union drafted laws permitting the taxation of African slaves as imports and as transfers from the West Indies. The taxation of African slaves confirms the fact that the economic framework of the slave trade expanded beyond simple supply and demand, allowing governments to fill their coffers with tax revenues derived from the heads of imported slaves.

GREAT BRITAIN AS A SLAVE POWER

The issuance of the asiento signaled a transformation in the transatlantic slave trade, from an unorganized endeavor characterized by kidnappings along the West African coast to a profitable enterprise sustained by law and brutality. Thus, the asiento gave the slave trade economic legitimacy as well as greater momentum. Competition developed between Portugal, Spain, Holland, France, and Britain as they sought to dominate the trade in slaves. In the Treaty of Utrecht (1713), Spain granted the British exclusive rights to transport slaves into Spanish colonies for 30 years, although Spain retained the power to issue the asiento. Simultaneously, Britain carried African captives to its British colonies in North America. Due largely to its naval prowess, the British established both military and economic supremacy over the slave trade, not merely in terms of transporting Africans into both Spanish and British colonies but also in terms of the associative trades in which it was engaged, including shipbuilding, gunmaking, manacle production, and the manufacture of cheap wares and trinkets traded for African captives in Africa.

The economic importance and feasibility of the trade were reflected in the fact that the Royal African Company, the Sierra Leone Company, and the Dutch West India Company formed to carry on the traffic in slaves, for which they minted their own coins to be exchanged for slaves and other commodities elsewhere in the Atlantic trade network. Britain's participation in the slave trade is cemented in the architecture of the private homes of former ship captains and in that of banks and other commercial buildings in Bristol, Liverpool, and London. In one manner or another, they bear the symbols of their builders' and owners' connections to the slave trade. The masonry entrance to Martins (now Barclays) Bank in Liverpool is embellished with the images of two "Negro" boys holding a ship anchor and other nautical instruments. Slavetrading was an expensive

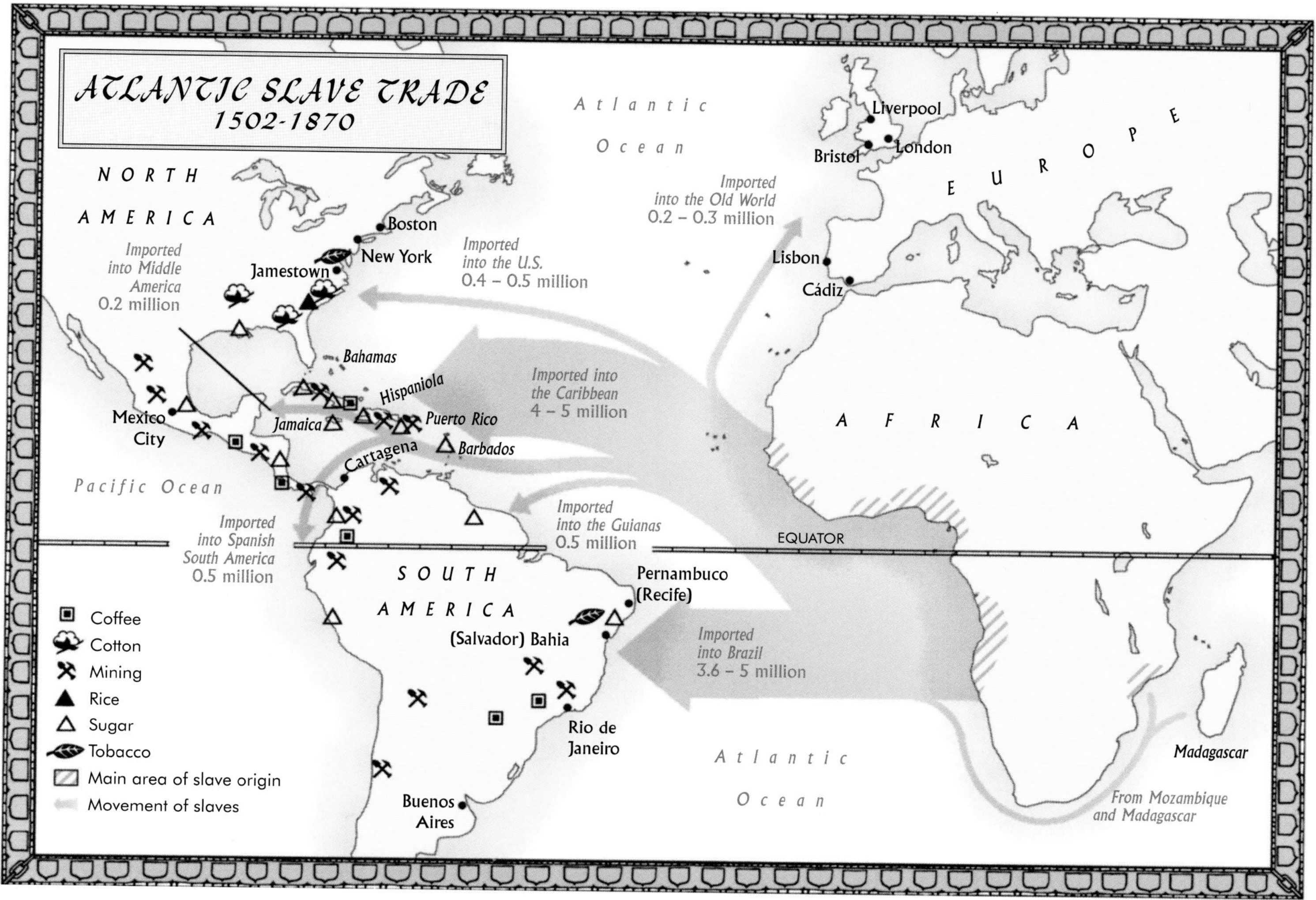

The transatlantic slave trade uprooted millions of Africans for more than three centuries, sending them to the Americas and parts of Europe.

endeavor engaged in by multiple investors operating under the auspices of one company, by wealthy individuals acting out of their personal interests, or by individuals financed by wealthy monarchs and citizens. The Englishman John Newton commanded the slave ships *Duke of Argyle* and *African* for J. Manesty & Co., a prominent slave-trading house in Liverpool. After several near-fatal experiences aboard the slave ship *Greyhound*, Newton penned the hymn "Amazing Grace." On the surface, it seems hypocritical that a slave ship captain would pen what became a very popular hymn. But the hypocrisy is rooted in the fact that Christianity was used to justify, and sustain, the slave trade. Moreover, slave ship captains prayed for safe passage to Africa, successful slave trading on the coasts of Africa, and a safe Middle Passage from Africa to the New World.

AFRICAN INVOLVEMENT

Underpinning the slave trade's transformation and growth was the reality that the asiento demanded more slaves than could be obtained by kidnapping alone. Necessarily, relations between Europeans and Africans were also transformed, some Africans taking on the role of suppliers of African captives to European and American slave buyers. In order to meet their quotas for African captives, foreign buyers needed the cooperation of African warriors and traders, who controlled the supply side of the trade. To avoid laying the

A 17th-century engraving shows Cape Coast Castle in Ghana, West Africa. Originally built by the Swedes, it became a British fort in 1663.

"Involuntarily I strolled to one of the windows a little before dinner, without the smallest suspicion of what I was about to see . . . between two and three hundred victims, chained and parceled out in circles, just satisfying the cravings of nature from a trough of rice placed in the center of each circle."

—*Anna Maria Falconbridge, Englishwoman visiting Bunce Island slave castle, Sierra Leone, 1791*

blame for the slave trade squarely on the shoulders of the African suppliers, it must be remembered that the transatlantic slave trade was buyer driven. The economic success of European plantation systems depended heavily on African labor and knowledge, so foreign buyers continued to call at African ports. Moreover, Europeans established slave forts on the East and West African coasts, including Gorée Island (Senegal), Elmina (Ghana), Cape Coast Castle (Ghana), the Portuguese Fort (Whydah, Republic of Benin), and Fort Jesus (Mombasa, Kenya), to regulate the exchanges of slaves and European-manufactured guns, which facilitated slave raids in the African interior.

Enslavement was a process that began at the point of capture, often located 200 or more miles from the point of sale. Pretexts for launching slave raids on specific villages included failing to pay taxes or tribute (human and material resources collected from vassal territories), competing or interfering in a rival's slave-trading activities, impeding a competitor's access to coastal slave markets, offending a group or nation, and insulting a reigning king. Typically, African warriors launched intercultural slave raids. Fon warriors of the kingdom of Dahomey (located in what is currently called the Republic of Benin) raided their Yoruba enemies in neighboring Nigeria, and vice versa. However, groups also engaged in intracultural slave raids, preying upon and enslaving their countrymen for acts of sedition, adultery, and witchcraft. Although slave raids often involved some preplanning, many Africans were abducted when they were simply walking along roads or working on their farms. Others were victims of more strategic slave raids on their towns and villages.

Confrontation between slave raiders and target groups was brutal, often fatal for undesirable individuals such as elderly or handicapped persons. For example, the Fon warriors of Dahomey were known to rip the jawbones out of the faces of resistors, decapitating them and retaining their heads as war trophies. Horrific sights of such carnage illustrated the power of the Dahomean empire, on the one hand, and frightened captives into submission, on the other. Capturing Africans represented an important component of the process of enslavement; evacuating captives to trans-Saharan or coastal markets constituted another component of that process. Captives who survived evacuation from their interior points of capture experienced a new set of psychological and physical trauma

Prince Among Slaves: Prince Abdul Rahman

"I was born in the city in the city of Tombuctoo. My father had been living in Tombuctoo, but removed to be King in Teembo, in Foota Jallo. His name was Almam Abrahim." Abdul Rahman Ibrahima Sori, King Almam Abrahim's son, was born a prince in Africa in 1762 and penned these words as a slave in America. He was born into the royal family in a region in west-central Africa that is now present-day Guinea. Raised as a Muslim, Abdul Rahman was educated in the African cities of Djénné and Timbuktu, both of which were thriving centers of Muslim culture and learning. After completing his education, he served as an officer in his father's military, rising to the rank of colonel at the age of 24. In 1788, while leading 2,000 warriors against a rival group known as the Hebohs, he and his army were defeated. Prince Abdul Rahman and his friend Samba were taken hostage and transported to the West African coast, where they were traded to British slavers for gunpowder, guns, tobacco, and rum. Ironically, he was captured while defending his own father's highly successful slave trade with Europeans.

Abdul Rahman was taken to a large slave market on the Mississippi River for transport to Natchez, Mississippi, where he and Samba were sold as slaves to a young cotton and tobacco planter named Thomas Foster for the total sum of $950. On Foster's plantation, Abdul Rahman began his transformation from African to African American and from prince to slave. The act of cutting off his long royal locks of hair and forcing him to do menial labor humiliated the young prince, and he ran away within weeks of his arrival on the plantation. After wandering around alone in the swamps for weeks, Abdul Rahman returned to the plantation. In an act of submission, he placed the foot of Foster's wife upon his neck and professed his loyalty in exchange for having his life spared.

True to his word, he settled into his new life in America. In 1794, he married Isabella, a devout Christian woman who was also enslaved on the Foster plantation and who served as the midwife and doctor. The couple had five sons and four daughters. Abdul Rahman drew upon his knowledge of farming gained while growing up in Africa and quickly rose to a position of authority. Eventually, Abdul Rahman was made overseer of the Foster plantation, in which position he earned the respect of the slaves under his care. Foster considered him to be trustworthy and allowed him to maintain a private garden and to sell his produce at a rural market. One afternoon in 1807 Abdul Rahman and another slave were selling vegetables at the market when a white man spoke his Arabic name to him. The man was Dr. John Cox, who had stayed with Abdul Rahman and his family in Timbo when he was stranded sick in the early 1780s. Grateful for the hospitality shown to him in Timbo, Cox and his son William appealed to Foster for Ibrahim's freedom but the prince's services and skills were indispensable to Foster, and he would not agree; it was not until about 20 years later that William teamed up with a local newspaperman to bring national attention to the prince's enslavement.

Foster finally agreed to sell Abdul Rahman and his wife with the condition that they be sent back to Africa immediately. "I feel sad, to think of leaving my children behind me. I desire to go back to my own country again; but when I think of my children, it hurts my feelings. If I go to my own country, I cannot feel happy, if my children are left. I hope by God's assistance, to recover them." A year later, after an unsuccessful campaign to raise money to buy his children and grandchildren, the couple set sail for Liberia, an African colony established by the American Colonization Society for freed slaves. Prince Abdul Rahman was now 67 and had lived more than 40 years as a slave. Tragically, before he could raise the money to free his children and before he could contact his family in Guinea, Abdul Rahman fell ill and died. Several years later, American supporters raised enough money to purchase two of the sons and their families and reunited them with their mother in Liberia. The seven children and grandchildren left enslaved in America were distributed among Foster's nine children upon his death in 1828. *D. W.*

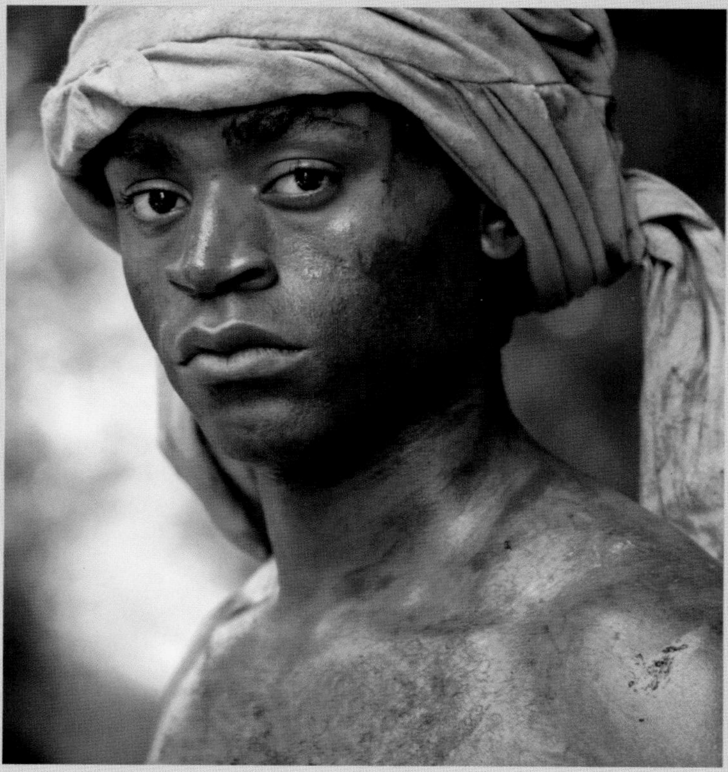

Actor Marcus Mitchell portrays Abdul Rahman in the 2008 PBS film Prince Among Slaves. *Born a prince in west-central Africa, Rahman spent more than 40 years as a slave in Mississippi before returning to his homeland.*

Right: Some Africans supplied slaves to European traders in exchange for weapons or goods. Here, captives are led to coastal trading centers.

Below: The slave collar, used to control captives, is one of many enduring symbols of slavery's brutality.

at the coasts, where they saw the sea, huge slave ships, and white people for the first time. At the coasts, captives were placed in European forts, warehouses, and barracoons, less fortified holding pens located along the beaches, until they were sold to European and American buyers.

TRANSPORTING SLAVES

Slavery would come to be referred to as the peculiar institution, due to the nature of the commodity on which it so heavily depended for its success. Simultaneously, the African was both a human being and a commodity. Oxymoronically, the "commodity" was a thinking, feeling being. The Africans were further objectified and commodified when they underwent a health inspection, a necessary component of the process of enslavement. Buyers wanted their human commodities to be free of debilitating diseases, handicaps, or other defects that would reduce their value in American and Caribbean markets. Ultimately, buyers aimed to purchase the most desirable, "No. 1," "Prime Negroes," who

Bringing the Family Together: Artemus Gaye

Artemus W. Gaye is a seventh-generation grandson of Prince Abdul Rahman Ibrahima Sori and his wife, Isabella (see page 65). In 2002, he helped to organize a Freedom Festival in Natchez, Mississippi, to bring together descendants of the prince, who had been captured in Africa and brought to America as a slave in 1788. Gaye's 92-year-old great-great-grandmother told him the story of his royal ancestor in the African oral tradition of the griot. It was 1990, and Gaye, 13, was fleeing with his family from war torn Monrovia, Liberia, to the western part of the country, where his great-great-grandmother lived. She used the curfew imposed on the region as an opportunity to teach Gaye and other children about their history and about ancestors. One of the stories she told was of the royal warrior prince's life as a slave in America and his return to Africa with his wife in 1829 as a freed man. Although seven of Abdul Rahman's nine children remained in America as slaves, American abolitionists were able to raise money to purchase the freedom of two of his children. Through their generous action, the abolitionists were able to reunite the children with their mother in Liberia following the death of the prince. One of the freed children was Gaye's great-great-great-great-grandfather, Simon, who fought against the slave trade. As a young boy, Gaye did not appreciate the story of these shadowy figures who had lived so long ago, preferring to play outdoors with the other children. Nevertheless, he found himself intrigued by the story.

In reality, Gaye had learned only part of the story from his great-great-grandmother. After spending his childhood in chaos in Liberia, he and his family escaped to Sierra Leone, a West African country bordering Liberia, then moved to Zimbabwe in the southern part of Africa. With the assistance of a college professor, he immigrated to the United States in 1997 and began a study program in counseling at a Michigan college. "It was the first time I got in touch with my own feelings. . . . You get in touch with your own pain, you can be more effective in dealing with the people you're trying to help. So one of the things I was told was to tell my story."

He began researching and writing the story told to him by his great-great-grandmother, combing through archival records for information about his ancestors. Starting with Simon, he was heartbroken to learn that slave names were close to impossible to find because slaves were considered property. Later, he found out that passenger lists were kept for ships leaving the States and was elated to locate Simon's name on a passenger list of the ship that carried him to Liberia. Gaye also made contact with Terry Alford, the author of *Prince Among Slaves*, which told the story of Prince Abdul Rahman. Alford used historical documents and oral accounts to piece together the life of the prince. With Alford's help, Gaye was able to connect the American side of the story with the African

Descendants of slave-prince Ibrahima, plantation owner Thomas Foster, and journalist Andrew Marschalk gather in Mississippi to celebrate the 175th anniversary of Ibrahima's liberation.

side. He was told that after abolitionists raised money to purchase the freedom of the prince and his wife, Abdul Rahman was unable to raise enough to free the rest of his children before he was sent to the Liberian colony in 1829, where he died shortly thereafter. His American enslaved children were distributed among the children of his former master, who died that same year, and they remained in the States after emancipation. None of the descendants on either continent had ever met until Gaye came to America.

On his visit he traveled to the plantation site in Natchez where his ancestors had been enslaved so many years before. "God, it was like a sacred moment in my life. As if I'd been longing, unconsciously, to come to that place. I could almost feel the presence of my ancestors and my grandmother with me. And I tell you, my experience in Natchez brought a deep sense of connection to the history of Africa, and the history of America." The festival brought together descendants from Africa and America. Gaye also invited the descendants of the slaveholder, Thomas Foster, to heal the wounds left by slavery. "His family's history did not begin in slavery, but in freedom," he says.

Gaye is currently pursing a Ph.D. in ethics from Loyola University. He is the founder and president of the Prince Ibrahima & Isabella F. Freedom Foundation, Inc. The nonprofit foundation promotes dialogue between people of African descent in Africa and in the United States and seeks to research and preserve the legacy of slavery on both continents. *Prince Among Slaves* was made into an award-winning PBS documentary in 2008, and it featured highlights of the reunion between Abdul Rahman and Foster descendants.

D. W.

Lives of Slave Ships

NATALIE ROBERTSON, PH.D.

The Slave Trade Acts of 1794 and 1807 criminalized the importation of "any negro, mulatto, or person of colour from any foreign kingdom, place, or country into the United States for the purposes of holding, selling, or disposing of such persons as slaves." Violators would be guilty of a high misdemeanor, punishable by five to ten years in prison. The acts inaugurated the "illegal period" in the transatlantic slave trade. By 1830, most slave-trading nations had abolished new importations. Despite these policies, illegal cargoes arrived in the United States via Havana, Cuba, a veritable smugglers' den, where American and Spanish ships could be outfitted and provisioned for slaving voyages in violation of international anti-smuggling laws. The infamous *Wanderer* has been popularized as "the last slave ship" to land a cargo of Africans in the Gulf states in 1859, but it is followed by the slaver *Clotilda*, which landed its cargo in Mobile, Alabama, in July 1860.

THE *BLACK JOKE* AND THE *DOS AMIGOS*

At Havana, Spanish and Portuguese captains obtained blank ship registries and American flags to use as protection against seizure by British naval officers at sea, exploiting the historic hostility between the United States and Great Britain over search and seizure rights.

The Spanish brigantine schooner *Dos Amigos*, under the command of Don Juan Ramon de Muxica, launched from Havana in 1830. On the West African coast, British naval officers aboard *Black Joke* watched *Dos Amigos* enter the Bay of Cameroon and sail up the Wouri River. To evade capture by *Black Joke*, Captain Muxica discarded *Dos Amigos'* human cargo and its copper kettles used to cook food for the captives, prima facie evidence of illegal slave trade in violation of the laws of Spain. American and Spanish smugglers used nimble Baltimore-built schooners and clippers to elude sluggish government cruisers as well as "clip" the sail time between West Africa and the Americas. Given the extensive slave-trading relationships between Baltimore shipbuilders and Spanish smugglers at Havana, and at Brazil, during the illegal slave trade, it is highly likely that *Dos Amigos* came from Baltimore.

Dos Amigos could not evade capture by *Black Joke* with its 18-pound pivoting cannon, and Captain Muxica surrendered. *Black Joke* escorted *Dos Amigos* to Sierra Leone, where a Court of Mixed Commission, composed mainly of members of the major European nations, adjudicated cases involving vessels labeled as slavers. Condemned vessels were sold at auction, after which many of them were redeployed under new names. In its former life, for example, *Black Joke* was the notorious Spanish slaver *Henriquetta*, owned by José de Cerqueira Lima of Bahia, Brazil. From 1825 to 1827, *Henriquetta* smuggled a total of 3,040 Africans into Brazil, sailing, on one occasion, under the flag of the United States. After loading a cargo of 569 slaves at Lagos, *Henriquetta* was captured by H.M.S. *Sybill*. In 1828, the British Navy purchased *Henriquetta* for 330 pounds and renamed it *Black Joke*.

Natalie Robertson studies slave ships as part of her research on the transatlantic slave trade.

In its second career, it served as a tender to British cruisers in the African Squadron to enforce anti-importation laws at sea by capturing slavers like *Dos Amigos*. *Black Joke* supplied provisions, communications, and transportation between shore and the larger vessels anchored offshore. This was a perfect role for the 256-ton *Black Joke*, capable of penetrating bays and smaller waterways such as the Wouri River, where she trapped *Dos Amigos*.

After the Court of Mixed Commission condemned *Dos Amigos* in 1831, the British

The H.M.S. Black Joke, *firing here on the Spanish slave ship* El Almirante, *was essential to ending the transatlantic slave trade.*

purchased it at auction. Subsequently, the *Dos Amigos* sailed to Portsmouth, England, the location of the Royal Navy's dockyard, where it was renamed *Fair Rosamond*. In Portsmouth, *Fair Rosamond* received its masts and was outfitted for its voyage to Sierra Leone, where it served as tender to H.M.S. *Dryad* in the African Squadron. Its first captain, Lt. Sir Henry Huntley, characterized her as "A fair schooner, superior to *Black Joke* when running free." From 1834 to 1836, *Fair Rosamond* overhauled several slavers, including *El Esplorado*, *La Mariposa*, and *La Pantica*.

STOLEN PEOPLES

At Douala, situated on the Wouri River, *Dos Amigos* acquired Bamileke, Bamun, and Fang peoples, who, in addition to being cultivators, are excellent wood-carvers. At Whydah, a slave port in the Republic of Benin, *Henriquetta* acquired Fon, Yoruba, and Ibo Africans, who are highly skilled metallurgists, carvers, herbalists, and cultivators of tubers, grains, and indigo.

Indeed, Africans were people before they were reduced to the status of slaves by way of a specific process that began in West Africa but that continued in the Americas, reinforced by laws and brutality. The length of time required to complete the Atlantic Passage from Africa to the Americas was influenced by several factors, including the speed of the slaver, the navigational skills of its captain, the weather, and the health conditions aboard ship. Slave trading was a precarious enterprise with high disease and mortality rates for both cargo and crew. The early routes traveled by European slavers formed a triangle that was sometimes called the notorious triangle, not merely because of the dangers associated with disease but because of the heinous predations that captains and crews perpetrated on their defenseless captives at sea. Thus, the slave ship was, at once, a floating crypt and a den of iniquity. Once aboard a slaver, however, most of the captives would never see their African homelands again, consumed by the treachery of the Atlantic Passage or forced to live the balance of their lives as slaves for the benefit of their owners in the New World. ■

An 1868 photograph shows East African slaves taken aboard the H.M.S. Daphne *after being rescued from a dhow in the Indian Ocean.*

would bring the highest prices in the New World. Young captives were preferred over aged ones, who had a shorter life expectancy and who were not as durable as their younger counterparts. Male captives were desired over female captives. In addition to possessing agricultural knowledge, male captives possessed woodcarving and metallurgical skills that increased their value to planters, in particular, and to plantations, in general. However, female captives were also desirable, because of their ability to serve as sexual objects for the gratification of their owners, their ability to bear children thereby increasing the wealth of their owners, and their ability to nurse the planters' children when the planters neglected that parental responsibilities.

Slave ship captains selected their captives based on their health, gender, and age and the preferences of European and American plantation owners, or those of the investors who financed the slave trading expedition. In cases where Africans were prepurchased, the initials of their European, American, and Caribbean owners, or the initials of the ships in which they would be transported across the Atlantic, were seared into the captives' flesh using a hot branding iron. African captives owned by the Royal African Company, for example, were branded with the initials RAC. The captives carried these psychological and physical wounds into the holds of slave ships, where they encountered new horrors. African captives were stored in the holds of ships in an efficient manner that capitalized on the ship's stowage capacity, calculated relative to their tonnage, as explained by Captain John Newton:

> *With our ships, the great object is, to be full. When the ship is there, it is thought desirable she should take as many as possible. The cargo of a vessel of a hundred tons, or little more, is calculated to purchase from two hundred and twenty to two hundred and fifty slaves. Their lodging-rooms below the deck, which are three (for the men, the boys, and the women), besides a place for the sick, are sometimes more than five feet high, and sometimes less; and this height is divided towards the middle, for the slaves*

Right: Faced with the trauma of slavery, African captives often risked their lives to escape bondage. Here, captives leap from a slave ship near the coast of Africa.

Below: Devices like the speculum oris, used to force-feed captives, ensured slaves wouldn't starve themselves to death en route to the selling markets.

A sea chest painted by a sailor from the brig Sultan, *circa 1850, shows a European standing side by side with an African.*

lie in two rows, one above the other, on each side of the ship, close to each other, like books upon a shelf. I have known them so close that the shelf would not, easily, contain one more. And I have known a white man sent down, among the men, to lay them in these rows to the greatest advantage, so that as little space as possible might be lost and our profit increased.

Motivated by profit, captains and investors did not always adhere to the stowage formula. They packed as many Africans into the holds of their ships as was possible. However, tight packing increased the instances of disease aboard ship. Cargoes were ravaged by fevers, ophthalmia (eye infection), yaws (syphilitic skin infection), and bloody flux (dysentery). Sickness placed heavy demands on water supplies. In 1781, Luke Collingwood, captain of the slave ship *Zong* bound for Jamaica, jettisoned 131 Africans who were suspected of having a contagious disease, to decrease the demand on the water supply that was insufficient, in part, because Collingwood did not provision the ship with an ample amount of water for a transatlantic voyage.

The *Zong*'s owners filed a claim with the insurance company that underwrote the voyage. John Lee, the solicitor-general, advanced the following argument on behalf of the *Zong*'s owners:

What is this claim that human people have been thrown overboard? This is a case of chattels or goods. Blacks are goods and property; it is madness to accuse these well serving honourable men of murder. They acted out of necessity and in the most appropriate manner for the cause. The late Captain Collingwood acted in the interest of his ship to protect the safety of his crew. To question the judgement of an experienced, well-travelled captain held in the highest regard is one of folly, especially when talking of slaves. The case is the same as if horses had been thrown overboard.

The case of the *Zong* demonstrates two important realities concerning the transatlantic

African Princess: Anna Madgigine Jai Kingsley

Anna Madgigine Jai Kingsley was born Anta Majigeen Ndiaye in Senegambia in 1793 to a distinguished family that owned land and slaves, and she is believed to have been a princess or a noblewoman. In 1806, her father was killed and she and other family members captured and enslaved by Tyeddo horsemen from the kingdom of Cayor in what is now Senegal. The captives were transported to Gorée Island, where Anta remained imprisoned until she was purchased and placed on the Danish vessel *Sally*.

When the *Sally* arrived on the Spanish-controlled island of Cuba, Zephaniah Kingsley, a wealthy slave ship owner, slave trader, and planter, purchased Anta along with two other women, molasses, and rum. Three months later he took them to his Florida plantation, Laurel Grove, by which time Anta was pregnant with his child. Rather than place her in the slave quarters, Kingsley brought her to live in his house. Laurel Grove contained more than 200 acres where more than 100 slaves worked in the fields and did carpentry, blacksmithing, and other skilled jobs. Kingsley also owned at least eight slave ships.

Although the Kingsleys had a polygamous relationship, Anna was the first wife and the primary manager of the estate. In 1811, Zephaniah emancipated Anna along with their three children. A year later, she established her own farm of five acres granted her by Spanish authorities and managed 12 slaves.

In 1819, Spain ceded control of Florida to the U.S., which began enacting stricter laws governing mixing of races, and Zephaniah moved his family to Haiti. To further protect his family Kingsley completed his will, leaving everything to Anna and the children. He died five years later at 78.

Anna returned to Jacksonville in 1860 to confront Kingsley's white relatives over her inheritance, which they sought to deny her and the children. The court upheld the rights of Kingsley's Black heirs, and they remained in Florida through the outbreak of the Civil War in 1861. Florida joined the Confederacy, and the Kingsley family, which sympathized with the Union, had to be evacuated north in 1862 while Union soldiers took control of Jacksonville. Anna was able to return to Florida a year later, and she died in 1870. *D. W.*

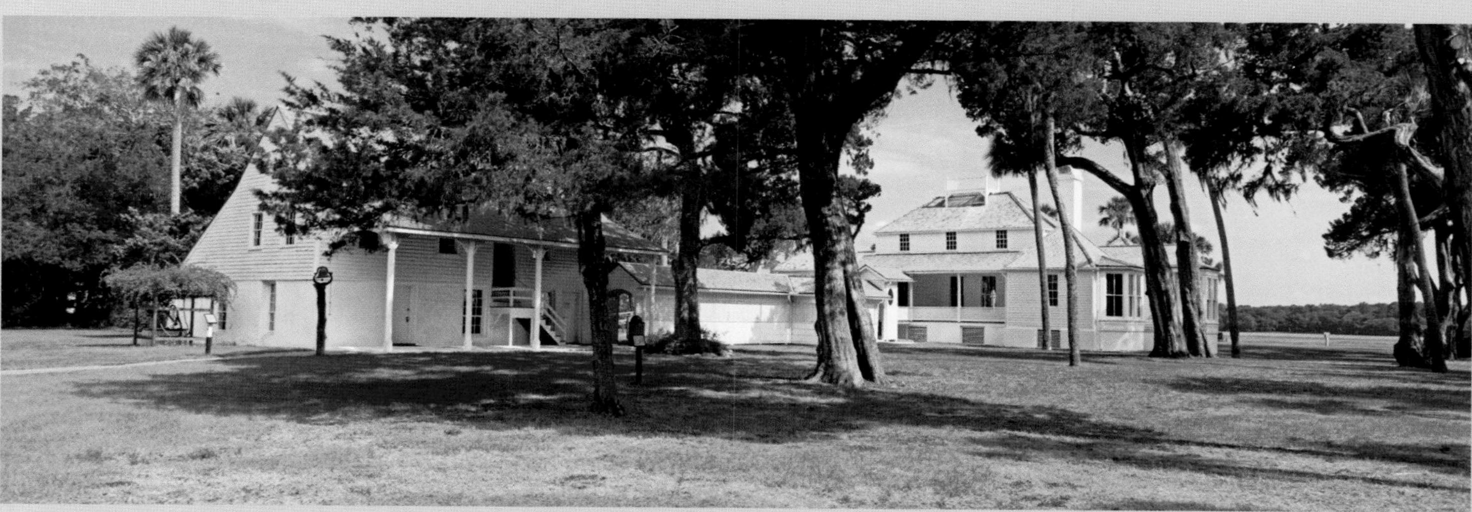

Anta Majigeen Ndiaye lived in Florida with plantation owner Zephaniah Kingsley as his wife. Slave quarters (top) show living conditions for other Africans on the plantation. Today the land is a state historical park, and an original house (above), built in 1798, still stands.

Right: An 1857 drawing, from the *Illustrated London News,* shows slaves in cramped quarters during a transatlantic crossing.

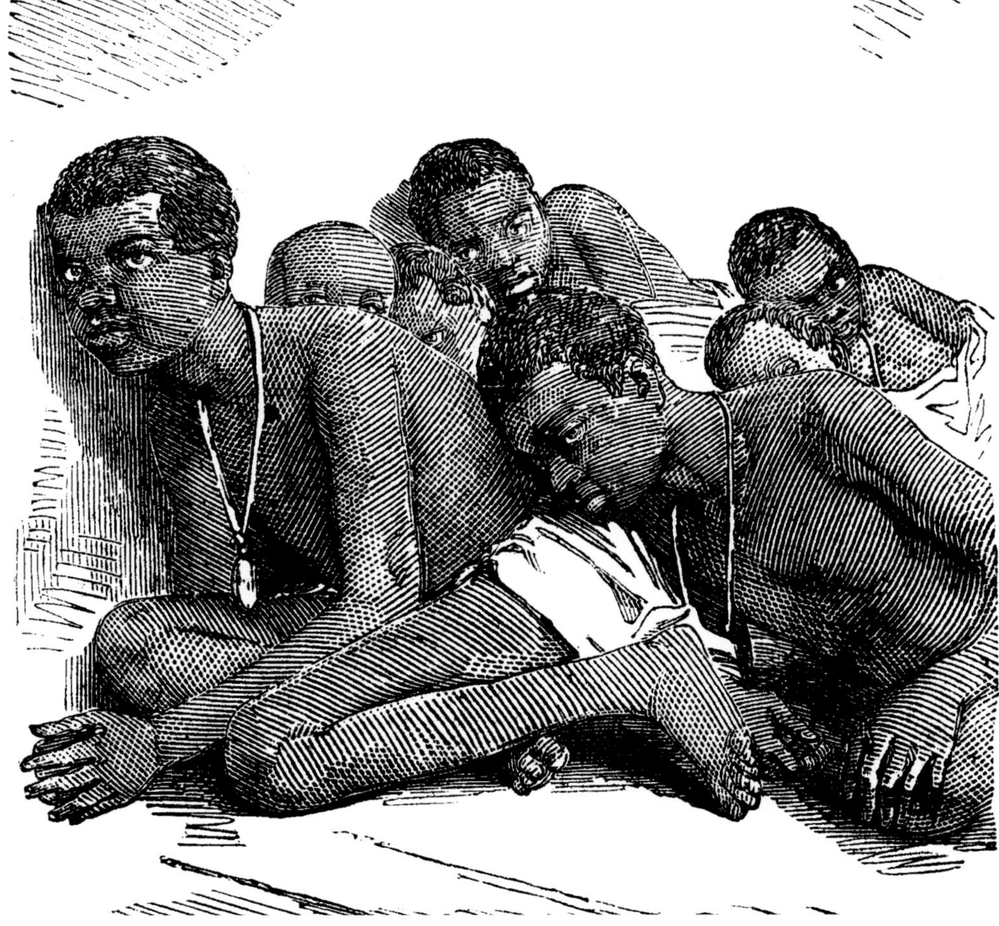

slave trade. First, the slave trade was a business in the strictest sense of the term, one that was a financial boon to insurance companies that underwrote policies for slaving ventures. Second, slave trading was a dangerous business, not only because of the prospect of a contagious disease breaking out aboard ship, but because of the ruthlessness of ship captains and crewmen who thought of the African captives as mere objects for base forms of exploitation.

That exploitation was both economic and sexual in nature. Men were shackled together, so as to prevent an insurrection. But women were left unshackled, making them easy targets for the sexual predations of the captain and his crewmen. John Newton's journal yields the following description of an incidence of rape aboard his slave ship *African*:

> *Monday 24 June. . . . Buryed a girl slave (No 92). In the afternoon while we were off the deck, William Cooney seduced a woman slave down into the room and lay with her brutelike in view of the whole quarter deck, for which I put him in irons. I hope this has been the first affair of the kind on board and I am determined to keep them quiet if possible. If anything happens to the woman I shall impute it to him, for she was big with child. Her number is 83. . . .*

As Number 83 in the cargo, the slave's value lay not in her humanity, but in the fact that she was pregnant with a child who, if bought to term, would increase the wealth of her

Above: The thumbscrew was one cruel punishment device.

Her Family's History: Peri Frances-Betsch

Peri Frances-Betsch was born on August 1, 1972, in Nashville, Tennessee, to Carol Creswell-Betsch, a retired psychologist and art gallery owner, and John Thomas Betsch, Jr., a jazz drummer and expatriate who currently lives in Paris. She is a direct descendant of Anna Kingsley (see page 73), an African noblewoman from Senegal who was enslaved and sold to a Florida planter. Kingsley fought to keep the land she inherited from her husband following his death, and during the Civil War she was heralded for her support of Union troops. Frances-Betsch's aunt MaVynee sparked her interest in learning her family history by relating the connection between Anna Kingsley and her great-great-grandfather, who was a co-founder of the Afro-American Life Insurance Company in Jacksonville, Florida, and the founder of American Beach, a seaside resort community for African Americans.

Frances-Betsch was a child of the seventies and was one of thousands who sat mesmerized when *Roots* aired on television. As a Spelman College student, she studied French and International Relations but was fascinated by the Francophone writers of the Negritude Literary Movement, which introduced her to French African writers and French-speaking African countries like Côte d'Ivoire, Mali, and Senegal, where Kingsley was born. After finishing Spelman in 1994, Frances-Betsch taught French, Spanish, and history and began traveling with her students to the countries she had studied in college.

Frances-Betsch began to delve more into her family history. Trips to Senegal and Ghana placed her on the path to self-discovery. "Traveling to Gorée Island, Senegal, for the first time in 1995 . . . knowing the name of my ancestor and the date she left the continent, feeling Anta's [Anna Kingsley's birth name] spirit there, knowing she passed through those doors, believing she brought me there. Talking to her, seeing how she has guided my path and passions in so many ways, even before I knew her story."

In her lectures, she relates the Kingsley story as well as her personal history. She is heavily inspired by other women in her family. Her aunt MaVynee Oshun Betsch, popularly known as the Beach Lady, was an activist and environmentalist. Her aunt Johnnetta Cole, president of Spelman College from 1987 to 1997, was the first African-American woman to serve in that position.

In addition to lecturing, Frances-Betsch leads tours to Senegal and has participated in the Kingsley Heritage Celebration, held annually in October since 1998 at the Kingsley plantation on Florida's Fort George Island. *D. W.*

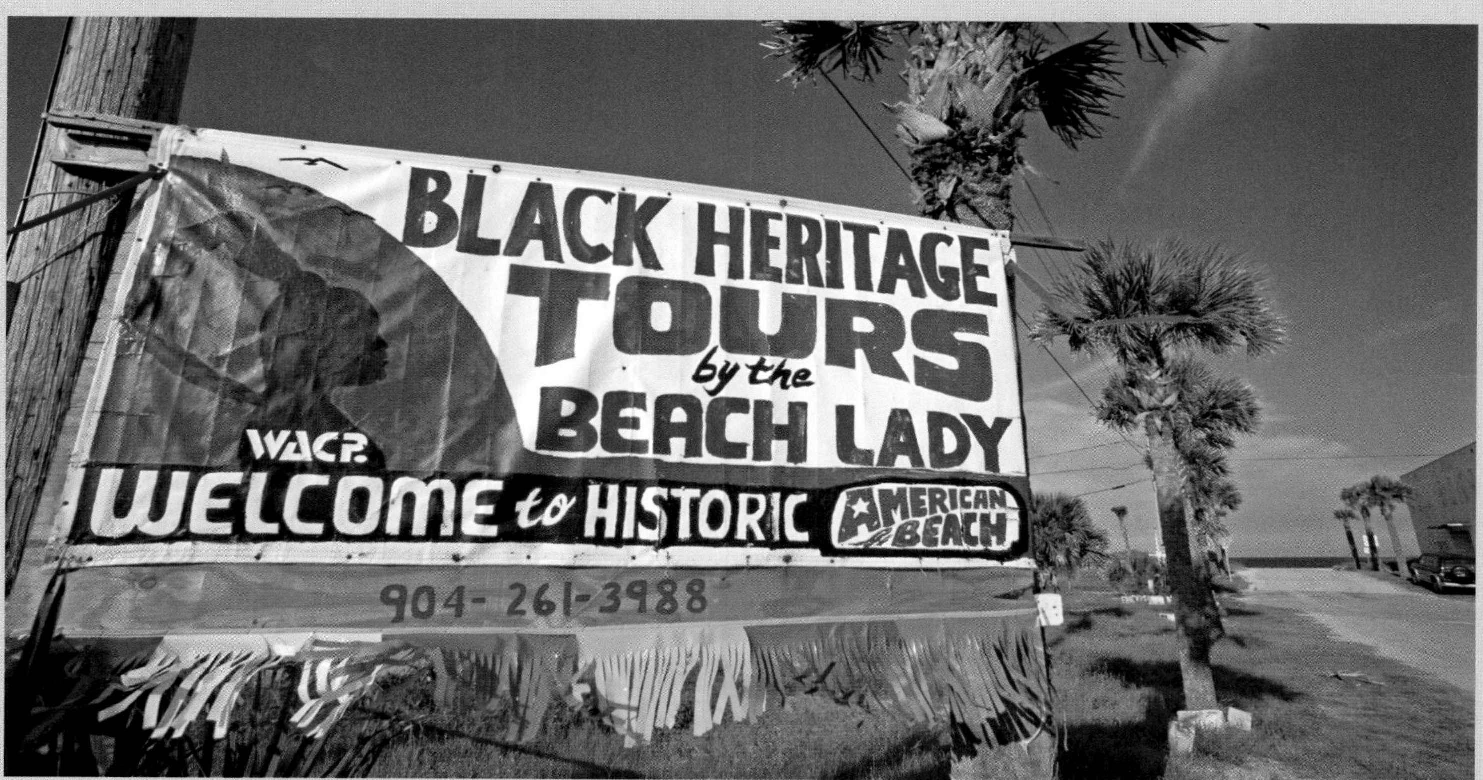

MaVynee Betsch, the "Beach Lady," inspired her niece, Peri Frances-Betsch, to research her family history in the U.S. and Africa. A sign on historic American Beach advertises MaVynee's tours of the quiet resort community, a relic from the days of southern segregation.

"I can still smell the
spray of the sea they made
me cross.
The night, I can't remember.
Not even the ocean itself
could remember. . . .
By chance, I have forgotten
neither my lost coast,
nor my ancestral tongue.
They brought me here and
here I have lived."

— Nancy Morejón, poet

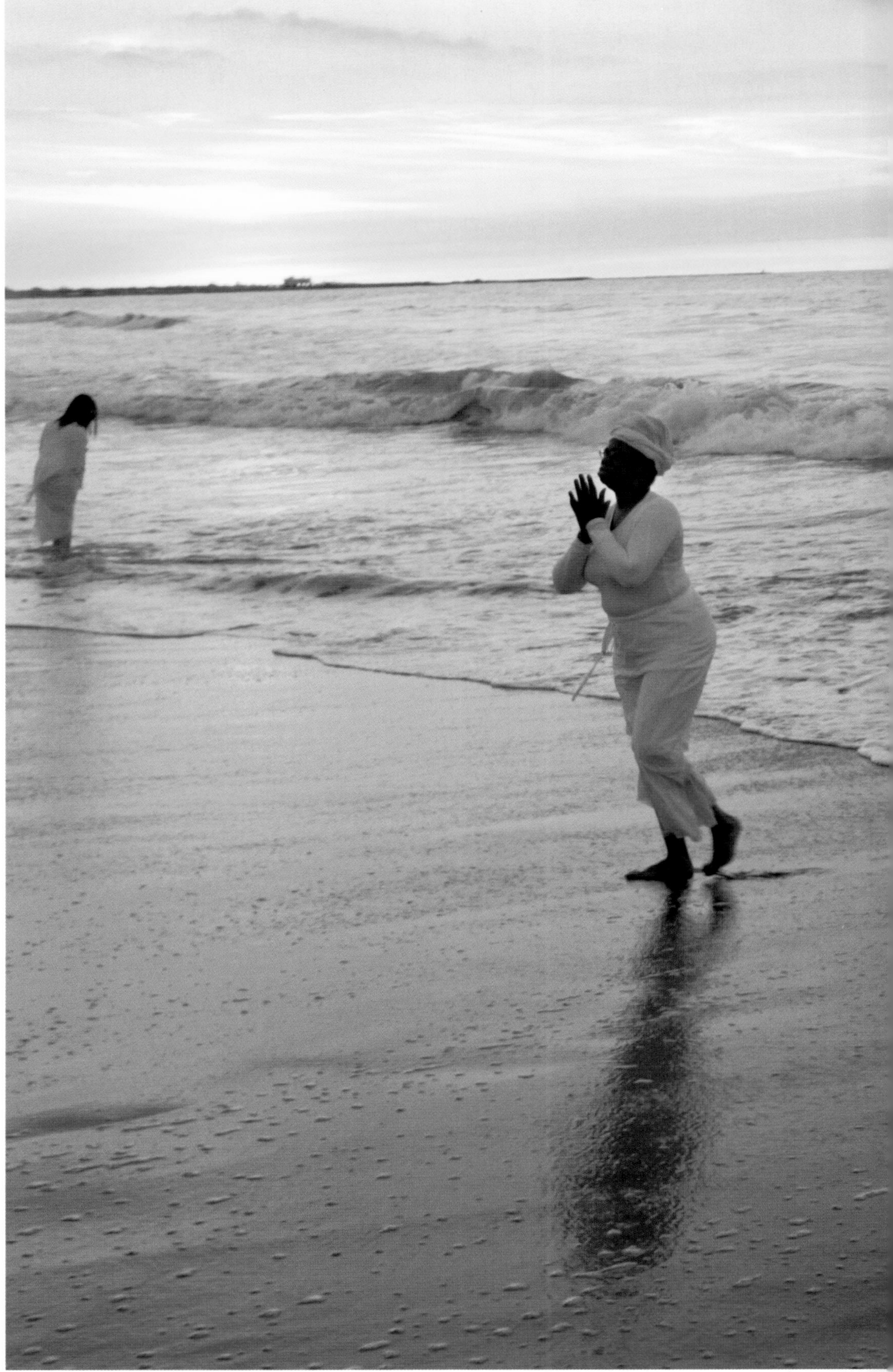

In a seaside commemoration, congregants of St. Paul Community Baptist Church in Brooklyn, New York, revisit the voyage to slavery.

> "While the East African drama of slavery was unfolding with the Arabs and later with the Portuguese as the protagonists, the larger drama in West Africa was changing the course of history."
>
> —*John Henrik Clarke, author, historian, journalist*

owner. Therefore, she would command a higher price at sale. To escape dehumanizing experiences at sea, Africans committed suicide by jumping overboard or by starving themselves. Captains endeavored to protect their profits by placing nets around their ships to ensnare those who jumped overboard, and they used a speculum oris (a scissor-shaped instrument inserted into the mouth to make the jaws open) to force food into the mouths, and down the throats, of those Africans attempting to starve themselves.

Africans used suicide and insurrections to free themselves from the horrors of the Middle Passage. Although some insurrections were successful, like that staged by Sengbe (Cinque) Pieh and his fellow Mende captives aboard the slaver *Amistad*, many more were unsuccessful and their plotters paid a heavy price for their bravery, as explained in the following excerpt from John Newton's journal:

> *Friday 28 June. . . . By the favour of Divine Providence made a timely discovery today that the slaves were forming a plot for an insurrection. Surprised 2 of them attempting to get off their irons, and upon farther search in their rooms, upon the information of 3 of the boys, found some knives, stones, shot, etc, and a cold chissel. Upon enquiry there appeared 8 principally concerned to move in projecting the mischief and 4 boys in supplying them with the above instruments. Put the boys in irons and slightly in the thumbscrews to urge them to a full confession. We have already 36 men out of our small number.*

Ship captains used thumbscrews and other instruments of torture to force confessions regarding insurrections and to punish Africans for their roles in them. The success of the transatlantic slave trade depended on a set of rules that were brutally enforced on both sides of the Atlantic, and at sea, for 400 years.

THE U.S. SLAVE TRADE

The transatlantic slave trade may be divided into two periods—legal and illegal.

Within the context of the legal slave trade, the first American-built slave ship was named *Desire* (1638), symbolic of New England's desire to make money as transporters of slaves into the various North American and Caribbean colonies. During the 18th century, New England produced several prominent slave-trading families, such as the Browns of Rhode Island. John Brown, the patriarch, was a plantation owner, an opium trader, a slave trader, and the proprietor of the slave ships *Delight*, *Hope*, and *Mary*. His descendants inherited the wealth generated by those businesses. A portion of that wealth existed in the form of land, some of which the Browns donated to Rhode Island College. In recognition of their generous gifts, the name of that college was changed to Brown University.

In 1794, and in 1807, the United States implemented slave trade acts that criminalized the importation of Africans for the purposes of making them slaves, selling them as slaves, or holding them as slaves. These acts ushered in the "illegal" period in the transatlantic slave trade. In 1820, the federal government implemented the Piracy Act, which defined slave smuggling as an act of piracy, punishable by death. By 1830, most European nations had abolished new importations of African captives into their territories. However, the demand for African laborers continued to grow in tandem with the exponential growth of cotton plantations in the Gulf states. As long as the demand for laborers existed, slave smugglers were willing to defy federal statutes to satisfy the demand well into the middle of the 19th century. The smuggling industry constituted an enterprise unto itself, replete with

An African slave ship hoists sail after sighting an English ship in the distance. The British Navy intercepted slave ships after the trade was abolished in 1807.

brash captains motivated, once again, by profit; rogue U.S. consuls who aided and abetted smugglers by selling blank ship registries that could be filled out to mask the ownership, the origin, or the destination of a ship engaged in the illegal slave trade; and fast-sailing schooners and clipper ships such as the *Dos Amigos,* the *Wanderer,* and the *Clotilda* (reputed to be the last American slaver to successfully smuggle Africans into the United States) that could elude capture by federal cruisers that made up the U.S. African Squadron patrolling Atlantic waters in search of smugglers. One final motivating factor included the reality that no one, with the exception of Nathaniel Gordon, who was tried as a pirate in 1862 and hanged, had hanged for smuggling Africans into the United States. Thus, for 42 years after the implementation of the Piracy Act, Americans were allowed to smuggle Africans with impunity, defying the laws of both the United States and humanity.

It is estimated that slave ships carried anywhere from 12 million to 20 million Africans across the Atlantic. Although some Africans escaped captivity by absconding or by committing suicide, the majority of them were taken to various southern plantations or forced to labor in northern industries such as shipbuilding. There was no aspect of labor that was not performed by a slave, whose agricultural expertise, technical skills, and craftsmanship served collectively as the economic foundation upon which the Caribbean and the Americas built their wealth.

African Burial Ground

A GALLERY

Until recently many people thought that slavery in the United States existed only in the South. A new treasure trove of evidence shows, however, that New York and other northern states had active, well-established African communities. Africans had begun arriving in what was known as the Dutch village of New Amsterdam in 1625. They came as laborers and servants, some free and others enslaved.

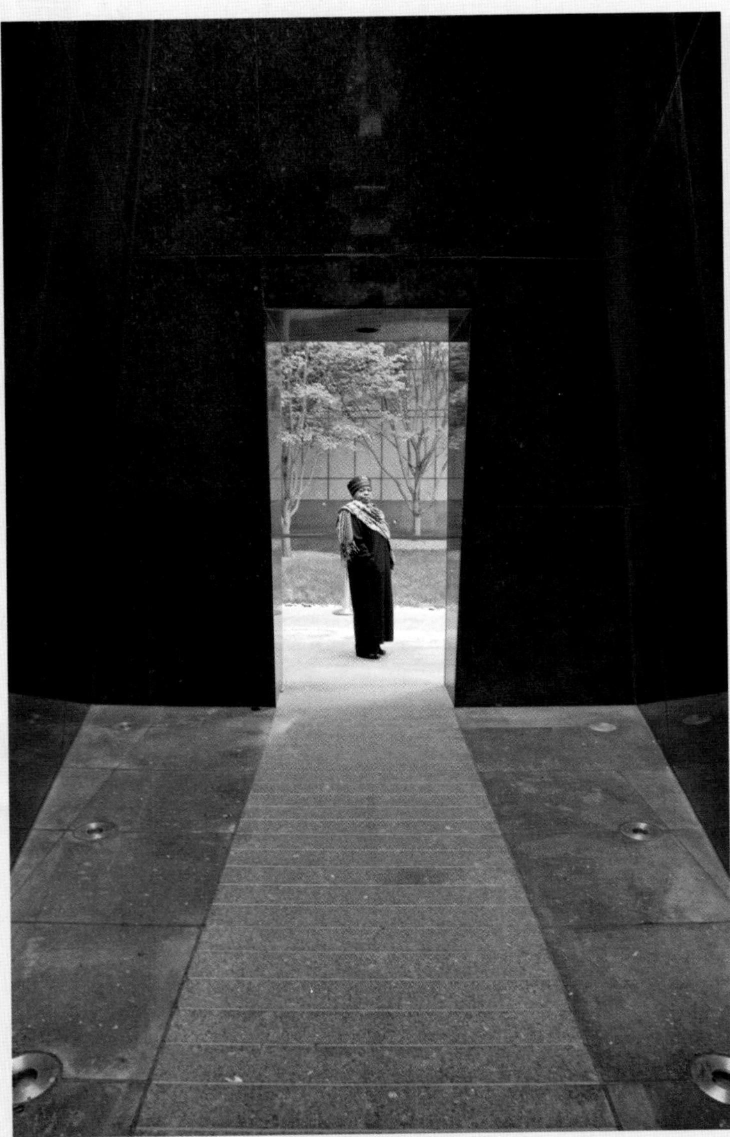

The "Door of Return," at the African Burial Ground Monument in New York City, marks the resting place of free and enslaved Africans.

In 1991, while a General Services Administration building project was under way in Lower Manhattan, construction workers near 290 Broadway discovered a burial ground that had been covered by landfill and development many years earlier. The 6.6-acre site contained approximately 15,000 free and enslaved African remains. The burial ground, which had been used from the 1690s to the 1790s, was a powerful discovery that held many secrets. The construction project was immediately suspended, while decisions were made about how the situation should be handled. Much disagreement ensued, and the African remains became a point of contention for many years.

Eventually, some remains from the burial grounds were removed and taken to Howard University in Washington, D.C., for anthropological and forensic study. According to the African Burial Ground final report, much can be learned by reading the findings in "The New York African Burial Ground Skeletal Biology Final Report," edited by Drs. Michael L. Blakey and Lesley Rankin-Hill. The results of the studies placed a real human face on what had earlier been seen merely as skeletal remains.

The reports read, in part:

> *1.1 Introduction*
>
> *When the archaeological team disinterred the remains of the woman later designated as Burial 340 in 1991, the waist beads and hourglass-shaped, filed incisors that had adorned her in life remained to define her culturally more than two centuries after death. Nearby, in Burial 254, a young child reposed in its final resting-place, with a silver earring strung like a pendant around its tiny neck. The man whose bones imprinted the soil in Burial 101 had been laid to rest in a simple coffin, but someone had painstakingly fashioned a heart-shaped object on its lid with brass tacks. And in Burial 25, a young woman's broken body—face shattered, wrist fractured, and rib cage penetrated by a still present musket ball—provided evidence of the violence that pervaded colonial New York. These four representatives of the community of African and African-descended peoples in the city, rendered anonymous as a consequence of their enslavement, remind us that even among those designated property, humanity prevailed. For in death (as in life) their membership in the human family resonated.*

Scientists and scholars spent many hours studying the remains before returning them to New York for interment. They decided to

African drummers in Philadelphia celebrate the establishment of the African Burial Ground. Five cities in which Africans played an important role historically, including Baltimore; Newark, New Jersey; Philadelphia; Wilmington, Delaware; and Washington, D.C., held ceremonies.

make coffins to hold the ancestors before returning them to New York. Artisans in West Africa made small coffins with elegant and important symbols carved on the outside to hold the remains. Several ceremonies were held, including one at Howard University's Andrew Rankin Memorial Chapel. The very moving service included singers, special blessings, and African ceremonies. A representative number of coffins were placed at the front of the sanctuary. At the end of the ceremony, pallbearers carried them out as attendees said prayers for the ancestors.

Other services and ceremonies were held in New York City. The National Park Service decided to make the official new burial ground one of their authorized sites. Various people who had worked for many years to make this dream a reality took pride in the outcome. The monument to the African Burial Ground stands as testament to the fact that a resilient people lived and died in the nation's North during and after colonial times. The evidence of these pioneers in our country is a source of pride for Americans everywhere.

After excavation, selected remains were reburied in small coffins designed by West African artisans, who decorated them with traditional symbols.

CHAPTER FOUR

Life in a New World

CHAPTER FOUR

1450 – 1860s

Life in a New World

Slavery in America is a separation of peoples that happened not once, but repeatedly throughout its history. Uprooted from distant villages, enslaved Africans were forcibly shipped from coastal trading centers many miles from their inland homes. Those who survived the Middle Passage may have spent a few years in the West Indies before another sale—another separation from family and friends—sent them to a small farm or town in New England, or a plantation on the Chesapeake or in the Carolinas. Bonds of family and friendship would soon be broken again, as the sons and daughters of the first generations of enslaved Africans were sold south to support the 19th-century expansion of America's slave economy into Alabama, Mississippi, Louisiana, and Texas. For these "many thousands gone," to use historian Ira Berlin's phrase, the New World held not promise but purgatory.

Of the many millions of Africans who arrived on America's shores in chains, just a few had the opportunity to later record their experiences of the New World. Olaudah Equiano, an enslaved Ibo born in Benin around 1745 and later a leading abolitionist in England, compared the brutalized Africans he encountered in the West Indies to subjects from Milton's *Paradise Lost*:

With shudd'ring horror pale, and eyes aghast,
They view their lamentable lot, and find
No rest . . .

"It was very common in several of the islands," he wrote, "for the slaves to be branded with the initial letters of their master's name, and a load of heavy iron hooks hung about their necks." In their relentless quest to convert human beings into commodities, slavers refined techniques to strip slaves of their identities. By being branded, given new names, and experiencing systematic degradation, once free African men, women, and children became America's unpaid workforce for nearly 250 years.

SEASONING AND SALE

As it did in Equiano's experience, the West Indies served as a brutal way station for millions of slaves, part of a "seasoning" process that lasted up to several years, during which they gradually adjusted to a life of forced servitude in a foreign land. Slave owners systematically used tools of torture and techniques of degradation to achieve a "seasoned" slave, one ready to submit in countenance, if not in spirit. "On the most trifling occasions," Equiano remembered, "they were loaded with chains, and often instruments of torture were added. The iron muzzle, thumbscrews, etc. are so well known as not to need a description, and were sometimes applied for the slightest faults." A seasoned slave knew how to tolerate

Left: In an early photograph, a line of men and women snakes through fields near Charleston, South Carolina, carrying the day's cotton crop.

Previous pages: Africans await their fate at a 19th-century slave market in Richmond, Virginia, in this 1852 painting by Eyre Crowe.

"A cargo . . . was first sorted into grades. . . . To each slave was attached a ticket bearing a number, while a corresponding ticket was deposited in one of four boxes. . . . the planters bought the privilege of drawing tickets from the appropriate boxes and acquiring thereby title to the slaves. . . ."

— Lucien Peytraud, historian

strange foods, communicate in a foreign language, live in dwellings barely suitable for livestock, endure the daily routine of forced labor, and somehow survive the crushing loss of freedom, friends, and family. For the slave owner, a seasoned slave was one who no longer sought release through starvation, suicide, flight, or outward resistance. For the slave, seasoning marked the beginning of a dual life: one face shown to the slave owner and most of white society, and another shown to loved ones with mostly black faces.

When slave traders prepared to sell their human cargo—whether from a ship's deck, auction block, slave market, or jail cell—they often resorted to salesmen's tactics and sleight of hand. Some even enlisted the aid of the slaves themselves to facilitate the sale. "While we were going to the vessel," Broteer, an enslaved boy from Guinea, remembered, "our master told us all to appear to the best possible advantage for sale." Whatever the six-year-old did to appear to "advantage" worked: He changed hands for "four gallons of rum and a snippet of calico cloth." His new owner renamed him Venture, "on account of his having purchased me with his own private venture."

To help him appear to "advantage," Venture and other new arrivals like him were most likely given an overdue bath (in truth, a cursory hosing or douse with a bucket) or a rubdown with oil or just "greasy water" to polish their skin to a sheen, and fattened up with ample food prior to the sale. These and other common tactics temporarily concealed symptoms of poor diet and ill health. Slaves suffering from illness were often forced to hide their condition from prospective buyers, and those with dysentery or diarrhea may have had plugs of tobacco inserted into their rectum to disguise the condition that all too frequently resulted from the impoverished diet, filth, and crowding of the Middle Passage.

Other transactions that sealed young Africans' fates were more degrading than Venture's seemed to have been. A practice known as the scramble also typically took place on shipboard yet resembled a livestock sale or lottery more than anything else. According to historian Ulrich B. Phillips, "A practice often followed in the British West Indian ports was to advertise that the cargo of a vessel just arrived would be sold on board at an hour scheduled and at a uniform price announced in the notice. At the time set there would occur a great scramble of planters and dealers to grab the choicest slaves."

Even more inhumane, if possible, was yet another sale method recorded by Equiano: "I have often seen slaves, particularly those who were meager, in different islands, put into scales and weighed, and then sold from three pence to six pence or nine pence a pound." In this way, malnourished and underweight slaves met their new masters and mistresses not as fellow men and women, but as commodities, bought and sold by the pound.

Following each sale came inconsolable loss as families were forcibly separated from each other. Thomas Branagan, a slave trader from Dublin who later became an anti-slavery pamphleteer, described families torn from each other's arms:

Children are torn from their distracted parents; parents from their screaming children; wives from their frantic husbands; husbands from their violated wives; brothers from their loving sisters; sisters from their affectionate brothers. See them collected in flocks, and like a herd of swine, driven to the ships; They cry, they struggle, they resist; but all in vain. No eye pities, no hand helps.

Torture masks prevented slaves from eating.

During the 250 years that enslaved Africans arrived in America, the leading slave ports and slave markets shifted from the West Indies to America's East Coast port cities. From among these, leading slave markets gradually shifted south and west, from Rhode

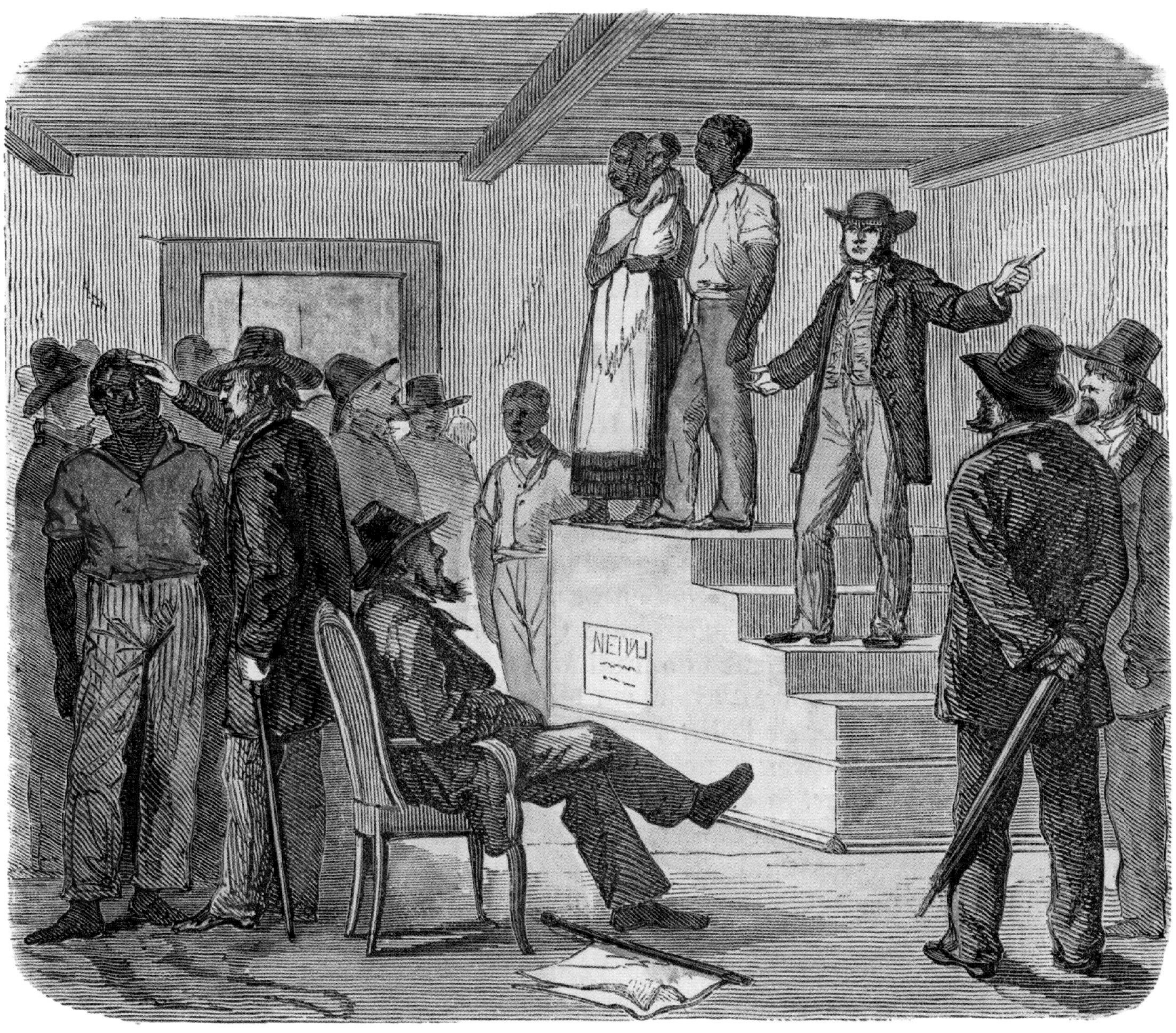

The French newspaper L'Illustration, Journal Universel *depicted Africans on display at an American slave auction. Before being sold, slaves were examined to determine their physical health and overall strength.*

Island and New York in the early 1700s to Baltimore, Washington, D.C., and the Chesapeake in the 1730s, and from Charleston and the Carolinas in the 1770s to New Orleans in the 1830s. The fates of millions were thus tied to market fluctuations and the expansion of the US. from 13 colonies to 33 angry states poised on the brink of Civil War in 1861.

THE BULLWHIP

Physical violence played a large role in the perpetuation of slavery. For the one very public beating of Senator Charles Sumner that took place on the floor of the U.S. Senate in 1858 when he denounced the institution of slavery, countless other beatings designed to perpetuate the institution had taken place outside the halls of government—behind closed doors, in open fields, and town markets with bullwhips, cat-o'-nine-tails, canes, sticks, and willow branches.

"My freedom is a privilege which nothing else can equal. Notwithstanding all the losses I have suffered by fire, by the injustice of knaves, by the cruelty and oppression of false hearted friends, and the perfidy of my own countrymen whom I have assisted and redeemed from bondage, I am now possessed of more than one hundred acres of land, and three habitable dwelling houses. It gives me joy to think that I have and that I deserve so good a character, especially for truth and integrity."

— Venture Smith, slave

In Virginia planter William Byrd's diary, "whipping" appears as a casual entry alongside prayer, dance, reading selections, and menu items:

> *February 8, 1709*
> *I rose at 5 o'clock this morning and read a chapter in Hebrew and 20 verses in Homer's* Odyssey. *I ate milk for breakfast. I said my prayers. Jenny and Eugene were whipped. I danced my dance.*
>
> *June 10, 1709*
> *Eugene was whipped for running away and had the bit put on him. I said my prayers and had good health, good thoughts, and good humor, thanks be to God Almighty.*
>
> *June 17, 1710*
> *I set my closet right. I ate tongue and chicken for dinner. In the afternoon I caused L-s-n to be whipped for beating his wife and Jenny was whipped for being his whore. In the evening the sloop came from Appomattox with tobacco. I took a walk about the plantation. I said my prayers and drank some new milk from the cow . . .*

When Byrd "caused" Jenny, Eugene, or "L-s-n" to be whipped, it may well have been that his slave driver wielded the bullwhip. Slaves had different names for their fellow slaves who carried out the masters' and overseers' agendas, among them whipping man, whipping boss, straw boss, overlooker, underlooker, headman, and foreman. Most, though, agreed on one general epithet—"mean as the devil."

In the 1930s, former slave Henry Cheatam looked back with undiminished anger at the overseer who shaped his youth as a slave in Mississippi during the early 1860s:

> *Old Miss had a nigger overseer and dat was de meanest devil dat ever lived on de Lord's green earth. I promise myself when I growed up dat I was a-goin' to kill dat nigger if it was de last thing I ever done. Lots of times I'se seen him beat my mammy, and one day I seen him beat my auntie who was big with a child, and dat man dug a round hole in de ground and put her stomach in it, and beat and beat her for a half hour straight till de baby come out right dere in de hole.*

Few items symbolize the tyranny of slavery more than the bullwhip. It lacerated the flesh, seared the soul, and too often, broke the will of thousands. "During the entire period of the cotton-picking season," recalled one former slave, "the crack of the lash, and the shrieking of the slaves, can be heard from dark till bed time."

"A SAD EPOCH"

Untold numbers of slave women like Henry Cheatam's mother and aunt suffered from another kind of systematic violation: rape and forced breeding. The former was a routine tool of oppression and control, the latter a deliberate strategy to increase personal wealth.

Frequent accounts of rape come from all sources: slave traders, enslaved men and women, and the slave owners themselves. Slaver Thomas Branagan witnessed husbands being separated from "their violated wives" before leaving the west coast of Africa. Ottobah Cugoano, who endured the Middle Passage, recalled that "it was common for the dirty filthy sailors to take the African women and lie upon their bodies." In 1861, Harriet Jacobs,

A Man of Many Hats: Rohulamin Quander, Esq.

Rohulamin Quander wears many hats: judge, historic preservationist, and author, among others, but he has achieved international acclaim for his documentation of the Quander family, believed to be one of the oldest African-American families in the United States.

Born in Washington, D.C., in 1943, Quander is the eldest of four siblings. His mother worked for the Department of Defense for 33 years, and his father, James W. Quander, who had had a career as a mathematical statistician, was ordained a permanent Catholic deacon in 1971. Considered one of the longest-living juvenile diabetics in the nation after he was diagnosed with the disease at the age of five, James Quander was also one of the first people to use insulin.

Rohulamin Quander was among the first children to integrate Sacred Heart Elementary School in September 1950 after the racial barrier was removed by the archdiocese, as was Carmen Torruella, who would later become his wife. He attended Howard University, studying political science and history, and remains an active and devoted member of the Omega Psi Phi Fraternity, the first Black national fraternal organization to be founded at a historically Black college.

While in law school he was elected the first-year class representative to the Student Bar Association, vice president in his second year, and president in his third year. He received his bachelor of arts degree in 1966 and his juris doctor, also from Howard, in 1969. In 1968, while still a student, he attended his first family reunion and became interested in the Quander family history.

Quander maintained a full-time private practice for 11 years. In 1985, he served as a hearing examiner in the Traffic Division of the D.C. Department of Motor Vehicles and joined the D.C. Department of Consumer and Regulatory Affairs in 1986. During the nineties, he worked in the capacity of judge, although under various titles, including attorney examiner, administrative law judge, and administrative judge, when he took a position in the D.C. Office of Employee Appeals. Today he is known as a senior administrative judge, given his length of service as a public official.

Quander lectures around the country on a variety of topics, including the history of Washington's distinctive neighborhoods and icons. His dedication to the research and preservation of history earned him a role as the city's agent for historic preservation, a position he has served in since 1998. In this capacity he presides over administrative hearings on the restoration and preservation of Washington's historic districts and landmarks.

However, it is his intense dedication to the documentation of the Quander family history that directs his life. "It has given me a focus, and a realization that I have a special mission in life . . . to tell the story and to keep telling the story, as different aspects and elements of the expanded Quander family's history unfold."

Rohulamin Quander, a descendant of one of George Washington's slaves, commemorates his ancestors' emancipation at Washington's Mount Vernon estate.

Inspired by Alex Haley's *Roots,* family members began documenting the family by creating a family tree, designing a coat of arms, and writing the history and life stories of their ancestors. "They were not all literate people, and many of them apparently had no formal education at all. But they possessed a certain dogged determination, a willingness to go the extra mile or two, to prove their right to be recognized as full citizens." This determination and desire to do more is what he identifies as the Quander quality. Before his father's death from complications of diabetes in 2004, Quander recorded his life experiences, which led to a biography entitled *The Quander Quality*. Currently he is working on a history of the Quander family. *D. W.*

An 1844 bill of sale for the estate of Clemment Wells (top) shows slaves listed among other household objects. Likewise, an 1848 tax receipt (bottom) for 1,621 acres of land in Natchez, Mississippi, declares 15 slaves as part of the owner's property.

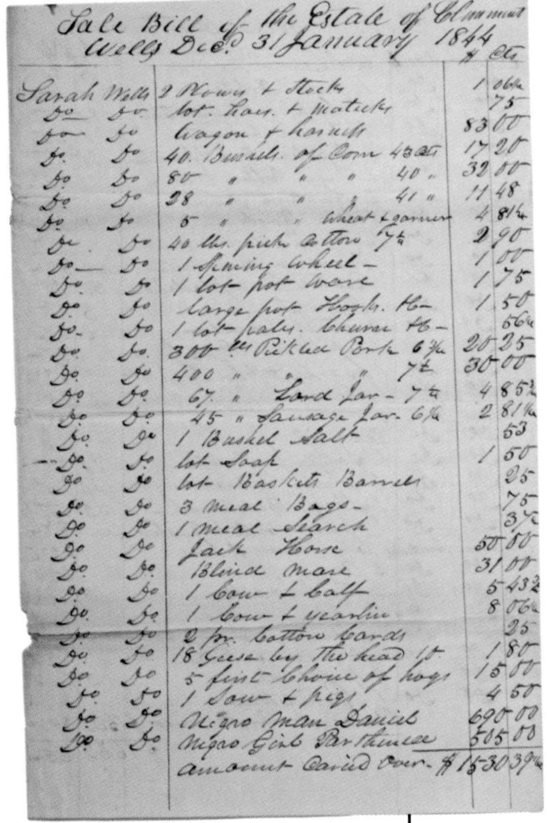

a former slave who wrote the first slave narrative by a woman under the pen name Linda Brent, unflinchingly recalled her own experience:

> *I now entered on my fifteenth year—a sad epoch in the life of a slave girl. My master began to whisper foul words in my ear. Young as I was, I could not remain ignorant of their import. . . . He peopled my young mind with unclean images, such as only a vile monster could think of. I turned from him with disgust and hatred. But he was my master. . . . He told me I was his property; that I must be subject to his will in all things.*

Although the resourceful Harriet managed to thwart her master's unwelcome advances, many others did not. Enslaved women and teenagers who became pregnant through rape were not the only ones who conceived children without their full consent. As the institution of slavery spread westward through territorial expansion and the domestic slave trade, some slaveholders (in Virginia and elsewhere) actively promoted "breeding" to supply slaves to these new markets. A planter might accomplish this aim in ways either subtle or overt, by encouraging multiple unions or by actively arranging for specific men and women to produce particularly robust offspring. Former slave Hilliard Yellerday, for example, remembered that "Master would sometimes go and get a large, hale, hearty Negro man from some other plantation to go to his Negro woman."

According to preeminent historian John Hope Franklin, "One respectable Virginia planter boasted that his women were 'uncommonly good breeders' and that he never heard of babies coming so fast as they did on his plantation. Of course, the very gratifying thing about it was that 'every one of them . . . was worth $200 . . . the moment it drew breath.'" Another planter's father advised him to "get as many young breeding-women as you can. . . . The increase of your negroes will make you rich." As former slave Fannie Moore recalled, good breeders commanded prices almost as high as prime field hands: "De breed woman always bring mo' money den de res', ebben

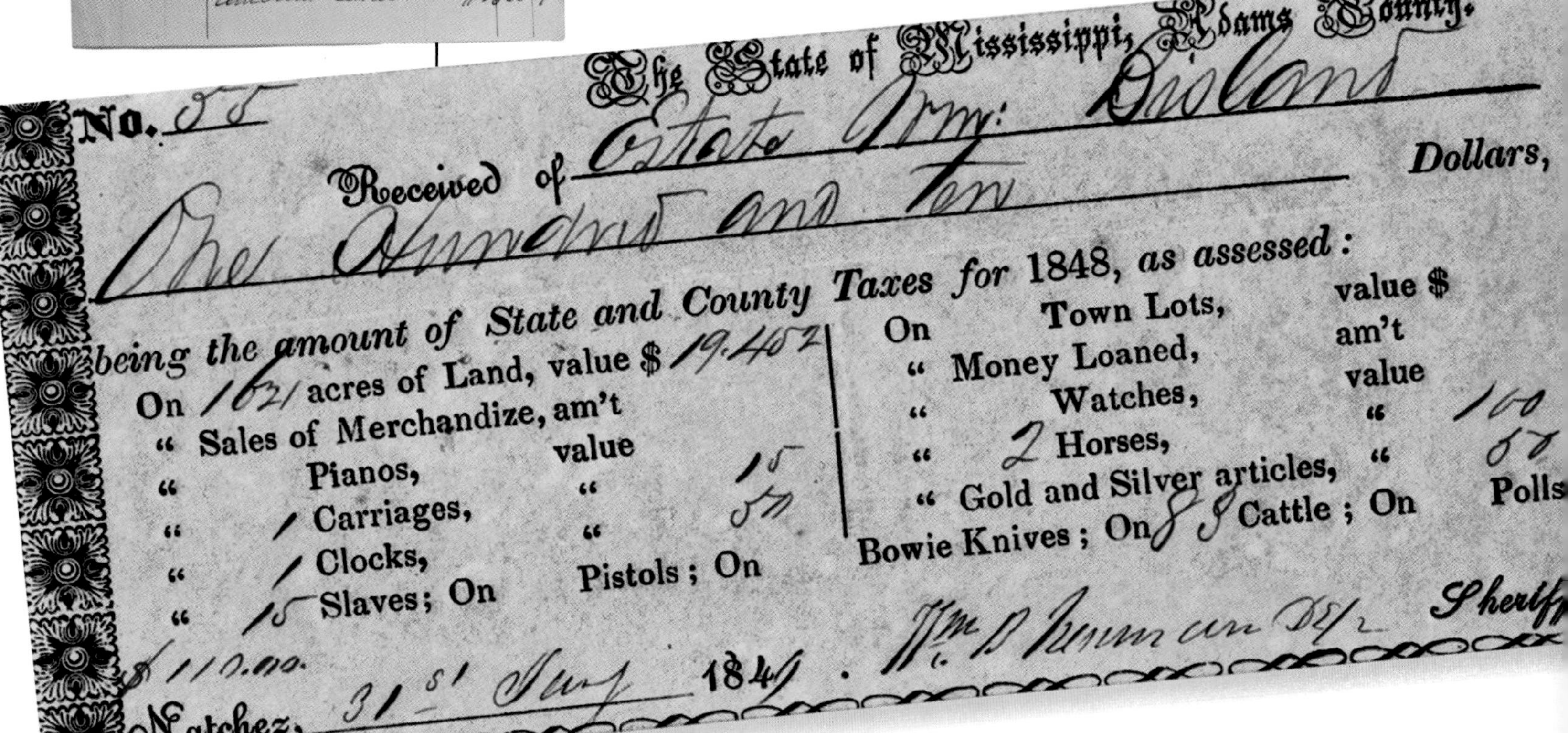
The State of Mississippi, Adams County.
No. 55
Received of Estate Wm: Daslans
One Hundred and Ten Dollars,
being the amount of State and County Taxes for 1848, as assessed:
On 1621 acres of Land, value $ 19.452
" Sales of Merchandize, am't
" Pianos, value
" 1 Carriages, " 15
" 1 Clocks, " 50
" 15 Slaves; On Pistols; On
On Town Lots, value $
" Money Loaned, am't
" Watches, value
" 2 Horses, " 100
" Gold and Silver articles, " 50
Bowie Knives; On 88 Cattle; On Polls
$110.00
Natchez, 31st Jany 1849. Wm B Tumman Sheriff

Strengthening Sisterhood: Nellie Quander

Although the presence of the Quander family in the United States dates back to the 1600s, it has an older lineage in Africa. The name is derived from the African name Amkwandoh, and the family has traced its roots back to the Fanti tribe in Ghana. According to family oral traditions, a slave named Amkwandoh fathered two sons. One was enslaved in southern Maryland and the other in northern Virginia. The descendants of the Virginia son found their connection in Nancy Quander, who was listed as a slave among the inventory of George Washington's Mount Vernon in 1799 and later freed in his last will and testament.

The Quander name continues to be held in high esteem in the Washington, D.C., metropolitan area, with many of Nancy's descendants carrying what they refer to as the Quander quality, which they define as "a composite of inner strengths and traits" that are admired by and inspire others.

One descendant who embodied the Quander quality was Nellie Quander, a former president of the Alpha Kappa Alpha Sorority, Inc., the oldest Greek letter organization established by African-American women in the country, and its first international president.

Nellie Quander was the daughter of Hannah Bruce Ford and John Pierson Quander, who was a direct descendant of Nancy and Charles Quander. Hannah was a descendant of West Ford, a slave who provided detailed information on the interior decoration of the Mount Vernon plantation when it was restored in the 1850s.

Nellie Quander graduated magna cum laude from Howard University in 1912 with a degree in history, economics, and political science.

Nellie Quander attended public schools in Washington, D.C., and graduated from the Miner Normal School with honors. She then pursued her academic dreams, entering Howard University to study history, economics, and political science. While still a student at Howard, she also taught at the Garrison Elementary School.

Quander became a member of the Howard chapter of Alpha Kappa Alpha in 1910 and served as the chapter president two years later. She graduated in 1912 with a bachelor of arts degree, magna cum laude. She began to demonstrate leadership qualities early on and after graduation served as an adviser to the Howard chapter of AKA.

As the organization grew, though, newer members wanted it to expand, with the addition of other chapters and increased programs. To protect the original agenda of AKA, Quander contacted other graduate members, and in January 1913, with her help, the sorority was nationally incorporated; the members who had sought a different direction left to form the Delta Sigma Theta Sorority.

Quander served as the sorority's president for six years, and under her direction it grew and began to play a more active role in the issues of the day, such as women's right to vote and financial aid for college-bound women. A second chapter was chartered in 1913 at the University of Chicago. At the first Boulé (an annual meeting of the governing body), which was held on Howard's campus in 1918, Quander was officially elected president but resigned a year later. During her tenure she wrote the preamble to the sorority's constitution. She also established a scholarship for seniors and later directed the North Atlantic Region. Quander was instrumental in expanding the organization to include undergraduate chapters, and she continued to act as graduate adviser to the Alpha chapter at Howard.

Throughout her life, Quander devoted her time and effort to education and civic activities, teaching in the D.C. public school system from 1901 through 1950. She began her teaching career as a first- and second-grade teacher but soon sought to teach slightly older students and moved to junior high schools. While at Shaw Junior High, in what is now the historic Shaw neigborhood, in Northwest D.C., she established the School Safety Patrol Unit. She was appointed special field agent to the Children's Bureau of the Department of Labor from 1916 to 1917. A board member and chairwoman of the Young Women's Christian Association, she served with Mary McLeod Bethune, Mary Church Terrell, and a young Dorothy Height. She also served on the board of the Business Professional and Industrial Committee of the Phillis Wheatley YMCA, located in Washington, D.C.

Nellie Quander died on September 24, 1961. During its 75th anniversary, the Alpha Kappa Alpha Sorority, Inc. recognized her for her intelligence, diplomacy, and leadership by establishing a scholarship endowment in her honor. In displaying her namesake quality, she acted, said her nephew Rohulamin Quander, as "a beacon for how she directed others to look for the good, the high ground, the roads that otherwise would not be taken."

D. W.

Asking "What If?"

BILL COSBY, ED.D.

One of the things that my wife Camille and I enjoy most is watching old movies. Most often our interest is focused on the entertainment element in them, but occasionally, we like to ask the question "What if?" in a given case and add our own analytical content to the story. We have found that we gravitate frequently to older films that are, among other things, message oriented and full of comic capers on the part of those who play supporting roles.

Recently, we reviewed and thoroughly enjoyed a Western entitled *The Undefeated* (1969). The film takes place just after the Civil War; two ex-colonels, one from the Union and the other from the Confederacy, are beginning new lives in Mexico. The film follows the usual format; its principal characters, male and female, continually remind us that good always triumphs over the not-so-good moral decision. John Wayne, the principal character, plays the Union ex-colonel John Henry Thomas. Rock Hudson plays the role of Confederate ex-colonel James Langdon, leading a group of Southerners who have lost their homes to northern carpetbaggers. Although they fought on separate sides of the Civil War, Thomas and Langdon are able to bond not only through their belief in the rules of war but also in the social bonding men normally pursue looking out for the common good. We observed several ideas in *The Undefeated* that caused us to pose our "What if" question about its content.

The son of a white father and a black mother, James Augustine Healy became the country's first black bishop in the late 19th century.

Camille and I sat back to analyze what really went on in the nation when these two disparate groups of people, the northern carpetbaggers and the defeated Confederates, took on the benevolent role of showing each other how to make do with the spoils of war. Most southern whites felt the brunt of northern intervention and considered it meddling. As far as the carpetbaggers were concerned, Southerners were selfish, favoring of their own interpretation of the law. We were somewhat surprised to see ex-Colonel Langdon torch his plantation house rather than sell it to a carpetbagger for little or nothing. His plans were to take his family and other like-minded ex-Confederate sympathizers to Mexico in search of a new and perhaps more prosperous life. Here is where Camille and I decided to ask our question: What if?

FELLOWSHIP

The question arose in my mind because there is an implied notion of common benevolence and camaraderie—brotherly fellowship, if you will—in the film between white gentlemen of culture, regardless of their differences during the war. However, there now seems to be the general understanding among them that they must work to promote the common good among themselves. We then asked ourselves if Northerners were really more sympathetic to African Americans in the period of Reconstruction than Southerners. The answer is not a simple yes or no. But the historical record will show that some southern plantation owners sent their mulatto children to the North to be educated—realizing the lack of opportunities for them in the recovering war-torn South. A case in point is James Augustine Healy, who was born in Macon, Georgia, in 1830 to a white father and a black mother. His father, an Irish American, sent James to school in New York and Massachusetts. He was ordained a Catholic priest in Paris in 1854 and became the nation's first black bishop, presiding over the Catholic dioceses of the state of Maine in the late 19th century. This is one example of little-known familial benevolence amid such racial conflict in the South. But there are many other examples of this kind of interest on the part of caring Southerners. One may rightly ask if such an act of benevolence on the part of a white man, as in the case of Michael Harris Healy, who was forbidden by law to marry across the color line, was a common occurrence. The answer is no. Most children born of mixed parentage in the South were reared as slaves.

One might also ask what would have happened if these two men, ex-Colonels Langdon and Thomas, had had a benevolent concern for the people they left behind. In ex-Colonel Langdon's case, we may rightly ask what were the slaves to do on their own, having been freed of human bondage without being given anything to live on? All they had was an unfriendly dismissal from their former owners. Is it possible that they would have chosen to accompany their ex-masters on the long and treacherous journey to Mexico if given the chance? And were these not the men, women, and children who had enabled ex-Colonel Langdon and his family to live the good life in the pre–Civil War South? Were they not the skilled artisans, architects, mechanics, and craftspeople in their capacities as builders and carpenters of the plantation houses who constructed the 20-foot columns that adorned the lofty buildings where they served with dedication? Were they not the carriage builders, the wheelwrights, the potters, the dressmakers, the bricklayers, and the basket makers—a craft so essential for gathering food and harvesting cotton in the South? How could life go on without them? In the film, neither ex-Colonel Thomas nor ex-Colonel Langdon could call on slave servants to build their new lives in Mexico.

ARCHITECTS OF THE AMERICAN SOUTH

These questions raised by the movie caused me to reflect on some important writings on slavery and Reconstruction by a number of eminent scholars. I went to our library and reread what art historian and artist David Driskell said about the work of the slaves who were left behind in situations such as we see in the film. In his celebrated book, *Two Centuries of Black American Art,* Driskell defines the salient role played by slaves on southern plantations, where they were experts at making objects of service and accustomed to providing solutions for many everyday problems. These included supplying medical remedies for sick children, taking care of numerous chores such as painting the houses, and shrinking the wood needed in construction, among other things. In a footnote on services slaves provided to their masters, Driskell points to the memoirs of J. M. Gibson stating with certainty the professional skills of his "mechanic slave," John Jackson, as being the designer and builder of the old 19th-century courthouse in Vicksburg, Mississippi. There must be hundreds of other such true stories out there that fit into our "What if?" scenario.

Lessons learned from the human experience in the film are relevant ones, but I would have been more comfortable seeing more personal interaction among the unacknowledged supporters and providers of the lifestyles of the ex-colonels as well as those who followed them to Mexico.

As an African American who remains cognizant of the social and racial divide in our nation, I am constantly in search of finding a means of delivering an informed message to everyone about the social history of our nation and how it continues to be portrayed on film and television and in the electronic media. My stance is one in which I wish to reserve the right to be participant and critic while reflecting on how the arts, in particular the film arts, have influenced our judgment about social mores, political correctness, and, in some ways, the economic situation in which we find ourselves at this time in history.

Actor-comedian Bill Cosby remains critical of the way the country's racial history has been portrayed in film, television, and electronic media.

So we return to asking what if ex-Colonel James Langdon had decided to take his entourage of ex-slaves with him to Mexico? Would their new life in Mexico have been better or worse? So what if a more benevolent attitude had been taken by Langdon toward his ex-slaves? If they had followed him on the treacherous trek down to Mexico would they have been welcomed with outstretched arms? I doubt it.

One real strength of the movie, we concluded, is that these two leading men portrayed roles of reconciliation in an unusually trusting manner. And having to resolve their differing points of view, they came together as a united team, pulling together to ward off outlaws and revolutionaries on both sides of the border in pursuit of their own newly sought freedom and safety. Now, what if Camille and I had not taken time to see *The Undefeated* for a second time? Would we have been prepared to add our insights to the salient meaning of the film and re-create its content with our own personal agenda? I think not. ■

Right: Female slaves, struggling to care for both their children and themselves, often faced cruelty and severe mistreatment from their male overseers.

The driver's whip unfolds its torturing coil.
"She only sulks — go, lash her to her toil."

de men. When dey put her on de block, dey put all her chillun aroun her to show fol'ks how fas she can hab chillun. When she sold her family nebber see her agin."

Slavery's constant companion was thus systematic violence and abuse of power. Without it, the flawed system would fall apart; with it, the system was simply intolerable. The Founding Fathers, most of whom also owned slaves, well understood this predicament. In 1820, near the end of his life, Thomas Jefferson wrote: "We have the wolf by the ear, and we can neither hold him, nor safely let him go."

Below: A typical slave whip was constructed of a wooden handle and a steel spring flail. Henry Louis Stephens's 1863 illustration (opposite) captures the cruelty of punishment by whip.

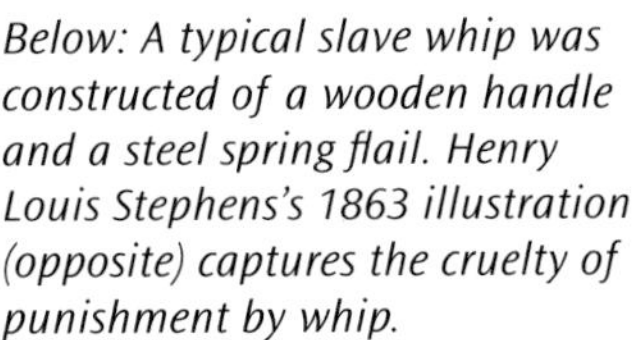

SLAVERY IN THE NORTH

As Venture Smith grew into manhood as an enslaved African in the North during the mid-1700s, he witnessed one scene of violence too many, especially between his master's wife and his own wife, Meg, and resolved to free himself. His path to freedom was indirect, lengthy, and arduous, but as he looked back in later years, he reflected: "I have many consolations; Meg, the wife of my youth, whom I married for love and bought with money, is still alive. My freedom is a privilege which nothing else can equal."

The means by which Venture obtained his entire family's freedom—hiring himself out, shunning all luxuries, scraping together the purchase prices of his wife, daughter, and two sons over periods of years—was more typical to slavery in the North than in the South. According to historian Ira Berlin, "slaves in society" are the hallmark of slavery in the North, whereas discrete "slave societies" evolved on the plantations of the South.

In the North, enslaved Africans typically experienced greater isolation from one another, as most northern slaveholders owned one to three slaves, instead of 100 times that many, as on the South's largest plantations. They also made up a much

Working anonymously in the bustling markets of late 18th-century New York City (top), Black men unpack casks alongside white seamen and merchants. A rare 1855 ambrotype (above) tells the story of a slave boy's journey to the free North.

smaller percentage of the overall population. "At its height," writes Berlin, "the black population totaled only 8 percent of the population of New Jersey and less than 4 percent in Massachusetts and Connecticut." This was in stark contrast to a Black population of 80 percent in the West Indies, or of 50 percent and greater in the Carolinas and Mississippi Delta.

Whether they lived on a rural farm, or in cities and town such as Boston, New York, Washington, D.C., or Providence, Rhode Island, northern slaves probably worked alongside, and shared close quarters with, white slaveholders and indentured servants. Berlin says that "slave farmhands were reduced to near invisibility by being stuffed into garrets, back rooms, closets, and outbuildings." Although she lived in a city, Sojourner Truth testified that she too lived in a cellar, and with other "inmates, of both sexes and all ages," slept on "damp boards, like the horse, with a little straw and a blanket."

Like shelter, food, clothing, and other necessities rarely surpassed the meager. Frederick Douglass (born Frederick Bailey), runaway slave, editor of the *North Star* newspaper, and eminent abolitionist, recalled a typical meal during his boyhood as a slave in Maryland during the early 1800s: "Our food was coarse corn meal boiled. . . . It was put into a large wooden tray or trough, and set down upon the ground. The children were then called, like so many pigs, and like so many pigs they would come and devour the mush; some with oyster-shells, others with pieces of shingle, some with naked hands, and none with spoons." Clothing, distributed once a year, consisted of rough linen and

An Ancestor's Roots: Kunta Kinte

Kunta Kinte is the main character in Alex Haley's *Roots: The Saga of an American Family* (1976) and in the resulting television movie (1977). The characters resulted from Haley's extensive genealogical research on his family, beginning with the capture and enslavement of Kinte. According to Haley's investigation, Kinte was his great-great-great-great grandfather on his mother's side.

Kinte was born around 1750 in Juffure, a town on the Gambia River in Gambia, West Africa. He was the eldest son of Omoro and Binta of the Mandinka tribe. They raised Kinte in Mandinkan tradition under the Islamic religion. At 17 or so, he was captured and transported to the U.S. aboard an American slave ship. Haley believes Kinte sailed on the *Lord Ligonier,* which left Gambia on July 5, 1767, and arrived in Annapolis, Maryland, on September 29, 1767, with 98 of its original 140 captured Africans.

After Kinte's arrival in Annapolis, he is sold to John Waller, who brings him to work on his plantation in Virginia. Kinte resists the slave breaker's attempts to force him to abandon his African ways and succumb to the will of his American master. He tries several times to run away from the plantation and even survives repeated lashes from the master's whip. After his fourth capture his foot is chopped off as punishment. Beaten and almost broken in spirit, he finally yields by accepting the American name Toby but refuses to abandon Islamic teachings. He is eventually sold to Waller's brother William and works as his driver and gardener. While enslaved on William Waller's plantation, Kinte meets and later marries a domestic slave named Belle.

For Haley, Kinte's unrelenting desire to maintain his African identity is the common thread throughout the saga. He continuously impresses upon other slaves the need to keep striving for freedom and to preserve their African roots. Kinte and Belle have a child named Kizzy, who grows up learning African words, culture, and family history from her father, who allegedly dies in 1810. Kinte's legacy is passed down through African oral traditions.

Scholars have speculated about how much of Haley's account is true. Haley proved he was a descendant of Kizzy, but others argue that there is no proof that a slave named Toby was her father, nor proof of the existence of Kunta Kinte. Regardless, Kinte embodied the slave experience for many Americans. More important, though, his depiction as proud, dignified, and courageous altered the prevailing image of the African slave forever. Haley's story played a major role in promoting dialogue about slavery and ignited a nation to search its roots. A memorial to both Alex Haley and Kunta Kinte stands at the dock where Kinte arrived in Annapolis, and the Kunta Kinte Heritage Festival is a two-day celebration of African- American, African, and Caribbean cultures held every September in Annapolis. *D. W.*

LeVar Burton portrays Kunta Kinte in the U.S. television show Roots, *a 1977 miniseries based on the book by Alex Haley. Part fiction and part fact, the story line is based on Haley's family history, beginning with the enslavement of Kinte in 1767.*

Four generations of an African family, all enslaved in the South, gather outside living quarters in Beaufort, South Carolina.

"A slave consumes in meat two hundred pounds of bacon or pork, costing, in Kentucky, Ohio, Indiana, Illinois, Missouri, Tennessee, and Western Virginia, $8; thirteen bushels of Indian corn, costing $2; this makes up his food. Now for salt and medicines add $1, and it runs thus: a year's food is $11."

—*Nathaniel Ware, slaveholder*

"negro cloth" shirts and trousers, just one set per season. When these wore out, Douglass recounted, slave children "went naked until the next allowance-day."

The one small boon many northern slaves leveraged to maximum advantage was exposure to a wide range of skills and access to a ready labor market. "Moving from job to job as labor demands changed," Berlin writes, "slaves found themselves in the field one day and in the shop the next, smithing horseshoes, tanning leather, making bricks, or repairing houses, barns, and furniture. On other days, they could be back in the field or driving a wagon, piloting a boat, or delivering a message." Proficiency in various skills meant that many northern slaves could be hired out by their masters, or hire themselves out. In this way, they had the opportunity to pocket the difference between what their employer paid and what their master kept. By receiving the value of their own labor directly, they could set aside a few cents a day, perhaps a dollar a month, and gradually accrue a small measure of wealth, and a priceless ticket to freedom.

In addition to mastering a variety of trades, many northern slaves also turned minimal free time to maximum advantage. As one Anglican missionary noted, most slaveholders gave their slaves "one Day a Week to clear Ground and plant it, to subsist themselves and Families." This day, typically Sunday, and sometimes half of Saturday, became not a day of rest, but a day of toil to clear a tiny profit. Toward the end of his remarkable

Discovering His Past: Alex Haley

Alex Haley's award-winning *Roots: The Saga of an American Family* is credited with generating wide interest in genealogy. The book was born out of stories passed down by Haley's maternal grandparents about an enslaved ancestor named Kunta Kinte. Haley spent years researching his family history while building his career as a journalist.

Born Alexander Murphy Palmer Haley on August 11, 1921, he was the oldest of three boys of Simon Alexander and Bertha Palmer Haley in Ithaca, New York. Shortly after his birth, he and his mother moved to Henning, Tennessee, to live with her parents while Simon completed graduate studies at Cornell University. It was here that Haley attended high school and learned from his grandparents how Kunta Kinte was brought to Annapolis, Maryland, with other Africans from Gambia and sold into slavery.

Haley finished high school at the age of 15 and enrolled in Alcorn College (now Alcorn State University) in Mississippi, the nation's first state-supported institution for the higher education of African Americans. He also attended Elizabeth City Teachers College in North Carolina but withdrew and returned home.

Observers gather around a statue of the late author Alex Haley in Annapolis, Maryland. The Kunta Kinte–Alex Haley Memorial marks the place where Kinte arrived by slave ship in 1767.

His father encouraged him to join the service, and in 1939 Haley left to join the U.S. Coast Guard as a mess boy. Working as an attendant in the mess hall was one of the few positions open to African Americans. He was promoted to petty officer third class. While in the service, Haley began honing his writing skills and was paid by other sailors to write love letters for them. He transferred into the Coast Guard's journalism unit following World War II, where he made petty officer first class in 1949. After 13 years, he was made chief journalist and achieved the rank of chief petty officer. He retired from the service in 1959 and began his writing career in earnest.

He published his first articles in 1962, beginning with an interview with the legendary trumpeter Miles Davis. Throughout the 1960s, Haley would conduct many notable interviews, including those with activist Martin Luther King, Jr.; boxer Cassius Clay (later Muhammad Ali); television personality Johnny Carson; and performer Sammy Davis, Jr. However, it was his 1963 interview with Nation of Islam leader Malcolm X that led to Haley's first book, *The Autobiography of Malcolm X: As Told to Alex Haley* in 1965, which bought him international recognition as a talented interviewer and investigator.

Haley returned to the stories he heard as a child about his enslaved ancestors. For 12 years he researched the collections of the Library of Congress and in the archives of Great Britain for information that would verify his grandparents' accounts. He also traveled to the small town of Juffure in Gambia and learned from a tribal historian that at 16 Kunta was in the woods searching for wood for a drum when he was captured and brought to America on a ship called the *Lord Ligonier*. In returning to the States, Haley slept on the hard wooden boards for ten nights in the hold of a cargo ship to experience what it was like for a slave to cross the Middle Passage in the cramped space of the ship's hold. Haley's subsequent description of his ancestor's journey illustrates the experience of millions of Africans who watched others die of illness and poor treatment during this initial stage of enslavement. To gain further insight into his ancestor, Haley stood on the spot in Annapolis, Maryland, where the *Lord Ligonier* had deposited Kunte Kinte some 200 years earlier.

Roots: The Saga of an American Family was published in 1976 and was immensely popular. Haley's research demonstrated that not all slaves gave up their African culture, and the book sparked generations of African Americans to trace their ancestry. However, its publication also led to charges that Haley fictionalized parts of the story. A year later Haley admitted to plagiarizing large passages from *The African* by Harold Courlander and settled out of court. Nevertheless, *Roots* won the Pulitzer Prize in 1977, and in the same year ABC created a 12-part miniseries based on the book that surpassed *Gone with the Wind* as the most-watched program, with 130 million viewers. In 1979, ABC aired *Roots: The Second Generation,* which continued the story of the descendants of Kunta Kinte.

Alex Haley died of a heart attack on February 10, 1992, and was buried near his childhood home in Tennessee. *D. W.*

"I would not be silent, and denounced the authors of my imprisonment, whoever they might be, as unmitigated villains."

—*Solomon Northup, enslaved freeman*

life, Venture Smith modestly described his legacy in terms of the labor he exchanged for eventual freedom: "I will be here remembered how much money I earned by cutting wood in four years."

Although slavery in the North took a form different from the one it took in the South, it was no less systemic, and just as prevalent. Churches, universities, banks, insurance companies, textile mills, shipyards, railroads, state and federal governments—all of these enterprises and institutions benefited both directly and indirectly from slave labor. Yet one by one, from 1777 (Vermont) to 1804 (New Jersey), northern states gradually abolished slavery, and although most Northerners continued to wear cotton, eat rice, and enjoy sugar that had been cultivated by slaves in the South, they no longer owned slaves themselves. Whereas the scale of the cotton and sugar economy supported large plantations in the South, the northern economy transitioned to a wage labor system, in which free Blacks competed for modest wages alongside whites and foreign-born indentured servants.

SLAVERY IN THE SOUTH

In many ways, the journey of New York–born Solomon Northup is like Venture Smith's, yet in tragic reverse. Born free, Northup was enslaved as an adult—a husband and a father—the victim of a kidnapping in the nation's capital. While his kidnappers pocketed $500 for his illicit sale into slavery in 1841, Solomon began a punishing regime on Edwin Epps's Louisiana cotton plantation. His account, *Twelve Years a Slave,* eloquently describes the South's "slave societies" during the 1840s and 1850s, when the U.S. led the world in cotton production, and slavery assumed its most brutal form. "Ten years I toiled for that man without reward," recalled Solomon. "Ten years I was compelled to address him with downcast eyes and uncovered head—in the attitude and language of a slave."

Solomon, a skilled musician and gentle soul, had little knack for picking cotton. When his sack repeatedly measured up short—"not half the quantity required of the poorest picker"—and whippings did not improve his dexterity, his owner declared him "not fit to associate with a cotton-picking 'nigger.'" Solomon, in other words, did not fit into a southern plantation's implicit caste system, based on work and a mirror of skin color.

In a hierarchy that mimicked plantation design and architecture, field hands occupied the lowest rung of the ladder. Next came those who tended and cared for horses, important as primary transportation. One or two steps up were the craftsmen who built houses, shod horses, crafted furniture, and made and repaired tools and agricultural implements. Closer yet to the "big house," coachmen dressed well, befitting those who ferried masters and their families to and fro. And at the top rung, inside the big house, lived and worked the house slaves, trusted by the white families and often very light skinned themselves.

Side by side, under one roof, within close earshot, yet sharply divided by race, slaves and masters shared an unmistakable intimacy. Those who paid most dearly were the enslaved women caught between master and mistress. For example, Solomon Northup feared for the spirit and safety of a young slave named Patsey on the Epps plantation. She was "a joyous creature" whose "back bore the scars of a thousand stripes . . . because it had fallen her lot to be the slave of a licentious master and a jealous mistress."

Despite daily tyranny and lifelong labor, enslaved Africans found ways to transcend their experience. Many practiced what Frederick Douglass preached: "A man's troubles are always half disposed of when he finds endurance his only remedy." The world they created, often invisible to whites, supported the undying dream of freedom they carried in their hearts.

Slave tags, like those shown above, identified Africans by number or place of ownership.

Camaraderie and an enduring spirit helped slaves to survive plantation life in the South. On Cockspur Island, Georgia (above), a group of slaves rests outside their plantation quarters. A 19th-century engraving (right) depicts life on a North Carolina plantation; women tend the rice fields while an overseer looks on.

Free Black Planters

A GALLERY

Among Virginia's famous 17th-century plantations, it has recently come to light that several Blacks purchased freedom from slavery for themselves and became landowners of large farms and small to medium-sized plantations. They purchased the land with money they had earned by various means, including from the sale of livestock, tobacco, and produce. The richer of these black planters also owned slaves and indentured servants, and their plantations rivaled the estates of their former owners.

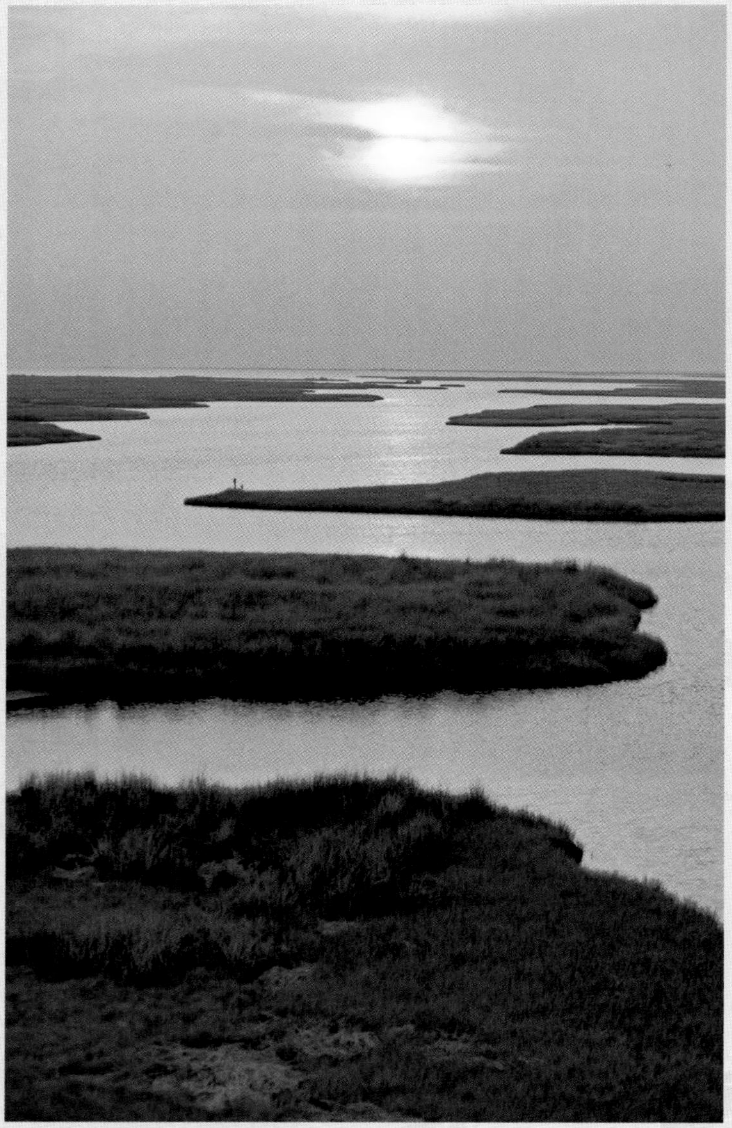

For a brief time in the 17th century, free black men could become landowners in the Chesapeake Bay area.

One prominent family was headed by Emmanuel Rodriggus (Driggus). His name implies that he could once have been enslaved by the Portuguese. During this era the Portuguese were well known as slave traders who captured "Atlantic Creoles," or inhabitants of Angola, and sold them to planters in Virginia.

Emmanuel Driggus is first mentioned on May 27, 1645, in the Northampton County court records located in Eastville, Virginia. He and his wife, Frances, became indentured servants to a white Virginia planter named Captain Francis Pott. Driggus signed a paper that declared Captain Pott, "who had newly come over the Baye with some servants whereby to make a cropp," his owner for a certain period of time. The paper further stated that his two daughters, Elizabeth and Jane, who had also been indentured to Pott, would be released at some date in the distant future. These two girls were not natural children of the Driggus couple, but he provided for them anyway. As events proved, he was eventually able to secure their release from service. He was not so fortunate, however, with other children that he and his wife had. They watched helplessly as one young son, Edward, and an older daughter, Ann, were sold away into service "for ever."

Perhaps spurred by these inhumane separations, Driggus purchased his and his wife's freedom from Potts. Once free, he worked hard to make a stable home and life for his remaining family. He eventually enlarged a herd of cattle to the point that he leased 145 acres of land from William Kendall, a wealthy white landowner in Northampton County. The land, which Driggus secured with 7,500 pounds of tobacco, was located on Kings Creek in Cape Charles. His lease was for 99 years and allowed him to sublease a 50-acre section of land to a white tenant. Driggus built his wealth by acquiring additional land, farming, and raising and selling livestock. His greatest wealth came from breeding horses.

After Frances Driggus died, Emmanuel married a white woman named Elizabeth. His holdings and his clan continued to grow. As with most of the free black families of the area, the family relationships were central to the lives of the people. As prosperous as Driggus was, he was still unable to purchase the freedom of some of his children. Because of this situation, he decided to give livestock to his free children in hopes that their holdings would allow them to remain free. This effort would be in vain.

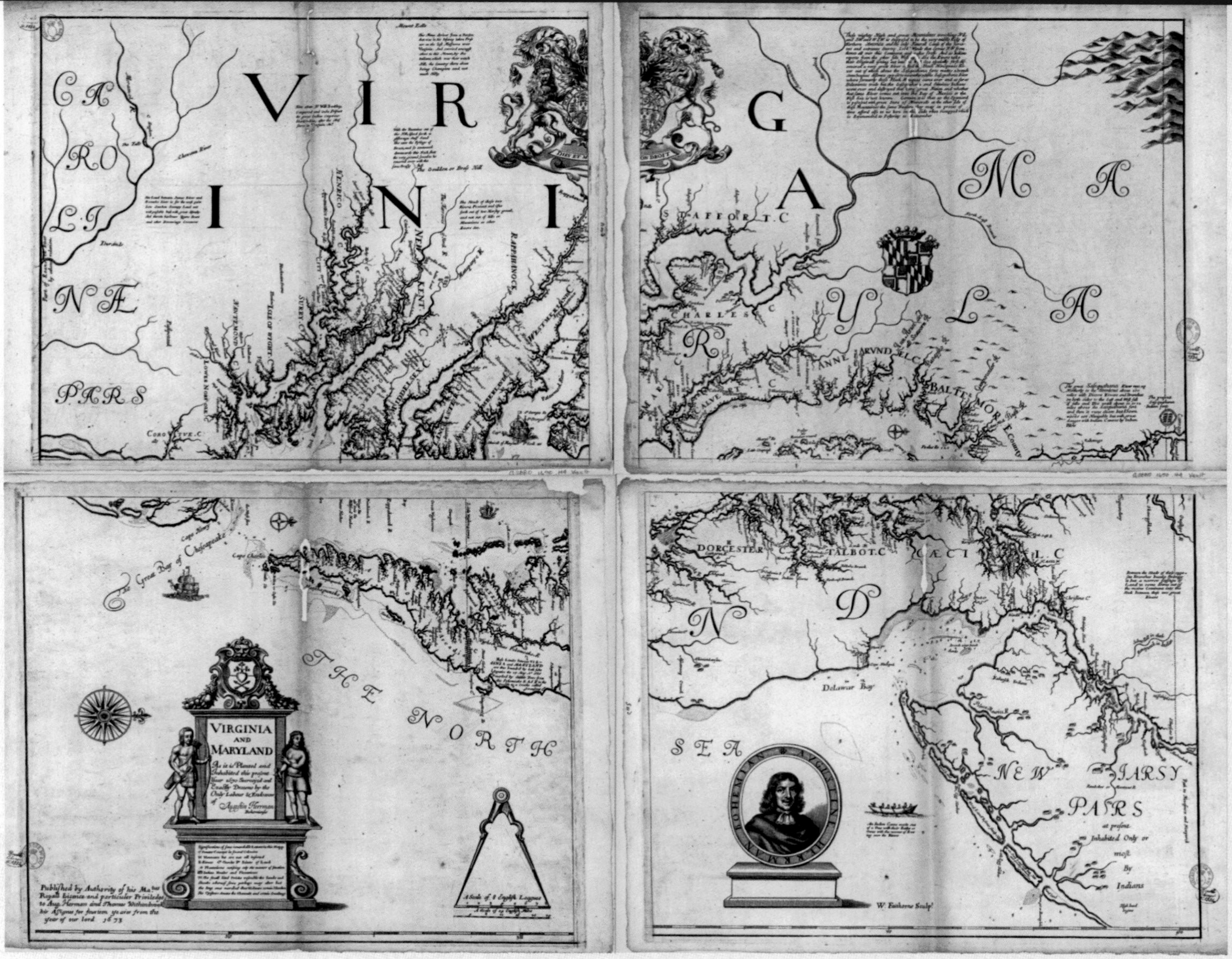

A 1670 map (above) shows land use in Virginia and Maryland. Emmanuel Driggus owned land in Northampton County, in the lower left quadrant. A 1670 court document (below) decrees that land owned by a Negro, now deceased, should revert to England.

One record in Virginia's Eastern Shore courthouse archives is a deed filed by Driggus that reads "one Bay Mare for my two daughters." It references his adopted daughters. Although they took ownership of their mare, both sisters became embroiled in legal fights that threatened their freedom for most of their lives.

After his death, life changed significantly for the free Blacks of Virginia and elsewhere. Uprisings led by runaway slaves from Virginia and throughout the South led to crackdowns. What had been a promising way of life soon disappeared for the vast majority of Blacks. Whites passed laws that took away Blacks' hard-earned freedoms and property. The phenomenon of the great black planter lasted for less than two generations, replaced by a new harsh reality that would last for more than 200 years. Ironically, the land that was once Driggus's plantation is now adjacent to a budding golf and gated community called Bay Creek Resorts. Some black residents still call it home.

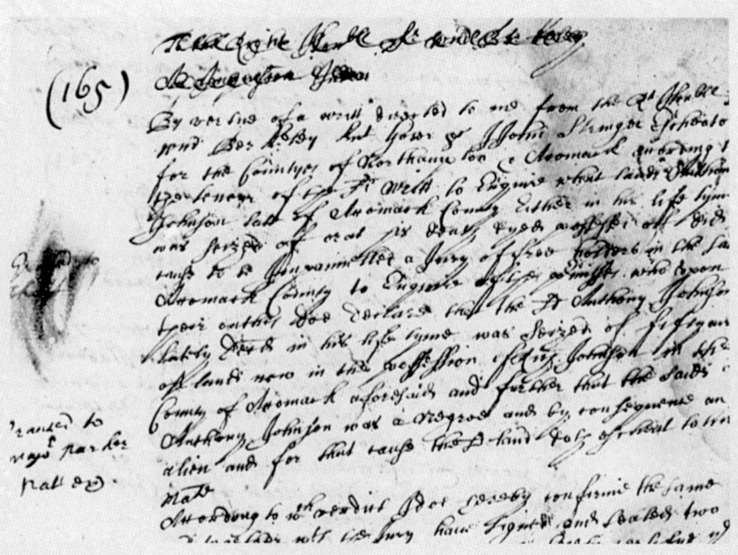

CHAPTER FIVE

Building a Culture

CHAPTER FIVE

1700s – 1860s

Building a Culture

Recent excavations of the slave quarters at Monticello, the stately Virginia plantation home designed and built by Thomas Jefferson between 1769 and 1809, have unearthed a small mystery. As archaeologists studied the foundations along Mulberry Row, the slave quarters adjacent to the main house, they discovered a series of small, rectangular pits that had once been overlain by the floorboards of several slave cabins. Similar archaeological finds have turned up on other plantations in Virginia and elsewhere on the Chesapeake. Most likely used to hide personal belongings or perhaps to store food and other necessities, these subfloor pits—dubbed slave safe-deposit boxes by some historical archaeologists—provide a metaphor for the private world that enslaved Africans created. These spaces in the foundations of slave cabins are at once hidden yet ubiquitous, silent yet significant. Much of the private world that slaves created was similarly self-made, crucial to survival, invisible to white society, and obscured by history.

Slaves endured and transcended forced servitude through strong family and kinship bonds, the quest for literacy, religious beliefs that sustained dreams of freedom, and cultural traditions that were carried from Africa. Despite a world that perpetuated racist myths at their expense, they created a cultural legacy that sustained and nourished them in the face of overwhelming odds. Emotional resilience, self-mastery, and agency in a white-dominated world were passed from one generation to the next through many small, daily miracles and practices: child-raising techniques that nourished self-esteem in spite of a master's cruelty and control; inventive ways for achieving literacy; clandestine gatherings to worship, sing, and dance; and a unique blend of American and African traditions.

"MAN IS BORN FREE"

By the time George Washington took office as the nation's first President in 1789, enslaved Africans and their descendants had been adapting to, and in turn redefining, the institution of slavery for nearly five generations. George Washington owned several hundred slaves who ran his plantation at Mount Vernon in Virginia, including many "dower slaves" who came from his marriage to wealthy Martha Custis Washington. He selected eight house slaves to accompany him first to New York for a year and then to Philadelphia for the remainder of his two presidential terms (1789-97). The nation's first family, in other words, included a "Second Family": slaves transplanted from Virginia to the North to serve the President and Mrs. Washington for eight years. Among them were Ona Judge Staines, who served as Martha Washington's chambermaid; a man called Hercules, who dazzled guests of state with his cooking; and William Lee, who served as Washington's valet, as he had throughout the protracted Revolutionary War.

Left: An aerial view of Monticello, Thomas Jefferson's Virginia plantation, shows gardens and orchards where slaves may have labored.

Previous pages: Strong family bonds enabled slaves to survive the harsh realities of everyday life. Sculptor Larkin J. Mead photographed this slave family in 1862.

"There is no subjugation so perfect as that which keeps the appearance of freedom for in that way one captures volition itself."

—Jean-Jacques Rousseau, philosopher

The contradiction inherent in a slave-owning democracy—a country founded on freedom yet divided by racial inequality—is painfully apparent in several of the nation's first Presidencies and in the private lives of many of its Founding Fathers. Thomas Jefferson's fabulous library at Monticello, whose shelves were undoubtedly dusted by black hands, included works by French Enlightenment philosopher Jean-Jacques Rousseau, who asserted without hesitation that

> *Man is born free; and everywhere he is in chains. One thinks himself the master of others, and still remains a greater slave than they. So, from whatever aspect we regard the question, the right of slavery is null and void, not only as being illegitimate, but also because it is absurd and meaningless. The words slave and right contradict each other, and are mutually exclusive. It will always be equally foolish for a man to say to a man or to a people: "I make with you a convention wholly at your expense and wholly to my advantage; I shall keep it as long as I like, and you will keep it as long as I like."*

Rousseau's bold truth did not appear in the Declaration of Independence, written by Jefferson in 1776. Instead, the Declaration's more subtle promise that "all men are created equal" actually kept the door to slavery open. For if all are born free, then children of slaves would automatically be freed upon birth. Yet if all are simply "created equal," not actually "born free," then enslavement is allowed to persist from one generation to the next. Jefferson, in whose life the contradiction of slavery in America was writ large, reflected on the meaning of the Declaration 50 years after he first penned it, stating that it represented a promise of equality rather than a guarantee. The Declaration, he wrote (in the last letter of his life), remained a powerful "signal arousing men to . . . the palpable truth, that the mass of mankind has not been born with saddles on their backs, nor a favored few booted and spurred, ready to ride them."

To justify inequality—which was entirely at odds with both Enlightenment philosophy and the promise of America—most of the nation's founders, and many of its first citizens, subscribed to racist beliefs. Somehow, they believed—or were able to convince themselves—that black men, women, and children, whose skin had simply evolved in such as way as to provide protection from Africa's searing equatorial sun, had to be fundamentally inferior to whites to merit such injustice.

Isaac Jefferson, Thomas Jefferson's slave, worked the Monticello estate for more than four decades. This photograph was taken when Isaac was 70.

This "less than" myth is actually encoded in the U.S. Constitution, made a tenet of federal law, in a clause establishing that for purposes of taxation and representation slaves counted as three-fifths of a person. Thus, five enslaved Blacks counted as three whites when taxes were calculated and congressional delegates allocated for the southern states.

Yet what did several of these "three-fifths" humans do during the nation's first Presidencies? What did the world look like to them, and how did they live in it? What became of Ona Judge, Hercules, and Billy Lee when they lived in Philadelphia, by then a largely free city? What became of Peter Fossett, an enslaved boy born and raised at Monticello, while Jefferson retired from public life yet reigned as the "Sage of Monticello"? The choices that they made to define their destinies, and in some cases defy very powerful masters, reveal much about the private lives of millions of other enslaved Americans during the 18th and 19th centuries. It is a world that requires effort to get to know, for it existed in the margins, shadows, and private spaces for centuries, much like the "slave safe-deposit" boxes discovered in the slave quarters at Monticello.

FAMILY TIES

Guests in President George Washington's executive home in Philadelphia agreed that his cook, Hercules, was truly a master chef. G. W. Parke Custis, the grandson of Martha Washington from her first marriage and later the adopted son of George Washington, described Hercules as "as highly accomplished a proficient in the culinary art as could be found in the United States." Hercules elevated traditional southern cuisine to new heights and leveraged his position to earn as much as "one to two hundred dollars a year" by selling leftovers from the President's kitchen. When he learned that the President wanted to transfer him from Mount Vernon to Philadelphia in 1790 to replace the less skilled chef who served Washington in New York, Hercules requested that his sons Richmond and Christopher come with him. He had raised his sons on his own following the death of his wife, known as Lame Alice, and his insistence on keeping his family together reveals a fundamental, yet overlooked, aspect of slavery. Family life was central to the slave experience, and though it could be broken apart or relocated on a master's whim, it nonetheless sustained and nourished millions of slaves from one generation to the next.

George Washington oversees his slaves' work at his Mount Vernon estate in 1797. Several hundred slaves ran the Virginia plantation.

Plans for Washington, D.C., were designed in part by Benjamin Banneker, the son of an enslaved father and a free mother.

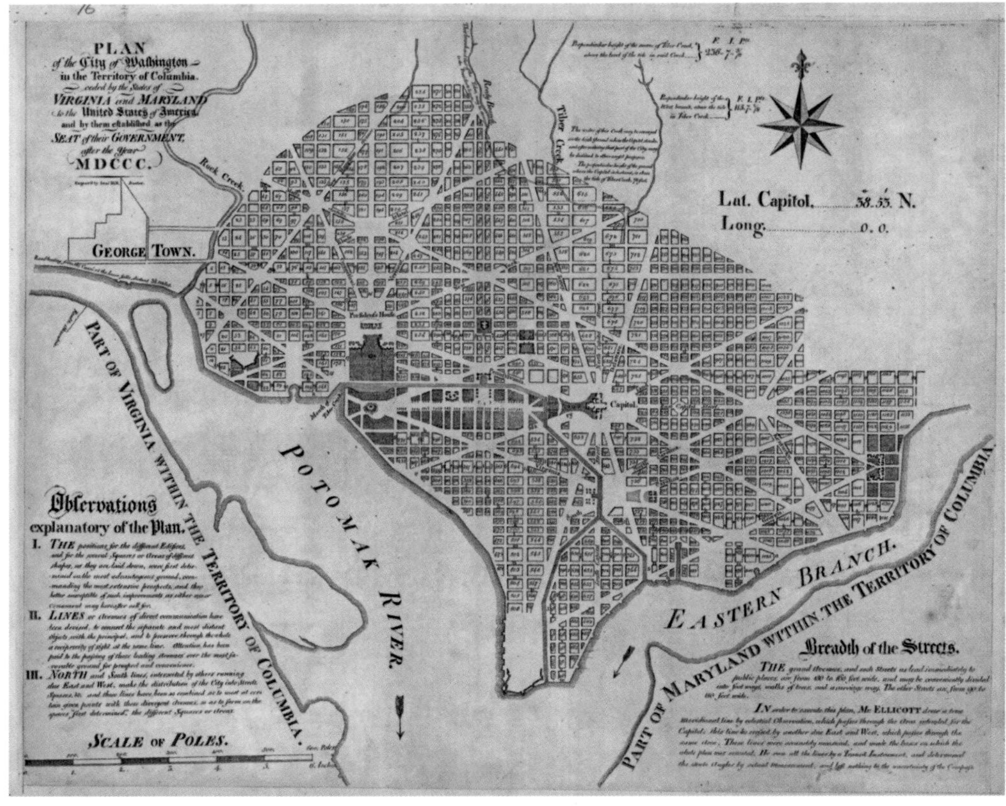

> "Deep has been the anguish of my soul when looking over my little family during the silent hours of the night, knowing the great danger of our being sold off at auction the next day and parted forever."
>
> — *Henry Bibb, slave*

Enslaved Americans made choices about marriage and child-raising within a context that defied conventional family structures. Slave parents faced a difficult challenge: how to raise their children in bondage, foster dreams of freedom, pass along practical and spiritual survival skills, and nourish in them a sense of self-worth despite a lack of power. According to historian John Blassingame, "Since slave parents were primarily responsible for training their children, they could cushion the shock of bondage for them, help them to understand their situation, teach them values different from those their masters tried to instill in them, and give them a referent for self-esteem other than the master."

Some slaves proved their love for their families by temporarily abandoning them. Henry Bibb, who lived in Kentucky in the early 1800s, explained his habit of running away within the emotional context of a husband and father: "My infant child was also frequently flogged by Mrs. Gatewood, for crying until its skin was bruised literally purple. This kind of treatment was what drove me from home and family, to seek a better home for them."

Hercules passed on more than his love and dedicated parenting to his children: He left behind an inspiring legacy of freedom. In 1797, as Washington returned to Mount Vernon at the end of his second term, Hercules escaped into the free Black community of Philadelphia and disappeared from public view. His daughter, born several years after his first wife died, told a visitor to Mount Vernon that she was "very glad" he was no longer there, "because he is free now."

Although President Washington did not make any attempt to have Hercules forcibly returned to Mount Vernon following his escape, the same cannot be said of Ona Judge following her risky bid for freedom a year earlier in 1796. As President Washington

Man of Science: Benjamin Banneker

Benjamin Banneker is believed by some scholars to have reconstructed the complete design of Washington, D.C., in two days after the firing of the project's manager, French architect Pierre L'Enfant. Even if this claim isn't true, most scholars agree that Banneker, the son and grandson of slaves, joined his neighbor, George Elliott, in creating important designs for what was to become the nation's capital. Impressed by Banneker's many talents and high level of intelligence, Elliott's cousin, Maj. Andrew Elliott, invited Banneker and others to join the team that had been charged with surveying the Federal District of what is now the city of Washington, D.C. L'Enfant drew up the actual architectural plans, and Elliott and his team completed the surveys.

Banneker was born in Maryland. The farm on which he grew up, called Bannaky Springs, was owned by his English grandmother, Molly Walsh, a former indentured servant who purchased the land after serving seven years of bondage as a maid. Along with the land, she purchased two slaves and promptly set them free. She married one of the men, Banna Ka, with whom she had several children. Their daughter, Mary Bannaky, married a slave named Robert. Robert and Mary had several children, including Benjamin, who was born in 1731.

Benjamin learned to read as a child when his grandmother taught him from the Bible, although much of his education was learned from a Quaker teacher who moved close to the Bannaky farm. The teacher, who changed Benjamin's last name to Banneker, set up a school for boys in the valley. Banneker attended, obtained a basic education, and went on to teach himself to become an astronomer, surveyor, and inventor. Borrowing from the design of a neighbor's pocket watch at the age of 21, Banneker took the timepiece apart and put it back together again. After finding it to be in fine working order, he designed a striking clock made completely of wood. This clock, which is believed to be the first striking clock designed and made in America, worked flawlessly for 40 years.

In addition to his other talents, Banneker's studies and calculations of the stars led him to compile six farmer's almanacs. These almanacs, published between 1791 and 1797, became top sellers from Pennsylvania to Virginia and into Kentucky. They were even recognized abroad, in France and England.

Banneker also distinguished himself as an early civil rights advocate. In his August 19, 1791, letter to Secretary of State Thomas Jefferson, he questioned why the "Father of Liberty" still held slaves. He challenged Jefferson to help him to get rid of "absurd and false ideas" that one race was superior to another. Banneker included with his letter a copy of his almanac, implying that he, as a black man, had alone calculated the complex contents in the book. Jefferson's reply, in part, included the following statement:

BANNAKER'S NEW-JERSEY, PENNSYLVANIA, DELAWARE, MARYLAND AND VIRGINIA ALMANAC, OR EPHEMERIS, FOR THE YEAR OF OUR LORD 1795; Being the Third after LEAP-YEAR.

BALTIMORE: PRINTED BY S. & J. ADAMS.

Banneker's Almanac, *which was filled with sophisticated astrological calculations and studies, gained widespread notoriety.*

". . . you exhibit . . . talents equal to those of the other colors of men." Jefferson, however, did not free any of his slaves in his lifetime.

Banneker died at his home in Maryland on October 9, 1806, at the age of 74. By then, he had sold his farm to the Elliotts but kept a life interest in the farmhouse. It burned to the ground on the day of his funeral, causing some people to wonder if the fire was deliberate. Of all of his many works, only two items survive today—a manuscript journal and published volumes of Banneker's *Almanac*.

C. J. C.

“To seize, and put [Ona] on board a Vessel bound immediately to this place, or to Alexandria which I should like better, seems at first view, to be the safest and least expensive.”

— *George Washington, President*

wrote in a letter that was sent via Secretary of the Treasury Oliver Wolcott to Joseph Whipple, the collector of the Port of Portsmouth, Ona “has been the particular attendant on Mrs. Washington since she was ten years old; and was handy and useful to her, being perfect Mistress of her needle.” In the letter the President doggedly pursued her safe return, even to the extent of suggesting that she be kidnapped. Yet Whipple politely disobeyed the President's instructions in what he called the face of Ona's “thirst for compleat freedom,” and Ona herself insisted that she “should rather suffer death than return to Slavery.”

Ona continued to thwart the President's attempts at recapture, married in 1787, and had two children with her husband Jack (also called John) Staines. She spent the rest of her days in relative poverty but never regretted choosing freedom, for it allowed her to learn to read and practice her faith freely. Toward the end of her life, Ona told an interviewer, “I am free, and have, I trust been made a child of God by the means.”

LITERACY

The quest for literacy—attained often at great risk and in the face of harsh anti-literacy slave code laws—reveals a nearly unquenchable thirst for knowledge. For example, a South Carolina slave code from 1740 levies hefty fines against anyone daring to teach slaves to read and write:

> *XLV. And whereas the having of slaves taught to write, or suffering them to be employed in writing, may be attended with great inconveniences; Be it enacted, that all and every person and persons whatsoever, who shall hereafter teach, or cause any slave or slaves to be taught to write, or shall use or employ any slave as a scribe in any manner of writing whatsoever, hereafter taught to write; every such person and persons shall, for every such offence, forfeit the sum of £100 current money.*

Reading and writing granted slaves greater internal agency as well as an external path to freedom. With literacy came the ability to forge a free pass (a document that slaves carried to prove they were traveling with their master's permission), study the Bible without interference from white preachers, and gradually unseat the power that held slavery in place.

While Ona used her freedom to attain literacy, thousands of others used their literacy to attain freedom. Some learned from white children, a few learned from masters whose purposes it served, and most stole away at night to learn from literate fellow slaves in “pit schools” that were held under oak trees and other covert meeting places. Frederick Douglass at first learned from his mistress, and then, when his master forbade her continued efforts, devised more cunning ways to master the language that would one day make him an orator of world renown:

> *The plan which I adopted, and the one by which I was most successful, was that of making friends of all the little white boys whom I met in the street. As many of these as I could, I converted into teachers. With their kindly aid, obtained at different times and in different places, I finally succeeded in learning to read. When I was sent of errands, I always took my book with me, and by going one part of my errand quickly, I found time to get a lesson before my return. I used also to carry bread with me, enough of which was always in the house, and to which I was always welcome; for I was much better off in this regard than many of the poor white children in our neighborhood. This bread I*

Low Country Saviors: P. Simmons and E. Campbell

Slaves who lived on the Sea Islands of North Carolina, South Carolina, and Georgia for more than 150 years became known as the Gullah. Their language, also called Gullah, had its roots in the Creole villages of Sierra Leone. Isolated from the mainland, they continued to practice the trades and crafts brought from West Africa. Among these was the practice of going to the marshes and gathering sweetgrass to make intricately designed baskets in the same patterns that their ancestors had created. They also heated and shaped metals for use in farmwork, particularly shoeing horses. These inhabitants then passed their culture on to their descendants.

One such beneficiary was Philip Simmons, born on Daniel Island in 1912. At 13 Philip began a blacksmith apprenticeship with a former slave named Peter Simmons. As automobiles became more prevalent, the business transformed from making horseshoes to making repairs to existing ironwork throughout Charleston. In time, the elder blacksmith retired and sold his business to his young protégé. Simmons began creating elaborate ornamental ironwork in the form of gates, wrought-iron fences, balconies, stair rails, and window grills in the late 1940s. He has gained recognition throughout South Carolina and in many other parts of the country, being awarded a National Heritage Fellowship and seeing his work appear in a number of museums.

Emory Shaw Campbell has crusaded for the preservation of the environment and the rich Gullah heritage, endangered by the onslaught of rapid development. Campbell was the executive director of Penn Center on St. Helena's Island for more than 20 years. Founded by northern missionaries as a school to help newly freed slaves, it later became a retreat and a meeting place to plan civil rights strategies. During Campbell's tenure, the school became a haven for preserving the culture of the Sea Islands. He has been recognized throughout South Carolina as a primary keeper of the Gullah culture. Campbell and his wife continue to live on Hilton Head Island, one of only a few of the original Black families, and he keeps Gullah history alive by operating tours of sites of importance to the Gullah people and culture. *C. J. C.*

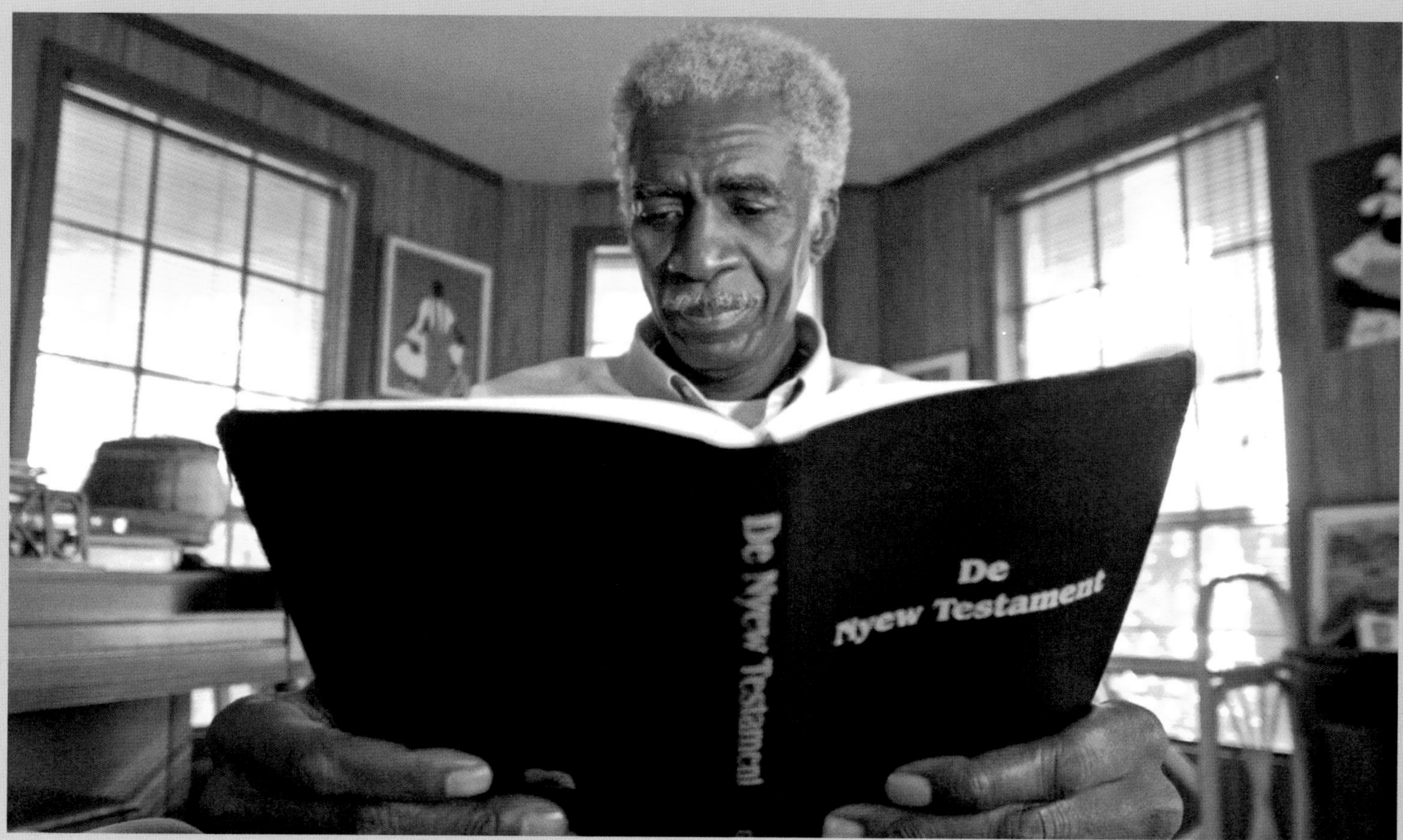

Emory Campbell's translation of the Bible from English to Gullah helped to preserve an endangered language and way of life. Although initially fearing that missionaries would look down upon his efforts, Campbell ultimately produced a work that honored his heritage.

Jubilee: Making Freedom

IRA BERLIN, PH.D.

"My Dear Wife it is with grate joy I take this time to let you know Whare I am," John Boston wrote in early January 1862. "i am now in Safety in the 14th Regiment of Brooklyn this Day i can Adress you thank god as a free man." Like most Black people, John Boston celebrated the moment when, as the "lord led the Children of Isrel to the land of Canon[,] So he led me to a land Whare fredom Will ranes in spite Of earth and hell." Wife Elizabeth was not as fortunate; she remained a slave. But John assured her "trust the time Will Come When We Shal meet again. . . . And if We dont met on earth We Will Meet in heven Whare jesas ranes."

The conflict that allowed John Boston to seize his freedom would eventually sweep slavery from the U.S. Boston was one of the first to be sheltered in federal lines, but thousands, then hundreds of thousands, and eventually millions would follow. Their numbers would grow, as federal edicts, congressional legislation, presidential proclamations, and finally, in December 1865, a constitutional amendment abolished slavery.

FROM SLAVE TO OFFICEHOLDER

For John Boston and the slaves that followed him to freedom, slavery's demise was the most important event in their lives, and Boston was not alone in comparing it to Jesus' Second Coming. After more than three hundred years of bondage, everything had changed. Between the spring of 1861 and the spring of 1867—the beginning of the Civil War and the beginning of Radical Reconstruction (when black men gained the vote and the right to hold office)—Black people went in quick order from slave to free, from free men to soldiers in the world's most powerful army, from soldiers to citizens in the world's greatest republic, and finally from citizens to officeholders. If a former slave—defined in law as mere property—could be transformed into a magistrate of the republic in a matter of years, imagine what could be done in a decade, in a lifetime, in a century? With good reason, black men and women believed the revolution to remake the world in accord with their own vision was upon them. With John Boston, they rejoiced at their Jubilee; it seemed that the time had come when Jesus would "ranes."

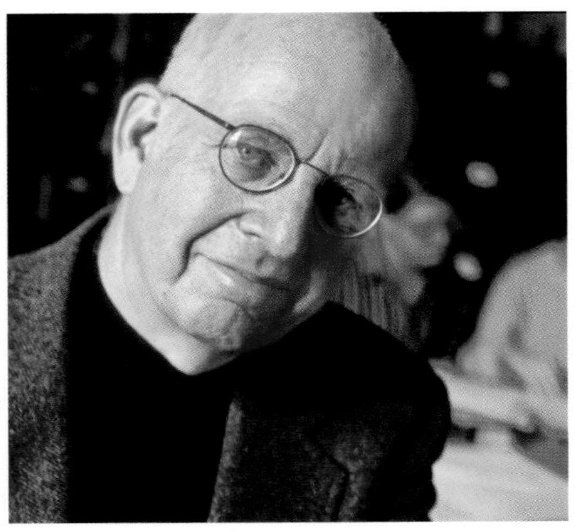

Through his studies of the history of slavery in North America, Ira Berlin captures the essence of early African-American life.

But revolutions not only go forward, they also go backward. The revolution that John Boston saw beginning when he reached the 14th New York Infantry turned against him and his people. At the end of the century, slavery was gone, but a new system of political domination and labor extortion had been put in its place. The refashioning of the shackles of subordination led many—especially those who viewed emancipation from the distance of the 21st century—to dismiss emancipation as a cruel charade. For them, the celebration was premature, if not mistaken. Former slaves had been naive about the possibilities of change and had vastly underestimated the power of the slave regime to maintain the old order. Emancipation had changed nothing of the essentials.

Even a cursory inspection of the arrival of freedom suggests otherwise. As slaves, black people had thought long and hard about freedom and what it meant. When freedom came, they were ready and they were anything but naive. The changes they put in place permanently transformed African American life. The slaves' ideas about freedom derived from their experience in slavery. Themselves property, they had been denied control over their labor. Without independent standing in the eyes of the law, they were subject to the whims of an owner. They could be sold, disciplined and transported without recourse, and they had no right to marry, educate their children or provide for their parents. They could not bear arms, assemble, hold property, and travel without their owner's consent.

Freedom would be different. If slavery had denied their humanity, it would be recognized in freedom. If slavery deprived them of control of their persons and progeny, freedom would allow them to organize their families and domestic life as they wished. If slavery permitted their owners to expropriate the fruits of their labor, freedom would guarantee compensation. As a free people, former slaves expected to be able to organize their lives in accordance with their own sense of right.

But freedom was not merely slavery's negative. Even before the war, slaves had established families, created churches, selected

At the center of Thomas Nast's circa 1865 tribute to emancipation, a freed family gathers jubilantly around the hearth. To their left, three scenes show the brutality of life under the Confederacy, while to their right, African Americans enjoy the benefits of their newfound freedom.

community leaders, and carved a small area of independent economy activity. Although denied the right to own property, slaves owned many things, which served as the basis for an elaborate network of kinship, with its own patterns of courtship, rites of marriage, parental responsibilities, and kin obligation. Likewise, slaves organized churches, where black ministers articulated their own distinctive notions of Christianity and, with other community leaders, orchestrated a complex politics.

LABOR NEGOTIATIONS

With freedom, black men and women took new names, found new residences, reconstituted families, and transformed their own labor into material independence. Institutions that had been clandestine—churches, schools, and burial associations—functioned openly, and leaders who had previously muffled their voices spoke freely or, at least, more freely than in times past. Freed people understood the symbols—a new name and residence—and institutions—family, church, and school—of freedom needed a substantial base. From the first, black people claimed the right to the land they had worked, in some places for centuries. The treason of former owners and wartime confiscations of Confederate property encouraged former slaves to believe that the federal government would expropriate their owners' property and give them—its ally—access to land. The idea of "40 acres and a mule" gained enormous force, fueling anticipation that former slaves would be given the resources to achieve independence. But as the evidence mounted that land would not be theirs, freed people reentered negotiations with their former owners over the terms on which they would work. Those negotiations would become the basis of a new labor system and with a new politics, articulated at the conventions of former slaves that met in the wake of emancipation.

The new world that former slaves had created in the aftermath of emancipation fell short of John Boston's hoped-for Second Coming. But it had profoundly transformed his life and the lives of other black men and women. If the world freed people made did not inaugurate a new Jerusalem, it set black people on a path that would enable Boston's descendants to fulfill his vision of freedom. ■

"No child, white people never teach colored people nothing, but to be good to dey Master and Mistress. What learning dey would get in dem days, dey been get it at night, Taught themselves."

—*Louisa Gause, former slave*

A plaque identifies the slave seller W. W. Wilber and advertises his goods— "strong healthy African blacks from Cape Coast Africa."

used to bestow upon the hungry little urchins, who, in return, would give me that more valuable bread of knowledge.

John Sella Martin, a slave originally from North Carolina who escaped in 1856, learned from his master, who went blind and asked that Sella read aloud to him to keep him abreast of news. More typically, slaves learned neither from white children nor from kindly or self-serving masters and mistresses, but rather on their own, at night, and in secret.

In 1815, soon after Thomas Jefferson sold his personal library to the U.S. Congress to replace books that had been destroyed by the British during the War of 1812, a boy named Peter was born at Monticello to the slave couple Joseph and Edith Fossett. Although Peter did not have the opportunity to take advantage of what became the nucleus of the Library of Congress—Mr. Jefferson's library of 6,700 books—he did learn to read "from white children" at Monticello. According to an 1898 newspaper interview with Peter Fossett much later in his life, "Mr. Jefferson allowed his grandson to teach any of his slaves who desired to learn, and Lewis Randolph first taught me how to read."

Upon Jefferson's death in 1826, many slave families from Monticello were sold on the auction block and separated. Peter's father was freed by the terms of Jefferson's will and managed to buy the freedom of most of his children, but Peter's new owner simply refused to sell him. Peter carried his literacy with him, though, and while owned by a Colonel Jones, taught others to read (in spite of Jones's threat of "thirty-and-nine lashes on your bare back" if he ever caught Peter with a book in his hands), forged free passes, and twice attempted escape on his own. "For the second time," Peter recalled, "I was put up on the auction block and sold like a horse. But friends from among my master's best friends bought me in and sent me to my father in Cincinnati, and I am here to-day." Able to rejoin his family in freedom, Peter became a well-respected caterer, preacher, and eventually, conductor on the Underground Railroad in Cincinnati.

While Peter lived with Colonel and Mrs. Jones in the 1830s, he experienced a spiritual conversion during a revival typical of the Second Great Awakening, which swept much of the eastern seaboard during the early 1800s. Mrs. Jones, he later said, "was called the mother of the Baptist church, and our house was the stopping place for all the preachers. It was here when they were holding these meetings that my eyes were opened." This experience, combined with Peter's already steady internal compass, guided him toward a life with sturdy spiritual roots.

As it did for Peter Fossett, literacy often supported another mainstay of slave life: the ability to practice religion freely. While most white preachers reminded slaves solely of their "Christian" duty to be obedient to their masters and mistresses, Black preachers spoke mostly of freedom, both in the here and now and the hereafter. The ability to read and interpret the Bible in its entirety, not just those few passages that served slave owners' interests, supported the evolution of what many historians call the invisible church.

Unlike the Baptist church in Cincinnati that Peter Fossett led, an invisible church had no fixed address. Much like the improvised schools that took place under oak trees during the cover of night, this church was an informal institution that existed outside white churches, far from white preachers, and despite slave owners' concerted efforts to make Christianity appear to be in harmony with slavery.

In fact, changing the status quo, seeking an end to injustice, was a key tenet of most slaves' religious practices. According to Charles Ball, a slave from Maryland who lived

Though many African-American slave children were educated in secret, a privileged few, like these photographed in New Bern, North Carolina, could publicly attend school.

during the late 1700 and early 1800s, "The idea of a revolution in the conditions of the whites and blacks is the cornerstone of the religion of the latter." To be "Free indeed, free from death, free from hell, free from work, free from the white folks, free from everything" was the fervent prayer of one old slave preacher, according to a member of his audience.

Different in purpose, the invisible church differed in practice as well. Praise meetings, shouts, spirituals, call and response—all these rituals and ceremonies made it unique

Worship rituals, such as the circle dance, or ring shout, pictured above, enabled Africans to forge a unique culture within the bonds of slavery.

and a powerful source of joy and sustenance. "The way in which we worshipped is almost indescribable," said James L. Smith. The black plantation preacher recalled all-night prayer meetings whose conclusion allowed slaves a mere hour or so of sleep before they had to begin working again. "The singing was accompanied by a certain ecstasy of motion, clapping of hands, tossing of heads, which would continue without cessation about half an hour; one would lead off in a kind of recitative style, others joining in the chorus. The old house partook of the ecstasy; it rang with their jubilant shouts, and shook in all its joints."

While Hercules and Ona both walked away from the Washingtons' home and servitude, William Lee, the President's valet, did not follow the same path. Instead, he returned to Mount Vernon, where he continued to live in freedom—the only slave Washington specifically freed in his will—for approximately 30 years after the President's death in 1799. Many visitors came to talk with him about his heroic service during the Revolutionary War and his days at the side of the nation's first President. Perhaps they

From Slave to Landholder: Coincoin

In 1742, Louisiana had a variety of unusual customs that governed the lives of descendants of Africa. Marie Therésè was born a slave in Natchitoches, Louisiana, and named Coincoin, which meant "second daughter" in their African language. At this time human beings were "rented out" for various purposes, and at the age of 25, Marie Therésè was rented to Claude Metoyer as his housekeeper.

Coincoin became far more than a housekeeper for Metoyer; she bore 13 of his children during her time with him. This was in addition to the five children that she had had before becoming his mistress. Although Metoyer's religious leaders pressed him to sell Coincoin and to stop living with her, he refused to accede to their demands. Defying them, he purchased enough land to build Coincoin a house. Eventually, Metoyer freed Coincoin and three of their children; three later children would be born into freedom.

Louisiana devised special classifications for its Black inhabitants. Women of African descent who had some degree of white blood were known by varying terms such as "mulatto," "quadroon," or "octoroon," depending on how mixed they were. For example, if a Black woman and a white man parented a daughter, she was considered a mulatto, that is, half Black and half white. These children might be given special privileges. Many became educated in the United States and abroad, and some were allowed to own land. Of particular interest is the term *plaçage,* which refers to a system starting in the 1800s wherein biracial women were placed in arranged relationships or common-law marriages with whites. They were mistresses of the wealthy white plantation owners, who usually also had white wives and children. Although the racially mixed children were recognized as the children of the white men, they were never considered to be equal to the white children in society. The Black women could, however, pass on some of their holdings to the children.

The property owned by Coincoin, which is now known as the Coincoin-Prudhomme House, is located on Cane Island near Natchitoches. Handed down to her descendants, it is considered a rare surviving example of a Norman-plan Creole plantation home from the middle antebellum era. It is also a classic example of a southern property that was built by slaves.

By the time she was in her mid-40s, Coincoin had been given a plot of land that was located farther away from the place where she had lived with Metoyer. Later, she purchased an additional 640 acres of land from Spain. She used that property to increase her ownership of livestock and farm production. She started to grow new crops, such as indigo and tobacco.

During her lifetime, Coincoin amassed more than 2,000 acres of land and 50 slaves. Her holdings grew even larger with the help of her descendants, until she owned more than 500 slaves. Just before Coincoin's death in 1816 at the age of 70, she sold much of her property, and eventually the slaves owned by Coincoin's family were set free.

According to a 2002 *Washington Post* article, Coincoin gradually bought all of her children—beginning with four Black offspring born before she met Metoyer—out of slavery. Her son Nicolas Augustin Metoyer founded and built the Church of St. Augustine, believed to be the first Catholic church in the U.S. built and supported by Blacks.

Although Coincoin's estate was diminished, her family maintained a portion of it until it was sold to the Prudhomme family in 1846. It became part of the historic holdings of the National Park Service after World War II.

C. J. C.

Nicolas Augustin Metoyer, Coincoin's oldest son, followed in his mother's pioneering footsteps to found the Church of St. Augustine.

"As it is absolutely necessary to the safety of this Province, that all due care be taken to restrain the wanderings and meetings of negroes and other slaves . . . and the using and keeping of drums, horns, or other loud instruments, which may call together or give sign or notice to one another of their wicked designs and purposes. . . ."

— *South Carolina Slave Code*

One of the earliest known African-American artifacts, this 18th-century Asante-style drum was likely brought to the Americas on a slave-trading voyage.

also learned about his private life, the traditions and folkways that shaped his boyhood and sustained him during adulthood. For most slaves who did not win emancipation, or whose self-esteem might have been harder won than William Lee's seemed to have been, spiritual sustenance came from cultural traditions carried from Africa and adapted to a new life in America.

Food, music, dance, language, and folktales contributed to a unique culture that lightened the load of daily oppression. Slave gardens, or patches, which some slaves were allowed to till on Saturdays, provided foods reminiscent of Africa and relieved an otherwise monotonous diet of cornmeal and salt pork. Spirituals and drumming became communication tools that were both pragmatic and beautiful. Lyrics had encoded messages—about the imminent approach of the overseer or upcoming meeting or secret barbecue—and drumming carried over long distances. In 1740 following the Stono Rebellion (the largest slave uprising in the colonies before the Revolution), a South Carolina law banned drumming and the use of other loud instruments, as whites believed they had been an essential part of the "slave underground," the communication network that rapidly spread news and plans across many miles. Many slaves learned about current events before their masters did: As they ran errands in town, or to neighboring plantations, they watched, listened, remembered, and reported.

On some plantations, the conjurer held a position of considerable power, used his or her knowledge of medicinal roots and herbs to win converts, and exercised no small measure of control over the superstitious, Blacks and whites alike. William Webb, a slave in Kentucky during the 19th century, learned how to become a conjurer from a skilled practitioner, and recounted that he soon obtained complete sway over the slaves on one plantation. If the conjurer represented a living trickster who asserted control over more powerful men and women, then stories featuring Br'er Rabbit and the Tar Baby offered an analogy in folklore, in which smaller, cleverer animals overcame the larger, more powerful ones through cunning and trickery. Many folklorists have traced these stories to similar trickster tales and legends from West Africa's Wolof, Ewe, the Asante, and Ibo peoples.

According to one former slave, the African tunes she sang at religious services in America were transformed into spirituals when picked up and added to by others in attendance:

I'd jump up dar and den and holler and shout and sing and pat, and dey would all cotch de words and I'd sing it to some ole shout song I'd heard 'em sing from Africa and dey'd all take it up and keep at it, and keep a-addin to it and den it would be a spiritual.

The same spiritual that signaled insurrection to whites, especially following Nat Turner's revolt in 1831, extended hope to Blacks:

A few more beatings of the wind and rain,
Ere the winter will be over—
Glory, Hallelujah!
Some friends has gone before me,—
I must try to go and meet them—
Glory, Hallelujah!
A few more risings and settings of the sun,
Ere the winter will be over—
Glory, Hallelujah!
There's a better day a coming—

The Garífuna Scholar: Joseph O. Palacio, Ph.D.

In discussions of slavery, the North American experience predominates. Yet many other countries had slaves, and their experiences help to bring the entire institution of slavery and its resulting legacy into clearer focus. When Christopher Columbus and others explored the Caribbean islands and Central America, these areas were populated by indigenous peoples known as Caribs. Of the numerous stories regarding the Carib people, those from Belize serve as examples of how slavery changed the cultural and physical aspects of a land and its people.

Anthropologist Joseph O. Palacio is one of more than 14,000 people of southern Belize who identify themselves as Garífuna. Palacio, who has studied the issue of cultural identity, was born in the small Garífuna village of Barranco and initially educated locally by his father and his brother, who were both teachers. He later earned degrees in the United States and Canada and taught for many years in the West Indies.

Palacio believes that the Garífuna stem from a mixture of Black Caribs, the descendants of the Arawak/Caribs, and Maroon Africans who escaped slavery. The Caribs inhabited southern Belize as aboriginals long before Christopher Columbus arrived.Their West African counterparts were en route to plantations in the New World when they were shipwrecked off Saint Vincent in 1635. Some of them ran away from their captors and intermingled with the Carib inhabitants of the area, giving birth to the people that we know as Garífuna.

The Garífuna were not allowed to live peacefully in their homeland. In the late 1700s the British, who waged war with them and with their French neighbors over land, sent the Garífuna as prisoners of war to an island called Baliceaux. There, more than half of the prisoners died after being exposed to harsh conditions. A year later, the British sent the survivors to Roatán Island off the coast of Honduras. Eventually, the Garífuna would inhabit Nicaragua, Guatemala, and Honduras, in addition to Belize.

The story of the Garífuna was told in a 2001 *National Geographic* magazine article that described the challenges they face in the 21st century as they work to preserve their culture. *C. J. C.*

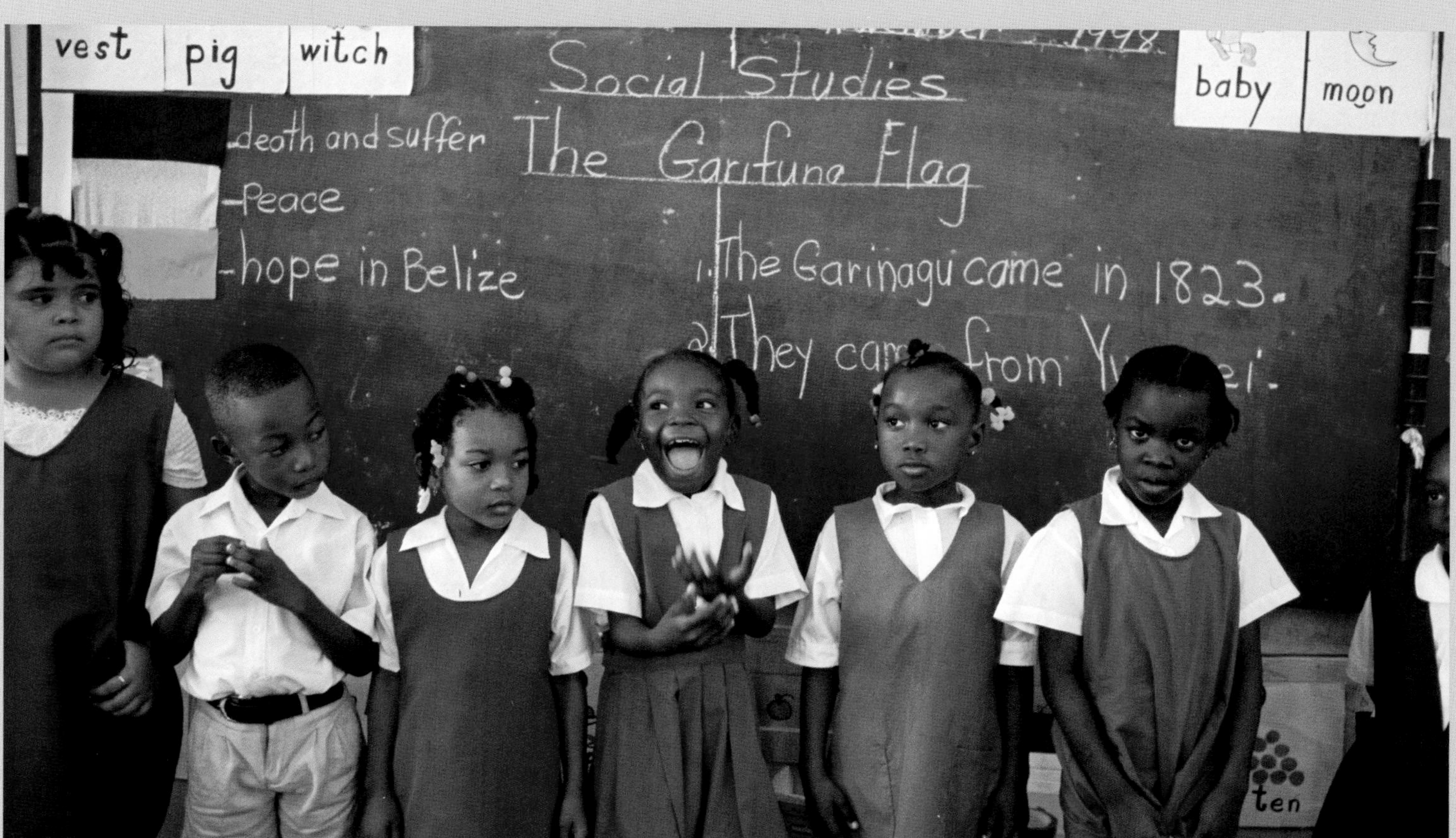

At an elementary school in Dangriga, Belize, schoolchildren learn the history of the Garífuna people and the legacy of slavery in the Caribbean.

"Many of the colored people in other places were in a situation nearly like those of Philadelphia and Baltimore, which induced us in April 1816 to call a general meeting . . . and taking into consideration their grievances, and in order to secure the privileges, promote union and harmony among themselves, it was resolved, 'That the people of Philadelphia, Baltimore, &c. &c., should become one body, under the name of the African Methodist Episcopal Church.' "

— Richard Allen, clergyman

There's a better day a coming—
Oh, Glory, Hallelujah!

Lyrics such as these encouraged persistence and, above all, kept the dream of freedom alive.

The hidden compartments found in the slave quarters of Monticello were a physical manifestation of the rich, yet often hidden, cultural world that slaves created. By adapting

Amid the horrors of plantation life, slaves found hope in community and traditions such as celebating the Sabbath, as depicted in this 1849 wood engraving.

African rituals, music, dance, stories, and myths from their homelands to their new circumstances in the United States, slaves constructed a vibrant cultural space from which they could draw strength and inspiration in the face of slavery's great cruelty and inhumanity. Gathering together in secret—whether to learn to read and write under an oak tree or to worship and praise in an invisible church—fostered a strong community to sustain the freedom in their hearts.

Keepers of the Gullah Culture

A GALLERY

Many legacies that trace back to the days of slavery can still be found today. Rice cultivation, ironworking, and sweetgrass basketmaking are among the lasting traditions of the Low Country, or the Sea Islands, which encompasses coastal towns and islands found mostly in South Carolina and Georgia. This area is home to the descendants of West African slaves whose culture has lasted since the 1700s. The Gullah/Geechee nation has survived largely because of the determination of a people and a common language, also known as Gullah or Geechee.

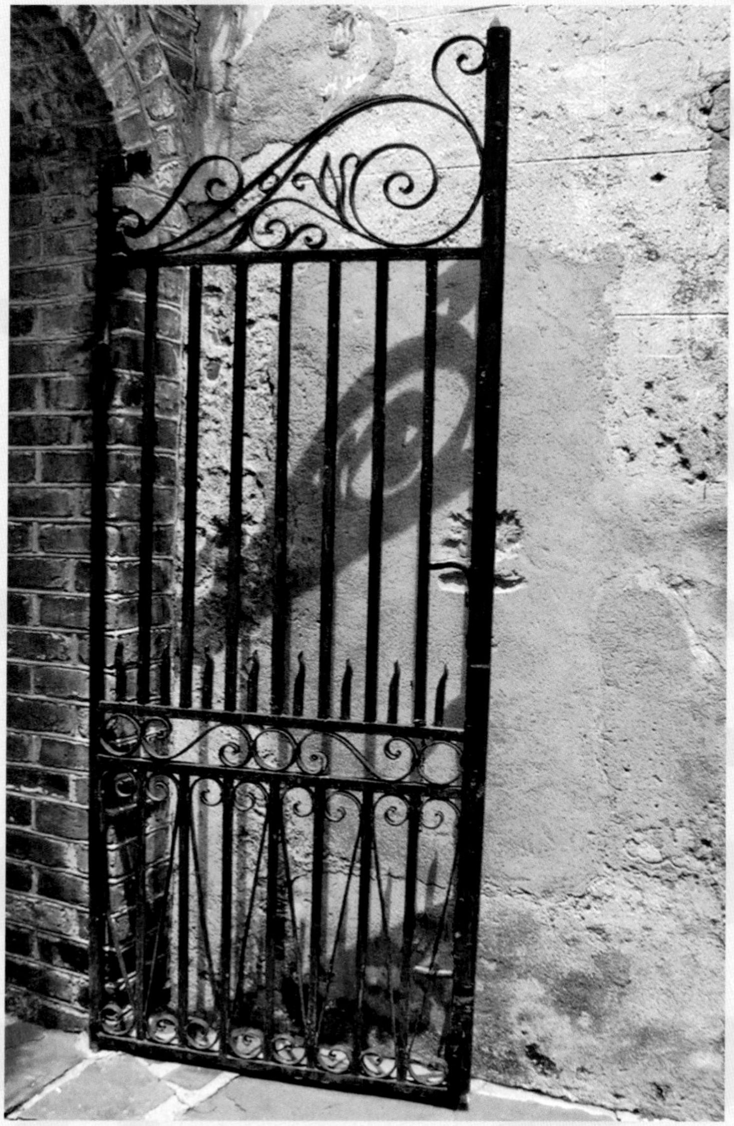

Philip Simmons has kept alive the Gullah tradition of ironworking; his first gate, pictured above, was built entirely from scraps.

The culture originated in the lands that housed the West African slave castles of Gorée Island in Senegal (Senegambia) and Bunce Island in Sierra Leone. Because of their areas of origin and the skills and knowledge that they possessed, certain slaves were gathered and stockpiled for shipment to specific buyers in the Sea Islands of South Carolina.

According to historian Daniel C. Littlefield, the author of *Rice and Slaves: Ethnicity and the Slave Trade in Colonial South Carolina,* "It is clear, then, that South Carolinians did place a positive emphasis on slaves from rice-growing regions. It has also been established that Africans possessed the technical knowledge to produce this crop and that from the earliest period of successful rice production in South Carolina a relationship developed between this region and rice-growing regions in Africa."

Littlefield also quotes a letter that was written to the Duke of Athold in 1768 by a slave owner named James Grant: "the Planter has Tradesmen of all kinds in his Gang of Slaves." Grant most likely was referring to the fact that slaves imported into the Low Country possessed the knowledge of myriad trades and crafts, including basketmaking, ironworking, shoemaking, bricklaying, carpentry, sailing, blacksmithing, fishing, sewing, tailoring, tanning, painting, plowing, cooking, cattle hunting, jewelry making, and much more. The men and women who provided this labor are largely responsible for the rich array of architecture and design still visible today in such Sea Islands as Hilton Head, Edisto, Jekyll, Port Royal, and nearly 100 others.

In October 2007, Congress voted to officially recognize a tradition, a culture, a way of life, and a region that are endangered by modern development. The recognition came in the form of an allocation of ten million dollars over ten years in a piece of legislation called the Gullah/Geechee Cultural Heritage Act. Representative James Clyburn of South Carolina, whose wife is of Gullah origin, spent eight years studying threats to the culture, crafting the legislation, and championing its passage.

One family living near Savannah, Georgia, discovered its African roots through a song that had been passed down by an ancestor. Mary Moran, who had learned the song from her mother, Amelia Dawley, became the last person living in the United States who

Inspired by the natural world, Simmons's wrought-iron designs adorn the drives, lawns, and homes of Charleston, South Carolina. This full-size driveway gate (above), commissioned in 1985, resides in the South Carolina State Museum.

knew it. Sixty years after Lorenzo Turner, an African linguist, recorded Dawley, scholars traced the song to Bendu Jabati of Senehun Ngola, Sierra Leone.

Moran and Jabati met in Africa in 1997, where they shared and reenacted the Mende funeral song, sung at funerals only by the women of Jabati's family lineage. The song united a long-separated family and contributed to the way in which the Morans remain keepers of the Gullah culture.

Other keepers of the culture gather sweetgrass and pine straw to make what was known as fanner baskets. Better known today as sweetgrass baskets, the rice-harvesting tools originated with enslaved West African rice growers. The people of the Gullah culture today make their baskets in the same styles as those found in the rice culture of West Africa. The baskets, which were also used for carrying laundry and storing food and firewood, have become expensive collector's items for tourists, who love the one-of-a-kind creations made by the remaining Gullah artisans who remember the craft.

Philip Simmons learned the traditional art of ironworking as a child from a former slave.

CHAPTER SIX

Resistance to Slavery

$2,500

REWARD!

RANAWAY, from the Subscriber, residing in Mississippi county, Mo., on Monday the 5th inst., my

Negro Man named GEORGE.

Said negro is five feet ten inches high, of dark complexion, he plays well on the Violin and several other instruments. He is a shrewd, smart fellow and of a very affable countenance, and is twenty-five years of age. If said negro is taken and confined in St. Louis Jail, or brought to this county so that I get him, the above reward of $1,000 will be promptly paid.

JOHN MEANS.

Also, from Radford E. Stanley,

A NEGRO MAN SLAVE, NAMED NOAH,

Full 6 feet high; black complexion; full eyes; free spoken and intelligent; will weigh about 180 pounds; 32 years old; had with him 2 or 3 suits of clothes, white hat, short blue blanket coat, a pair of saddle bags, a pocket compass, and supposed to have $350 or $400 with him.

ALSO---A NEGRO MAN NAMED HAMP,

Of dark copper color, big thick lips, about 6 feet high, weighs about 17
pounds, 36 years old, with a scar in the forehead from the kick of a horse; had
lump on one of his wrists and is left-handed. Had with him two suits of clothes
one a casinet or cloth coat and grey pants.

Also, Negro Man Slave named BOB

Copper color, high cheek bones, 5 feet 11 inches high, weighs about 150 pounds
22 years old, very white teeth and a space between the centre of the upper teet
Had a blue blanket sack coat with red striped linsey lining. Supposed to hav
two suits of clothes with him; is a litte lame in one ancle.
$1,000 will be given for George----$600 for Noah---$450 for Hamp---$45
for Bob; if caught in a free State, or a reasonable compensation if caught i
a Slave State, if delivered to the Subscribers in Miss. Co., Mo., or confined i
Jail in St. Lonis, so that we get them Refer to

JOHN MEANS &
R. E. STANLEY.

ST. LOUIS, August 23, 1852.

(PLEASE STICK UP.)

Resistance to Slavery

What did freedom mean to slaves in America during the 17th, 18th, and 19th centuries? And how did the enslaved actively strive for it? Slavery having been unsuccessfully tried with native populations and indentured whites, landed squarely on the shoulders of Africans stolen from their homeland and families. Freedom for Africans, slaves, and so-called free Blacks meant the ability to exercise control of their lives and to enjoy the privileges afforded others in the new land. They sought the same social, economic, and political goals as their right conferred by being an inhabitant and later a citizen of the new land.

The active quest for freedom was always central to the daily existence of slaves in America. From the first recorded revolt in 1526, in a town on the Pedee River in South Carolina, to the last shot fired before the fall of Richmond in 1865 during the American Civil War, slaves desired freedom and often paid dearly for it. Moreover, from the earliest days of American slavery, Africans captured in their homeland destined for enslavement in the colonies resisted and fought valiantly in the slaveholding pens as well as on the slave ships during the 10-to-12-week transatlantic crossing, often called the "Middle Passage."

MUTINY

Some of the first recorded accounts of slave revolts occurred aboard the English slave ship *Eagle Galley* in 1704. Even before the ship left the west coast of Africa on the River of Old Calabar in the Bay of Guinea, several of the more than 400 slaves aboard attacked the ship's crew with their bare hands. Their attempt failed because of their captors, yet slaves' desire for freedom continually burned in their souls.

It is estimated that, between 1699 and 1845, hundreds of slave revolts occurred on slave ships in spite of the fact that only about 55 were documented. Women and children often aided in mutinies, although the punishment was equally as brutal for them. In many instances, slaves simply starved themselves to death or jumped overboard to the waiting sharks that regularly followed slave ships, rather than live to endure slavery.

Perhaps the most highly publicized mutiny aboard a slave ship is the story of the 1839 *Amistad,* which held captive 53 African slaves from the Mende region of Sierra Leone, West Africa. When told by the ship's cook that they would be killed and eaten upon arrival at their destination, the Africans revolted by killing the captain and the cook. They ordered the ship's remaining crew to sail the ship back to Africa, but the white crewmembers redirected the ship's route at night, and the ship ended up off the coast of Long Island, New York. The ship's owners charged the slaves with murder and piracy, and the case went all the way to the U.S. Supreme Court. John Quincy Adams argued on behalf of the

Left: An 1852 poster from Missouri offers rewards ranging from $450 to $1,000 for the capture of four escaped male slaves.

Previous pages: Abolitionist and heroine Harriet Tubman, clutching a revolver at center, leads a group of slaves northward to freedom.

"Insurrection aboard a ship did not happen as a spontaneous natural process. It was, rather, the result of calculated human effort—careful communication, detailed planning, precise execution. Every insurrection, regardless of its success, was a remarkable achievement. . . . For those who ran the slave ship, an insurrection was without a doubt their greatest nightmare. It could extinguish profits and lives in an explosive flash."

—Marcus Rediker, historian

Opposite: Cinque, at top, leader of the uprising aboard the slave ship La Amistad, *inspired his fellow captives to fight for their freedom. Upon the ship's arrival at Culloden Point, Long Island, the remaining white crew and African slaves were met by the U.S.S.* Washington, *below.*

Africans. The surviving 36 Africans were freed in 1841, and eventually returned to their African homeland.

RETRIBUTION

During the Middle Passage era, approximately 30 percent of the transported Africans died before they even reached the Americas. Another 20 percent died during the first year of their seasoning and acculturation. Seasoning was a process of physically and psychologically breaking the spirit of recently arrived slaves so that they would be more manageable once placed on southern plantations. The goal of seasoning was to destroy African values and to adopt servile submissiveness to the New World of inhumane chattel slavery.

For many of the newly arrived Africans, this attempt at dehumanization only increased their desire to escape to freedom and/or exact revenge and retribution on slave masters, overseers, or their families and property. Historian William Loren Katz reports, "The slaves who labored in the fields destroyed tools and crops and sometimes tried to poison masters and overseers. For example, in 1732 slaves were accused of poisoning the grandfather of the architect of the U.S. Constitution, James Madison, at his estate in Montpelier, Virginia. Similarly, they set so many fires that some companies refused to insure homes in slave states. The slave pretended to be lame, sick, blind, or insane and they often pretended stupidity or clumsiness to avoid work." By the same token, slaves were accused of setting fire to most of the commercial buildings in New York City in 1741.

Why would Africans risk their very lives and bodies to be free? The answer is twofold: First, slaves understood the financial value of their bodies as a source of labor; therefore, depriving the slave masters of a body reduced their profit. Secondly, many slaves believed that, by dying or committing suicide, they would return to their homeland in the afterlife.

If there is a single explanation for the slaves' capacity to continually endure the indignities and suffering of slavery, it would be the innate "spirit of freedom" that they nurtured daily in their hearts and minds through songs and secret religious gatherings. This spirit energized their ingenuity and an indomitable courage to hold fast to dreams of freedom, even if that came only in the afterlife. Moreover, incredible as it may seem, slaves also

believed that the colonists' talk of independence and freedom may have included freedom for them.

FIGHTING FOR FREEDOM

Two very significant late 18th-century events occurred that forever recast the sordid path of slavery in North America: the American Revolution and the invention of the cotton gin.

The perspective of the slave on the issue of the American Revolution is one of the most neglected and misconstrued chapters in American history. The slave population in the American colonies was well aware of the strong connections, in their minds, between independence and freedom. Conventional history has recorded the number of Blacks who fought in the American Revolution (both Army and Navy) at 5,000. Many hoped

"The year 1800 is the most important one in the history of American Negro slave revolts. For it is the birth year of John Brown and of Nat Turner, the year in which Denmark Vesey bought his freedom and it is the year of the great Gabriel conspiracy."

— Herbert Aptheker, historian

that the promise of freedom would be extended to them when the colonies had at last achieved independence.

But Eli Whitney's 1793 invention of the cotton gin revolutionized the cotton industry in America and further prolonged slavery's existence in the new nation. The gin could do the work of 50 slaves working by hand to separate out the seeds from the cotton. However, slave labor became more valuable and entrenched during the first half of the 19th century

For slaves in the American South, running away offered a chance at freedom but also guaranteed a long and risky hunt, as depicted in this 19th-century engraving.

Escape in Broad Daylight: Ellen and William Craft

In December 1848, two men—one black and one white—boarded a northbound train in Macon, Georgia. The white gentleman appeared to be sickly and frail, his right arm bound up in a sling; he was remarkably civil to the slave accompanying him, so much so that it attracted attention. For five days, the two traveled together by train, steamer, and mail coach to Philadelphia. Along the way, many questioned the gentleman's decision to bring a slave to a northern city noted for its sympathy to runaway slaves. But the two men were not what they appeared to be: the sickly man was actually a light-skinned African-American woman named Ellen Craft, and the slave was her husband, William. Using a brilliant disguise, the two hid in plain sight to embark on a daring escape to freedom.

Ellen Craft was born in Clinton, Georgia, in 1826, to a slave woman named Marie and her owner Major James Smith, a cotton planter. Ellen, a quadroon (one-quarter black), had skin so light that she was often mistaken for one of Major Smith's white children. When she was 11 years old, Major Smith gave Ellen to his daughter, Eliza, as a wedding present, and Ellen moved with her to Macon, Georgia, in 1837.

In Macon, Ellen encountered William Craft, a slave apprenticed to a cabinetmaker. William's skill made him very valuable; he was treated with more respect than many other slaves, owned his own clothing, and had a dwelling that gave him a degree of self-sufficiency.

In 1846, the two married. Initially, Ellen had not wanted to marry or to bear children because she knew that they all would be enslaved. They thought of ways to escape but did not follow through because they feared being caught if they attempted to cross the 1,000 miles of slave states that lay between them and freedom. After marrying, Ellen became more convinced that, even though it seemed too much to undertake, God would help them with their greatest dream. The couple longed for a life of freedom.

In a clever plot to escape to the North, former slave Ellen Craft, a quadroon, disguised herself as a young white male slave owner. Her husband, William, posed as her slave, and the two were able to travel in plain sight to Philadelphia.

Accounts say that William devised their audacious escape plan. In December 1848, he posed as a slave, and Ellen posed as his young, white male slave owner (a white woman traveling alone with a black slave would have aroused too much suspicion at that time). Ellen created a disguise to partially cover her face and neck; she cut her hair short and wore green spectacles to shade her eyes. Gloves hid her hands, and a sling held her right arm to hide her inability to write. They traveled in full view of everyone and ventured north by train, steamer, and ferry through parts of Georgia, the Carolinas, Virginia, and Maryland, until they safely reached Pennsylvania. In all, the trip took eight days.

Upon arriving in Philadelphia on Christmas Day, the Crafts made their way to an abolitionist-run boardinghouse where they met free Black abolitionists William Still and Robert Purvis. They arranged for the Crafts to stay with a Quaker family outside of Philadelphia. Soon after, the Crafts relocated to Boston, where William found work as a cabinetmaker, and Ellen earned money as a seamstress. They became very active in the local antislavery movement, publicly telling their story to encourage others to escape. Their newfound popularity attracted unwanted attention from their former owners who had learned how the couple escaped. The passage of the Fugitive Slave Law in 1850 made it possible for the Crafts to be kidnapped from Boston and taken south.

After a close call with bounty hunters hired by their former owners, Ellen and William decided leaving the country would be safer. The Crafts first moved to Halifax, Nova Scotia, Canada, and then traveled to Liverpool, England in 1850. There, the Crafts continued their antislavery work and also began furthering their own education, learning to read and write. Ellen bore four children. In 1860, they also published *Running a Thousand Miles for Freedom*, an account of the daring escape they embarked on so many years before. The Crafts eventually returned to America in the late 1860s, well after the end of the Civil War and the abolition of slavery. *C. J. C.*

"*I* should arise and prepare myself, and slay my enemies with their own weapons."

— *Nat Turner*

as the southern cotton crop increased from 160 million pounds to 2,300 million pounds. Because more cotton could be processed mechanically, more slaves were needed to pick the cotton.

The Louisiana Purchase of 1803 allowed the institution of slavery to rapidly expand westward. Thus, with tobacco in Virginia, Kentucky, and the Deep South, cotton in Mississippi and Georgia, rice in South Carolina, and sugar in Louisiana, prime business owners in these states partnered with ambitious northern industrialists. The labor of slaves became the primary labor force. Suffice it to say, America's emergence as an international power in the early 19th century rested squarely on the shoulders of its three million slaves. Disappointed by the empty promises inspired by the Declaration of Independence and the Revolutionary War, and then betrayed in the 1789 ratification of the U.S. Constitution, slaves fought back through a series of revolts.

REVOLT

One of the poorest nations in the Western Hemisphere is Haiti, a predominately Black country in the Caribbean. A French colony since 1697, Haiti achieved independence in 1804, through the efforts of rebellious slaves led by Toussaint L'Ouverture. Between 1791 and 1804, Haitian slaves fought and defeated two of the most powerful colonial powers in the world, France and England. In so doing, Haiti became the first and only free Black nation in the Western Hemisphere. Slaveholders in the United States feared L'Ouverture's revolution because of the potential this event had to encourage and incite an already disgruntled American slave population to organize and rise up in insurrection in the United States. In spite of slaveholders' best efforts to keep this information from the slaves, the news of the Haitian rebellion spread like wildfire between the slave and free Black populations in America.

Accounts of these rebellions are scant in the annals of United States history, but thousands of such incidents occurred throughout the North and South, and, with each event, slaves were more emboldened to persist regardless of the risks. Most of the leaders of these revolts were captured and executed, but this did not deter the masses from continuing to resist.

In 1800, Gabriel Prosser, a slave in Henrico County, Virginia, along with approximately 1,000 other slaves, gathered six miles outside of Richmond to execute their revolt. However, two of Gabriel's partners revealed the existence of the planned insurrection,

A handwritten voucher for sheriff's fees rewards the capture of an African American in Lincoln County, Kentucky, on November 14, 1812.

The Commonwealth of Kentucky To Bartlett Greenwood Constable of Lincoln County — — — Dr
14 Novr 1812 To Apprehending Daniel a Negroe man Slave the property of John Tadlock on a charge of felony — — — — — $2.00
Bartlett Greenwood Cons

The Quilt Messages: Viola Canady

Founded in 1979, the Daughters of Dorcas and Sons is a quilting group with a membership of more than 200. The group is named after Dorcas, a woman who made garments and distributed them among the poor in Joppa, a biblical city in Israel. After Dorcas died and the poor mourned her death, the disciple Peter was moved by their grief and brought her back to life. Viola Williams Canady, the 80-year-old co-founder and president of the group, says that she was a devout student of the Bible as a young girl and always remembered the story of Dorcas.

Canady learned to sew when she was a child living in a rural area outside of Goldsboro, North Carolina. She was born to a family of sharecroppers on November 3, 1922. Sharecropping was an agricultural system in which landowners would lease a house and land to sharecroppers in exchange for a share of the proceeds made from selling the crops. In many cases, landowners took the bulk of the proceeds, and the sharecroppers and their families were left with barely enough food to sustain them until the next growing season. Life was hard for sharecroppers, and the Williams family was no exception.

The entire family worked the fields early in the morning, and the children who were not needed attended school afterward. The house they lived in was large, and Viola's parents rented a room to teachers from town. The teachers stayed during the week to teach at a nearby one-room school for African-American children, then went back to town for the weekend. Viola's mother and grandmother were also seamstresses, and they sewed, washed, and ironed for white families in the community between planting and harvest seasons.

Viola was the eldest of nine children. Her mother died when she was nine, and she took on her mother's responsibilities in addition to going to school and working in the fields. "When I got out of high school, I was twenty. I couldn't go to school until crops were in. Rainy days I could go. I was the one who had to cook, iron, patch, and everything, then go to white people's houses when not working the fields. Plant in the morning, go to school, then come home to do chores."

Viola was fascinated by the colorful pieces of fabric that people would give her mother, and she began collecting scraps to make quilts for the family to keep warm during the winter. Nothing was wasted, not even cloth from old worn-out clothing. A large quilting rack was tied to ropes and hung from the living room ceiling in the evening. In the morning, it was brought down, and a group of four or five women would work on one quilt. Besides helping to make each other's quilts, they supplied quilts for the church, for poorer families, and as gifts to newlyweds and parents. She learned many of the patterns—such as the Wagon Wheel, the North Star, Crossroads, and the Bear's Claw—that slaves passed down. She learned later that these patterns represented the Underground Railroad, which fugitive slaves used to escape.

Shortly after graduating high school, Viola moved to Washington, D.C., where she married Cliff Canady a year later. She worked briefly for the telephone company, but left to raise her two children, Evelyn and Vernon. She continued to supplement the family income with her sewing and even studied design for two years at Livingstone Academy of Arts and Sciences, where she learned to create her own patterns and quilting designs. She and a friend started a crocheting and sewing circle and, remembering the story from the Bible, named it the Daughters of Dorcas. When her daughter turned 12 and was old enough to get herself ready for school, Canady took a job as a tailor/seamstress for the Department of the Army, and the group disbanded.

Her tenure with the government lasted almost 20 years. Not only did she sew slipcovers, bedspreads, clothing, and uniforms for the military, she also did sewing for the White House and for members of Congress. Her most memorable experience was being specifically requested by General Westmoreland to sew a flag for which she was rewarded. At her retirement, the U.S. Army Color Guard attended in her honor.

She re-formed the Daughters of Dorcas as a quilting group in 1979. Canady added *and Sons* to the name when Raymond Dobard, a nationally known quilter and author of a book on African-American quilting, joined. Canady and members of the group were featured in *A Communion of the Spirits: African-American Quilters, Preservers, and Their Stories* by photographer Roland Freeman. Canady no longer sews but continues to teach and to meet with her quilting group. *D. W.*

Five members of the Daughters of Dorcas and Sons, including co-founder Viola Canady (far right), quilt an original design by Roland L. Freeman.

Collecting Our Culture

CHARLES BLOCKSON

What makes a collector collect? The hoarding instinct? A fascination and curiosity about the past? The desire for immortality? People have different motives. My path to collecting books and documents relating to people of African descent began in a most inauspicious way during my childhood in my hometown of Norristown, Pennsylvania. Though more than 60 years have passed since then, I remember it as if it were yesterday.

One morning in school our subject was the nation's Founding Fathers. As I listened to a litany of their deeds, it struck me that all the historic achievements that we had learned to date had been credited to white Americans. When I asked my fourth-grade teacher to relate some notable contributions of black people, she betrayed no hint of uncertainty in her answer, "Negroes have no history, they were happy on the plantations." She continued, "They were born to serve white people." I sat in stunned silence.

For a few moments after her response, I was dreadfully aware of the sea of white faces surrounding the three or four African Americans in that classroom. I had never before been confronted with such flagrant prejudice. I felt numb, sensing more than knowing that her assessment had to be inaccurate. A blaze had been sparked by my teacher's remarks, one that ignited a fire in my soul to learn more of the history of African-American people.

As I grew older, I frequented rummage sales, church bazaars, flea markets, auction houses, and antiquarian bookstores in search of books and texts on the subject. I still remember my first three acquisitions purchased at the Salvation Army for 15 cents each: Booker T. Washington's *Up From Slavery*, James Weldon Johnson's *God's Trombone*, and Rackham Holt's *George Washington Carver: An American Biography*. I began to search for my ancestors long before the 1977 publication of Alex Haley's landmark book, *Roots,* on his family history; that was the same year I published my own chronicle of genealogical research, *Black Genealogy*, the first how-to book for African Americans seeking to trace their lineage.

FINDING MY PAST

Beginning my 20-year odyssey into the past, I started with my own family's oral history and our Bible. Through them, I discovered that our familial enslaved roots began in Accomack County, Virginia, and in the Eastern Shore region of Delaware and Maryland. This same region produced many great leaders of the 18th and 19th centuries, including African Americans such as Reverend Richard Allen, Reverend Absalom Jones, Frederick Douglass, Harriet Tubman, and others. I discovered that the original spelling of my family's enslaved name was Bloxom, named after the slaveholding family who settled in Accomack County in the 17th century and funded the town of the same name. In 1810, one member of this family relocated to Seaford, Sussex County, Delaware.

I turned to the Hall of Records in Dover, Delaware, where I found my great-great-grandfather Spencer's name listed in his owner's will. Spencer was listed along with barley, animals, and furniture. He was listed as property. When I read that, I cried and pounded the oak table where I sat. Spencer's parents, Harry and Polly, were also listed with a price tag next to their names—their monetary worth!

In 1856 and 1858, several of my relatives from the Eastern Shore of Delaware and Maryland escaped to Saint Catharines, Ontario, Canada, with Harriet Tubman. A portion of my family's connection with the Underground Railroad is documented in William Still's book *The Underground Railroad*. A Philadelphia African-American agent who kept a record of his activities, Still authenticated my family's passage on the freedom network. This book remains one of my most cherished possessions.

CREATING COLLECTIONS

By 1984, the bookshelves and boxes in my home were overflowing with materials. At that time, I decided to donate a comprehensive assemblage from this personal

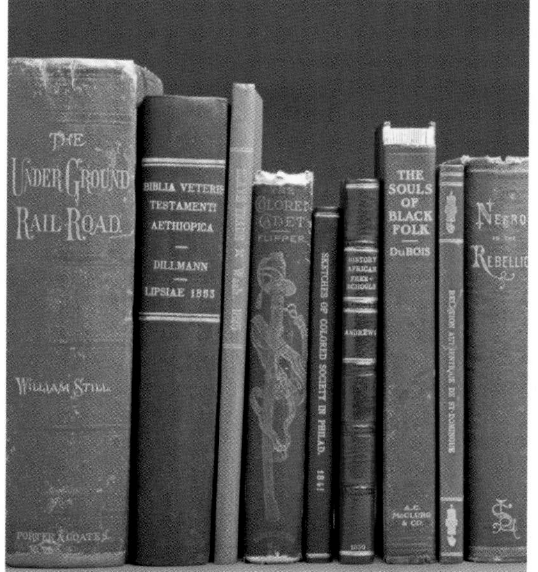

Charles Blockson's collection ranges from the great works of African-American writers and thinkers to more obscure documents, maps, and narratives.

collection—nearly 20,000 items documenting the African diaspora through four centuries—to Temple University in Philadelphia. The Charles L. Blockson Afro-American Collection, as it is now known, laid the foundation for what has evolved into a leading national research center where anyone can begin a journey to uncover more about the African-American experience. Today, its holdings contain more than 500,000 prints, photographs, books, pamphlets, letters, posters, maps, newspapers, and musical scores. The collection includes an impressive compilation of African and Caribbean Bibles, a wide selection of slave narratives (representative works are the writings of Phillis Wheatley, Benjamin Banneker, Olaudah Equiano, Ignatius Sancho, Nat Turner, Frederick Douglass, Harriet Tubman, Sojourner Truth, and others), and items representing some of the most painful graphic moments of African people's history. One of the most unusual and gruesome books in the collection is *Lincoln: The Unknown*. A portion of the binding for this particular volume was made from human skin, "taken from the skin of a Negro" at the Baltimore Hospital and tanned by the Jewell Belting Company.

There are also hundreds of taped proceedings, oral history, and radio programs of African-American history and culture. The collection is also representative with literature of the Harlem Renaissance and the writings of contemporary authors.

After my donation to Temple, I still continued to gather more materials relating to the African-American experience. In October 2007, I donated another portion of my private auxiliary collection—comprised of nearly 12,000 items—to my alma mater, Pennsylvania State University. The collection is known as the Charles L. Blockson Collection of African Americans and the African Diaspora. Materials from all over the world—in many languages—are included as well. In attempting to find the answers I sought, I understand well the agony and the ecstasy that mark the trail of the collector.

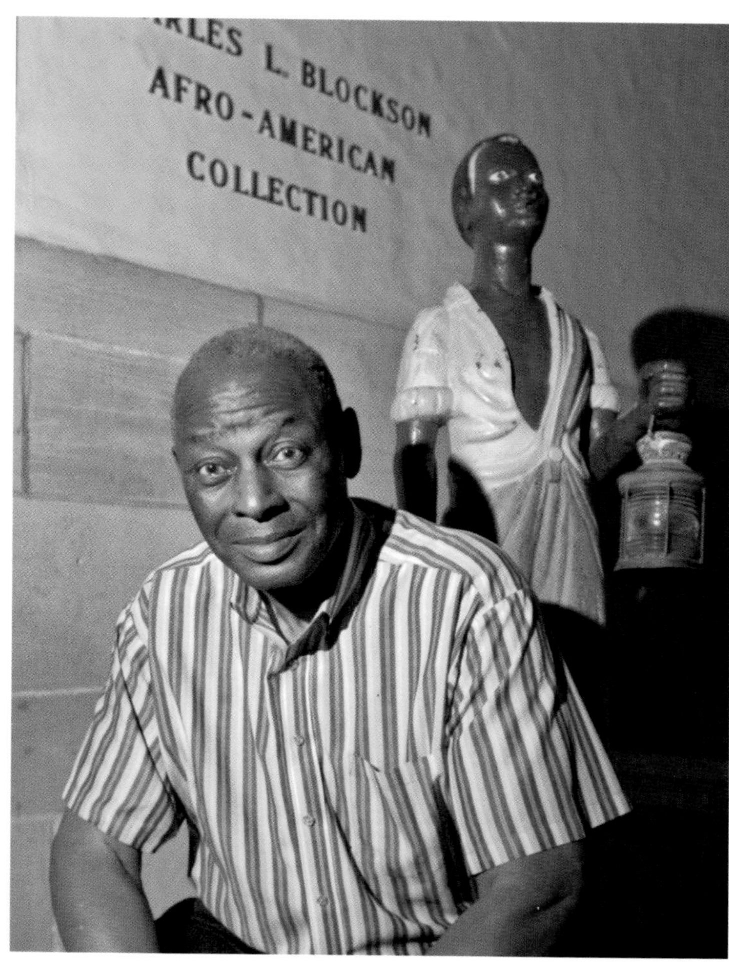

The renowned Afro-American Collection at Temple University in Philadelphia began with Blockson's donation of more than 20,000 books and documents.

A RETURN TO AFRICA

From childhood the lure of Africa captured my fancy. I sensed that part of my soul—a very old part—belonged there. I felt a great sense of regret and sadness that I did not know where my ancestors had lived in the vast continent. But recently, through DNA ancestry testing, I was able to document my Igbo Nigerian heritage. This discovery ignited a deep interest in Igbo African history and culture; I learned much from books about how their fierce pride and unshakable courage sustained unremitting resistance in the homeland and even on slave ships whose holds were filled with other enslaved African peoples. Igbos were not desired because they were proud, inclined to escape, and the source of revolts, which became the eternal dread of slave owners.

Ultimately, I was able to visit West Africa and make the ritual pilgrimage of return that every person of African descent should make to reconnect with the ancestral home from which we were stolen.

Contrary to what a fourth-grade teacher espoused that day so many years ago, the significant cultural, philosophical, and historical contributions of African Americans shine forth from history. A lifetime of collecting has helped me to bring that fundamental truth to light. Of course, much has been lost through the centuries, but enough still remains to remind us of what was endured and how, despite obstacles of enslavement, African peoples have been able to triumph even when an oppressive environment works against them.

It seems as if destiny has a special mission in mind for Governor Douglas Wilder. Here I speak of his vision, the United States National Slavery Museum, respectfully dedicated to the memory of our ancestors and a place that will collect and house items that bear witness to the story of slavery. The museum represents the defining challenge of our age and a treasured gift to Americans in general and people of African descent in particular. It is a vision that thrills the heart and soul as it does the mind. ■

"Brethren, arise, arise, strike for your lives and liberties. Now is the day and the hour. Let every slave throughout the land do this, and the days of slavery are numbered. You cannot be more oppressed than you have been. You cannot suffer greater cruelties than you have already. Rather die free men than live to be slaves. Let your motto be resistance, resistance, RESISTANCE."

—Henry Highland Garnet, abolitionist

and the revolt failed. Gabriel and 35 of his comrades were executed. Denmark Vesey, a freed slave in Charleston, South Carolina, planned one of the most extensive slave revolts in American history, one that involved roughly 9,000 slaves. Again, betrayal from within led to the crushing of the revolt, and Vesey and his most trusted comrades were hanged.

In 1831, 31 years later, Nat Turner, a slave in Southampton, Virginia, planned and executed a revolt that resulted in the deaths of approximately 60 whites. Turner, along with 13 other slaves and three free Blacks, were hanged. To say that these revolts failed would be woefully inaccurate because they were simply the overt manifestation of the wishes and desires of millions of slaves who strengthened their resolve to pick up the mantel of freedom in honor of their fallen comrades. When asked why he had participated in Gabriel's revolt, a slave said, "I have nothing more to offer than what General Washington would have had to offer had he been taken by the British officers and put on trial by them. I have ventured my life in endeavoring to obtain the liberty of my countrymen, and am a willing sacrifice to their cause, and I beg as a favor that I may be immediately led to execution. I know that you have pre-determined to shed my blood, why then all this mockery of a trial?"

If we fast-forward 59 years to John Brown's rebellion in 1859, we see the national tension and division over slavery becoming so intense that the Civil War two years later was all but inevitable. Many whites assisted Blacks in their rebellion efforts, but none were more famous than fiery abolitionist John Brown. Brown spent years planning a revolution that he hoped would attract thousands of slaves from several states surrounding Virginia. He had discussed his plans with Frederick Douglass and Harriet Tubman, two of the best-known Black abolitionists of the time. John Copeland, Jr., a black man in Brown's raid, wrote a letter to his parents that captures the strong resolve of Blacks to be free of slavery at any cost:

Dear Parents,

My fate as far as man can seal it is sealed but let this not occasion you any misery for remember the cause in which I am engaged, remember that it was a "Holy Cause", one in which men who in every point of view better than I am have suffered and died, remember that if I must die I die in trying to liberate a few of my poor and oppressed people from my condition of servitude which God in his Holy Writ has hurled his most bitter denunciations against and in which men who were by color of their faces removed from the direct injurious affect, have already lost their lives and still remain to meet the same fate which has been by man decided that I must meet.

ESCAPE

An equally disruptive and resistive slave activity was running away. Most slaves who ran away were recaptured, but many, particularly men, repeatedly fled five or six times. Most of the runaways—particularly the fugitives—were literate, a basic requirement when moving outside the plantation grounds. Even though it was illegal for slaves to read and write for more than 150 years before the Civil War, more than a few—perhaps 15 percent—mastered these skills.

Although the exact number of slaves who ran away during the 230 years of chattel slavery is inexact at best, runaways posed enough of a profit-loss problem for slave owners to mount extraordinary mechanisms to recapture runaways, as well as to retrieve fugitives who had successfully reached free territories. Successful runaways greatly encouraged other slaves

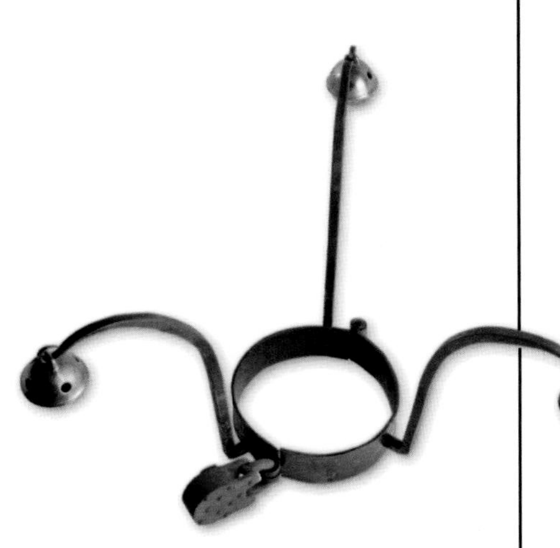

A slave collar with bells prevented runaways by making quiet escapes difficult.

Leading an Insurrection: Denmark Vesey

By the year 1730, South Carolina held the distinction of being the only state where the number of slaves was greater than the number of slave owners. This preponderance was troubling for the white slaveholders, who had reason to fear Black uprisings. Slaves lived in deplorable circumstances, suffered from widespread malaria and other diseases, and worked in inhumane conditions.

When a young slave named Denmark Vesey arrived in Charleston in 1783, he was outraged by what he saw. Most of the 260,000 slaves worked in rice fields under the command of cruel white overseers. Of the 3,000 free Blacks, who were confined to Charleston, many worked at the docks, in the homes, and in the shops of whites.

A white slave trader from Bermuda named Joseph Vesey had captured the new immigrant, Denmark Vesey. Denmark had become an avid reader and often cited passages against slavery that he found in the Bible. He soon managed to buy his freedom for $600 from $1,500 that he won in an East Bay Street lottery. He later earned more than $8,000 by working as a carpenter. This was quite a large sum of money for a black man to have at the time. After he had become prosperous, he decided to do something about the injustices that he saw. His plan, later called a conspiracy by the whites, was to end slavery in South Carolina.

Vesey enlisted the help of other disgruntled Blacks in a bid to overthrow the white owners. They held meetings in which they discussed other revolts. They were impressed by the Haitian Revolution of 1791, and one of Vesey's co-conspirators, Monday Gell, wrote two letters to the president of Santo Domingo asking for support for the revolt. Another co-conspirator, Gullah Jack Pritchard, an African priest from Mozambique, was one of Vesey's staunchest allies in planning the revolt. They also studied the lessons from another slave uprising in Virginia, in 1800, led by a black man named Gabriel Prosser.

Vesey and members of his inner circle first settled on the date of May 30, 1822, to carry out an uprising involving 9,000 slaves, though they later tried to change the date from May to July. In any event, their planned insurrection was thwarted when a member of their group, George Wilson, informed his master that thousands of Blacks—free and enslaved—were planning a revolt. Wilson believed that being an informant would gain him great favor with his master.

Officials from Charleston moved quickly to end the planned revolt once the plot was revealed. After a lengthy trial, Vesey and 36 others were hanged. Some conspirators were deported to unknown locations. J. Hamilton, Charleston's mayor, wrote and published an account of Vesey's rebellion in August 1822. The preface stated, in part:

> *I have not been insensible . . . as to what it might be politic either to publish or suppress. . . . I have deemed a full publication . . . as the most judicious course. . . . there can be no harm in the salutary inculcation of one lesson, among a certain portion of our population, that there is nothing they are bad enough to do, that we are not powerful enough to punish.*

Despite the outcome, Vesey remained admired as much in death as he had been in life by many of the African Americans of South Carolina. *C. J. C.*

CLASS No. 1.

Comprises those prisoners who were found guilty and executed.

Prisoners Names.	*Owners' Names.*	*Time of Commit.*	*How Disposed of.*
Peter	James Poyas	June 18	Hanged on Tuesday the 2d July, 1822, on Blake's lands, near Charleston.
Ned	Gov. T. Bennett,	do.	
Rolla	do.	do	
Batteau	do.	do.	
Denmark Vesey	A free black man	22	
Jessy	Thos. Blackwood	23	
John	Elias Horry	July 5	Do. on the Lines near Ch.; Friday July 12.
Gullah Jack	Paul Pritchard	do.	
Mingo	Wm. Harth	June 21	
Lot	Forrester	27	Hanged on the Lines near Charleston, on Friday, 26th July.
Joe	P. L. Jore	July 6	
Julius	Thos. Forrest	8	
Tom	Mrs. Russell	10	
Smart	Robt. Anderson	do.	
John	John Robertson	11	
Robert	do.	do.	
Adam	do.	do.	
Polydore	Mrs. Faber	do.	
Bacchus	Benj. Hammet	do.	
Dick	Wm. Sims	13	
Pharaoh	— Thompson	do.	
Jemmy	Mrs. Clement	18	
Mauidore	Mordecai Cohen	19	
Dean	— Mitchell	do.	
Jack	Mrs. Purcell	12	
Bellisle	Est. of Jos. Yates	18	
Naphur	do.	do.	
Adam	do.	do.	
Jacob	John S. Glen	16	
Charles	John Billings	18	
Jack	N. McNeill	22	
Cæsar	Miss Smith	do.	
Jacob Stagg	Jacob Lankester	23	Do. Tues. July 30.
Tom	Wm. M. Scott	24	
William	Mrs. Garner	Aug. 2	Do. Friday, Aug. 9.

A record from 1822 shows that 35 Black men were executed for conspiracy, including Denmark Vesey, the leader of the uprising plot.

Runaway

Face down to the earth
My ear pressed to its back
Spirits rise singing songs
along the spine
of old plantation yards
Empty fields echo
work songs
blues rifts
chanted to the cadence
(of) shuffling feet
An elemental dirge
Composed of sorrows
Long forgotten memoir
A distant memory of
shackled days
fugitive nights
A flight North
To freedom's lair
A voyage to a life
Unfettered by the
specter of bondage

— Karl W. Carter, Jr., lawyer

to do likewise. For this reason, recaptured slaves were punished severely, often enduring heinous whippings, mutilation, and limb amputations to frighten others into not following their example. Author Alex Haley recounts a prime example: his great-great-great-great-grandfather, Kunta Kinte, a slave in Maryland in 1776, had his foot chopped off as punishment for running away.

The mythical Underground Railroad is most often associated as being the main vehicle of runaway slaves to achieve freedom. Indeed, some slaves were aided by the "railroad," but most relied on their own knowledge and ingenuity, as well as secret networks of escape: sailing ships, stowaways, Maroons (established hidden communities in the swamps), and the welcome extended by American Indian tribes hostile to whites, particularly the Seminoles of Florida. Between the 1820s and 1850s, the United States government fought three major wars with the Seminole Nation, expending more money than had been used in all preceding wars combined. This potentially lethal coalition between runaway slaves and native populations who were also being abused by whites proved to be extremely dangerous for the country, so it was essential to thwart the effort.

NEGRO HUNTERS

Nothing depicts best the severity of the runaway problem than the nomenclature associated with it: Negro Stealers, Negro Hunters, and Negro Dogs. The stealers were usually antislavery whites who engaged in elaborate schemes to free slaves. Virginian John Fairfax was such a person. Over 12 years in the early 1800s, he freed hundreds of slaves, including those owned by his father and uncle. He was imprisoned on several occasions but persisted in his freedom efforts.

Negro Hunters were local white patrollers who established themselves as businessmen adept at recapturing runaway and fugitive slaves. Included within this group were northern

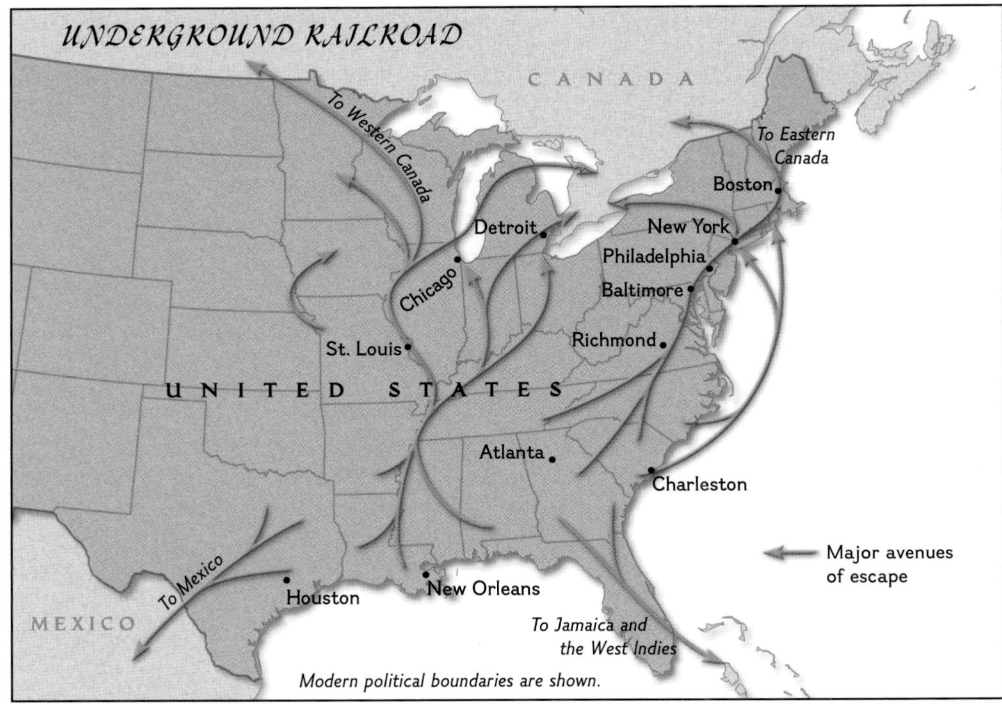

The Underground Railroad, whose main routes out of the South are depicted, carried slaves to lives of freedom in the North, Canada, Mexico, and the Caribbean.

whites who could easily identify fugitives, turn them in, and then share in the profits of rewards with their southern cohorts.

The Negro Hunters could not have been as effective as they were without "Negro Dogs." These were dogs specially and exclusively trained to hunt and savagely attack runaways. Historians John Hope Franklin and Loren Schweninger report that a southern slave master stated, "He had dogs trained on purpose to run after niggers, and never let out for anything else."

Moreover, slave catchers who owned Negro Dogs prominently advertised their business in newspapers and by word of mouth. In the decade leading up to the Civil War, Tennessee slave hunter David Turner advertised in the local paper that "I have two of the finest dogs for catching Negroes in the Southwest. They can take the trail twelve hours after the Negro has passed and catch him with ease." Nevertheless, slaves continued to run away up until the end of the Civil War.

Fugitive slaves (top) escape to freedom on horseback. Plantation police, wearing badges such as the one from South Carolina pictured above, made their journey more dangerous.

QUIET RESISTANCE

Discussion of freedom for slaves and the various methods used to pursue freedom would be incomplete without including a form of psychological resistance characterized

"My master! and who made him my master? That's what I think of—what right has he to me? I'm a man as much as he is. I'm a better man than he is. I know more about business than he does; I am a better manager than he is; I can read better than he can; I can write a better hand,—and I've learned it all myself, and no thanks to him."

— George, slave in Uncle Tom's Cabin

as passive acceptance. This concept means that, when a person is in a subordinate, disempowered position, it is very functional to feign subservience and total complicity rather than reveal a true revulsion over the imbalance in the current power relationship. Essentially, it becomes an active manipulation of a potentially threatening situation that conveys the exact opposite emotion or affect to the situation at hand.

The most prominent example of this type of behavior is attributed to the main character in Harriet Beecher Stowe's classic work, *Uncle Tom's Cabin,* published in 1852. The novel itself was a fictional but accurate indictment of the cruel and inhumane institution of slavery in the South. The main character, Uncle Tom, emerges as the strongest and most morally upright person in the story. Yet over the years and even today, the term "Uncle Tom" carries a negative emotionally charged meaning.

DEFINITION OF *UNCLE TOM*

1) "pious and faithful black slave in Uncle Tom's Cabin *(1851-52) by Harriet Beecher Stowe (1922). 2) A black who is overeager to win the approval of whites (as by obsequious behavior or uncritical acceptance of white values and goals. 3) A member of a low-status group who is overly subservient to or cooperative with authority."*

The term has come to mean something completely different than what is present in the content and context of Stowe's novel. The passage of the 1850 Fugitive Slave Act, which totally altered the antislavery mind-set in the North and South, was motivation for Stowe's writings. Specifically, after this law's passage, Northerners were required by law to aid in the pursuit and return of fugitive slaves to southern slave masters.

Moreover, the burden of proof of ownership greatly shifted in favor of the slave owners. A simple statement of ownership sufficed, where in the past, courts decided ownership. Stowe and her family were staunch abolitionists and had sheltered runaway slaves in their home. Stowe's book was more fact than fiction, and, in response to blistering negative attacks on her claiming that the book was based on contrived exaggerations and abolitionist rubbish, she published the results of her firsthand research documenting the assertions in the book. "A Key to *Uncle Tom's Cabin*" was published in 1853. This 259-page report temporarily silenced some of her critics.

So it is within this complex social and political antebellum society that the slave, Uncle Tom, has operated. Contrary to popular opinion then and now, Tom was neither a coward nor a servile pawn. He was courageous, religious, self-sacrificial, and the embodiment of humaneness. It would have been easy for Tom to run away and leave his family; he did not. He could have revealed the escape plans of runaway slaves; he did not. He could have killed his tormenting owner, Simon Legree; he did not. Accordingly, Tom became the conduit for freedom for family members and fellow slaves while at the same time believing that he would at some point experience a better life, even if it would be in the afterlife. The spirit of freedom burned deeply in his life and allowed him to passively accept his earthly plight.

More often than not, whites viewed slaves as ignorant and incapable of thinking in ways that suggest intelligent intellectual processing. Many slaves played this role well while plotting for freedom, unbeknownst to their slave masters. It is widely believed that the fugitive slave Josiah Henson was the model for Stowe's book. She wrote the preface in his 1858 autobiography.

Freedom Fighter: Stokely Carmichael (Kwame Toure)

Flamboyant and outspoken, Stokely Carmichael (aka Kwame Toure) was a leading voice of the Black Power movement during the 1960s. Carmichael was born in Port of Spain, Trinidad and Tobago, on June 29, 1941. At the age of two, he was left with his grandmother when his parents immigrated to New York City. In 1952, after finishing elementary school in Trinidad, Carmichael rejoined his parents, moving to the predominately Jewish and Italian East Bronx, where he attended the Bronx High School of Science, a school for gifted children.

While Carmichael was in high school, the civil rights movement went into full swing. Emmett Till, who at 14 was the same age as Carmichael, was abducted and killed in Mississippi for allegedly whistling at a white woman. In Carmichael's senior year, four freshmen students from North Carolina Agricultural and Technical College (A&T) staged a nonviolent sit-in at the local Woolworth lunch counter after they were denied service. Carmichael was influenced by these activities and began attending the lectures of civil rights activists such as Bayard Rustin in New York, and participated in sit-ins in other parts of the South.

Although he received a number of scholarships from white universities after graduating in 1960, Carmichael elected to attend historically black Howard University in Washington, D.C. There, he studied philosophy and was influenced by sociology professor Nathan Hare, who believed that the university was out of touch with the Black community. At Howard, Carmichael became more involved in the civil rights movement. He joined the university's student chapter of the Student Nonviolent Coordinating Committee (SNCC), which was founded on the campus of Shaw University in North Carolina in 1960, following the Greensboro sit-in.

Carmichael was also active in the frequent sit-ins and Freedom Rides to southern states in protest against segregation on buses and in bus terminals. His apartment was a regular meeting place for fellow student activists. He was arrested numerous times throughout his student years, but he graduated from Howard with a degree in philosophy in 1964, before fully immersing himself in the civil rights movement. He remained in the South and continued to picket, participate in sit-ins, and to register Blacks to vote.

The same year he graduated from Howard, he was made regional director of the SNCC headquarters and helped to organize the multiracial Mississippi Freedom Democratic Party. When the party was refused seating during the Democratic National Convention, he became disillusioned by the nonviolent freedom rhetoric of older movement leaders like Martin Luther King, Jr., and was instead influenced by the vision of Malcolm X, spokesman for the Nation of Islam, and Pan-Africanist Kwame Nkrumah. In May 1966, he replaced moderately conservative John Lewis as chair of SNCC. A few weeks later, he gave a speech during a rally in Jackson, Mississippi, that changed the tone of the civil rights movement when he uttered the words "Black Power."

The SNCC evolved into a more radical entity under Carmichael's leadership. Young people around the country adopted "Black Power" as their rallying cry. Yet within the organization, members believed Carmichael's celebrity status undermined the goals of the organization. For this reason, he was asked to leave the organization in 1967. Still strong and passionate about his beliefs, he wrote *Black Power: The Politics of Liberation* with Charles V. Hamilton, which further clarified his philosophy of politics and race. "As children, we joined the Freedom Rides, to break the back of segregation and apartheid in interstate transportation in the United States. Today, we ride on the front of the bus, we charter buses to take one million men, women and children to marches in Washington, Philadelphia, New York and Atlanta. And we will never turn back."

He was made an honorary prime minister of the Black Panther Party, but had totally distanced himself from that group by 1969. He and his wife, singer Miriam Makeba, moved to Conakry, Guinea, where he worked for both Prime Minister Ahmed Sékou Touré and former Ghanaian President Kwame Nkrumah. He changed his name to Kwame Toure in honor of both African leaders.

In 1971, he published a collection of his later writings and speeches in *Stokely Speaks: Black Power Back to Pan-Africanism*. Until his death in 1998, Carmichael defined internal racism and the flaws that guided Black middle-class logic regarding equality for all. He died of prostate cancer in Guinea, West Africa, at the age of 57.

D. W.

Stokely Carmichael, pictured in 1967, called for a more radical course to Black equality and inspired a generation of followers.

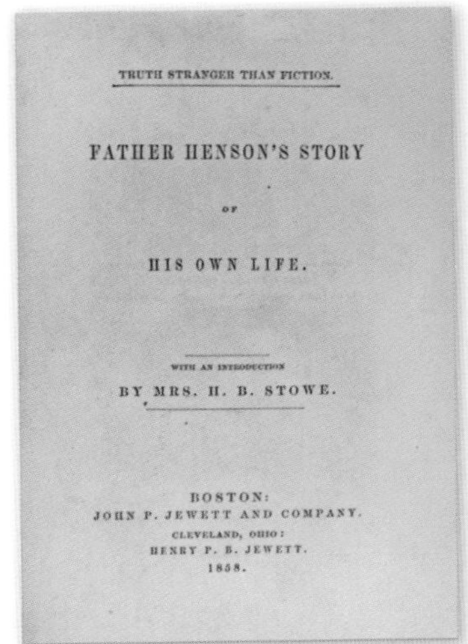

TRUTH STRANGER THAN FICTION.

FATHER HENSON'S STORY

OF

HIS OWN LIFE.

WITH AN INTRODUCTION

BY MRS. H. B. STOWE.

BOSTON:
JOHN P. JEWETT AND COMPANY.
CLEVELAND, OHIO:
HENRY P. B. JEWETT.
1858.

Above: The title page of Father Henson's Story of His Own Life *announces an introduction by "Mrs. H. B. Stowe." Right: Harriet Beecher Stowe drew her inspiration for the groundbreaking* Uncle Tom's Cabin *from the life of runaway slave Josiah Henson, pictured here in 1877 with his wife.*

"Liberty was a glorious hope in my mind; not as an escape from toil, for I rejoiced in toil when my heart was in it, but as the avenue to a sense of self-respect, to ennobling occupation, and to association with superior minds."

—Josiah Henson, slave

QUEST FOR FREEDOM

Slaves in North America were willing to pay the ultimate price for the prize of freedom. Slaves gained freedom in a multitude of ways, including revolt, rebellion, arson, poisoning, running away, and ingenuity, but the end result was the same. Slaves sought to be able to control their lives, enjoy all of the rights and privileges accruing to persons free to roam and interact as they pleased, and to have these rights protected by law.

A lithograph by Charles Bour (top), from Stowe's Uncle Tom's Cabin, *depicts the flight of Eliza. Stowe's novel was immensely popular in its time, as evidenced by an 1859 advertisement (inset).*

The extremes to which slaves were prepared to go graphically point out the inhumane indignities, and physical and psychological brutality visited upon them daily by men, women, children, and fellow slaves symbolically placed in minimal positions of overseers and drivers. This latter divisive strategy worked very well because the majority of unsuccessful slave revolts failed because fellow slaves told of the plans to their masters. Some slaves took years to plan their activities, and betrayal by a "trusted" comrade destroyed the plan at the last minute.

Africans began their resistance on the shores of their homeland, on the oppressive transatlantic ships, in the seasoning pens of the Caribbean, on the auction block, in the kitchens, and in the fields. Furthermore, slaves petitioned state legislatures for their freedom and some succeeded. Yet it took a civil war between countrymen to arrive at a beginning resolution. Slaves fought to demonstrate that all men are in fact created equal with certain inalienable rights.

Symbols of Freedom

A GALLERY

The vestiges of slavery left by former slaves or by their abolitionist helpers can be found in large cities and in small towns, from the South to the North and even up into Canada. Some of these symbols hold profound meaning. Others appear to be ordinary buildings such as houses, museums, renovated plantations, and office buildings located on a busy street. Yet by digging deeper, more profound stories emerge in places like Old Town Alexandria, Virginia, in Plymouth Meeting near Philadelphia, or in Saint Catharine's in Ontario, Canada.

Prime examples of slavery's legacy include:

THE FIRST AFRICAN BAPTIST CHURCH, SAVANNAH, GA.
Front View, from Franklin Square.

Within the walls of the First African Baptist Church in Savannah, Georgia, lies a remarkable history, including escape tunnels and tribal symbols.

THE FIRST AFRICAN BAPTIST CHURCH OF SAVANNAH, GEORGIA

Here, symbols are as profound as a series of lines and curves or an intricate pattern of designs carved on the sides of church pews by slaves who were eager to show fellow captives their tribal affiliations. These drawings, along with another remarkable set of symbols composed of a diamond-shaped pattern of holes that had been bored into the floor of the second chapel of a church in Savannah, Georgia, are still visible today. These air holes—36 in total—lead to secret chambers that are located beneath the floor. These chambers in turn connect to 14 tunnels that branch out from the church. The tunnel entrances remain hidden to this very day.

AFRICAN BURIAL GROUND WALL

This new edifice, which is maintained by the U.S. Park Service in New York, is a moving memorial that includes eloquent symbols from West Africa.

FRANKLIN AND ARMFIELD SLAVE OFFICE

A former slave pen and sales office located on Duke Street in Alexandria, Virginia, is now the office of a Black organization, the local Urban League.

QUILTS

The quilt patterns, used in a certain order, relayed messages to slaves preparing to escape. Each pattern represented a different meaning. Some of the most common were Monkey Wrench, Star, Crossroads, and Wagon Wheel. Quilts slung over a fence or windowsill, seemingly to air, passed on the necessary information to knowing slaves. Quilts hung out to air was a common sight on a plantation, so neither the plantation owner nor the overseer noticed anything suspicious. It was all part of a day's work for the slaves.

Numerous other symbols and reminders include interior and exterior architecture such as iron gates at the statehouse, airport, and additional sites in South Carolina; everyday inventions used by millions, such as the traffic light; spirituals and related sheet music/coded music such as "Follow the Drinking Gourd"; poetry by Paul Laurence Dunbar

An Emancipation Proclamation Day Celebration (above), held in 2008 at the First African Baptist Church, drew a large and ebullient crowd. The church still bears the marks of slavery, including ventilation holes in its floor for slaves held underneath (below).

and others that refers to early Black culture in the United States; and Benjamin Banneker's surveys of the national capital, Washington, D.C.

NATIONAL COUNCIL OF NEGRO WOMEN BUILDING

This point, which is located at Sixth Street and Pennsylvania Avenue N.W., between the United States Capitol and the White House, was at one time one of the largest slave auction sites in the nation's capital. The building that occupies much of the location today is the headquarters of an organization comprising more than four million black women members, worldwide. It is also the only building of its size in Washington, D.C., that is owned by black women.

SHEILA JOHNSON AND MIDDLEBURG, VIRGINIA

Black people were among Middleburg's earliest inhabitants. After the Civil War, men continued as stonemasons, general contractors, blacksmiths, and horsemen, and women as cooks, caterers, seamstresses, midwives, and domestic workers. By the 1940s and 1950s, African-American businesses thrived in Middleburg and in the surrounding

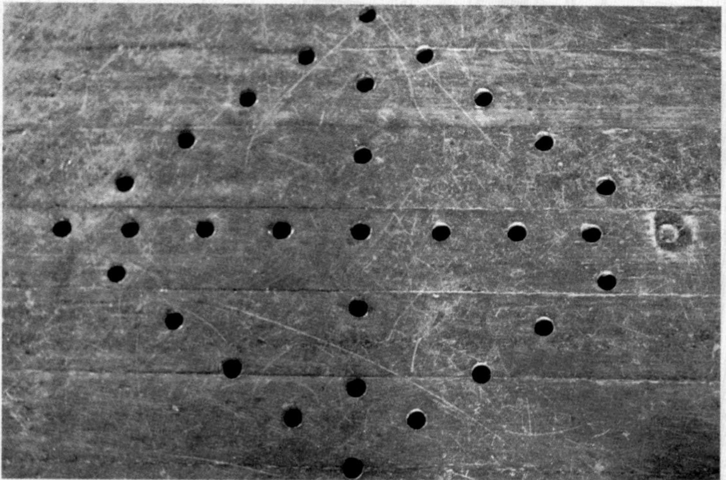

areas. Today, the legacy of African-American business ownership in Middleburg is exhibited by America's first black female billionaire, Sheila Johnson, whose enterprises include a performing arts center, a market, a 168-room resort and spa, and a 200-acre farm.

CHAPTER SEVEN

Quest for Freedom

Quest for Freedom

The status of indentured Africans compared to indentured whites in 17th-century colonial America shifted considerably between 1640 and 1660, after John Punch became the first black person to be declared a slave for life. In 1640, he and two white indentured runaways were captured; his white companions received one-year extensions of their indentureship, but Punch was declared the permanent property of his owner. In 1660 and 1661, Massachusetts, Virginia, and Maryland enacted slave laws that relegated African servants to lifelong slaves.

Africans had become an ideal source of free labor in perpetuity. Author Vincent Harding best captures the uniqueness of slavery in early colonial North America, "So in the course of the 17th century, the freedom-loving English colonies developed a series of laws and judicial rulings to define the black situation. . . . They were followed by laws prohibiting black-white intermarriage, laws against the ownership of property by Africans, laws denying blacks all basic political rights (limited as they were among whites at the time). In addition, there were laws against the education of Africans, laws against the assembling of Africans, laws against the ownership of weapons by Africans, laws perpetuating the slavery of their parents to African children, laws forbidding Africans to raise their hands against whites even in self-defense."

This marked the beginning of slavery in North America that, over the course of more than two centuries, solidified involuntary servitude as the social, economic, and political foundation of what would become the most powerful nation in the world. Historian Howard Zinn refutes the notion that the American slave traders were only doing what the Africans had begun in their slave activities. He states, "African slavery lacked two elements that made American slavery the most cruel form of slavery in history: the frenzy for limitless profit that comes from capitalistic agriculture: the reduction of the slave to less than human status by the use of racial hatred, with the relentless clarity based on color, where whites are masters, blacks are slaves." This also marked the beginning of the Africans' quest for freedom, because the hope that the end of five- to seven-year terms of indenture would result in freedom was now nonexistent.

Early on, slavery also established the racial psychosocial protocol that would exist between all Blacks and all whites, regardless of a particular strata held in society. To this day, we see remnants of color distinctions established in the 17th century and modern racism as an enduring legacy of slavery. Historians Christopher and James Collier state, "Southerners, by and large, believed that if slavery was abolished, their economy would collapse. Moreover, they had subtle and complex emotional ties to slavery. Not only those who owned slaves but those who did not could get from slavery a host of psychic rewards—a sense of superiority over other human beings, the wielding of command, which many of them would not otherwise enjoy and for males was an endless supply of irresponsible sex."

This sense of false superiority therefore established a myth of equality among all whites (rich and poor), because the Black population was relegated to an inferior social, economic,

Left: Antislavery conventions, like this one in Cazenovia, New York, around 1845, drew prominent abolitionists such as Frederick Douglass.

Previous pages: At Fort Lincoln, outside the District of Columbia, the Fourth U.S. Colored Infantry stands ready to defend the cause of freedom.

"She was born a slave and remained a slave for nearly thirty years. She could neither read nor write yet in her own sphere she had no superior or equal. She neither wasted time nor property. She never violated a trust nor failed to perform a duty. In every situation of domestic trial, she was the most efficient helper, and the tenderest friend. Good mother, farewell."

— Gravestone of Mum Bett

and political position based on a unity of whiteness. The subtle duplicity of the founders was established on the notion that whites in positions of power and authority would operate in the best interests of lesser positioned whites, often at the expense of Blacks, both slave and free alike. The Colliers state, "In fact Madison's idea of 'people' was not precisely what we would take the phrase to mean. Blacks would not vote, indentured servants would not vote, and the propertyless mob of sailors, vagrants, day laborers and criminals who swarmed the cities would not vote. Perhaps only ten percent of the population would be enfranchised."

Despite being technically free, free Blacks had little guarantee of personal safety or protection of their civil rights. At any given time, in any place in the country, they could be kidnapped and sold south into slavery. In the 18th century, the Fugitive Slave Law of 1793 facilitated this practice, and the 1850 Fugitive Slave Law was more punitive than the 1793 law. Historian Ira Berlin best captures this point: "The line between slavery and freedom was never quite what some abolitionists made it out to be. Once free, blacks generally remained at the bottom of the social order, despised by whites, burdened with increasingly oppressive racial proscriptions and subjected to verbal and physical abuse. Free Negroes stood outside the direct governance of a master, but in the eyes of many whites their place in society had not been significantly altered. They were slaves without masters."

Accordingly, the quest for freedom was a crusade for all black people in the country. The commonality of this struggle served as a point of solidarity among Blacks, regardless of where they lived as well as their condition of physical or mental servitude. Contrary to popular opinion and historical distortions, Blacks sought to abolish slavery long before the formal creation of the first white abolitionist movements in America and England alike.

PETITIONS

Petitioning was among some of the earliest attempts of slaves to achieve their freedom by legal means in colonial America. Primarily in the North, slaves petitioned the courts and governors for their freedom, often making passionate and compelling arguments on their behalf. Signers of these petitions were not only those directly affected by slavery but also people who were sympathetic to the cause of freedom.

Some petitions were individual, but most were signed by several slaves. Although many petitions were denied or tabled, it is noteworthy that slaves chose a literary, legal route to freedom when it was illegal for slaves to demonstrate any minute semblance of literacy in most states, particularly in the South.

Another petition was submitted to the governor of the province of the Massachusetts Bay in 1773. The petition stated, "We presume not to dictate to your EXCELLENCY and Honors, being willing to rest our Cause on Your Humanity and Justice. . . . We have no Property! We have no Wives! No Children! We have no City! No Country."

Another interesting slave petition was submitted to the colony of Massachusetts Bay in 1777. Clearly, elements of this document reflect the slaves' familiarity with the 1776 Declaration of Independence. It stated, "Your petitioners apprehend we have in common with all other men a natural and unalienable right to freedom which the Great Parent of the universe hath bestowed equally on all mankind." Although few petitioners succeeded in achieving freedom, slaves were not discouraged and continued their efforts for the next 80 years.

A 1781 case that exemplifies this element of the nonviolent quest for freedom is that of Mum Bett, a Massachusetts slave who petitioned the local court for her freedom based on the preamble in the new Massachusetts Constitution that stated that "all men are born free and equal." A local white attorney, Theodore Sedgwick, represented her. The all-white jury found in her favor, and Mum Bett immediately renamed herself Elizabeth Freeman. Freeman later

Dover June 4. 1777—
This may certify all Persons that I Otis Baker do hereby give to the within named Cato his freedom & discharge him from my Service and the Service of my heirs forever Otis Baker

Witness Jeremy Belknap

On the back of a bill of sale, a document signed by Otis Baker in 1777 (top) discharges his slave, Cato, from service, thereby granting Cato his freedom. Mum Bett (above) earned her freedom by petitioning a white judge and jury in Massachusetts.

stated, "Any time while I was a slave, if one minute's freedom had been offered to me, and I had been told I must die at the end of the minute, I would have taken it just to stand one minute on God's airth a free woman."

THE FIRST ABOLITIONISTS

Conventional American history most often identifies the beginning of the abolitionist movement with white advocates such as William Lloyd Garrison and Levi Coffin, as well as the Pennsylvania Anti-Slavery Society founded in 1775. The primary purpose of the abolitionist movement in America was to permanently end the enslavement of Blacks in the United States and to develop a plan for the slaves' future after being freed. In reality, the abolitionist movement began long before 1775. It began among Blacks when they recognized why they were being forcibly removed from their homeland and shipped thousands of miles across the Atlantic Ocean to become the property for life of American slaveholders. Black abolitionists first began to organize during and immediately after the American Revolution and ratification of the Constitution in 1789, when it became clear to them that their interests were not incorporated in the future of the new republic.

These early Black abolitionists served as inspiration for a later generation of 19th-century activists, such as Frederick Douglass, Sojourner Truth, Harriet Tubman, William Wells Brown, and others. Central among them were freed slaves Richard Allen and Absolom Jones, founders in 1787 of the Free African Society, which paved the way for the creation of the African Methodist Episcopal Church. Other early Black abolitionists included James Forten, a successful Philadelphia entrepreneur; Prince Hall, founder of the Black Masonic organization;

Like many former slaves, Martha Rix, shown here in Liberia in the 1890s, found refuge in her homeland of Africa.

and David Walker, a Boston antislavery militant who published what was considered the most incendiary document ever in terms of encouraging Blacks to rise up and fight for their freedom—even if it meant killing their masters. Historian Richard S. Newman describes their important legacy: "By living as free men in the Age of Revolution, building communities and institutions, and expressing their rights as citizens (even when laws denied them citizenship), they defined America as an interracial republic from the very beginning."

If in fact there was any doubt that the white founders had forsaken Blacks during the Revolution and after, it is clearly evident in the 1787 Constitutional Convention. By all accounts, it certainly appears that there existed a "gentleman's agreement" that, because the issue of slavery was so polarizing, it would not be discussed or even considered in any of the intense and delicate deliberations that occurred in Philadelphia between May and September 1787. What further incensed Blacks was that some of the same white leaders present at the

The Lion of Anacostia: Frederick Douglass

Frederick Douglass was one of the most influential African-American figures of the 19th century. As a slave who became free, he spent his life speaking out against the rationalizations used to justify the enslavement of people of African descent. Born in 1817 on Maryland's Eastern Shore, he—and his mother—belonged to Aaron Anthony, a supervisor on the plantation of Edward Lloyd V, one of the richest men in Maryland. When his mother was hired out to work on another plantation 12 miles away, Douglass was left in the care of his grandparents. He had only fleeting memories of his mother waking him up at night and sleeping with him until the morning, when she had to walk back to the other plantation. When she had not visited in a long time, he heard that she had died. When he was six, his grandmother took him to the Lloyd mansion, where she introduced him to his three siblings. He was never allowed to return to the home of his grandparents. This was when he first understood the harsh cruelty of slavery. "I didn't know I was a slave until I found out I couldn't do the things I wanted."

At the age of eight, Douglass was sent to Baltimore to live with Sophia and Hugh Auld. Hugh was the brother of Thomas Auld, who was married to Lucretia Anthony, the daughter of Douglass's master. Sophia noticed Douglass's intelligence and began teaching him to read until her husband forbade her, because he believed reading encouraged slaves to want freedom. Although the lessons stopped, Douglass's appetite to learn was whetted by the experience, and his determination to seek his freedom was born.

A former slave who escaped and bought his freedom, Frederick Douglass spoke eloquently and tirelessly against the institution of slavery in the U.S.

Upon the death of Anthony Aaron, followed by the death of Aaron's daughter Lucretia, Douglass was returned to Thomas Auld to work in the fields. Douglass attempted an escape but was captured and jailed. Upon Douglass's release, Auld sent him back to Baltimore to live with Auld's brother, Hugh. He was employed in the shipyards on Fells Point, where he was allowed more freedom than he ever had as a field hand. He found time to socialize with the free Black residents of Baltimore, and attended church services and social organizations, where he honed his debating skills. All the while, Douglass continued to long for his freedom. With money he borrowed from his fiancée, Anna Murray, a free woman, and the free seaman papers and uniform of a black sailor, Douglass escaped north to New York City, where he was reunited with and married to Anna.

The Douglasses subsequently moved to New Bedford, Massachusetts, where Anna gave birth to two children. Douglass's first step toward abolitionism was his subscription to the antislavery newspaper, the *Liberator,* published by William Lloyd Garrison. The two met several years later after Garrison heard Douglass's powerful oration about his experience as a slave. Garrison hired Douglass as a speaker for the Anti-Slavery Society. From that point on, Douglass traveled all over the country, debating the evils of slavery and demanding freedom for his enslaved brethren.

After supporters purchased his freedom from Auld, Douglass started his own antislavery newspaper, the *North Star,* and also published his first autobiography. He was outspoken and unflagging in his pursuit of freedom for all people, regardless of race. He helped with the recruitment of black soldiers to fight in the Civil War, even offering two of his sons as the first to sign up. As the Civil War came to a close and slaves were emancipated, Douglass settled into a life as a speaker and public servant. He moved to Washington, D.C., in 1870, as editor of the *New National Era* newspaper, and he became president of the Freedmen's Savings and Trust Company in 1874. The President of the United States appointed him as a U.S. marshal in 1877, and Recorder of Deeds for Washington, D.C., in 1880. Anna, his wife of 46 years, died two years later. Amid a firestorm of protest, Douglass married a white woman named Helen Pitts in 1884. The couple lived in the Anacostia neighborhood of the city. His last position as public servant was as general consul to Haiti, which he resigned in 1891. Douglass died at home in 1895. *D. W.*

Prominent African Americans of the 19th century include: Maj. Martin Robinson Delany, a Union officer (top); activist Sojourner Truth (middle); and abolitionist Henry Highland Garnet.

Constitutional Convention had attended the First Continental Congress 13 years earlier and had fervently professed their abhorrence of slavery and the slave trade.

Therefore, it is quite understandable that Black loyalty in the Revolutionary War was to neither competing side but to the principles of freedom and equality. Once the U.S. Constitution was ratified in 1789, it was very clear to Blacks that their total exclusion from the democratic principles in the document would begin a social and political struggle that would eventually result in a civil war that would claim 700,000 American lives more than 70 years later.

COLONIZATION

The complexity of the American abolitionist movement in terms of racism, ideology, and patriotism remains an obscure chapter in U.S. history. However, to more fully understand the African Americans' quest for freedom would be incomplete without a more full examination of the struggles Blacks endured simply to be treated as equal partners in the antislavery crusade during the decades leading up to the Civil War.

Vincent Harding best captured the black-white ideological dilemma in the abolitionist movement. He stated, "From this white vantage point, the fight against slavery was, on the one hand, a negative battle against an evil which was undeniably immense, but in most cases not very close to them; and on the other hand, a positive struggle for the honor of America, in which they felt great personal involvement, not only to right the wrongs of the present, but also to vindicate their divinely inspired forefathers. . . ." The Black abolitionists, on the other hand, prefaced their struggle not only as philosophical and ideological tenets but also through identifying slaves not merely as inanimate objects but as mothers, fathers, uncles, sons, and daughters. Accordingly, no price was too high to pay for the freedom that these human beings sought, given their horrific experiences as slaves.

The first white abolitionist societies of the late 18th century and early 19th century refused to accept Blacks as members. Similarly, the religious group most closely associated with abolitionism, the Quakers, did not welcome Blacks into their churches in the late 18th and early 19th centuries, and some even owned slaves early on. The initial strategy of the white abolitionists was to send free Blacks out of the United States to locations they would select in the Caribbean, South America, or Africa. Although a few Blacks did entertain the thought of colonization, the suggestion offended many and galvanized their commitment to seek freedom in the land where they had toiled, lived, and died for more than 150 years. By the 18th century, they had come to claim the United States as their country as well.

Following the ratifications of the U.S. Constitution and its designation of slaves as property, Black anger and insurrection activity intensified. In fact, the main slave revolts in American history occurred during this period (1800–1830). Whites therefore became increasingly concerned about the intense emotions among the slaves and decided that the best way to defuse this tinderbox was to deport freed slaves out of the country. To this end, Robert Finley, the son of an immigrant Scottish merchant and a Presbyterian minister, founded the first colonization organization in America.

Within a month of the founding of the American Colonization Society (1816), Black abolitionists James Forten and Bishop Richard Allen issued the following statement: "We will never separate ourselves voluntarily from the slave population in this country; they are our brethren by the ties of consanguinity, of suffering, and of wrong, and we feel that there is more virtue in suffering privations with them than fancied advantages for a season."

In 1829, abolitionist David Walker was even more profound and direct in his rejection of Black colonization. He stated, "Let no man of us bridge one step. . . . America is more ours than it is the whites. The greatest riches in all America have arisen from our blood and tears."

Professional Soldier: Gen. Colin Powell, Retd.

After a long and storied military career, Colin Luther Powell was unanimously confirmed by the U.S. Senate and sworn in as the 65th secretary of state on January 20, 2001. Having been nominated by President George W. Bush, Powell was the first African American to serve in this distinguished Cabinet post.

Born in Harlem in 1937, Secretary Powell grew up in the South Bronx, the son of Jamaican immigrants. His parents, Luther and Maud Powell, valued education. Secretary Powell attended New York City public schools, graduated from City College of New York, and earned a master's degree in business administration from George Washington University in Washington, D.C., in 1971.

During his 35-year career as a professional soldier, Secretary Powell held numerous command and staff positions, culminating in his appointment as four-star general. His military career began in Fort Benning, Georgia, where he received his basic training. After being assigned for two years in West Germany, his next post was in Massachusetts, where in 1962 he met his future wife, Alma Vivian Johnson of Birmingham, Alabama.

A few months after his marriage, Secretary Powell was sent to Vietnam. Now holding the rank of captain, he was wounded and awarded a Purple Heart. After earning the rank of major in 1968, he went back to Vietnam for a second tour, where he once again showed great bravery in saving several comrades from a burning helicopter. Again he was wounded and earned a second Purple Heart along with a Soldier's Medal.

By 1977, Secretary Powell had been promoted to brigadier general. He continued to rise through the ranks during the 1980s, until he became the 12th Chairman of the Joint Chiefs of Staff. In this position, he held the highest military position in the Department of Defense. During his tenure, he oversaw 28 crises, including Operation Desert Storm, which ended in victory in the 1991 Persian Gulf war.

Powell is the recipient of numerous civilian and U.S. and foreign military awards, including the Congressional Gold Medal, two Presidential Medals of Freedom, the President's Citizens Medal, and the Secretary of State Distinguished Service Medal. Upon his retirement from the military, Powell wrote his best-selling autobiography, *My American Journey,* which was published in 1995. After stepping down from his post as secretary of state in 2004, he has pursued a career in public speaking, where his services are in great demand.

C. J. C.

As U.S. secretary of state, Colin Powell (center) met with Sudanese vice president Ali Osman Taha (left) and rebel leader John Garang in 2005 in Nairobi, Kenya, over the conflict in Darfur, where hundreds of thousands of Sudanese have died or been displaced.

A Time to Teach

BEN VEREEN

Upon learning about the plans for the U.S. National Slavery Museum from my daughter, Kabara, I instantly felt that I must become a part of it. My passion for the education that this project will bring to the people of America is overwhelming.

When I grew up as Negro, colored, black, and African American, the only relevant thing I saw during Negro History Week was a paragraph about how once there were slaves and they were freed by President Abraham Lincoln. It was as if nothing else happened regarding African Americans; it seemed as though the only time we could even be mentioned was during that one week when it was OK to be black.

THE POWER OF *ROOTS*

This was not the first time that I had felt so strongly about a project in the making. When I first heard about Alex Haley's *Roots,* in the 1970s, I knew I had to be a part of it, as well. During and after the showing of *Roots,* we saw it affecting people all over the world. Because of *Roots,* we learned that people were hungry for the truth. The same is true of the U.S. National Slavery Museum. We can unveil the truth right here in America.

The time has come to let the world know that we are taking responsibility for the museum. Just as our Jewish brothers and sisters embraced the Holocaust Museum right here in America with the intention that such atrocities will never happen again, we must do the same thing in regard to the Slavery Museum. The world must know that slavery is our Holocaust and that this is our Holocaust Museum—the museum is for all of us. The enslavement of human beings must never happen again.

Architect of the U.S. National Slavery Museum C.C. Pei (right) poses with Richmond, Virginia, mayor L. Douglas Wilder (left) and actor Ben Vereen.

This museum will serve many purposes. It will honor the mother who was beaten as her children were torn away from her side. It will be for the father who stood helplessly as his family was sold away, never again to be seen by him. This museum will enable our children to know more about our past than what I learned as a child—that black people were not only slaves or people like Sojourner Truth, Fredrick Douglass, Nat Turner, and Harriet Tubman, but also those unmentioned heroes who stood for the freedom of the slaves, whose voices could not be silenced.

When I think of the reproduction of a slave ship in the museum, I think of the day that I viewed the Tall Ships sailing into New York Harbor several years ago. In viewing those ships, it was clear that many people of years gone by had taken great pride in sailing in those ships. Black people, however, did not have the luxury of sailing into America in comfort in such ships. Instead, our ancestors were shipped as cattle, and that story must be told. The museum's slave ship will be a vivid reminder of the conditions that our forebears actually had to endure.

Alex Haley did a wonderful thing when he told the story of his family's past. Now let us revisit the story so no one will again have to go through such ordeals. This pertains not only to African Americans but to every American. When I played the role of Alex Haley's ancestor, Chicken George, I had to call upon the elders, who told me the stories of slavery in every detail. I sat for days learning the truth that had been hushed up, sugarcoated, and denied all of my life. I was determined to teach the world through my portrayal of Alex Haley's forefather. It is my strong desire that the people of America will come to the Slavery Museum often, learning something new and unique as a result of each visit.

With the opening of this museum, we will celebrate the lives of the men, women, and children whose stories are told in this book and whose lives will be represented in the museum. It is a tribute to those sung and unsung heroes. ■

Ben Vereen portrayed Alex Haley's ancestor Chicken George in the television series Roots.

"This for the purpose of this celebration is the 4th of July. It is the birthday of your National Independence and of your political freedom. I am not included within the pale of glorious anniversary! Your high independence only reveals the immeasurable distance between us. The blessings in which you, this day, rejoice, are not enjoyed in common. The rich inheritance of justice, liberty, prosperity and independence, bequeathed by your fathers is shared by you, not by me. The sunlight that brought light and healing to you has brought stripes and death to me."

—Frederick Douglass, abolitionist

19TH-CENTURY ABOLITION

White abolitionist William Lloyd Garrison is still considered by many to be the "father" of the American abolitionist movement. He was an immigrant from Nova Scotia who, under the tutelage of Quaker Benjamin Lundy, began his antislavery crusade in 1828. In 1830, he founded one of the most influential antislavery newspapers, the *Liberator,* and invited Black abolitionists to express their views.

Yet many within the African-American community of the 19th century strongly disagreed with Garrison and publicly expressed their dissent. Black abolitionist Thomas Van Rensselaer was central among these critics. He rejected the notion that whites could solve the ingrained problems experienced by Blacks in America and rejected white organizations proclaiming to operate in the best interest of Blacks, when the very problems they professed to abhor were, in fact, created by whites themselves.

Vincent Harding stated, "By that time [1830s], too, white abolitionist organizations, springing from different roots, had established themselves as significant elements in the life of America. Most often these white anti-slavery groups built on the base that the independent black struggle for freedom had prepared, for blacks had provided the first abolitionists, the first martyrs in the long battle, starting in the slave castles, on the ships of the middle passage, continuing on the soil of the new land."

Perhaps the most famous Black abolitionist was Frederick Douglass, who escaped from slavery in Maryland in 1838, and settled in New Bedford, Massachusetts. He was instrumental in desegregating the white abolitionist societies and established the antislavery newspaper the *North Star.* Another daring, well-known antislavery activist was Harriet Tubman. After escaping from slavery herself in 1849, she reportedly helped guide some 300 runaway slaves to freedom. She also served in the Union Army during the Civil War as a spy and scout. Sojourner Truth, born a slave named Isabella, ran away in 1827. From then up until the Civil War, she walked through Long Island, New York, and Connecticut preaching about abolition of slavery and suffrage rights for women. Near the end of the Civil War, she collected signatures on a petition for the creation of a free "Negro State" on western public lands.

In addition to these more familiar names, there were a number of lesser-known, heroic Black abolitionists, such as:

- Martin Delany (1812–1885). Activist, critic, physician; worked with Frederick Douglass on the newspaper, traveled internationally on behalf of abolitionism, and was the first Black major in the U.S. Army. Author of *The Condition, Elevation, Emigration, and Destiny of the Colored People of the United States Politically Considered,* 1852.
- David Ruggles (1810–1849). Travel agent for the newspaper *Emancipator;* staunch supporter of Black-only organizations; considered the press the primary modality for promoting abolitionism, Black pride, and uplift.
- Charles Remond (1810–1873). Attended 1840 World Anti-Slavery Society Convention in England and spent 18 months in British Isles collecting 60,000 signatures in support of antislavery activities in America. Also toured the United States with Frederick Douglass.
- Henry Highland Garnet (1815–1882). Strong advocate of militancy to end slavery, most eloquent orator on abolitionism; sought to turn American traditions of liberty to the cause of Black freedom, called for violent slave uprising in 1843 Black convention.
- Mary Ann Shadd Cary (1823–1893). Co-founded the *Provincial Freeman* in 1853, thereby becoming the first black woman editor in North America. An outspoken educator, journalist, and women's rights advocate, she recruited black soldiers for the Union during the Civil War.

In a call for freedom, a kneeling slave (top) and a commemorative bronze medal (bottom) ask, "Am I Not a Man and a Brother."

- Sarah Forten (1814–?). Youngest daughter of abolitionists James and Charlotte Forten; founding member of the Philadelphia Female Anti-Slavery Society; challenged American religions' hypocrisy on slavery via poetry and verse.

By the mid-19th century, Blacks were somewhat appreciative of the work of white abolitionists, particularly martyrs such as Elijah Lovejoy and John Brown. Yet the prevailing attitude of Blacks was one of self-help, self-reliance, and self-advocacy, using petitions to legislative authorities and Black conventions and establishing all-Black organizations as in the traditions of Richard Allen and Absolom Jones in 1787.

Similarly, the colored convention movement, which began in 1830 in Philadelphia, Pennsylvania, was another moderately effective mechanism for freedom and equality in 19th-century America. Historian Benjamin Quarles states, "The [convention] movement was an expression of protest against the status of the Negro in American life. By 1830 Negroes had come to the conclusion that concerted action was necessary to make clear their plight and their recommendations for bettering it."

Rallying fellow abolitionists to their cause, antislavery settlers in the new Kansas Territory sought out delegates to a "Free State" convention.

FREE STATE

CONVENTION!

All persons who are favorable to a union of effort, and a permanent organization of all the Free State elements of Kansas Territory, and who wish to secure upon the broadest platform the co-operation of all who agree upon this point, are requested to meet at their several places of holding elections, in their respective districts on the 25th of August, instant, at one o'clock, P. M., and appoint five delegates to each representative to which they were entitled in the Legislative Assembly, who shall meet in general Convention at

Big Springs, Wednesday, Sept. 5th '55,

at 10 o'clock A. M., for the purpose of adopting a Platform upon which all may act harmoniously who prefer Freedom to Slavery.

The nomination of a Delegate to Congress, will also come up before the General Convention.

Let no sectional or party issues distract or prevent the perfect co-operation of Free State men. Union and harmony are absolutely necessary to success. The pro-slavery party are fully and effectually organized. No jars nor minor issues divide them. And to contend against them successfully, we also must be united.—Without prudence and harmony of action we are certain to fail. Let every man then do his duty and we are certain of victory.

All Free State men, without distinction, are earnestly requested to take immediate and effective steps to insure a full and correct representation for every District in the Territory. "United we stand; divided we fall."

By order of the Executive Committee of the Free State Party of the Territory of Kansas, as per resolution of the Mass Convention in session at Lawrence, Aug 15th and 16th, 1855.

J. K. GOODIN, Sec'y. **C. ROBINSON, Chairman.**

Herald of Freedom, Print.

"ARTICLE III.—This Society shall aim to elevate the character and condition of the people of color, by encouraging their intellectual, moral, and religious improvement, and by removing public prejudice, that thus they may . . . share an equality with the whites, of civil and religious privileges; but . . . will never . . . countenance the oppressed in vindicating their rights by . . . physical force."

—*American Anti-Slavery Society Constitution*

The colored convention movement lasted for approximately 20 years and provided Blacks with an opportunity to discuss, debate, and plan how best to measurably improve the plight of all black people in America, slave and free alike. Some of the great orators and activists in the abolition movement regularly participated in these events—men like Frederick Douglass, Henry Garnet, Martin Delany, Richard Allen, and others were regular participants.

Although this movement was organized and guided primarily by free Blacks in New England, the rampant racist ideology of Black inferiority and white superiority had infected most if not all elements of the decades between the American Revolution and the Civil War. Accordingly, so-called free Blacks lived in constant fear of being kidnapped and sold into slavery, not only in the South but also in the western area of the nation that doubled in size as a result of the 1803 Louisiana Purchase. Quarles states, "The doctrine of white supremacy was held almost as tenaciously above the Mason-Dixon Line as below. Though by 1830 slavery had been virtually abolished in the North, the Negro still bore the indelible mark of a degraded inferior; he was regarded as a threat to the general welfare, if not an outright liability. Somewhat like a self-fulfilling prophecy, this attitude toward the Negro gave rise to a concerted effort to limit him to roles which fell to those of lesser breed."

Ironically, the southern slaves may have been afforded more protection than the free Blacks in many ways, because slave owners were very assiduous in protecting their economic investment in human capital, whereas free Blacks had no such buffer.

THE TRUE CAUSE OF THE CIVIL WAR

There has been an interminable debate about the causes of the Civil War, and slavery remains the primary focus in the minds of many. Although this is a simplistic and moderately believable theory, the reality is that the real cause of the war seems to be the manner in which the United States Constitution was written, promoted, and ratified in regard to slavery. Although the word "slavery" is mentioned nowhere in the Constitution, the political, economic, and social elements of slavery are ever present throughout. For example, slaves would be counted as three-fifths of a white man for purposes of political representation and taxation (Article I section 2). Similarly, James Madison was instrumental in gaining passage of abolition of the

The Dream Endures: Rev. Martin Luther King, Jr.

Thought by many to be one of the world's greatest leaders, Dr. Martin Luther King, Jr., led the fight in the 1950s and 1960s to end discrimination and institutionalized segregation in the United States. He was the youngest man ever to be awarded a Nobel Peace Prize.

Dr. King developed a strong determination for justice during his childhood years. He credited his sense of obligation to the influence of his father, Reverend Martin Luther King, Sr. Practically every man in his family was a preacher, including his father, grandfather, great-grandfather, uncle, and his only brother. Dr. King, Jr., believed that he had no choice other than to become a preacher.

Dr. King, Jr., was born on January 15, 1929, at the Williams/King family home on Auburn Avenue in Atlanta, Georgia. His parents were devout Christians who held middle-class values, including a strong belief in education. That belief had led Dr. King's father to leave the fields in which he worked and to attend Atlanta's Morehouse College.

Following in the footsteps of his father and his grandfather, Dr. King, Jr., graduated from Morehouse in 1948. He went on to complete his religious studies at Crozer Theological Seminary in Pennsylvania in 1951. After being awarded a scholarship, he enrolled in a doctoral program at Boston University. He received his doctorate degree in 1955 and married Coretta Scott.

Dr. King's father had a powerful influence on him in the area of civil rights. Rev. King had been president of the National Association for the Advancement of Colored People (NAACP) in Atlanta. Dr. King followed in his father's footsteps in his efforts for social reform. He came to feel that the two culprits that must be defeated were social injustice and economic injustice. These were the two social platforms that he would build his life around.

By the mid-1950s, Dr. King had become a member of the executive committee of the NAACP. This position gave him the opportunity to take the lead in the December 1955 bus boycott, which is considered by many people as the first great Black nonviolent demonstration. This successful boycott, which lasted for 382 days, led to a Supreme Court decision on December 21, 1956, declaring the laws that required black people to sit in the rear of buses to be unconstitutional.

Dr. King's participation in the boycott caused him to be arrested, his home to be bombed, and earned him much personal abuse. It was the beginning of his long fight for equality for all of Black America. His 1957 election to the presidency of the Southern Christian Leadership Conference catapulted him to the forefront of the civil rights movement in America.

Dr. King's accomplishments of the 1960s include his "Letter from Birmingham Jail," arguing against unjust laws; his 1964 Nobel Peace Prize; his Lincoln Memorial "I Have a Dream" speech; and his 1965 march from Selma to Montgomery, Alabama, demanding voting rights.

Martin Luther King, Jr.'s message of nonviolence and his tireless fight for equality laid the groundwork for decades of progressive change.

Nearly 20 years of nonviolent protests, marches, speeches, and sermons, including his famous "I Have a Dream" sermon made this Baptist preacher's name well known all over the world. After fighting for and inspiring millions of people, Dr. King was assassinated on a motel balcony in Memphis, Tennessee, on April 4, 1968. He had been preparing to lead a march to demand better working conditions and salaries for African-American garbage workers. Thousands of people returned to the location of Dr. King's death to commemorate the 40th year of his passing and to celebrate all that has been accomplished, while remembering all that is yet to be achieved for African Americans and others. Dr. King's life and legacy will be memorialized on the United States Mall in Washington, D.C., when his MLK, Jr., National Memorial is built sometime in the next few years. This memorial will be the first major monument in the nation's Capitol to celebrate the achievements of an African American. It will be part of the legacy that honors the contributions of Dr. King, much like the MLK, Jr., national holiday. *C. J. C.*

"By every consideration which binds you to your enslaved fellow—countrymen, and the peace and welfare of your country; by every aspiration which you cherish for the freedom and equality of yourselves and your children; by all the ties of blood and identity which make us one with the brave black men now fighting our battles in Louisiana and in South Caroline, I urge you to fly to arms, and smite with death the power that would bury the government and your liberty in the same hopeless grave."

— Frederick Douglass, abolitionist

importation of slaves into the United States after 1808. He oversaw the committee work and incorporated the action (in Article I, Section 9).

Slavery's existence benefited the North and the South economically, industrially, and politically, and political expediency and mutual economic self-interest prevailed in the end. A deliberate decision was made to exclude any mention of slavery in the Constitution. This strategy appeased the North and the South, and freedom for Blacks became an expendable annoyance. Thus, the seeds of the Civil War were sown in Philadelphia in 1787, but the dire need to unite the 13 colonies into 13 states superseded the unintended consequence that would occur over 60 years later in the war between the states.

As the United States continued to expand its territory between 1789 and 1861, slavery found itself at the center of the discussion concerning the growth and expansion of the new democratic republic. Would slavery be legal in the new territories? The 1803 Louisiana Purchase was in part a response to the 1787 Northwest Ordinance that prohibited slavery in the territory above the Ohio River. The Louisiana acquisition opened up the entire Southwest for the expansion of slavery. Similarly, the acquisition of Florida from Spain in 1819 eliminated the major refuge for runaway slaves from deep southern states such as South Carolina, Georgia, and Mississippi. The ensuing three Seminole Wars (1818–1858) were specifically fought to soundly defeat the American Indian tribe made up of lower Creek native people and runaway slaves.

The 1820 Missouri Compromise, however, only forbade slavery in the territory north of Louisiana (36° and 30'). A most important element of the Missouri Compromise is that it established the congressional protocol for admitting new states to the Union in groups of two: one slave and one nonslave. This arrangement would ensure a semblance of proportional representation in the United States Congress between slave and free states. New lands continued to be acquired after the United States provoked a war with Mexico to annex Texas as a slave state in 1845. The 1854 Kansas-Nebraska Act however overrode the Missouri Compromise by establishing the right of inhabitants within these two new states to determine the presence or absence of slavery. Kansas became a bloody battlefield, and the lines of war were clearly drawn. Kansas, in fact, was the site where white abolitionist John Brown reportedly murdered Kansas slaveholders.

The complexity of the decades leading up to the Civil War is immense, and at the center were over three million slaves still struggling to be free in America. Abolitionism, petitions, conventions, and revolts were occurring at the same time as the seminal national events described earlier. The final confirmation of exclusion for all Blacks in this inevitable quest were the 1850 Fugitive Slave Act and the 1857 Dred Scott Supreme Court decision. The slave act legally required all northern states and localities to help locate and return runaway slaves to their masters. The Scott decision stated that black people in America had no rights that whites were bound to honor. Two years later, John Brown and 20 others, including two of his sons, died in a slave revolt at Harpers Ferry, Virginia. After President Abraham Lincoln's election in 1860 and South Carolina's secession, the irrepressible conflict caused by the 1787 Constitutional Convention had come to pass. The Civil War had begun.

EMANCIPATION

Slaves and free Blacks welcomed this moment in history as a defining watershed in their quest for freedom and equality. Long before Lincoln issued his 1863 Emancipation Proclamation, thousands of slaves had begun deserting plantations and claiming their freedom. Black historian John Hope Franklin states, "Shortly after the Civil War began, slaves realized that it might bring them freedom. Thus, they began to leave the plantation in large

Called by God: Bishop Vashti Murphy McKenzie

In 2000, Vashti Murphy McKenzie became the 117th bishop of the African Methodist Episcopal Church, the first woman elected to the office in the 200-year history of the AME Church.

Bishop McKenzie was born in 1947 and grew up in Baltimore, Maryland. Her family had founded the *Baltimore Afro-American* newspaper. She was born into a family of leaders, such as Vashti Turley Murphy, who gained prominence as one of the founders of the Delta Sigma Theta Sorority at Howard University in 1913. Turley Murphy, who had graduated from the first public high school for Blacks in the United States, the M Street High School in Washington, D.C., was an ardent supporter of the major political issue of the day—voting rights for women. Following in her footsteps in the sorority, Bishop McKenzie serves today as its national chaplain.

McKenzie is a graduate of the University of Maryland, College Park, and has earned a master of divinity from Howard University School of Divinity, along with a doctor of ministry degree from United Theological Seminary in Dayton, Ohio.

Among Bishop McKenzie's positions, she was the chief pastor of the 18th Episcopal District in southeastern Africa, which includes Lesotho, Swaziland, Botswana, and Mozambique. While working in these countries, her accomplishments included starting a wide assortment of new churches and church buildings, instituting computer labs, creating start-up business projects, and building group homes for children orphaned or affected by the HIV/AIDS pandemic.

Back home, Bishop McKenzie led her church, Payne Memorial, for more than ten years. During that time, she served as pastor to more than three churches, including one where the membership grew from 7 to 1,700 parishioners. There is a good reason for this. Her preaching style has been characterized as electrifying. One recent story states that, due to Bishop McKenzie's delivery, "the congregation could be heard screaming their praises in awe at the sermon delivered to them. . . . Some were brought to tears. Others rejoiced. . . ."

Bishop McKenzie has also written three books that are related to leadership and professional growth for women, personal growth for women, and leadership concerns for women.

Bishop McKenzie currently serves as president of the Council of Bishops. In this position, she is the highest-ranking woman and the titular head of the majority Black Methodist denomination. Bishop McKenzie is also the presiding prelate of the 13th Episcopal District, which includes the state of Tennessee and the Commonwealth of Kentucky. *C. J. C.*

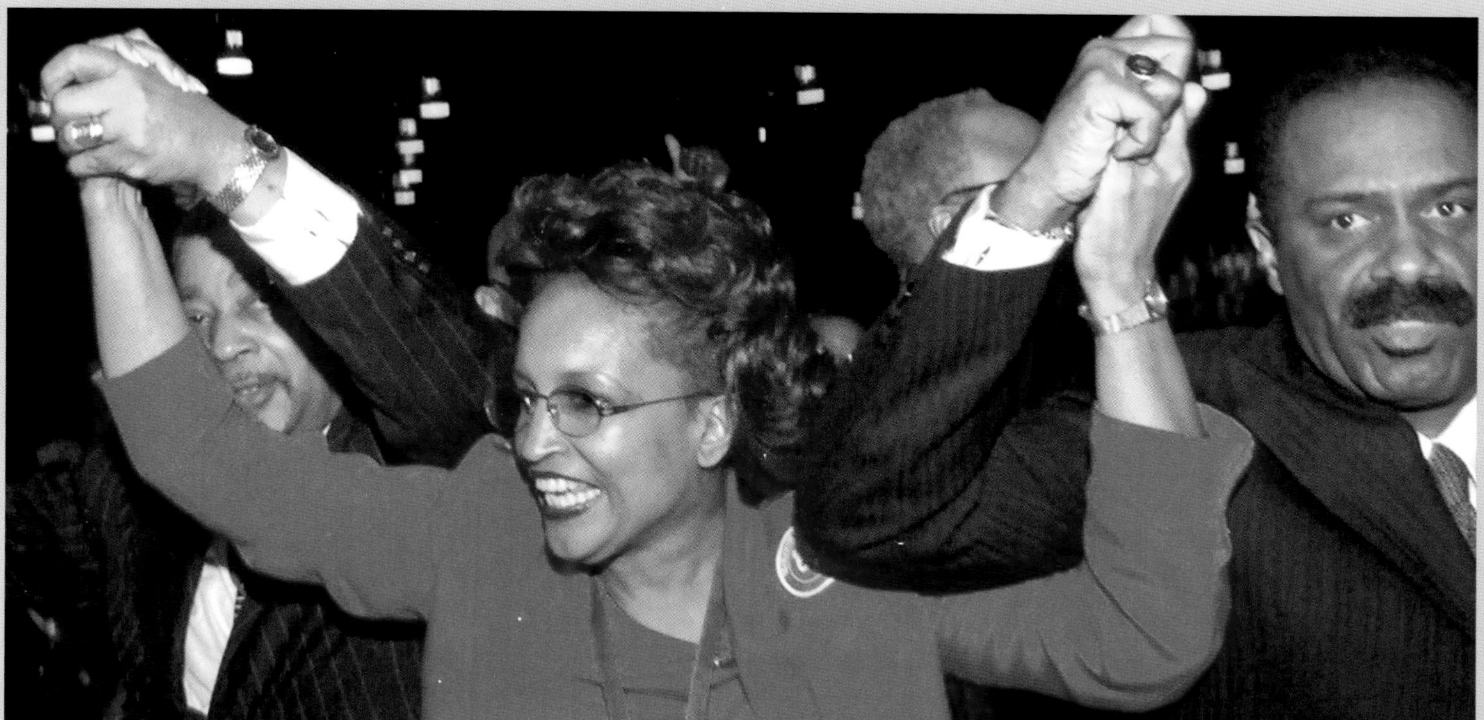

The Rev. Vashti McKenzie became the first woman bishop of the African Methodist Episcopal Church at a 2000 convention in Cincinnati, Ohio.

"The slaves and the free Negroes in the Confederacy expressed their hopes, dreams, and fears in the oral tradition because the written word was illegal for so many years. Music, oratory, informal education, and religion became the channels through which African-American leaders and their followers in various communities rebelled, debated, discussed, and sermonized on every aspect of their lives."

— Michael Frazier, Ph.D., historian

numbers. One historian, Bell I. Wiley, said that blacks that remained on the plantation were not the rule but the exception."

Numerous were the instances where slaves sensing that their freedom was finally imminent revealed their disdain and revulsion of slavery by acting in ways that most slave masters sincerely felt they were incapable of acting. States tried to enact laws to punish slaves for abusive and insulting language. Yet these feeble acts of white desperation were totally meaningless to the slaves. They had begun to taste the fruits of freedom, and the mental shackles of subservience and blind submission were shattered forever. The following scenario aptly captures the prevailing mood of the times. The Richmond newspaper *Enquirer* reported after the Proclamation that a trusted slave coachman, upon learning of his freedom, boldly entered his master's living quarters and donned the master's best clothes, watch, chain, and walking stick. He then confronted his former master in his parlor and announced that he would have to drive his own coach in the future. This incident is even more significant when recognizing that, in the plantation slave hierarchy, the coachman held a high position of authority and "freedom." They were trusted to care for the master's prime steeds and could travel far and wide in their transportation duties. A North Carolina white is reported to have said in 1864, "Our Negroes are beginning to show that they understand the current state of affairs, and insolence and insubordination are quite common."

ON THE BATTLEFIELD

From the beginning of the nation's history, Blacks had fought in the major wars between 1776 and 1861. Their payout in terms of freedom and equality was infinitesimal. Yet the issue of Black courage and valor in war became a topic of discussion leading up to the Civil War. Harding describes the situation thusly: "The black abolitionists offered wartime service by their people as evidence of a deserving status, yet knew the black men should not have to prove their right to freedom by their capacity to kill in white men's war." Moreover, in describing the nation leading up to the Civil War, he continues, "What it did not face was that all America was a slave society, that between the white north and the white south the ties of sentiment, consanguinity, and capital were deep, that they would not be broken by anything less than profound and bloody trauma, if even then."

Although Blacks were initially not allowed to take up arms in the Civil War, the Union did relent in 1862. It took the Confederacy three more years before officially permitting slaves to enter the fighting forces of the South. President of the Confederacy Jefferson Davis signed the authorization on March 13, 1865, but it was too late. The South surrendered a month later.

Franklin stated, "Enlistment of blacks was, however, a notable success: more than 186,000 had enrolled in the Union army by the end of the war. From the seceded states came 93,000, and from the borders slave states, 40,000. The remainder, approximately 53,000, were from free states. It is possible that the total figure was larger, for some contemporaries insisted that many mulattoes served in white regiments without being designated as blacks."

The issue of Black courage and valor is best captured in excerpts from the farewell address given by Lieutenant Colonel C. T. Trowbridge to the Blacks in his 33rd United States Colored Troops on February 9, 1866: "And from that little band of hopeful, trusting, and brave men, who gathered at Camp Saxton, on Port Royal Island, in the fall of 1862, amidst the terrible prejudices that then surrounded us, has grown an army of a hundred and forty thousand black soldiers, whose valor and heroism have won for your race a name which will live as long as the undying pages of history shall endure; and by whose efforts, united with those of the white man, armed rebellion has been conquered, the millions of bondmen have been emancipated, and the fundamental law of the land has been so

Black soldiers of the U.S. Colored Infantry, 84th Regiment, fought valiantly in campaigns throughout Louisiana, as memorialized on their regimental colors.

altered as to remove forever the possibility of human slavery being re-established within the borders of redeemed America."

He concludes with these words: "Soldiers, you have done your duty, and acquitted yourselves like men, who, actuated by such ennobling motives, could not fail; and as the result of your fidelity and obedience, you have won your freedom. And O, how great the reward!"

Thus the 78-year struggle between 1787 and 1865 ended with kernels of freedom and equality having been sown in the soil of mid-19th-century America. Though slavery had ended, its insidious vestige of racism would haunt Black America well into the next century. However, black men, women, children, families, churches, and organizations were accustomed to the struggle. So they pressed on, undaunted, though sometimes weary, but nevertheless freedom and equality were in sight. For them, turning back was not an option.

Teachers, Inventors, Liberators

A GALLERY

Before and after the Civil War, slaves and freed black people made significant accomplishments as freedom fighters, educators, enlisted soldiers, educators, doctors, inventors, preachers, and more. Prominent among those contributors to society include Catherine (Katy) Ferguson, Harriet Tubman, and Norbert Rillieux.

CATHERINE FERGUSON

Born around 1744 on a schooner en route from New York to a new slaveholder in Virginia, Catherine (Katy) Williams was taught the scriptures by her mother, contravening the approved dictates of the time. Yet Ferguson was soon separated from her mother. After being purchased by an abolitionist sympathizer at the age of 16, Katy was given enough money to pay for her freedom. She married a man named Ferguson at the age of 18. In 1793, after the deaths of her husband and two children, she began holding Sunday school classes—the country's first—for children in her home. She later moved her classes to the basement of the home of her pastor, Dr. Mason. He provided her with assistants who taught secular courses while she taught the scriptures to her students. The schoolrooms became known as the Murray Street Sabbath School, over which Ferguson supervised the teaching and welfare of students for more than 40 years. She died in 1854 of cholera, but her legacy lived on as New York City named a facility for her in 1920, the Katy Ferguson Home for unwed black mothers.

A former slave, Catherine Ferguson started the country's first Sunday school in her home and continued educating for more than 40 years.

HARRIET TUBMAN

One of 11 children, Harriet Tubman was born Araminta Ross in the early 1820s on a plantation in Bucktown, on Maryland's Eastern Shore. She encountered her owner's whip from the tender age of seven.

Harriet initially worked in the master's home, or the "big house," but was demoted to work in the fields and on the woodpiles because she was thought to be simpleminded. Even as a child, she worked from sunup to sundown. At age 15, she intervened in a scuffle between a runaway slave and an overseer. For her troubles, the overseer hurled a two-pound iron weight at her, striking her in the forehead. She was left for dead in the field. Although she survived, the injury caused her to suffer sleeping seizures and dizzy spells for the rest of her life.

Five years after Harriet married a freed slave named John Tubman in 1844, she feared that she would be sold to another plantation owner. She ran away, following the North Star by night. She made her way to Philadelphia, where she worked and saved her money. When she felt that the time was right, she made several dangerous treks back to the old plantation and other locations in the South and rescued her brother, sisters, nieces, and others. She also rescued other slaves, which earned her the nickname of "Moses," referring to the Bible and Negro spirituals. She tried to rescue her husband during one of her trips but found that he had remarried. These incursions came to be known as traveling on the Underground Railroad.

Harriet went on to become a "conductor" of the Underground Railroad, a spy for the North during the Civil War, and a freedom fighter. She led more than 300 slaves to freedom, earning for herself an honored place in history. Harriet was proud to say that she never lost a passenger. She retired to Albany, New York, where she is buried near Frederick Douglass, another great freedom fighter.

Harriet Tubman (above), standing on the far left with Gertrude Davis Watson, Nelson Davis, and others, freed more than 300 slaves in her lifetime. Born free in Louisiana and educated in Paris, Norbert Rillieux (below) revolutionized the sugar industry.

NORBERT RILLIEUX

Sugar was not always a staple in American homes. It was originally an upper-class luxury item, until 1843 when Norbert Rillieux invented the multiple-effect vacuum pan evaporator. His invention became widely used in the sugar-refining industry, increasing efficiency and escalating the rate of production, thus causing a reduction in its price.

Rillieux was born in New Orleans, Louisiana, in 1806 as a free man. His mother was an African American, and his father was a French engineer and plantation owner. Rillieux was educated as a chemical engineer at École Centrale in Paris. After graduating, Rillieux became the school's youngest instructor in his department. While there, he published many papers on the technology involved in steam mechanics.

After Reconstruction, conditions for African Americans in Louisiana were so oppressive that Rillieux decided to return to Paris. He became headmaster at École Centrale and went on to study Egyptology, helping to decipher hieroglyphics.

CHAPTER EIGHT

Legacy of Slavery

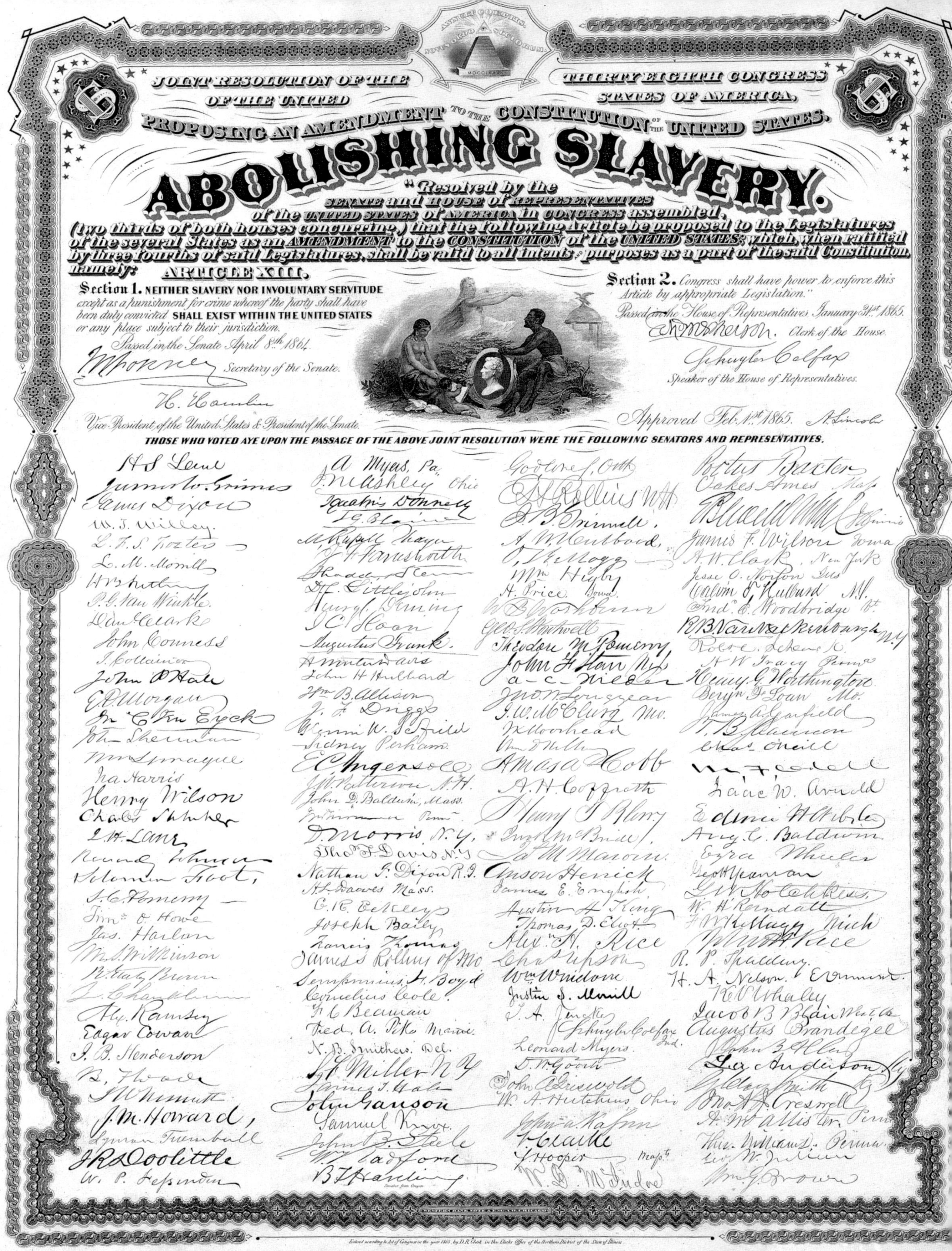

ANNUIT COEPTIS
NOVUS ORDO SECLORUM
MDCCLXXVI
JOINT RESOLUTION OF THE THIRTY EIGHTH CONGRESS OF THE UNITED STATES OF AMERICA,
PROPOSING AN AMENDMENT TO THE CONSTITUTION OF THE UNITED STATES.
ABOLISHING SLAVERY.
"Resolved by the SENATE and HOUSE of REPRESENTATIVES of the UNITED STATES of AMERICA in CONGRESS assembled, (two thirds of both houses concurring,) that the following Article be proposed to the Legislatures of the several States as an AMENDMENT to the CONSTITUTION of the UNITED STATES: which, when ratified by three fourths of said Legislatures, shall be valid to all intents and purposes as a part of the said Constitution, namely:
ARTICLE XIII.
Section 1. NEITHER SLAVERY NOR INVOLUNTARY SERVITUDE except as a punishment for crime whereof the party shall have been duly convicted SHALL EXIST WITHIN THE UNITED STATES or any place subject to their jurisdiction.
Section 2. Congress shall have power to enforce this Article by appropriate Legislation."
Passed in the Senate April 8th 1864.
Secretary of the Senate.
H. Hamlin
Vice President of the United States & President of the Senate.
Passed in the House of Representatives January 31st 1865.
Clerk of the House.
Schuyler Colfax
Speaker of the House of Representatives.
Approved Feb. 1st 1865. A. Lincoln
THOSE WHO VOTED AYE UPON THE PASSAGE OF THE ABOVE JOINT RESOLUTION WERE THE FOLLOWING SENATORS AND REPRESENTATIVES.

Legacy of Slavery

The year 1865 marked the end of the Civil War and the beginning of an era known as Reconstruction, a period of rebuilding on political, social, and economic levels in the aftermath of war. Reconstruction was also a period in which former slaves began to exercise their newly won freedom granted by the 13th Amendment to the U.S. Constitution (ratified in 1865). Thus, Blacks embarked upon a quest for civil rights and education, tantamount to their survival after slavery. While Blacks made notable gains in these areas, they did so under threats of reenslavement and domestic terrorism that characterized the Reconstruction era.

Blacks achieved political distinction at the state and federal levels. In 1868, John Willis Menard of Louisiana became the first Black to be elected to the U.S. Congress, but the federal government refused to seat him. In 1870, Joseph H. Rainey of South Carolina became the first Black to serve in the House of Representatives (1870- 1879). In that same year, Hiram R. Revels of Mississippi became the first African-American U.S. senator. Because he occupied the seat vacated by Jefferson Davis, Revels did not serve a full term. Blanche K. Bruce of Mississippi became the first Black to serve a full term in the U.S. Senate (1875- 1881). Menard, Revels, Bruce, and Rainey embodied the struggles of African-American people. Menard, Bruce, and Rainey were born into slavery, but they rose above their conditions. Bruce, in particular, escaped slavery in Virginia. As former slaves, they had insight into the problems faced by Blacks in freedom. Although Revels was a free Black, he was no less cognizant of the struggles of former slaves. To expedite slavery's demise, Revels recruited Blacks to serve in the Union Army. As legislators, Menard, Revels, Bruce, and Rainey championed civil rights legislation. For example, in the House of Representatives, Rainey introduced the Ku Klux Klan Act (aka Civil Rights Act) of 1871, in order to curb the violence that the Klan unleashed on proponents of civil rights. In April 1871, President Grant signed the Ku Klux Act designed to destroy the Klan.

Blacks viewed political enfranchisement and education, two forms of enfranchisement that had been denied them as slaves, as being inextricably linked to their survival in the Reconstruction period. Two notable teachers, Charlotte Forten and Mary S. Peake, laid the instructional foundation for Black education during Reconstruction. Charlotte Forten became the first black teacher at Penn Center, located on St. Helena Island, South Carolina, that began to provide education to Blacks as early as 1862. Forten might also be hailed as the first to offer formal instruction in Black history, teaching her pupils about historical figures such as Toussaint L'Ouverture. Blacks began to receive higher education with the founding of what are now called historically black universities and colleges (HBCUs), such as Hampton Normal and Agricultural Institute (currently known as Hampton University). Emancipation Oak, located on

Left: Souvenir copies of the 13th Amendment, signed by President Abraham Lincoln and members of Congress in 1865, commemorated the abolition of slavery.

Previous pages: Freedom did not guarantee an easier life for African Americans in the South, as this circa 1901 photograph depicts.

"It seemed to me a great hardship that I was born poor, and it seemed an even greater hardship that I should have been born a Negro. . . . Later I . . . came to see that, along with his disadvantages, the Negro in America had some advantages, and I made up my mind that opportunities that had been denied him from without could be more than made up by greater concentration and power within.."

— Booker T. Washington, educator and author

African-American students congregate outside the main hall of Howard University in Washington, D.C., one of nine Black colleges founded after the Civil War.

Hampton's campus, provided the shade for the first public reading of the Emancipation Proclamation in 1863. Listed on the National Register of Historic Places, Emancipation Oak is also significant because, under its canopy, Mary S. Peake delivered educational instruction to Blacks in the vicinity of Fort Monroe as early as 1861. Mary S. Peake and Emancipation Oak are significant to Hampton's early history that is "rooted" in the education of former slaves, their descendants, and Native Americans. From Hampton's roots sprang notable graduates such as Booker T. Washington, first president of Tuskegee University (née Normal School for Colored Teachers in 1881), and educator Robert Russa Moton, Tuskegee's second president. In fact, Moton raised more than ten million dollars for Tuskegee, and he prevented whites from seizing control of the

institution's Veterans Hospital that remained under the supervision of Blacks. From Tuskegee's roots sprang George Washington Carver and the Tuskegee Airmen. As a botanist, Carver is credited with reviving the southern economy by discovering new applications for peanuts, soybeans, and yams. The Tuskegee Airmen were Black fighter pilots who successfully escorted U.S. bombers to various European destinations during World War II, without losing any bombers to enemy fire.

The education of Blacks was not the exclusive domain of schools, for ordinary citizens felt it their collective responsibility to "uplift the race" through education. In this regard, Hiram Revels served as an educator before he became a U.S. Senator, and Joseph Rainey sought federal aid for education. Many Blacks received their first reading and writing

An 1872 lithograph shows the country's first African-American senators and representatives; they served in the 41st and 42nd U.S. Congress.

lessons in the homes of people within their respective communities, or they received them in their churches wherein the Bible served as their first text. In the education of Blacks, the role of the Black church must not be overlooked. Historically, the church has served multiple functions in the Black community, rendering educational, economic, and social services that the larger society denied Blacks. Services not obtained from the church were received from mutual-aid societies and fraternal lodges. For example, Blacks initiated burial societies to cover the costs of burying family members. They could not obtain burial loans from white lenders, and they could not bury their dead in cemeteries reserved for whites. Hence, Blacks faced racial segregation in life and in death.

Within Black communities, self-help and communalism were encouraged as modes of survival. Outside of the Black communities, the Freedmen's Bureau (The Bureau of Refugees, Freedmen, and Abandoned Lands) was the major federally supported institution to which Blacks turned for assistance. The Freedmen's Bureau supplied teachers and funding to Black schools. Although the Freedmen's Bureau helped Blacks obtain employment, bureau officials drafted labor contracts in favor of plantation and business owners, to the detriment of black laborers. Racial discrimination, internal corruption, and collusion between ex-Confederates and U.S. President Andrew Johnson, a former slave owner who originally opposed the implementation of the Freedmen's Bureau, contributed to the dismantling of the bureau.

"One ever feels his two-ness,—an American, a Negro; two souls, two thoughts, two unreconciled strivings; two warring ideals in one dark body, whose dogged strength alone keeps it from being torn asunder."

— *W. E. B. Du Bois, educator, writer*

"THE NEGRO PROBLEM"

In freedom, Blacks were eager to exercise their physical mobility in the quest for rights and resources. Exercising that mobility, however, left former plantations, mills, and mines without adequate labor forces. Economically, the war ended, but cotton continued to grow; lumber continued to be milled; railroads continued to be built; and coal continued to be mined. Without adequate labor, none of these industries were very productive. Herein emerged the second of what was dubbed "The Negro Problem" in America. Essentially, the problem involved creating a supply of cheap, expendable

The Truth Teller: Ida B. Wells Barnett

In May 1884, schoolteacher Ida B. Wells and two of her sisters boarded the ladies' coach of a Chesapeake and Ohio train bound for Memphis, Tennessee. Born in 1862 to former slaves in Holly Springs, Mississippi, Wells had been a schoolteacher in Mississippi and had secured a higher-paying position at a school in Memphis. She and her sisters would take the train to Memphis to stay with their aunt. Along the way, an encounter with segregation would change Wells's life forever, inspiring her to become a journalist, to dedicate her life to exposing the plight of black people in the United States, and to champion the causes of civil, economic, and women's rights.

As the three sisters took their seats in the coach, the conductor informed them that they had to relocate to the segregated coach. Wells refused: "As I was in the ladies' car, I proposed to stay." After a scuffle with the conductor, she and her sisters were forcibly removed from the train. Wells sued the railroad company for refusing to honor her first-class ticket. Initially, she won the case and was awarded $500, but unfortunately, the state supreme court reversed the decision on appeal and ruled in favor of the railroad company, saying that it had satisfied the statutory requirements by providing "like accommodations." The court's decision drove Wells to pen her first journalistic piece, an account of her experiences that appeared in the *Living Way*, a religious weekly. Ida's career as a publisher had begun, and became her primary venue for exposing the horrors of lynching and for advocating for equal rights.

In 1891, Wells put aside teaching and devoted herself full-time to journalism, a career she had been pursuing since 1889, when she accepted the editorship of the Memphis *Free Speech and Headlight*. In its pages, she first wrote about the evils of lynching after three close colleagues of hers were shot and hanged by a mob. She continued to write about lynching, and her work drew national attention as it exposed the gruesome details that would eventually move people to act against the practice. Her articles attracted great danger; the *Free Speech* offices were destroyed by a white mob while Wells was away on a speaking tour. Refusing to be intimidated, Wells continued her campaign for antilynching laws.

Wells eventually left Memphis and relocated to Chicago in 1894. In 1895, she married Ferdinand Lee Barnett, a lawyer and founder of Chicago's first Black newspaper, the *Conservator*. In that same year, she published *A Red Record*, a definitive statistical work on lynching in the United States that disproved the myth that lynching was a means to protect white women from assaults by black men. The book launched a nationwide antilynching campaign with Wells squarely at the front of it.

Wells toned down her rhetoric as she raised her children. She spoke out whenever atrocities occurred. She appealed to a responsive Black community to support her efforts with the Anti-Lynching Bureau.

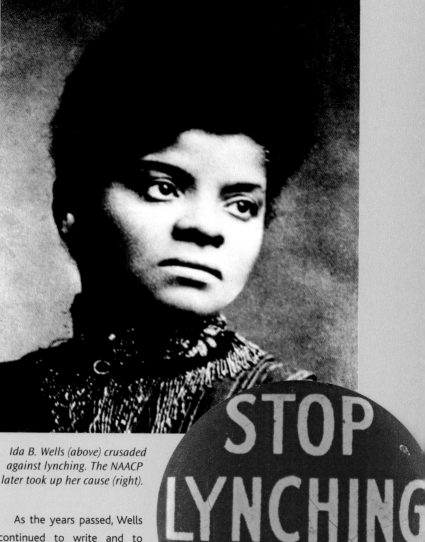

Ida B. Wells (above) crusaded against lynching. The NAACP later took up her cause (right).

As the years passed, Wells continued to write and to come to the aid of poor people who needed to have their stories told. She campaigned for women's suffrage and co-founded the National Association for the Advancement of Colored People (NAACP) with W. E. B. Du Bois in 1909. She encouraged all Black citizens—rich and poor—to overcome their fears, to organize, and to take the lead in fighting for freedom over segregation and racist oppression. When she died in 1931, her many relentless campaigns, writings, and speeches cemented her place as one of the most influential advocators for social change in U.S. history.

C. J. C.

"Section 1. Neither slavery nor involuntary servitude, except as a punishment for a crime whereof the party shall have been duly convicted, shall exist within the United States, or any place subject to their jurisdiction. Section 2. Congress shall have power to enforce this article by appropriate legislation."

—Amendment XIII, U.S. Constitution

laborers who could revitalize plantations and industries to productive levels. The solution, once again, hinged on legal apparatus used to facilitate the reenslavement of black men, women, and children. In this context, the language of the 13th Amendment to the U.S. Constitution (ratified in 1865) is extremely troublesome because it prohibited slavery and involuntary servitude, on the one hand, but, on the other, it allowed for the reenslavement of freedmen as a punishment for "a crime whereof the party shall have been duly convicted." In instances where ex-slaves accused of committing crimes were being adjudged and convicted by ex-Confederates, former masters, and labor-starved plantation owners, their convictions were both duly and automatic.

Increasingly, Blacks were warehoused within prison walls, constituting reservoirs of cheap convict labor that could be tapped as necessary. Such reservoirs included Alabama State Penitentiary (aka "The Walls"), Parchman Farm (Mississippi), and Angola Prison Farm (Louisiana). Parchman and Angola began their histories as plantations. In particular, Angola was named for the West African country from which Africans were exported to North America for the purposes of slavery. The fact that Parchman and Angola are still extant speaks to their conversion from plantations to prisons. Where slavery ended, the prison-industrial complex emerged to warehouse massive numbers of Blacks for the purposes of exploitation via convict-leasing schemes. The scheme worked as follows: Blacks were arrested on the charges of vagrancy, stealing, or something as vague and amorphous as insulting whites. In other cases, the charges were simply trumped-up; they were given harsh, lengthy sentences for minor infractions; and prison officials, with the political backing of the governor, leased black men, women, and children to anyone who would pay good money for them.

Convict leasing became a major industry during Reconstruction, one that supplied cheap labor to those who needed it and one that generated revenue for county coffers, magistrates, governors, and wardens of prisons. "By 1890, the convict lease [system] in Alabama had become a huge operation, supplying bodies like the slave trade of old. Black males, age twelve and older, went directly to the mines; black women, black children, and 'cripples' were leased to lumber companies and to farms," according to Oshinsky. With numerous arrests, the jails and prisons could remain stocked with laborers, much like the European factories along the African coasts were stocked with slaves during the slave trade, the major difference being that as a slave, black people were valuable property, but as convicts, they were expendable. Many Blacks died inside the walls of prisons, and they died in labor situations that denied them treatment for diseases including malarial fevers, dysentery, pneumonia, poisoning from their iron shackles, and gunshot wounds received for refusing a work detail, for attempting to escape, or for insulting the guard or overseer. Thus, imprisonment was a veritable death sentence for many Blacks, genocide by proxy.

LEGAL PROBLEMS

While Confederate states had agreed to extend civil rights and other protections to Blacks as a condition of readmission to the Union in theory, they did not honor that condition in practice. Thus, the conflict that developed during Reconstruction is between legislating laws such as the Civil Rights Act of 1875 and upholding them. A secondary legal problem developed relative to the extent to which ex-Confederates and former slave owners occupied seats in various federal and state legislatures, affording them unique positions from which to reinterpret, and manipulate, the laws to carry out their agenda, namely, the reduction of Blacks to peonage. Confederates, angered by the fact that they had lost

A Noose's Power: The Jena Six

On September 1, 2006, students at Jena High School found several nooses hanging from a tree on school grounds. Following several related incidents, including an attack of a white student by six black students, Jena High School caught the attention of a nation and the six students became known as the Jena Six.

The school is located in the small segregated town of Jena, Louisiana. White students congregate under a large tree in the school yard, while black students typically gather on the bleachers near the school auditorium. During a school assembly on August 31, a black male student asked the principal for permission to sit under the tree and was told he could sit wherever he wanted. After the assembly ended, he and his friends sat under the white students' tree. The next morning, the nooses were found hanging from one of the branches. To many, the noose remains a disturbing and frightening symbol of white racism in America.

Three white students were found responsible, but the board of education concluded that the nooses were a prank and the students did not understand the racial overtones of their actions. Black students reacted by staging a sit-in until law enforcement officers were called in.

Throughout the fall, racial tension heightened. On December 4, six black students attacked a white student who was taunting them with racial slurs. The white student was taken to the hospital with minor injuries and was released. The six black students were expelled and later arrested.

Five of the Jena Six—Robert Bailey, Jr., Mychal Bell, Carwin Jones, Bryant Purvis, and Theo Shaw—were 18 and under, but were charged as adults with attempted second-degree murder. Jesse Rae Beard was only 14 and was charged as a juvenile. Only Mychal Bell was convicted by an all-white grand jury because of past criminal activity. His trial was set for September 20, 2007, and, on that date, roughly 15,000 protesters marched in Jena. Seven days later, Bell was released but rearrested to face 18 months in a juvenile facility.

On July 31, 2007, the tree was cut down and removed from school grounds.

D. W.

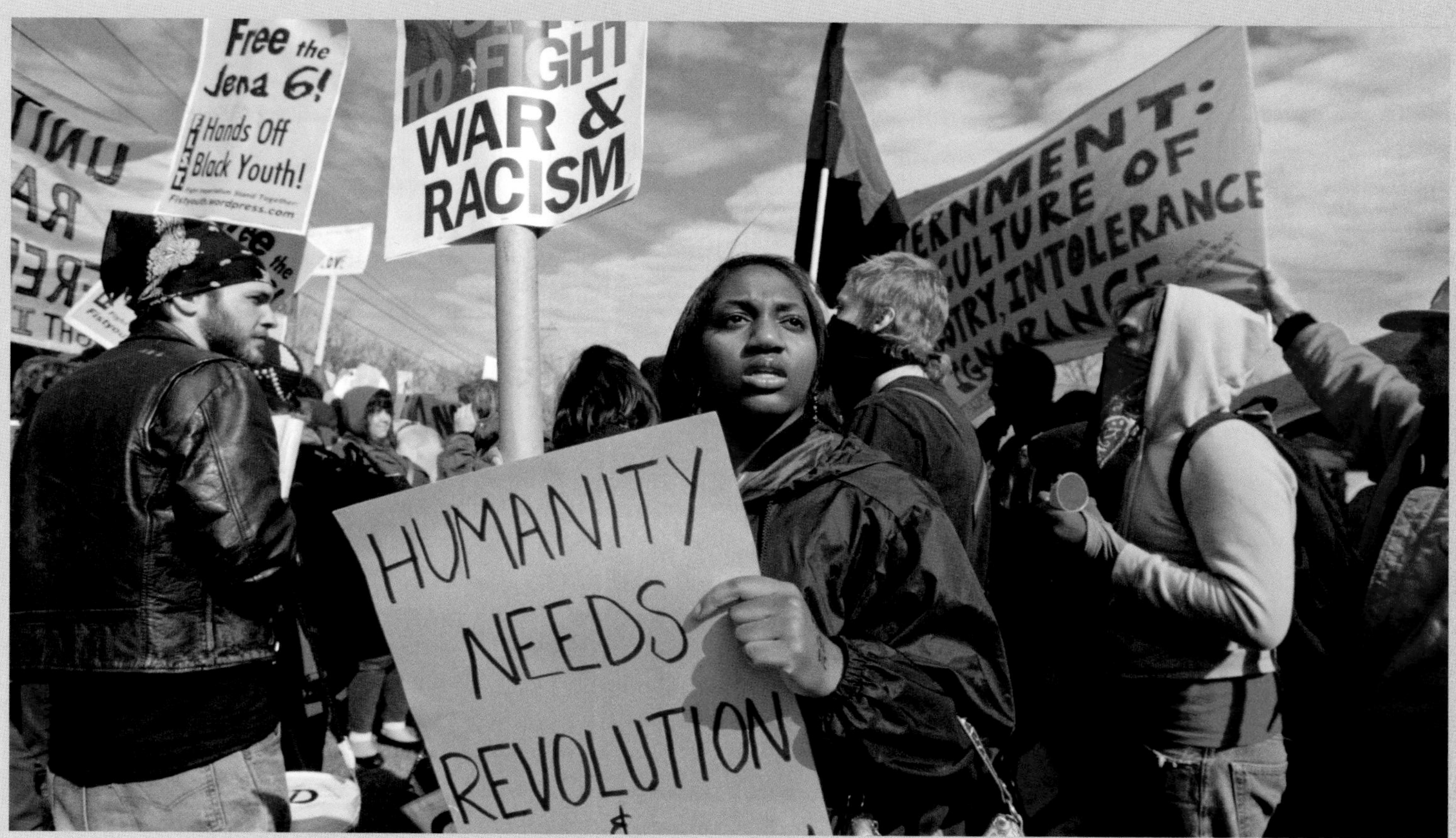

Student protestors rally behind the Jena Six in Jena, Louisiana. The case, which charged six black students at Jena High School with attempted second-degree murder, drew national attention to the racial tensions of a small town and persistent racial bias in the legal system.

Freedom Denied, Freedom Gained

GERALD A. FOSTER, PH.D.

There is an erroneous perception that something magical happened on April 9, 1865. On that day, chattel slavery ended along with the Civil War. With the Confederacy's surrender at Appomattox Courthouse, four million slaves became free. So what did it mean from the perspective of the slave on April 9, 1865, to be free at last?

Freedom for the slaves meant regaining control over their lives and the lives of those dependent on them. No longer would they have to yield to the inhumane dictates of brutal masters and overseers; no longer could they be beaten with impunity for no good reason; no longer would wives, sisters, and daughters be violated and abused; no longer would families be ripped apart and auctioned away; no longer would they be forced to work from sunup to sundown; no longer would they be pursued by men and dogs seeking to capture them as they ran away from the daily cruelty of slavery.

Therefore freedom meant the end of past atrocities, but what did it mean for the future? Where exactly would the slaves go upon leaving the plantation; how and where would they live?

PROTECTION

In the midst of these dilemmas, the primary goal of the freed slaves was to reconnect with long-lost family members. So, many wandered hither and yonder in search of kindred spirits. Few fully understood the practical implications of the 13th, 14th, and 15th Amendments to the U.S. Constitution; however, they did know that they were protected by the presence of federal troops in the defeated South, initially at least. One of the more important lessons of the century following the Civil War was the relative impotence of the Supreme Court to enforce its democratic principles. This power rested almost exclusively with state legislatures. In the South, these legal bodies were committed to returning African-American citizens to their former state of servile dependency by any means necessary—legal or illegal. To help fully understand the legacy of slavery, one needs to view the interconnectedness of the 1857 *Dred Scott* v. *Sanford* Supreme Court decision, the 1896 *Plessy* v. *Ferguson* decision, and the 1954 *Brown* v. *Board of Education of Topeka* decision. *Scott* declared that Blacks had no rights that whites were bound to respect; *Plessy* found that the existing Jim Crow laws were in fact legal and that Blacks and whites could be segregated in all circles of life; *Brown* struck down *Plessy* but again needed the 1964 Civil Rights Act and the 1965 Voting Rights Act to offer any real relief to the fourth-generation progeny of the four million slaves freed a century earlier in 1865.

Gerald A. Foster has studied the struggle for African Americans to gain a foothold on freedom in the decades following the Civil War.

OVERCOMING OBSTACLES

People who labored tirelessly and courageously in relative obscurity to ensure that Blacks attained the freedom articulated in the U.S. Constitution made invaluable contributions. White men of conscience, in spite of the racist terror tactics of the times, are included in this progressive cadre. On May 19, 1856, Charles Sumner, a staunch abolitionist senator from Massachusetts, delivered one of the most powerful and controversial antislavery speeches in the U.S. Congress. For his audacity, a South Carolina congressman who was offended by Sumner's speech beat Sumner mercilessly at his Senate desk. The senator never fully recovered from the assault, but continued undaunted in his abolitionist crusade. In 1862, he greatly influenced Abraham Lincoln's Emancipation Proclamation.

Over 100 years later in the state of Alabama, a little-known white defense attorney, Frank M. Johnson, Jr., successfully convicted two white men for the enslavement and murder of a black man, Herbert Thompson, who had been held against his will on a large plantation in Sumter County, Alabama. An all-white male jury found two white brothers guilty of peonage (involuntary servitude) under federal statutes adopted during Reconstruction to "protect the rights of freedmen." Presiding Judge Seybourn Lynne told Johnson, "You will be the last United States Attorney in the South to get a conviction for slavery." The Monday following Johnson's case, the U.S. Supreme Court unanimously ruled in the landmark *Brown* v. *Board of Education* case. Johnson went on

Thurgood Marshall (left) assists client Donald Gaines Murray, an African-American student who was denied entry into the University of Maryland Law School, in proceedings at the Maryland Court of Appeals. The case, Murray v. Pearson, *was decided in favor of Murray.*

to become the youngest federal judge in the country when President Eisenhower appointed him to the middle district court in Alabama. Over the next two decades, Johnson—amid death threats and bombings of his home—fought racism and discrimination.

In the Black legal arena, the most influential force in skillfully crafting the strategy leading up to the Brown decision success was Charles Hamilton Houston. Although other Black attorneys received much more acclaim, Houston worked tirelessly behind the scenes to ensure judicial success in May 1954. Houston, by far the most brilliant visionary of the legal team that ultimately ended segregation in America, died four years before the landmark *Brown* decision. Houston taught, trained, and mentored all of the key lawyers involved in the *Brown* victory. The strategic plan for dismantling segregation in America began in 1929, when Houston was appointed vice-dean of the Howard University Law School. The school had been denied accreditation, but through Houston's tireless efforts, accreditation was received a year after his arrival. Houston's best student was Thurgood Marshall, who succeeded him as special counsel for the NAACP and eventually successfully argued the *Brown* case before the Supreme Court. Houston's failing health, which included tuberculosis, exhaustion, and a bad heart, eviscerated his body, but his mind remained strong until the end.

FREEDOM DELAYED

In spite of the social, economic, and political impediments cast in their paths, many Blacks managed to succeed. They educated themselves, created businesses, self-help organizations, and churches, and lived in vibrant all-Black communities where doctors and teachers lived beside railroad conductors and janitors. The freedom that was denied them in the courts only galvanized their dreams of freedom pounding restlessly in their hearts and minds.

In the end, slavery's legacy was not freedom denied, but freedom delayed. In spite of terrorism, peonage, lynching, Jim Crow laws, and insurmountable social, economic, and political impediments, Blacks prevailed and began to exercise more control over their daily lives. They refused to be returned to a mentality of slavery and resisted attempts to discourage and intimidate them on all fronts. ■

A bloodstained Ku Klux Klan robe (above) suggests the violence for which the white supremacist group, meeting around a burning cross at right, was known.

KKK

Chain gangs, popular in the post-Reconstruction South, reenslaved African-American convicts by forcing them into harsh labor and dangerous working conditions.

the Civil War and the very property over which the war was fought—the slave—avenged the loss via racial discrimination and violence against freedmen. In American culture, Reconstruction is often discussed as a period of freedom and enfranchisement for Blacks. But the discussion must address the degree to which Reconstruction was also a period of reenslavement and domestic terrorism. Blacks had been terrorized by sadistic masters, slave patrols, slave catchers, and slave snatchers, but the terrorism became genocidal during Reconstruction.

In 1866, one year after Reconstruction began, the Ku Klux Klan formed in Pulaski, Tennessee, under the leadership of Nathan Bedford Forrest, an ex-Confederate. The Klan used intimidation, fearmongering, and murder to deprive Blacks of freedom, enfranchisement, and social mobility. The United States became a killing field in which black men, women, and children were lynched on various pretexts and often without provocation. Although various pieces of legislation had been passed to protect the rights of Blacks, that legislation could not save Blacks from the ravages of vengeful Klansmen, members of White Citizens' Council, White League, and rifle club, as well as other domestic terrorists who were angered by the loss of their master status, defined by the slave who was no longer in their possession. From its inception, the process of

A Great American Intellect: W. E. B. Du Bois

William Edward Burghardt Du Bois is considered one of the most influential African-American men in history. Ranked with such 19th-century giants as Frederick Douglass and Booker T. Washington, Du Bois sharply disagreed with the latter on strategies that freed slaves should employ for social and economic progress.

Born in the small Massachusetts town of Great Barrington in 1868, Du Bois and his mother were nearly the only African-American residents of the town. Du Bois moved to Nashville, Tennessee, to attend Fisk University, a historically Black institution, then attended Harvard University, where he earned a bachelor's degree in 1890. Further studies took him to the University of Berlin. He was becoming an intellectual force and solidified this position by returning to Harvard to become its first African American to earn a Ph.D. in 1895, writing his dissertation on the suppression of the African slave trade.

Unable to find a teaching position at any of the leading white universities, Du Bois taught for a year at a small Black college called Wilberforce in Ohio. He was then invited to take a post at the University of Pennsylvania. Du Bois began his research and teaching career in the area of sociological studies of Philadelphia's Black neighborhoods. His findings were soon published, along with his first collection of essays, *The Souls of Black Folk*, which was released in 1903. Many scholars have called this book the most important African-American publication of all time. In it, he dismisses the accommodating stance taken by Booker T. Washington and identifies "the color line" as the central problem of the 20th century. He wrote, "[Mr. Washington] does not rightly value the privilege and duty of voting, belittles the emasculating effects of caste distinctions, and opposes the higher training and ambition of our brighter minds . . . we must unceasingly and firmly oppose [him]."

In an effort to secure full civil rights for African Americans, in 1905 Du Bois joined William Monroe Trotter, the outspoken editor of the Black newspaper *Boston Guardian,* in forming the Niagara movement. This movement, though short-lived in its efforts to secure full civil and voting rights for African Americans, did serve as an impetus for Du Bois and others to found the most influential civil rights organization of the 20th century, the National Association for the Advancement of Colored People (NAACP). The early organization was made up mostly of white leadership, and Du Bois was the only black officer, serving as director of publications and research while living in Atlanta.

In 1910, Du Bois moved to the NAACP's New York headquarters, where he founded the association's magazine, *The Crisis*. As editor, he published the work of the literary luminaries of the Harlem Renaissance, including Langston Hughes, Countee Cullen, and others. His editorials revealed an evolution of his intellectual thoughts over the 20-plus years that he remained at the helm.

Moving beyond American race relations, Du Bois embraced international economics and politics. He helped to organize the Pan-African Congress of 1919, wrote many publications on matters of race, including one called *The Talented Tenth*, and was at the forefront of many conflicts and controversies. Du Bois worked toward international peace, visiting England, Holland, China, Russia, and other counties. He moved to Ghana with his wife, writer Shirley Graham Du Bois, in 1961, after attending the presidential inauguration of his friend Kwame Nkrumah. Du Bois died in Ghana at the age of 94, six months after receiving full citizenship in 1963. He remained active in political and intellectual pursuits throughout his long life, and his legacy still casts a shadow on pressing debates of our day.

Du Bois's Talented Tenth theory called for 10 percent of educated Blacks to reach back to help others in the group. Its relevance sparked a debate that still rages today. Du Bois died believing that his theory failed. However, a vast number of educated Blacks remain active in service and mentoring programs. *C. J. C.*

W. E. B. Du Bois, pictured here around 1911, became one of the most influential leaders of his time and one of the most significant thinkers in American history.

Seeking greater freedom and quality of life, many African Americans in the South migrated to the midwestern frontier in the decades following the Civil War.

"This nation . . . having closed its eyes to the cruelties, the injustice and oppression within its own border, has . . . gone off over the seas, in the interest of humanity, so called, to correct the wrongs of other nations, far less cruel and unjust than those being committed, by our own citizens, for whom there is no protection in county, state or nation, in THIS LAND OF LIBERTY AND EQUAL RIGHTS. TRULY A PHENOMENAL PARADOX."

—*Chas. H. Williams, an open letter to the* Chicago Tribune

All Colored People

THAT WANT TO

GO TO KANSAS,

On September 5th, 1877,

Can do so for $5.00

HISTORICAL SOCIETY

IMMIGRATION.

WHEREAS, We, the colored people of Lexington, Ky,. knowing that there is an abundance of choice lands now belonging to the Government, have assembled ourselves together for the purpose of locating on said lands. Therefore,

BE IT RESOLVED, That we do now organize ourselves into a Colony, as follows:—Any person wishing to become a member of this Colony can do so by paying the sum of one dollar ($1.00), and this money is to be paid by the first of September, 1877, in instalments of twenty-five cents at a time, or otherwise as may be desired.

RESOLVED, That this Colony has agreed to consolidate itself with the Nicodemus Towns, Solomon Valley, Graham County, Kansas, and can only do so by entering the vacant lands now in their midst, which costs $5.00.

RESOLVED, That this Colony shall consist of seven officers—President, Vice-President, Secretary, Treasurer, and three Trustees. President—M. M. Bell; Vice-President—Isaac Talbott; Secretary—W. J. Niles; Treasurer—Daniel Clarke; Trustees—Jerry Lee, William Jones, and Abner Webster.

RESOLVED, That this Colony shall have from one to two hundred militia, more or less, as the case may require, to keep peace and order, and any member failing to pay in his dues, as aforesaid, or failing to comply with the above rules in any particular, will not be recognized or protected by the Colony.

enslavement, along with its interdependent components (justification, codification, and enforcement), relegated African-American men, women, and children to the status of inferior beings. Dark skin was equated with inferiority, and this racist ideology was utilized to legitimize and sustain slavery over a period of 400 years, as W. E. B. Du Bois, the first Black to receive a doctorate degree from Harvard University, explains:

> *In order to establish the righteousness of this point of view, science and religion, government and industry, were wheeled into line. The word "Negro" was used for the first time in the world's history to tie color to race and blackness to slavery and degradation. The white race was pictured as "pure" and superior; the black race as dirty, stupid, and inevitably inferior. . . .*

Race-based slavery had deleterious implications for former slaves and former masters who resented the idea of having to compete with Blacks for jobs, housing, and other

The Audacity of Hope: Barack Obama

Barack Obama, Jr., is the first African-American man elected to the U.S. Senate since the election of Edward Brooke from Massachusetts. Senator Brooke, who served from 1967 to 1979, had been the first African American to hold that office since Reconstruction.

Obama was born in Honolulu, Hawaii, in 1961. He was born to a white mother from Kansas, Ann Durham, and a black father of the Luo ethnic group from Kenya, Barack Obama, Sr. Durham's family had been active in the antislavery movement in the 1800s. Obama Sr.'s ethnic group had been active in Kenya's struggle for independence in the 1950s.

The marriage between Obama's parents, who had met when they were college students at the University of Hawaii's Manoa campus, lasted only two years. Obama's father, a government economist, left Hawaii to attend graduate school at Harvard in pursuit of a Ph.D. in economics. Although both Baracks wrote to each other occasionally, the younger Obama met with his father only once, at the age of ten, after his parents divorced. The senior Obama returned to Kenya eventually and died in an automobile accident in the early 1980s.

Ann Durham remarried and moved with her new Indonesian husband to a location near Jakarta when Obama was six years old. Obama lived with his mother and stepfather until he was ten, when Obama's mother gave birth to his half sister, Maya. At that time, Obama's mother sent him back to Hawaii to live with her parents. Shortly after his arrival, his mother and sister joined him. Obama was enrolled in a prestigious private academy called the Punahou School, where he was an average student. By his own admission, he did not become serious about school until he reached college.

Obama attended Occidental College in Los Angeles before transferring to Columbia University. After graduating in 1983, he attended Harvard Law School. He holds the distinction of being the first African American to hold the position of president of the *Harvard Law Review.* He graduated magna cum laude in 1991.

In between college and graduate school, Obama had been actively involved as a community organizer in Harlem. In 1985, he moved to Chicago, where he worked for a church-related group to improve the living conditions of people in poor neighborhoods plagued by crime and unemployment. Upon graduation from Harvard, he was a civil rights attorney in Chicago from 1991 to 1996. In addition, he taught at the University of Chicago from the early 1990s to 1994. Obama was elected Illinois state senator, and served in that capacity from 1996 to 2005. He was elected as junior United States senator in 2005, making him the second African American from Illinois to hold that office, after Carol Moseley Braun.

On June 3, 2008, with his wife, Michelle, by his side, Barack Obama became the Democratic Party's first African-American presumptive presidential nominee.

C. J. C.

Barack Obama (D-Ill.), shown in Kenya in 2006, is the first African American to be the presidential nominee of a major political party.

"Is it not strange, that now, 28 years after Emancipation—after the Amendments to the Constitution—after settling as we thought forever the question of our citizenship, in this country we helped to make and save, that insult is added to injury by the traitorous men who sought to destroy this government, banding themselves together for the avowed purpose of disfranchising, ostracising, and by some means or other, getting rid of 8,000,000 of the most loyal, patriotic, and inoffensive people on this continent, simply because of their color."

— Hon. James M. Townsend, Emancipation celebration, 1891

resources. The racial roots of slavery spawned a legacy of divisiveness in American society, and many whites came to hate and fear the "Negro" and "Negroness." Consequently, Blacks were forever made to feel their "two-ness": They were Black, and they were American: they were American, and they were second-class citizens; they were human, and they were inferior to their white counterparts.

The notions that Blacks were inferior to whites, and that they were unfit for inclusion in American society as free persons, were views held by President Johnson who demonstrated his anti-Black sentiment by using his presidential powers to undermine the progress of Blacks. Early in his administration, he pardoned the Confederates who secured seats in state legislatures. Thus, the Confederates were empowered to implement a series of Black Codes designed to disenfranchise Blacks economically and politically. Specific codes also denied Blacks access to adequate education, and they prohibited Blacks from marrying or cohabitating with whites, classified as a felony. Secondly, Johnson dismissed Edwin M. Stanton, the secretary of war, who supervised the implementation of the Reconstruction Act of 1867 that placed various southern states under martial law, in order to, among other things, curb violence against Blacks. Such a political move left Blacks exposed to revenge and racial killings. Many black men, in particular, were lynched and castrated after being accused of raping or insulting white women. Ida B. Wells, who championed the cause against lynching, articulated the nature of, and the reasons for, lynching in the following manner:

> *It flourishes most largely in the states which foster the convict lease system, and is brought to bear mainly against the Negro. The first fifteen years of his freedom he was murdered by masked mobs for trying to vote. Public opinion having made lynching for that cause unpopular, a new reason is given to justify the murders of the past 15 years. The Negro was first charged with attempting to rule white people, and hundreds were murdered on that pretended supposition. He is now charged with assaulting or attempting to assault white women. This charge, as false as it is foul, robs us of the sympathy of the world and is blasting the race's good name.*

Between 1889 and 1918, American citizens perpetrated 3,211 lynchings. While black men constituted the majority of the lynching victims, women and children were also victimized. In 1901, a mother and her two children were lynched on the accusation that they failed to report a murder before it was committed. Between 1918 and 1927, 11 black women were lynched (three of them were pregnant). In one instance, the fetus was cut out of the abdomen of a woman in her eighth month of pregnancy. As late as 1981, Michael Donald, a young black male, was ambushed and lynched by Klansmen as he walked to a local store in Mobile, Alabama, where a street has been named in remembrance of him.

While Blacks made some political and educational gains during Reconstruction, they did so in an atmosphere of prejudice and racial violence that characterized the period. Significant numbers of Blacks were relegated to the periphery of American society, reduced to sharecropping and other forms of peonage. As president, Johnson vetoed several Reconstruction bills, the Civil Rights Act, and bills meant to extend suffrage to Blacks. Thus, Black progress was seriously impeded by individuals who not only held anti-Black sentiments, but who used their political power to perpetuate an anti-Black agenda. Blacks' hopes for a better life were dashed by the election of Rutherford B. Hayes to the Presidency in 1877. Hayes's legacy is that he withdrew federal troops from the

In this 1940 painting, "Early Morning Work" by William Johnson, African Americans struggle to make the best of rural life.

South, where martial law had been imposed under the Reconstruction Act of 1867. The removal of federal troops meant that Blacks were left without any protection from hate crimes, and the commandeering of seats in the state legislatures by Confederates ensured Blacks' political disfranchisement. These events contributed to the general failure of Reconstruction, relative to the progress of black peoples.

The long history of racial injustice that characterizes American society has undermined black peoples' ability to imagine being simultaneously black and American, having been historically denied full access to rights and privileges enjoyed by white citizens. Racial injustice has also robbed its perpetrators of knowledge of, and an appreciation for, the diversity of the human family. Still, racism persisted in America after Reconstruction, largely because it was deeply rooted in slavery, but also because it had an economic purpose; and it buttressed a pseudodemocracy that reserved life, liberty, and the full pursuit of happiness for only some, contrary to democratic ideals.

Buffalo Soldiers, Tuskegee Airmen

A GALLERY

The period following the Civil War is known as Reconstruction, also called the Second American Revolution. The United States began to rebuild the South in all aspects, including physically, politically, and socioeconomically. African Americans were allowed to vote, own property, and participate in civil society. Progress was not assured, however, because many whites were not in favor of the new social order. They resented the idea of Blacks having the same opportunities and privileges as whites.

In an effort to engage wholly in the experience of being free Americans, many Blacks joined the military. In addition to having fought in the Civil War, African Americans distinguished themselves in two other military arenas during the 19th and 20th centuries.

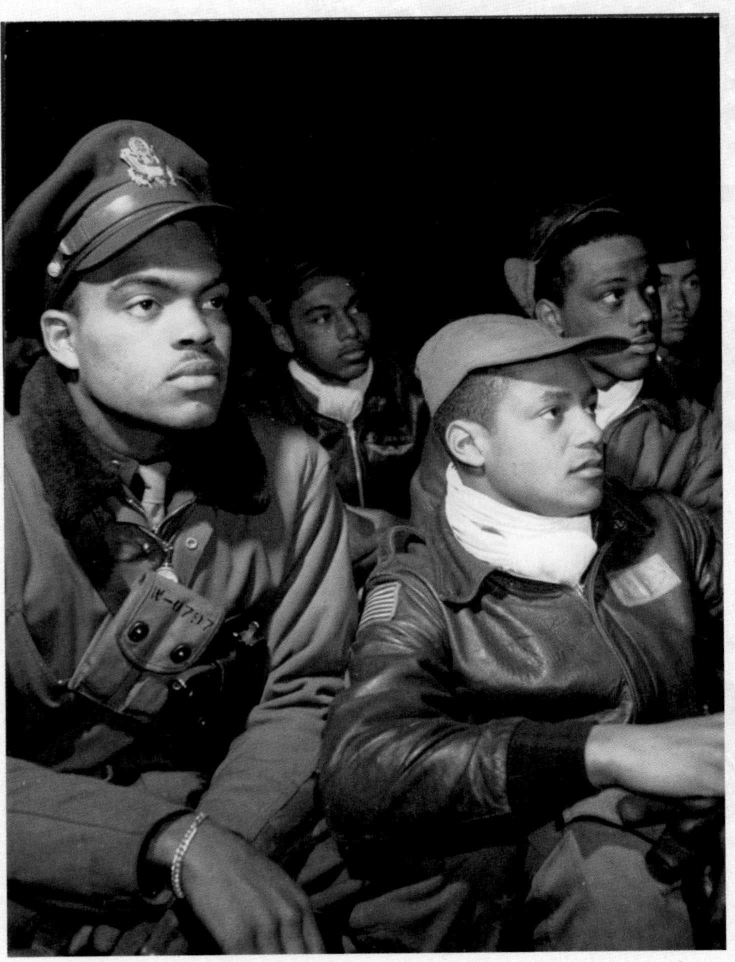

At a briefing in Ramitelli, Italy, in March 1945, members of the all-Black 332nd Fighter Group, also known as the Tuskegee Airmen, prepare for battle.

BUFFALO SOLDIERS

Following the Civil War, African-American cavalry and infantrymen fought in the American West. They were enlisted to aid the U.S. government in its campaign to forcibly remove Native Americans from the land that white settlers wanted to own. The U.S. government made promises of compensation to Native American communities, only to break these treaties. Native Americans often reacted with violence to the constant white invasions and broken promises.

Hundreds of thousands of Native Americans were removed from their homelands, and the so-called Indian Wars ensued. By 1866, Congress designated the Ninth and Tenth U.S. Cavalry as all-Black regiments. Blacks, consisting of former slaves, freedmen, and Civil War soldiers, quickly joined the units. Their benefits included salaries of $13 a month, free room and board, and an opportunity for education in the form of army-taught reading and writing, as stipulated in the bill.

The soldiers' fight took them from the Mississippi River to the Rockies and from the Rio Grande to the Canadian border. Because of their fierce tenacity and their curly hair, American Indian soldiers called the African-American soldiers "Buffalo Soldiers," after the animal that the Indians admired and honored. This reference to the buffalo prompted the Tenth Cavalry to add the animal to its official insignia. Elements of the Buffalo Soldiers went on to fight in the Spanish-American War, including the charge up San Juan Hill, and the subsequent Philippine insurrection. Due to their bravery during the Spanish-American War, 23 received the Medal of Honor. In later years, some were commanded by General Benjamin O. Davis, Sr., at Camp Funston, Kansas, as a part of the Fourth Cavalry Brigade in 1941. The Buffalo Soldiers were disbanded in 1944.

TUSKEGEE AIRMEN

Segregation did not stop the famed Tuskegee Airmen from fighting in America's battles for freedom and democracy. Forming U.S. Air Force units of African-American fighter pilots in Europe, the Tuskegee Airmen performed feats of valor in World War II. Undeterred by a 1925 study commissioned by the Army War College claiming that African Americans were unable to operate aircraft because of their inferiority and cranial capacity, Blacks pressured the military to accept them.

In 1939, Congress passed Public Law 18, calling for a major expansion of American air forces. The bill established training programs for African Americans at several Black colleges. Although this program only allowed Blacks to serve in support capacities, another program

Buffalo Soldiers (above), so nicknamed by the Native Americans they fought against, led campaigns throughout the American West. Decades later, across the Atlantic, Tuskegee Airmen (below) fought valiantly on the European front.

authorized the training of Black pilots. This program, established at the 66th Air Force Flying School, was based at Tuskegee Institute in Tuskegee, Alabama.

The NAACP and the Black press pressured the War Department to create an all-Black unit, the 99th Pursuit Squadron, which later became the 99th Fighter Squadron. Eventually young African-American soldiers from every part of the U.S. were allowed to enter the program. They received rigorous training from white officers who largely expected them to fail. The first class of five men, including Benjamin O. Davis, Jr., graduated in June 1942. Davis, a West Point Academy graduate, later rose in rank to become the nation's first black three-star general.

By 1946, 994 men won their wings, becoming trained pilots, and another 1,000 served in support capacities. Those pilots allowed to fly during the war amassed an impressive record. Assigned to Italy, their fighter planes escorted U.S. bombers in 1,578 missions and 15,552 sorties, never losing a bomber. They destroyed or damaged 409 enemy planes and sank the German destroyer *Trieste*. The Airmen had lost 66 men by the end of the war and the unit was awarded 100 Distinguished Flying Crosses. Even so, they returned home to face strong bigotry. The government disbanded the units and closed the Tuskegee base on September 5, 1946. Their success and courage led President Harry S. Truman to sign Executive Order 9981 in 1948, which ended racial segregation in the U.S. Armed Forces and became a model for racial integration.

CHAPTER NINE

I, Too, Am America

I, Too, Am America

After Reconstruction, de jure and de facto racism persisted in American society, denying Blacks ways to raise their social standing. Blacks who sought the right to vote were met with resistance from ex-Confederates, Klansmen, segregationists, and others who would not accept that they were now free. Nor would they permit Blacks to compete for jobs, adequate housing, and public accommodations reserved for whites.

De facto racism consisted of social practices designed to restrict Blacks' mobility or their access to public resources. Some examples of de facto racism included requiring Blacks to show deference to whites, such as yielding the right-of-way to white pedestrians. Blacks were required to enter restaurants via the back door. Blacks were denied patents for their inventions. More commonly, Blacks were falsely accused and arrested, and law enforcement officials followed Blacks on the suspicion that they were stealing or even "out of place." Hate crimes were perpetrated against Blacks for violating the "color line" that separated them from whites in almost every sector of American society. Such callous treatment extended to refusing to bring one of the greatest scholars in American history, John Hope Franklin, requested archival materials because he was black. In the economic sphere, banks practiced redlining, refusing to grant mortgage or other loans to residents of Black communities. Many of these practices hinged upon racist theories and stereotypical notions that assumed African Amerians were inferior to whites and unworthy of first-class citizenship.

De facto racism was enforced by de jure racism perpetrated via state-sanctioned Black Codes and Jim Crow laws; these legalized segregation in public accommodations. In almost every facet of public life, Blacks were excluded or given separate and unequal treatment. For example, Blacks were forced to sit in inferior train cars that were separate from those cars reserved for whites. In 1896, Homer Plessy tested the legality of such segregationist practices when he sat in a car reserved for whites, in violation of a Louisiana statute. Plessy was a very fair-skinned black man, described in trial transcripts as having "one-eighth African blood." As an "octoroon," his race was not readily discernible. Yet the train's conductor categorized Plessy as a "Negro" and forced him to move to the car that was reserved for them. When Plessy refused to do so, he was arrested and imprisoned. By refusing to sit in the car reserved for "colored" people and refusing to identify himself as a "Negro," Plessy not only challenged Louisiana's Jim Crow laws, he challenged Louisiana's social, often bizarre, notions of race. Plessy petitioned the court to dismiss his case on the grounds that the segregationist statute under which he was arrested was unconstitutional. After having his appeal dismissed in federal district court, Plessy took his case to the U.S. Supreme Court. But the Supreme Court ruled against Plessy, issuing the following opinion: "The power to assign to a particular coach obviously implies the power to determine to which race the passenger belongs, as well as the power to determine who, under the laws of a particular state, is to be deemed a white, and who a colored, person. . . .We consider the

Left: Singing freedom songs and calling for equality, members of the Student Nonviolent Coordinating Committee join the August 1963 March on Washington.

Previous pages: Under an overcast sky, hundreds of activists march from Selma, Alabama, to Montgomery in 1965 in support of civil rights.

"Segregation of white and Negro children in the public schools of a State solely on the basis of race . . . denies to Negro children the equal protection of the laws guaranteed by the Fourteenth Amendment."

— Brown v. Board of Education of Topeka, Kansas

underlying fallacy of the plaintiff's argument to consist in the assumption that the enforced separation of the two races stamps the colored race with a badge of inferiority." This ruling reveals the arbitrary nature of racial categorization. More important, the landmark *Plessy* v. *Ferguson* case legalized the separate but "equal" doctrine for another half a century.

TESTS OF THE LAW

Viewed as inferior beings, Blacks also had their rights as citizens denied by law and by violence. The Civil Rights Act of 1866, the Reconstruction Act of 1867, and the Enforcement Act of 1870 sought to protect Blacks who attempted to vote in elections. In addition, the Enforcement Act prohibited persons from using intimidation, force, or violence to deny Blacks their constitutional rights, including the right to vote. However, de facto and de jure racism combined to deny Blacks their voting rights. These tactics included requiring them to pay a poll tax and physically moving polling stations to remote locations out of their reach. One pernicious statute required them to abide by the grandfather clause, which denied registered males the right to vote just prior to upcoming elections, but granted the right to their sons and grandsons who, by virtue of their age, were also denied the vote.

The law's power was tested in 1873, when William Cruikshank led a mob of 100 whites to attack a group of Blacks attempting to vote at the Colfax, Louisiana, courthouse. After setting the courthouse ablaze, the mob shot several Blacks attempting to flee the fire, plus several who had surrendered. Cruikshank was indicted for conspiracy under the Enforcement Act. He was convicted of 322 counts, including conspiring to deprive "citizens of African descent and persons of color" their right to peaceful assembly, their right to bear arms for a lawful purpose, their right to due process of law, and their right to vote at any election. However, the U.S. Supreme Court overturned the convictions on a technicality. It argued that although the victims in this case were identified as African and colored, it had not been explicitly charged in the indictments that they were denied their rights on the basis of race. The court was truly "color-blind" in reversing the convictions, but Cruikshank and his conspirators were not color-blind in their murderous attack against Black citizens. After all, no white citizens had ever been murdered when attempting to vote in Louisiana or any other state.

Segregationist practices, civil rights abuses, and violence against Blacks persisted into the 20th century without federal protections, prompting W. E. B. DuBois to remark, "The problem of the 20th century is the problem of the color line." Blacks and whites were not merely divided, but Blacks were denied equal advantages. Nowhere was this more visible than in the area of education. Linda Brown, a black student in Topeka, Kansas, was forced to walk a mile, through a dangerous railroad switchyard, to attend a school designated for Blacks, even though a school existed closer to her home. However, that school was reserved for "whites only." Her father sued the Board of Education of Topeka, claiming that such segregationist practices were unconstitutional. Thurgood Marshall, who later became the first black Supreme Court justice, successfully argued the case before the Court, which declared "separate, but equal" practices in education unconstitutional in 1954.

The *Brown* v. *Board of Education* ruling in Topeka had little impact at the state level, in part because certain U.S. senators of former slave states refused to recognize it. In fact, as an adult, Linda Brown Smith sued the Topeka Board of Education a second time in 1979 because segregation in education remained a problem in Topeka. The problem continued to plague the entire nation as well. In 1956, Harry F. Byrd, Sr.,

Collectibles, such as this salt and pepper shaker set from the mid-20th century, promoted stereotypes of African Americans.

SHORT'NIN' BREAD

Song

for Voice and Piano

By JACQUES WOLFE

High Medium Low

Price, 50 cents, net, in U. S. A.

Piano Transcription, Simplified	.30
Piano Concert Version—Wolfe-Savino	.50
Two Pianos—Complete Set	$1.00

Also published for

Mixed, Men's, or Women's Chorus

HAROLD FLAMMER

INCORPORATED

Like Aunt Jemima, the smiling, Black woman on the cover of "Short'nin' Bread" sheet music fed traditional notions of white superiority.

senator from Virginia, endorsed *The Southern Manifesto*, which opposed racial integration. Prince Edward County, Virginia, was a microcosm of the national problem. In opposition to integration, it closed all of its public schools in 1959. Subsequently, county officials built Prince Edward Academy, a private school that restricted enrollment to white students. Black students, on the other hand, were denied the benefit of a public education, although their parents paid taxes. Vonita Foster, a black student enrolled in the Prince Edward County school system in 1959, summed up her feelings about the school closings by saying, "In the summer of 1959, everything to me seemed so unfair. My mother tried hard to help me understand, but how do you explain to a child that 'separate but unequal' was the meaning of democracy for African-American citizens in the United States of America."

Opposition to integration was, in large measure, fueled by perceptions of Blacks as inferior, subhuman, and lazy. Collectively, these stereotypes buttressed racial discrimination by providing justifications for the practice. Stereotypes were perpetuated in various forms of popular culture, including a form of entertainment known as the minstrel show. Typically performed by whites in blackface, minstrel shows conveyed to white audiences the idea that black people, as inferior, shiftless, and stupid beings, were unfit for social integration with whites. The popular appeal of minstrel shows in the post-slavery period was that, on the one hand, they degraded Blacks, and, on the other, justified society's treatment of them as second-class citizens. To a greater extent, they reinforced whites' feelings of dominance over Blacks, reminiscent of the days of slavery. One of the most popular minstrel characters

Subjected to a system that benefited whites in nearly all aspects of daily life, an African-American man uses the back entrance of a movie theater in Depression-era Missouri.

One of the "Big Six": James Farmer, Jr.

Minister and civil rights leader James Farmer was a subject of *The Great Debaters*, a movie based on the true story of a debate team at Wiley College in Texas. The movie chronicled his early years living in Texas in the 1930s and some of the encounters he had with racism that later sparked his interest in fighting discrimination. Living near a college campus, however, protected him from the extreme racism encountered by the wider community beyond.

He was born James Leonard Farmer on January 20, 1920, in Marshall, Texas, to teacher Pearl Marion Houston and to James Leonard Farmer, Sr., a minister and scholar who taught in southern colleges. His father is believed to be the first African American from Texas to receive a doctorate. Farmer recalls an incident when he was three that first made him aware of Texas's racial climate. His family was living in Holly Springs, Mississippi, at the time, where his father taught at Rust College. After he and his mother went shopping, she had to explain to him why he could not go into a drugstore to buy a soda after seeing a white child go in. "Until then, I had not realized that I was colored." The incident made him determined to do something about racism.

Entering Wiley College at the age of 14, he considered both medicine and the ministry as possible vocations and opted for a degree in chemistry. He continued to face discrimination and remembers separate balcony seating for Blacks in local movie theaters.

After completing his undergraduate work, Farmer did graduate work at Howard University's School of Divinity, where he was influenced by the teachings of Gandhi. His father was also on the faculty. Farmer graduated in 1941, and took a job as race relations secretary for the Fellowship of Reconciliation (FOR), a New York–based pacifist group. He relocated to Chicago as part of his work for FOR and traveled throughout the Midwest speaking on pacifism. Some of his time was allocated to helping to organize southern unions.

Farmer is best known as the principal founder and a fierce leader of the Congress of Racial Equality (CORE), which he founded with University of Chicago students in 1942. CORE is where he put the Gandhi strategy for nonviolence to practice, introducing sit-ins. CORE went national within a year, and its membership topped 60,000 with more than 70 chapters by 1945. Some CORE projects included protesting school closings during the aftermath of *Brown* v. *Board of Education*. Farmer organized Blacks all over the South to stand in lines at public venues from which they were barred, and they facilitated the Freedom Rides in the early '60s. Supporters were often attacked and injured, and buses were firebombed. Farmer himself was often placed in personal danger in his efforts to organize peaceful demonstrations.

A member of CORE (above) pickets in Bogalusa, Louisiana. Besides supporting workers' rights, CORE lobbied to end lynching.

He resigned from his CORE director's job in 1965, but he remained affiliated with the organization until he formally broke with them in 1975, because he believed the organization had a strong Marxist faction. He devoted his full time to his memoirs, *Lay Bare the Heart* (1985), then taught at several universities. He began teaching at Mary Washington College in Fredericksburg, Virginia, where he maintained the largest student roster than any other history teacher at the college. President Clinton awarded him the Presidential Medal of Freedom in 1998 for his civil rights activities. James Farmer died the following year on July 9.

D. W.

Like these workers heading to New Jersey to pick potatoes, many African Americans migrated from South to North in search of a better life.

"No person or corporation shall require any White female nurse to nurse in wards or rooms in hospitals, either public or private, in which negro men are placed.

The warden shall see that the white convicts shall have separate apartments for both eating and sleeping from the negro convicts.

No colored barber shall serve as a barber (to) white girls or women."

—State Jim Crow laws

was called Jim Crow, created to caricature Blacks as imbecilic and as an embarrassing stain on America's social fabric. Because the character served as a metaphor for what lawmakers viewed as the larger "Negro Problem" in the post-slavery period, the name was adopted for the entire body of segregationist laws meant to restrict their upward mobility. In 1905, W. E. B. Du Bois formed the Niagara movement in Canada, having been refused a venue for his initial meeting in New York to protest Jim Crow segregation, among other things. "We must protest against the 'Jim Crow' car, since its effect is and must be to make us pay first-class fare for third-class accommodations, render us open to insults and discomfort and to crucify wantonly our manhood, womanhood and self-respect," asserted Du Bois.

The Jim Crow car was symbolic of the larger segregationist society that branded African Americans unequal to whites and unworthy of social integration. At worst, Blacks were portrayed as menaces to society. The Ku Klux Klan, the White Citizens' Councils, and other domestic terrorist groups felt it their self-appointed duty to neutralize the threat. Toward that end, Thomas Dixon published a white-supremacist treatise entitled *The Clansman*, a blueprint for abating the perceived threat and the basis for W. D. Griffith's film *Birth of a Nation* (1915). In the film, a "Negro," who, in actuality is portrayed by a white actor in blackface, stalks a white female to the edge of a cliff. However, "heroic Klansmen" ride in to save the woman—and by extension, the white race—from the ravages of the black man. More than mere entertainment, the film was a propaganda tool for recruiting individuals who would take up the cause of protecting the white woman and defending white supremacy against the Black threat. Enrollment in the Klan increased exponentially in the wake of this film that exploited well-established fears of the black male as a crazed sexual fiend. Although such fears were rooted in the days of slavery, they became the pretext for lynching black men after slavery. In the 20th century and even today, minstrel shows, Broadway musicals, films, songs, literature, memorabilia, advertisements, and product brands have been vehicles for the most pernicious stereotypes of Blacks, contributing to their persistence in American society. Some of these examples include Agatha Christie's *Ten Little Niggers*, Al Jolson's "Mammy," a

The Female Talented Tenth: Mary Church Terrell

After the Civil War, 95 percent of African descendants living in America were illiterate. The vast majority of them had been forbidden by their owners to learn to read or write. Only a few families, mostly the children of white plantation owners, were allowed to become educated and in some cases own property and businesses.

Two people that prospered after the war, mostly from real estate dealings, were former slaves, Robert Reed Church and Louisa Ayers Church of Memphis, Tennessee. Their daughter, Mary Eliza Church, was born in 1863. The Churches—the first Black millionaires in the United States—lived a life of privilege, and Robert Church expected his daughter to follow his example as a member of the fledgling Black elite.

Mary, however, wanted to become a teacher. Her father sent her to Oberlin College to earn a degree, expecting that she would return home to live after her studies were completed. She graduated from Oberlin College at the head of her class in 1884. Once Church's father learned that his daughter still intended to become a teacher, he threatened to disinherit her. Yet she followed through with her plan to teach, and as a result became estranged from her father for a time.

While she was still part of the Black elite, she did not live in that manner. She met numerous other Blacks, including teacher and lawyer Robert Terrell, who later became one of the first black judges appointed in the Washington, D.C., court system. They married and she went on to study for two years in Europe. Other advocates for educating the masses were her former classmate at Oberlin and later president of Frelinghuysen University, Anna Julia Cooper, educator and activist W. E. B. Du Bois, and many others. Du Bois's eloquent speech in 1903, called The Talented Tenth, spurred Terrell and others to educate and liberate their people.

According to Du Bois's theory, the Talented Tenth was to be a representative group—10 percent of educated African Americans—who would propagate education among the remaining 90 percent of Blacks. This view was in direct opposition to that of another prominent educator of the time, Booker T. Washington. Washington believed that African Americans should embrace vocational learning, as espoused by many of the whites of the era. The views of Washington and Du Bois were so dissimilar that they became staunch opponents in the arena of education.

Terrell continued to teach and to give major speeches to audiences all over the world, such as the International Congress of Women in Berlin. She spoke out against all types of injustices, including the horrific practice of lynching black men and women. From education to antidiscrimination, Mary Church Terrell was never without a cause. Her causes ranged from women's rights to boycotting segregated establishments. She was active in the founding of organizations such as the National Association of Colored Women and the National Association for the Advancement of Colored People (NAACP).

One of her greatest legacies lies in her active role in changing the world of segregation. Terrell was key in forcing the abolishment of laws that barred black people from sitting down and eating in Washington, D.C., establishments in the 1950s. Terrell launched a campaign to reinstate antidiscrimination laws. On February 28, 1950, she and several colleagues entered segregated Thompson Restaurant. When they were refused service, they promptly filed a lawsuit. In the three years pending a decision in *District of Columbia* v. *John R. Thompson Co.*, Terrell targeted other restaurants, this time using tactics such as boycotts, picketing, and sit-ins. Finally, on June 8, 1953, the court ruled that segregated eating places in Washington, D.C., were unconstitutional.

In this way, she lived her life as a person who not only excelled, but who advocated for the other 90 percent of African Americans. She fought for her beliefs until 1954, when she died at the age of 89. *C. J. C.*

Mary Church Terrell, shown here between 1890 and 1900, worked tirelessly to increase and improve education among African Americans.

Working with Mary McLeod Bethune

DOROTHY HEIGHT, PH.D.

Mary McLeod Bethune was called to Washington by President Franklin Delano Roosevelt to serve as his adviser on minority affairs and as director of the National Youth Administration. In 1935, Mary McLeod Bethune said that, from her vantage point in the federal government during the Roosevelt Administration, she could not rest to see the unharnessed woman power among us. She said that African-American women, the trained and untrained alike, stood outside the American mainstream of influence, opportunity, and power.

We have come a long way since those days, but we still have a long way to go. Even today, we have to work on some of the same issues that were challenging the position of women and African Americans in society. African-American women still have to deal with the double problem of race and sex.

Mrs. Bethune knew who she was, and she was proud of it! She said that she was proud to be black because, had she been born white, she would not have been able to do as much.

"COME BACK, WE NEED YOU"

On November 7, 1937, as assistant executive of the Harlem branch of the YWCA, I had an assignment to escort Eleanor Roosevelt into a meeting Mary McLeod Bethune was holding in the building. It turned out to be a meeting of the National Council of Negro Women (NCNW). As I was assisting Mrs. Roosevelt, as she was leaving, Mrs. Bethune asked me my name and said, "Come back, we need you." I have been back ever since!

When I returned to the meeting, Mrs. Bethune appointed me to the Resolutions Committee. The first resolutions that I ever wrote had to do with child labor and the minimum wage. In the face of today's child abuse and with so much happening to children that has come out from under the rug, I am still working on children's needs and on the minimum wage.

African-American women have advanced in every field where women have advanced in general, yet we are predominantly at the bottom of the social and economic order. Our lives seem to be characterized by rising expectations and rising frustrations. Even the progress made through the civil rights movement seems more tentative than we ever thought.

In founding the NCNW, Mrs. Bethune said that we did need another organization, but one that would bring organizations together. She always used her fingers to illustrate her point. She said: "If I touch you with one finger, you may not know that you have been touched. If I use two fingers, you just might feel it. But if I bring all my fingers into a fist, I can give you a mighty blow!" And this was the way in which she illustrated the importance of a council of women's organizations working together in unity with power. Years later, seeing Stokely Carmichael raise his fist, I told him that long before he was born, I saw a woman raise her fist as a sign of power.

MAKING A VISION A REALITY

For 72 years, the National Council of Negro Women has been working to make Mrs. Bethune's vision for humanity a reality. I often marvel that a woman who was born in 1875 of slave parents could have been networking and collaborating and coalition building long before the concepts were fully developed. I have been working through NCNW, knowing that whatever we do, we have to get beneath the surface to find the cause. For instance, we must tutor but also take time to understand why the tutoring is necessary—what is wrong with the educational system and what it would take to change the system. Working with Mrs. Bethune made clear to me that the task of advocating and serving has to give direction for every day.

I always say that African-American women are very special women because we seldom do just what we want to do, but we always do what we have to do—we know how to get it done. We have had to work hard to overcome disparities in order to have access to services and educational opportunities. In fact, disparities seem to drive our work! Mrs. Bethune always urged us to "leave no one behind."

Through the civil rights movement, we opened doors and gained confidence as we sang "We Shall Overcome." We have to regain that confidence as we seek the fulfillment of civil rights laws in the face of threats to policies such as affirmative action.

THE BETHUNE LEGACY

In her last will and testament, Mrs. Bethune left the challenge to work with people of all races and to have a worldview. Her philosophy prompted NCNW to initiate its international work in 1975—the 100th anniversary of her birth. We have joined with others to

Dorothy Height, president of the National Council of Negro Women, poses next to a portrait of herself in Washington in 1997.

help strengthen the world community. We have also learned that, while we have something to contribute, we also have a great deal to learn as we work with people around the world.

STRENGTHENING FAMILY LIFE

In the face of negative projections of the African-American family, NCNW has taken the initiative to strengthen family life and celebrate the historic traditions and the value traditions of the African-American family. Even as many of our white sisters questioned whether we were feminists, because we dealt with the whole family, we realized that we could not separate that way. NCNW has always had to work on strengthening family life and improving the quality of life for women and girls. The NCNW program focus today includes education, health, and family life.

In Montgomery, Alabama, at the celebration of the 45th anniversary of the birth of the Montgomery boycott sparked by Rosa Parks, it was exciting to find young people who, for the first time, understood the meaning of the boycott.

There is a tremendous job in helping new generations understand what the struggle has been and the challenge of her legacy of responsibility to our young people. As they go through open doors, they will be stronger if they know how those doors were opened, and understand their own responsibility to keep them open and to open them wider.

The heart of the Bethune legacy is love, faith, and hope. She said quite clearly, "I want to see my people go as high as they can, but never forget to help one another as they go along." It is in this spirit that we continue to work to fulfill the dream of Mary McLeod Bethune. ■

"You had the Varsity Theater, Carolina Theater, in Chapel Hill. Then we had a Rialto Theater in Carrboro, on the main street. That was a black theater. But here again, if it left scars on me . . . it's the fact that I would have to pass these theaters to go to the Rialto Theater."

— Fred Battle, Oral History Program Collection, University of North Carolina at Chapel Hill

Life in segregated communities, such as Chicago's South Side, could still bring delight. At right, African Americans enjoy an Easter Sunday movie in 1941.

Adults
CHILDREN 10¢
Total 44¢
FLASNOW PLAY
HOLLYWOODS
NO.1 ACTOR of 1940
JAMES STEW
Plus
E PICTU

"I, too, sing America.

I am the darker brother.

They send me to eat

in the kitchen

When company comes,

But I laugh,

And eat well,

And grow strong.

Tomorrow,

I'll be at the table

When company comes.

Nobody'll dare

Say to me,

'Eat in the kitchen,'

Then.

Besides,

They'll see how beautiful

I am

And be ashamed—

I, too, am America."

— Langston Hughes, writer

song that he performed in blackface, Darkie brand toothpaste, Uncle Ben rice, Aunt Jemima pancake mix, "Mammy" cookie jars, and black lawn jockeys.

In an effort to escape rampant discrimination and lynching in the South, and seeking to fill the labor void created by white males who left to fight in World War I, many traveled to northern cities. This mass exodus out of the South was known as the Great Migration. To some extent, Blacks expected northern cities to be free of the South's racism. They were disillusioned, however, when they met with racism in employment, housing, entertainment, and other aspects of life in northern cities. The progress of northern Blacks was hindered by their "Negroness" and by segregationists' perception of it. On some levels, life in the North was just as harsh at it had been in the South. The North was rife with segregationist practices. Blacks were allowed to rent tenement housing only in certain parts of the cities; a street, bridge, or other landmark served as the dividing line or, in Du Boisian terms, "the color line." For example, most black immigrants settled on the South Side of Chicago because they had been historically restricted to that section of the city. Such segregationist practices prompted Langston Hughes, dubbed the poet laureate of the Harlem Renaissance, to write, "I, too, am American," inspired by an incidence of de facto racism in which Hughes, rather than being allowed to sit in front, was forced to eat his meal in the restaurant's kitchen.

As in the South, Blacks paid first-class rates for second- and third-class treatment in the North. Blacks were not allowed to sit in the audience as patrons in various nightclubs, such as the Cotton Club, where they were only allowed to work as entertainers. The North was not free of racial violence. Many Blacks were physically assaulted by segregationists on a persistent basis. These attacks culminated in a series of bloody race riots, prompting James Weldon Johnson, a writer, musician, and composer of the Black national anthem, "Lift Every Voice and Sing," to label those months the Red Summer of 1919.

Even black soldiers who served honorably in World War I were disgraced when they returned to the United States, where they were called "coons" and "darkies" in uniform.

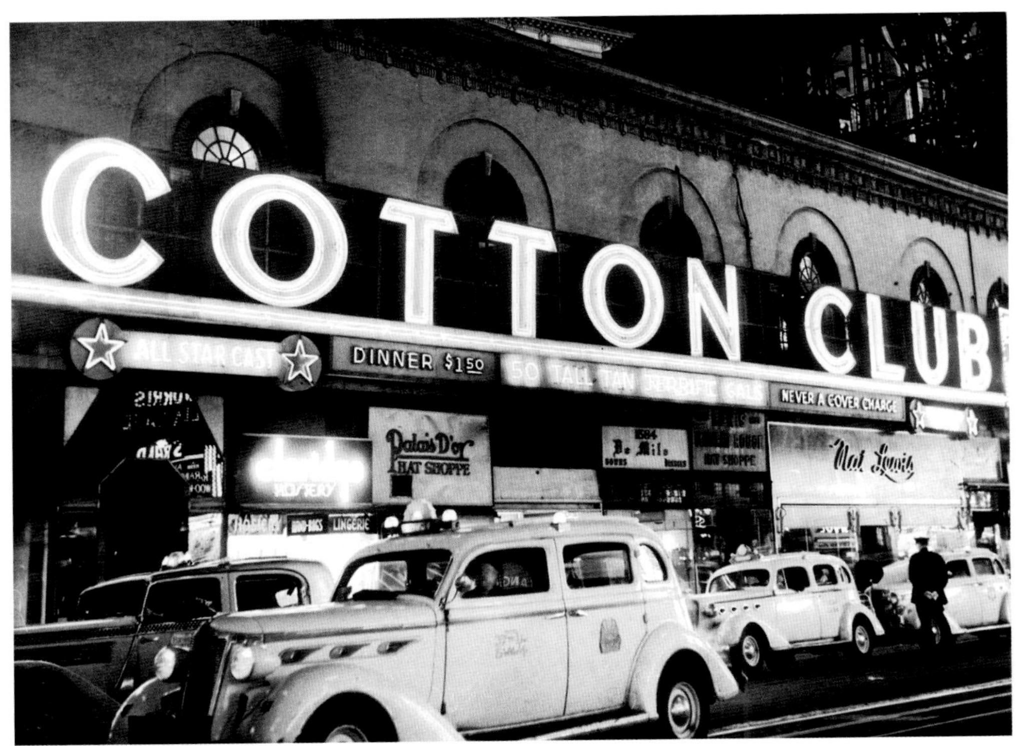

The Cotton Club, a popular Harlem nightspot in the 1920s and '30s, featured the most prominent Black musicians of the day but allowed only whites as audience.

Studying the Black Family: E. Franklin Frazier

Esteemed sociologist and writer Edward Franklin Frazier was born in Baltimore, Maryland, in 1894. Frazier's father taught him that education was the key to both being a success and obtaining social justice. Frazier graduated from the Colored High School in 1912, earning the school's annual scholarship to Howard University in Washington, D.C. He graduated with honors from Howard University in 1916 and began his doctoral studies at the University of Chicago in 1927, after studying in Massachusetts and Denmark. He later became a professor at Fisk University in Nashville, Tennessee, and next at Morehouse College in Atlanta, Georgia. By 1934, he had become department chair and professor of sociology at Howard University, where he remained until his retirement in 1959.

Early in life, Frazier studied the writings of W. E. B. Du Bois, and this led to his taking a number of public stands. He was jailed for picketing D. W. Griffith's *Birth of a Nation,* a movie that promoted demeaning stereotypes of African Americans. He became active with the National Association for the Advancement of Colored People (NAACP), and he publicly defended Du Bois and Paul Robeson during the McCarthy era of the 1950s, for which he was labeled a Communist.

During his career, Frazier was a prolific writer who wrote about a wide variety of subjects, including the African-American family, their church experience, their neighborhoods, and about culture and race. He authored nine books and contributed more than 100 articles and essays to books and journals. In his most controversial book, *The Black Bourgeoisie*, he wrote a stinging critique of the Black middle class. Frazier's studies in this 1957 publication concluded the Black middle class had earned "status without substance" and criticized affluent Blacks for trying to become part of the American elite. His findings caused many to criticize him and to accuse him of racial disloyalty.

Frazier's conclusions were based on his research findings about the origins of the Black bourgeoisie. He reported that, before the Civil War, the ownership of land or real estate was the main way for free Negroes to acquire wealth. He gave examples of two land acquisitions by freed Negros in Philadelphia and Washington, D.C., totaling $800,000 and $660,000, respectively. He wrote that failed plantations, which had been subdivided into small farms, led to land acquisition by free Negroes in Virginia and Maryland in the 1800s.

One of his most striking conclusions was about the free Negroes, or *gens de couleur*, of New Orleans. He found that, by 1860, their holdings in real estate and slaves were estimated to total $10 million to $15 million. His research revealed that, other than farming, successful African Americans opened small enterprises, including shops and banks in the Black community. His overall conclusion was that after emancipation, the roots of the Black elite were firmly lodged in the Negro spirit of modern business enterprises. He indicated that Negroes of his time had lost sight of this important principle.

E. Franklin Frazier, shown at his desk at Howard University in March 1957, launched significant debates on race and class in America.

Frazier traveled around the world, conducting studies related to Blacks in Brazil, the Caribbean, the continent of Africa, and elsewhere. He was named an international authority on racial issues by the United Nations Education, Scientific, and Cultural Organization (UNESCO) in 1944. In his work with UNESCO, he traveled to Paris, Africa, and the Middle East. In the United States, he was the first African American elected president of the American Sociological Association.

He was in the forefront of the development of African studies in the United States, as evidenced by the African Studies department that he helped found at Howard University. In his later years, he focused on the struggle of the African people and those of African descent in their struggle to achieve equality. He also wrote on religion, and his last book, *The Negro Church in America*, was published posthumously. E. Franklin Frazier died in 1962, leaving a legacy as one of Black America's most influential scholars and as one of the nation's leading intellectuals.

C. J. C.

Aaron Douglas's 1927 painting "The Creation" shows off his use of traditional African shapes and design. An artist of the Harlem Renaissance, Douglas stressed the importance of heritage.

"Harlem . . . Harlem

Black, black Harlem

Souls of Black Folk

Ask Du Bois

Little grey restless feet

Ask Claude McKay

City of Refuge

Ask Rudolph Fisher

Don't damn your body's itch

Ask Countee Cullen

Does the jazz band sob?

Ask Langston Hughes

Nigger Heaven

Ask Carl Van Vechten

Hey! . . . Hey!

'. . . Say it brother

Say it . . .'"

— Frank Horne, poet

Several black soldiers were the victims of hate crimes perpetrated by white supremacists who rejected the idea and the reality of Blacks wearing the uniforms of various branches of the armed services that also practiced segregation. Despite these challenges, or perhaps in consequence of them, the social, cultural, artistic, and intellectual landscapes of New York, Detroit, and Chicago were transformed by the Mississippi Delta blues and other forms of expressive culture introduced by southern Blacks. In New York, these transformations contributed to a phenomenon known as the Harlem Renaissance.

The Harlem Renaissance was a period of high intellectual and artistic creativity, one that produced black men and women of distinction in literature, music, fine arts, and architecture. Their experiences yielded fresh material or subject matter for their artistic, literary, and musical expression. For example, Claude McKay's poetry aggressively

Black Entrepreneurs: A'Lelia Walker and A'Lelia Bundles

Entrepreneur, philanthropist, and social activist Madam C. J. Walker was born on December 23, 1867, in Delta, Louisiana, to former slaves. Born Sarah Breedlove, she married early and became a mother at 17. Yet she was not content to live in poverty, and when she was 21, she moved to St. Louis, leaving her husband behind. She worked as a washerwoman and cook for the next few years. After developing a scalp condition called alopecia, which causes patchy baldness due to diet, stress, and damaging hair treatments, she began experimenting with several products to relieve her malady. This eventually led Walker to take a job working for a company that produced the product that relieved the condition. After selling the product door-to-door, she recognized that the hair care business could be her salvation.

After moving to Denver in 1905, she decided to go into business for herself. She changed the formula and persuaded members of Denver's Black community to try her product. This led to overwhelming success, prompting her to expand and move her business to Pittsburgh, then to Indianapolis, and finally to New York.

While living in Indianapolis, Walker gave $1,000 to the YMCA to be used toward building a center for African Americans. This gift, the largest ever given to a cause by an African-American woman, gained her national attention and made her name synonymous with the word "philanthropist." In a short time, Walker became active with social issues of the day, including antilynching, and she contributed $5,000 to an antilynching campaign led by the NAACP.

With increasing wealth, Madam Walker supported additional African-American charities. Among her selected charities in Indianapolis were Flanner House, Alpha Home, and Bethel AME Church. Elsewhere, her support included Mary McLeod Bethune's Daytona Educational and Industrial Training School for Negro Girls in Florida (now Bethune-Cookman University), Palmer Memorial Institute in North Carolina, and Haines Institute in Augusta, Georgia.

Madam Walker's interests extended beyond making financial contributions. She began a lawsuit in 1915, protesting discrimination at an Indianapolis theater. She believed in several causes, including ending the terrible practice of lynching. In 1917, she urged the Benevolent Association to do their part to end lynching in the South. During World War I, she went to Washington with a delegation to meet with President Wilson to protest segregation that was practiced by the War Department.

Madam Walker saw herself as a leader of her people. On occasion, she became concerned that some people did not extend to her the same honor as had been given to Booker T. Washington. Because she championed social causes, she expected to be shown the same respect as her contemporaries.

Walker's only child, Lelia (later changed to A'Lelia), had already moved to New York. She and her mother lived in grand homes and were associates of the most important African Americans of the time. They held salon events and social gatherings that included guests who were part of the social and political world and the great Harlem Renaissance.

By 1919, when her mother died, A'Lelia became president of Walker Company, the business that she helped to start in New York. She continued to run the business and to travel all over the world, including Africa, Europe, and the Middle East. She visited royalty wherever she traveled and continued to make a name for herself and her products.

The legacy of the Walkers is guarded and carried on by A'Lelia's great-granddaughter and namesake, A'Lelia Bundles. A seasoned journalist, Bundles has chronicled her family's storied lives, traveling extensively to tell their story. Bundles is the keeper of the flame of her forebears, two women who were the first African-American female millionaires. *C. J. C.*

Madam Walker built her 34-room mansion, the Villa Lewaro, in Irvington, New York, in 1918, where it functioned as a meeting place for black leaders and entertainers.

"I am a woman who came from the cotton fields of the South. From there I was promoted to the washtub. From there I was promoted to the cook kitchen. And from there I promoted myself into the business of manufacturing hair goods and preparations. ... I have built my own factory on my own ground."

— Madam Walker, entrepreneur

addressed racism and segregation; Archibald Motley's paintings documented the vigor of African-American social life in the cities; and the jazz music of Louis Armstrong, Cab Calloway, and Fletcher Henderson both mimicked and motivated the fast pace of life in the North. Like the social and cultural landscapes of the cities, Blacks were transformed by their northern experiences, giving rise to the designation "New Negro."

THE CIVIL RIGHTS MOVEMENT

Almost 100 of years of struggle against racial discrimination after the Civil War provided a historical platform from which the civil rights movement of the 1950s and '60s was launched. The civil rights movement represented a watershed in American history, a defining moment in which black people, joined by many white citizens, took a collective, more organized approach to fighting for their civil rights. Typically, the civil rights movement is divided into two camps—nonviolent and violent. It should be remembered, however, that groups such as the Black Panthers did not perpetuate violence for the sake of violence alone. Rather, they were "counterviolent," defending themselves and their communities from police brutality. It should also be remembered that the Black Panthers implemented various cultural, educational, and social programs in Black communities. While the civil rights movement addressed the injustices perpetuated by the larger society, it allowed African Americans to develop a collective consciousness regarding their approach to ending rampant discrimination. Nowhere is the demonstration of collective consciousness more evident than in the Montgomery bus boycott.

In 1955, Rosa Parks refused to yield her bus seat to a white man, in accordance with Montgomery's segregationist practices, which required black passengers to sit in the rear of the bus. Parks was arrested, an event that sparked a massive boycott of the Montgomery Bus Company. Angered and galvanized by her arrest, African Americans walked, cycled, and carpooled instead. Their collective action had a major economic impact on the bus company. In the end, it agreed to end its segregationist practices.

For all of the well-known personages of the civil rights movement, there are many unsung heroes and heroines, including Irene Morgan Kirkaldy, who, 11 years before the Montgomery bus boycott, refused to yield her seat to whites on a Greyhound bus traveling through Virginia. Kirkaldy was issued an arrest warrant in Saluda, where she tossed the warrant out of the window. Subsequently, she was jailed. Her case reached the level of the U.S. Supreme Court, which defined segregation in interstate travel as unconstitutional, a landmark ruling that signaled the dismantling of Jim Crow laws. President Clinton awarded Kirkaldy the Presidential Citizens Medal in 2001.

There are three overarching narratives of the Black experience in America. The first narrative tells of the trials and tribulations of enslaved people. The second narrative relates to Blacks' struggles to overcome oppression and racial discrimination in the Reconstruction period in particular, and in the post-slavery period in general. The third, and greatest, narrative speaks to their ingenious ability to draw on their African heritage, intelligence, skills, and talents to rise above their oppressed conditions, exemplified by the triumphant lives and accomplishments of many Blacks, including Madame C. J. Walker, an entrepreneur who became the first black female millionaire in the United States; Ernest Everett Just, a talented biologist who made important scientific contributions to the field of biology in egg cell morphology and fertilization; and Garrett A. Morgan, who invented the traffic signal in use throughout the United States and abroad. Given the racial and social hostilities with which Blacks were confronted in America, such achievements are truly remarkable, and they reflect an indomitable spirit.

For African Americans in the mid-20th century, securing the right to vote was the key to securing equality. The Selma to Montgomery civil rights march (above), led by Martin Luther King, Jr., in 1965, rallied hundreds to the cause of Black suffrage. Activists train Black and white students in Canton, Ohio (right), to register Black voters in the Jim Crow South.

Moving People Forward

A GALLERY

Although the story of Black social organizations such as the Prince Hall Masons and the Order of the Eastern Star is as old as the country, at the start of the 20th century, several African-American women and men began to develop new organizations to help push black people forward in society. Those organizations include the Alpha Kappa Alpha Sorority (established 1908), the Omega Psi Phi Fraternity (1911), and the Links (1946). Among the hundreds of organizations that have taken root in the United States, the ones included here show the breadth of such groups.

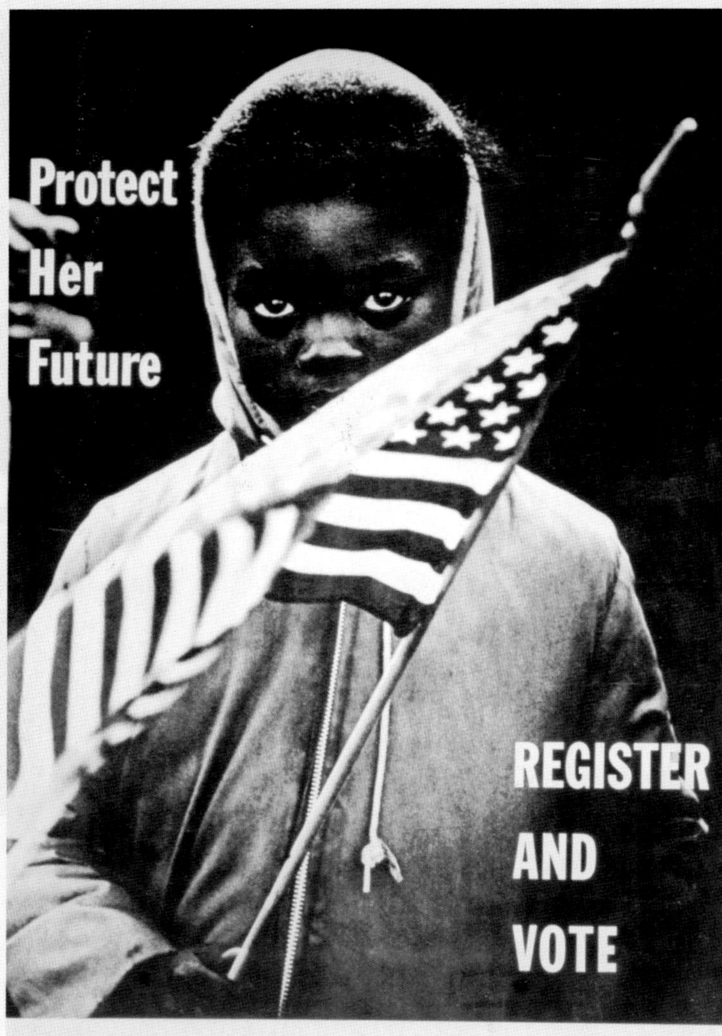

Protect
Her
Future
REGISTER
AND
VOTE
BLACK IS BEAUTIFUL - BUT YOU LOOK
PRETTIER WHEN YOU ARE REGISTERED
NATIONAL ASSOCIATION FOR THE ADVANCEMENT OF COLORED PEOPLE

An NAACP poster encourages Blacks to register to vote as part of its mission to ensure equality and end discrimination.

PRINCE HALL MASONS

Black Freemasonry began in 1775, when Prince Hall and 14 other free black men were initiated into Lodge No. 441 at Boston Harbor by the Irish Constitution. When the British Army left Boston in 1776, this lodge granted Hall and his brethren authority to meet as African Lodge #1. On March 2, 1784, Hall petitioned the Grand Lodge of England for a warrant or charter. The Prince of Wales appointed Hall Provincial Grand Master in 1791. Their mission included dispensing charity, promoting family values, and aiding in uplifting humanity.

THE ORDER OF THE EASTERN STAR

The Order of the Eastern Star was established in the United States in 1778, as a charitable and fraternal organization offering comfort, protection, and aid. The Order endeavors to diffuse the principles of morality and friendship and to improve the condition of widows and orphans. Historically, it has also offered assistance to "distressed female travelers."

NATIONAL COUNCIL OF NEGRO WOMEN

Founded in 1935 by Mary McLeod Bethune, the NCNW is devoted to leading, developing, and advocating for women of African descent. NCNW fulfills this purpose through research, advocacy, and national and community-based services and programs on issues of health, education, and economic empowerment in the United States and Africa. With its 39 national affiliates and more than 240 sections, NCNW has an outreach to nearly four million women.

NAACP

In 1909, W. E. B. Du Bois was among the founders of the National Association for the Advancement of Colored People. From 1910 to 1934, Du Bois served as its director of publicity and research, a member of the board of directors, and editor of *The Crisis*, its monthly magazine. The mission of the NAACP is to ensure the political, educational, social, and economic equality of all people and to eliminate racial hatred and racial discrimination.

Groups like the Prince Hall Masons (above), whose roots date back more than 200 years, and the National Council of Negro Women (below), founded 73 years ago, have in common a goal of human betterment.

DELTA SIGMA THETA

Founded in 1913 by 22 students at Howard University, Delta Sigma Theta Sorority is a private, nonprofit organization whose purpose is to provide assistance and support through established programs in local communities throughout the world. With a sisterhood of more than 200,000 predominantly black college-educated women, the sorority currently has over 900 chapters located in the United States, England, Japan, Germany, the Virgin Islands, Bermuda, the Bahamas, and the Republic of Korea.

KAPPA ALPHA PSI

Kappa Alpha Psi is a college fraternity composed of undergraduate and alumni chapters on major campuses and in cities throughout the country. The constitution of the organization is dedicated to the principles of achievement through a truly democratic fraternity.

JACK AND JILL OF AMERICA

Jack and Jill of America, founded in 1938, is the oldest and largest African-American family organization in the United States. It provides cultural, social, civic, and recreational activities. Jack and Jill, with a membership base of more than 9,500 families, is committed to ensuring that all children have the same opportunities in life.

CHAPTER TEN

Truth and Reflection

Truth and Reflection

Slavery in American history is far more than a thread that runs through a great tapestry. It is the loom, warp and woof, and weavers combined. The economic and geographic expansion of this country rests on the contributions of millions of anonymous men, women, and children who clothed the world in cotton, converted vast tracts of wilderness into farmland, and positioned the United States to reap vast rewards in the sweepstakes of the industrial revolution.

How can such fundamental contributions be so often ignored? American history has long been viewed through the lens of racism, the same set of beliefs that permitted slavery to take root and fuel the country's growth. This "original sin," as many historians call it, cannot be erased from memory or fact. However, the central place of slavery in American history can be acknowledged and applied to a new understanding of human relations in the 21st century.

As Dr. Martin Luther King, Jr., first envisioned in 1963—100 years after slavery ended, yet while its legacy of racism still gripped the nation—America in the 21st century is becoming a postracial society, a place where its citizens "will not be judged by the color of their skin but by the content of their character."

THE SHADOW OF SLAVERY

While still on the coast of his homeland in West Africa, the recently enslaved Olaudah Equiano feared he had entered "a world of bad spirits," in which his captors "were going to kill him." Nearly 250 years later, Governor L. Douglas Wilder, a grandson of slaves and Virginia's first black governor since Reconstruction, visited the slave castle on Gorée Island off the coast of Senegal. Wilder's reverse journey through this "door of no return" marked a new understanding of racism in American politics and society. While standing at the slave castle, closer to the shades of his ancestors, Wilder vowed to bring the untold story of American slavery to light and thus help the nation face its future unburdened by its shameful past.

"Through greater knowledge and understanding of the history of slavery," Wilder later said, "our nation can hope at long last to become free of its legacy." Racism is a complicated set of emotions, beliefs, attitudes, and associated political and economic barriers that resulted from equating skin tone with human potential. It is also an outmoded belief system. New genetic research, combined with decades of enhanced opportunities for and swift achievements by Blacks since the civil rights movement, have proven earlier race theorists wrong, biased by the perspective of their time, and long overdue for correction.

When John Punch attempted to escape with two white fellow indentured servants in Virginia in 1640, slavery, race, and inequality in America became inextricably linked. All three were beaten, but Punch, the only African American in the group, received a sentence of lifelong servitude, while his white companions received only four additional years. From this point on, an expanding body of laws, such as the Slave Codes of 1705 in Virginia and 1740 in South

Left: As they jump rope on the sun-filled city streets, the future looks hopeful for Harlem's youth.

Previous pages: Hunting on the Kalahari dunes, a San Bushman contemplates a traditional way of life in modern-day Africa.

"A black, after hard labour through the day, will be induced by the slightest amusements to sit up till midnight, or later, though knowing he must be out with the first dawn of the morning. They are at least as brave, and more adventuresome. But this may perhaps proceed from a want of forethought, which prevents their seeing a danger till it be present."

— Thomas Jefferson, Third U.S. President

Carolina, protected the practice of race-based slavery. Soon after Thomas Jefferson drafted the Declaration of Independence in 1776, a number of European physical anthropologists and natural scientists involved in classifying species proposed that humanity could be divided into five races: Caucasian, Ethiopian, American, Mongolian, and Malay. While some, such as Carolus Linnaeus and Comte de Buffon, believed that racial characteristics were a function of climate and environment, others, such as Johann Blumenbach and Francis Galton, believed a higher principle was at stake. These northern European scientists, immersed in their own culture, argued for a natural hierarchy among the races, and although "innumerable varieties of mankind run into each other by insensible degrees," one variety was more "perfect" than the others. This form of perfection, according to these European scientists, was exemplified by what they called the "Caucasian" race.

At the same time that natural scientists embarked on classifying flora and fauna around the globe, Enlightenment-era philosophers provided the moral tinder for social reform and revolutionary fervor in Europe and America. When America embarked on its quest for independence from Britain in 1776, many overseas observers waited in anticipation, hopeful that a new model of government would be proved and applied to their own monarchies and nation-states. After seven years of the Revolutionary War, America gained independence, yet its enslaved workforce did not. The promise that "all men are created equal" was now cast in shadow. Black men and women were deemed inferior to whites, not worthy of equal treatment.

None other than Thomas Jefferson advocated this race-based belief system. In his *Notes on the State of Virginia,* written in 1781, he advanced the thought "as a suspicion only, that the blacks, whether originally a distinct race, or made distinct by time and circumstances, are inferior to the whites in the endowments of both body and mind." He went on to doubt the viability of emancipation: "This unfortunate difference of color, and perhaps of faculty, is a powerful obstacle to the emancipation of these people."

Several years before Jefferson died in 1826—when Peter Fosset and other slaves from Monticello were sold on the auction block—he had a final visit with the Marquis de Lafayette, whose support for the Revolutionary War contributed greatly to its success. Jefferson's slave and expert blacksmith Israel (who took the surname Jefferson) observed a final conversation between the two aging revolutionaries: "Lafayette remarked that he thought that the slaves ought to be free; that no man could rightly hold ownership in his brother man; that he gave his best services to and spent his money in behalf of the Americans freely because he felt that they were fighting for a great and noble principle—the freedom of mankind—and that instead of all being free a portion were held in bondage." Israel later told an interviewer that Jefferson, "replied that he thought the time would come when the slaves would be free, but did not indicate when or in what manner they would get their freedom. He seemed to think that the time had not then arrived."

During Jefferson's lifetime, race-based slavery and racism became more entrenched, and the distance between the clarion call of the Declaration of Independence, crafted in 1776, and the compromised language of the U.S. Constitution, ratified in 1787, was considerable. The declaration kept the door to freedom ajar, but the Constitution slammed it shut, with clauses specifically allowing the slave trade to continue until 1808 (Article I, Section 9) and declaring enslaved Blacks equivalent to three-fifths of a white person (Article I, Section 2).

Once this racial injustice was embedded in the Constitution, many historians believe the Civil War became inevitable. Even though the letter of the law emancipated black slaves in 1865, the spirit soon faltered, then failed. The heady period of equality during Reconstruction soon dissipated, and a climate of renewed, and even more virulent, prejudice followed. Variations on race theory first articulated in the late 1700s persisted for nearly two more

A European-built fortress on Gorée Island, like others up and down Africa's western shore, imprisoned African captives while they awaited passage to the Americas. The dungeons marked the first grueling chapter in the life of a slave.

centuries. As recently as the 1990s, social scientists Richard Herrnstein and Charles Murray set forth a race-based explanation for statistical data on IQ test results in *The Bell Curve*. The controversial best-seller triggered a lively national debate and swift rebuttals. Noted biologist Stephen Jay Gould, for example, responded to *The Bell Curve* with "Mismeasure by Any Measure," in which he mused: "How strange that we would let a single and false number divide us [the factor 'g' used quantitative intelligence tests], when evolution has united all people in the recency of our common ancestry thus undergirding with a shared humanity that infinite variety which custom can never stale."

That "evolution has united all people" has been borne out by a new window into the past made possible by cracking and mapping the human genetic code. At last, rather than basing judgments about character and ability on external attributes such as skin tone, facial features, stature, and bone structure, the truth hidden in DNA reveals a far more profound assessment of humanity: We are far more alike than we are different, and we all share a direct lineage to ancestors living in Africa approximately 60,000 years ago.

Spencer Wells, director of the Genographic Project, has identified a few key mutations of the Y chromosome (present in all men and not subject to change in male offspring based on their mother's genetic makeup) that trace an arc of human migration that is truly breathtaking in scope and simplicity. In other words, when millions of Africans came in chains to America during the 17th, 18th, and 19th centuries, they were enslaved by people of common ancestry. Race is thus not a reality but a belief, a cultural artifact. "Race has never been about color," according to Gerald Foster, scholar in residence of the United States National Slavery Museum. "Instead, it is about attitudes that have been unique to America

A Japanese storeowner in Oakland, California, proudly displays his patriotism after the Japanese attack on Pearl Harbor. His sentiments echo those of many ethnic minorities in the U.S.—in times of crisis, the question of what constitutes "American" falls squarely on minority shoulders.

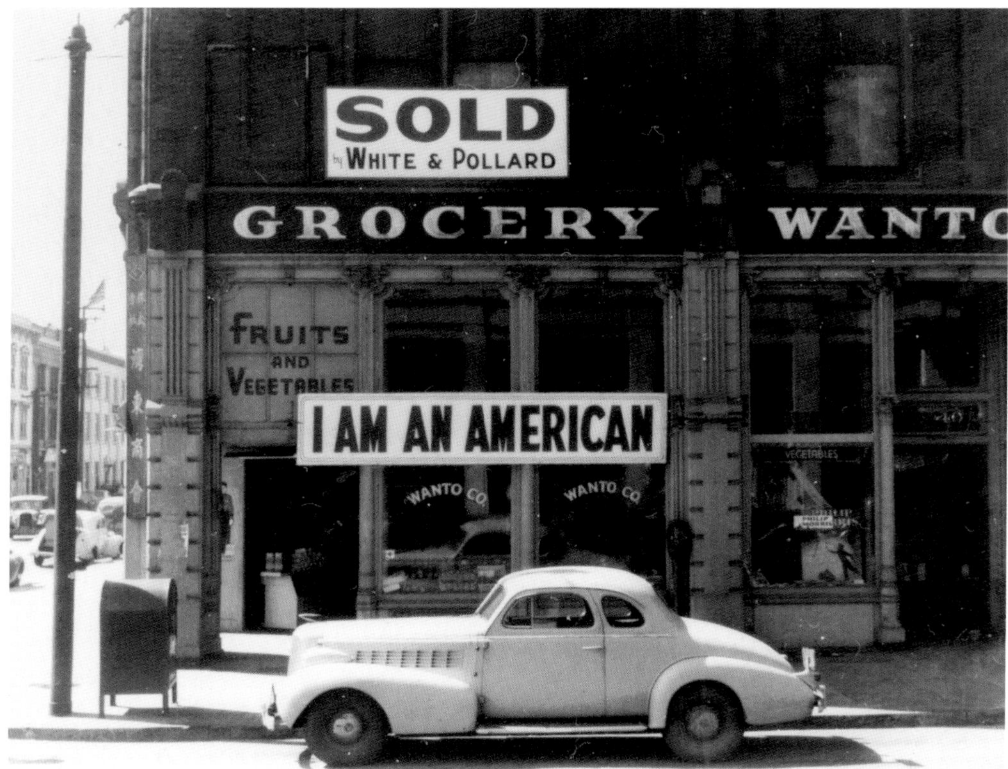

"It is a fact that, if a person is known to have one percent of African blood in his veins, he ceases to be a white man. The ninety-nine percent of Caucasian blood does not weigh by the side of the one percent of African blood. The white blood counts for nothing. The person is a Negro every time."

—Booker T. Washington, educator and author

to justify second-class treatment of blacks." No specter associated with racism caused more alarm among many whites than miscegenation, intermarriage between black and white people. Virginia passed the first law banning marriage between blacks and whites in 1661. Thirty years later, Virginia upped the ante for white women who bore mulatto children: a fine or "indentured servitude for five years for herself and thirty years for her child."

Maryland followed suit in 1715, and, on the eve of Civil War, "at least five states had enacted anti-miscegenation laws." Yet even as laws forbidding intermarriage became more commonplace, so did births of mulatto children. According to the Organization of American Historians, "Between 1850 and 1860, the mulatto slave population increased by 67 percent; in contrast, the black slave population increased by only 20 percent."

Antimiscegenation laws stayed on America's legal books for more than 300 years. In the 1960s, several states still prohibited intermarriage, yet due to the civil rights movement, the U.S. Supreme Court agreed to hear cases that challenged race-based penalties (*McLaughlin* v. *Florida*, 1964) and antimiscegenation statutes (*Loving* v. *Virginia*, 1967).

In 1958, Perry Loving, a white man, and Mildred Jeter, an African-American and American-Indian woman, wed in Washington, D.C., and returned to their Virginia home with a framed marriage certificate. Yet as police informed them early one morning after their return, their union was not recognized in Virginia, just across the Potomac River. They were arrested, put in jail, and came before a Virginia judge who gave them an ultimatum: spend one year in jail or leave the state. His reasoning harkened back to the race theorists of a bygone era:

> *Almighty God created the races, white, black, yellow, malay and red, and he placed them on separate continents. And but for the interference with his arrangement there would be no cause for such marriages. The fact that he separated the races shows that he did not intend for the races to mix.*

Senator from Mississippi: Blanche Kelso Bruce

Reconstruction, lasting from 1865 to 1876, was a federal program that attempted to resolve the equal rights issues created by the end of the war. In southern states, where voters were predominantly Black, a number of African Americans were elected to office. Blanche Kelso Bruce was the first to serve a full term in the U.S. Senate. Bruce was born to a white plantation owner and a house slave on March 1, 1841, near Farmville, Virginia. After his father legally freed him, Bruce parted ways at the start of the Civil War to enlist in the Union Army but was rejected because the Army was not recruiting African-American soldiers at the time. He found work teaching and is credited with founding the first school for African Americans in Hannibal, Missouri, in 1864. After two years of study at Oberlin College in Ohio, Bruce took a job as a steamboat porter, then moved to Bolivar County, Mississippi, in 1869, where he become a wealthy and influential property owner. He served as the state senate's sergeant at arms in 1870. In Bolivar County, he served as a sheriff, county school superintendent, and on the Board of Mississippi Levee Commissioners. In Tallahatchie County, he was the registrar of voters and tax assessor. On March 4, 1875, he was elected to the U.S. Senate as a Republican. Senator Bruce served on three committees: Education and Labor, Pensions, and the Committee on River Improvements, which he chaired. He also chaired the Select Committee to investigate the collapse of the Freedman's Savings and Trust Company. He fought for desegregation of the Army and for the protection of voting rights for African Americans. He supported a more humane treatment of American Indians and for the increased distribution of western land grants to African Americans. In 1879, Bruce was the first African American to preside over the U.S. Senate. Following the end of his term in 1881, Bruce remained in Washington, D.C., and held several public offices. On March 17, 1898, he died from diabetic complications at the age of 57. *D. W.*

The first African American to serve a full term in the U.S. Senate, Blanche Kelso Bruce, of Bolivar County, Mississippi, devoted his career to the education and rights of African Americans in the Reconstruction-era South.

"The common road of hope which we all traveled has brought us into a stronger kinship than any words, laws, or legal claims."

— Richard Wright, author

As the U.S. Supreme Court struck down the Virginia court's decision, Chief Justice Earl Warren decreed: "Under our Constitution, the freedom to marry or not marry a person of another race resides with the individual and cannot be infringed upon by the State." Perry Loving and Mildred Jeter could at last live in peace, and antimiscegenation laws in all other states were nullified.

Six years before the Lovings enjoyed their hard-won victory, a baby boy was born to a "father from Kenya and a mother from Kansas" in Hawaii. Forty-six years later, Senator Barack Obama ran for the Presidency of the United States. In March 2008, Obama delivered a historic campaign speech about the history of slavery, race, and America's democratic process. He delivered his address in Philadelphia, the city where the Constitution that both permitted slavery and delivered the tools to overcome it was drafted:

> *Of course, the answer to the slavery question was already embedded within our Constitution—a Constitution that had at its very core the ideal of equal citizenship under the law; a Constitution that promised its people liberty, and justice, and a union that could be and should be perfected over time.*
>
> *And yet words on a parchment would not be enough to deliver slaves from bondage, or provide men and women of every color and creed their full rights and obligations as citizens of the United States. What would be needed were Americans in successive generations who were willing to do their part—through protests and struggle, on the streets and in the courts, through a civil war and civil disobedience and always at great risk—to narrow that gap between the promise of our ideals and the reality of their time.*

Traditional African clothing, such as this garment on display in the National Slavery Museum, evokes a proud heritage for many African Americans.

WHO IS "AMERICAN"?

Nearly 150 years after slavery ended, and after generations of willing arrivals came from Europe, Asia, and South America during the 19th and 20th centuries, 6.8 million Americans reported that they were of more than one race. In West Coast cities such as Los Angeles, San Francisco, and Seattle, many young Americans of the early 21st century needed four or more words to accurately describe their ethnic and racial makeup: Scotch-Irish-Filipino-American, or African-Hispanic-Jewish-American, or Japanese-Hawaiian-Norwegian-American. In California, one in every six births was a child of mixed race. Reflecting this new demographic reality, the 1990 and 2000 censuses allowed respondents to write in their own racial identity. In 1990, "Americans using the write-in blank self-identified nearly three hundred races, six hundred American Indian tribes, seventy Hispanic groups, and seventy-five different combinations of multiracial ancestry." Thus, 200 years after Johann Blumenbach decided that humanity could be divided into five distinct races, Americans described more than a thousand variations on the theme. Ultimately, the architect of race theory was proved right on one account: "innumerable varieties of mankind run into each other by insensible degrees." By the 21st century, race in America became so nuanced, so subtle, and so personal as to lose its former significance.

Combating Slavery Now: Condoleezza Rice, Ph.D.

Secretary of State Condoleezza Rice was born in Birmingham, Alabama, in 1954. She earned her bachelor's degree in political science, cum laude and Phi Beta Kappa, from the University of Denver in 1974; her master's from the University of Notre Dame in 1975; and her Ph.D. from the Graduate School of International Studies at the University of Denver in 1981.

Rice had a prominent career in academe as well as government, serving for six years as Stanford University's provost. In government, she served in the George H. W. Bush Administration as director and then senior director of Soviet and East European affairs in the National Security Council. She has also served as special assistant to the President for National Security Affairs. She joined the administration of George W. Bush in 2001 as national security adviser.

Rice became secretary of state in 2005 after Gen. Colin Powell stepped down from that post. Powell and Rice were the first and the second African Americans to hold that position.

It is in this capacity that Rice has overseen the Office to Monitor and Combat Trafficking in Persons. The practice of human trafficking, according to the State Department's June 12, 2007, *Trafficking In Persons Report*, involves 800,000 men, women, and children annually. These include, however, only those who are trafficked across national borders. The total does not include the millions who are trafficked within their own countries. Approximately 80 percent of transnational victims are women, and up to 50 percent are minors. This practice is defined by the U.S. State Department as "The recruitment, harboring, transportation, provision, or obtaining of a person for labor or services, through the use of force, fraud, or coercion for the purpose of subjection to involuntary servitude, peonage, debt bondage, or slavery."

Through her position, Rice pressures other countries to end the practice of human trafficking, largely through placing the worst offenders on related lists. As the country's top diplomat, Rice has a mighty platform to use in fighting the enduring evil of slavery. *C. J. C.*

As U.S. secretary of state under President George W. Bush, Condoleezza Rice has encouraged an end to human trafficking.

Civil Rights: Lessons and Truths

JUAN WILLIAMS

History's judgment of the modern civil rights movement is now coming into view. Fifty years later, the answer to questions about the impact of the movement can be found in books but also in the actions of today's political and cultural leaders.

In 2004, the nation, North and South, celebrated the 50th anniversary of the landmark Supreme Court decision that ended legal segregation in public schools, *Brown* v. *Board of Education*. And 2008 marks 40 years since Martin Luther King, Jr., died in Memphis after leading a civil rights movement that gave the nation the 1964 Civil Rights Act and the 1965 Voting Rights Act. With a half century having passed, the truth can be seen clearly now: The Black American civil rights movement stands as the greatest social movement in American history.

The power of the 20th century's civil rights movement stirred controversy, and shifted politics and residential patterns. In many cases, it left emotions raw. With the smoke and static long gone from riots in big-city Black ghettoes, as well as from the murders and beatings by segregationists, there is now an emerging consensus about the movement. It has been the basis for the tremendous strides America made on race relations and beyond over the last half of the 20th century.

It set the framework for nonviolent protest strategies used to achieve social progress for women, for Latinos, for gay people, for the disabled, and even for both sides in the heated abortion debate.

The modern Black civil rights movement began during World War II. A. Philip Randolph, the labor leader, pressed President Franklin D. Roosevelt to integrate the factories and federal bureaus and then pressured President Harry Truman into fully integrating the U.S. military. Another milestone occurred when Major League Baseball allowed Jackie Robinson to play. That was followed by the bigger fight to end school segregation and then the transforming struggle to open the voting booth to black people.

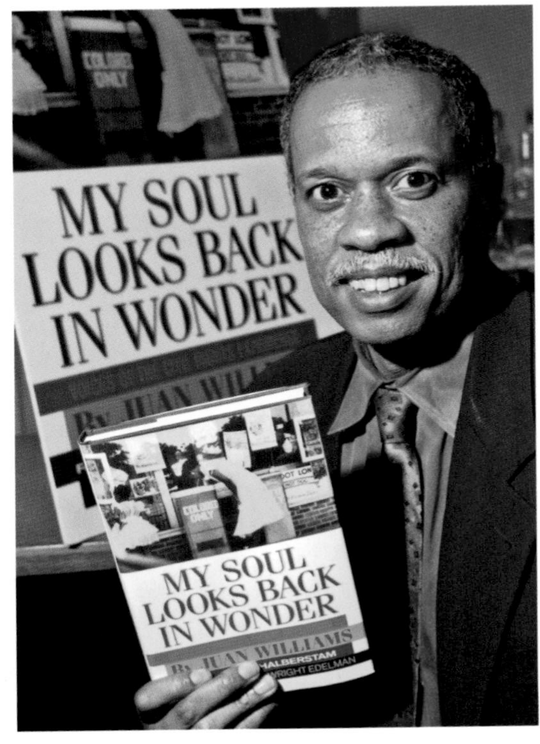

Journalist Juan Williams collected eyewitness accounts from the civil rights movement into a 2004 book, My Soul Looks Back in Wonder.

Big cities, including New York, Los Angeles, and Chicago, all saw Black political power rise up in the years that followed. Black people sat on school boards, became members of their city councils, and won mayoral elections. State politics saw historic numbers of Black legislators, and two states—Virginia and Massachusetts—saw their first Black governors since Reconstruction. The Congressional Black Caucus has grown to record numbers with more than 40 black people elected to Congress, including nearly a dozen from majority white districts. There have been two black men on the Supreme Court, and a black man and a black woman have served as the nation's secretary of state, representing America to the world.

Levels of Black high school and college graduation have also reached new heights. That has created the largest Black middle class ever seen in the nation's history and the wealthiest group of black people in the world. Today a majority of Black families have middle-class incomes because they earn more than twice the level of income that qualifies for poverty. By comparison, only one percent of Black Americans could claim to be in the middle class in 1940.

TODAY'S CHALLENGES

Today's civil rights issues include a poverty rate among Black Americans that is still 25 percent. The schools serving black children remain among the worst in the nation. Test scores show a sizable "achievement gap" between black and white high school students; on average, black students are graduating the 12th grade with reading and math skills equal to white eighth graders. Failing schools have many consequences, including adding to a rising number of black people ending up in prison.

Thirteen percent of the total U.S. population is black, but roughly 40 percent of the country's prison population is black. It is estimated that 60 percent of the inmates are basically illiterate. This awful reality plays out in family and street violence, and is reflected by aspects of hip-hop culture that

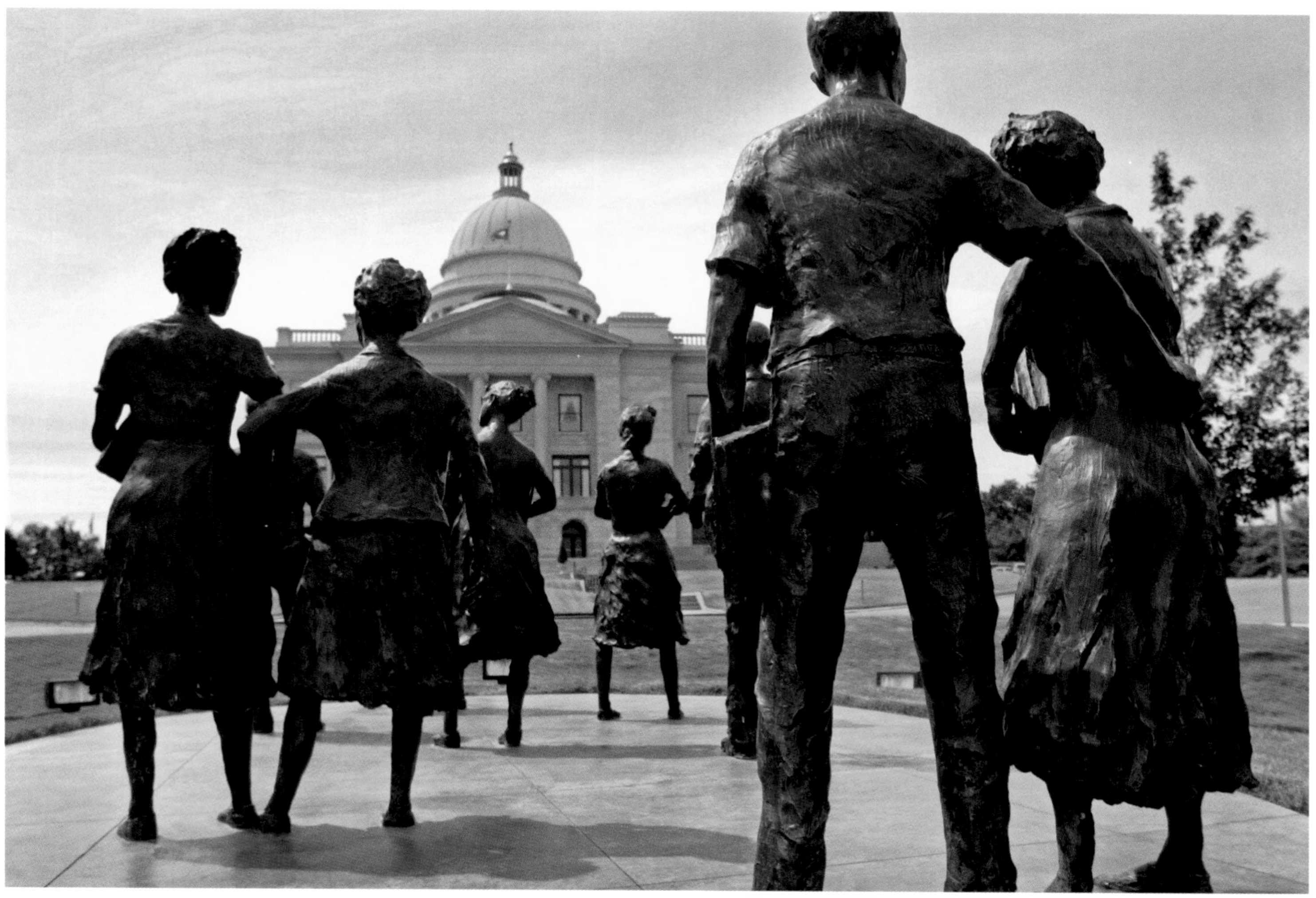

On the grounds of the Arkansas State Capitol, statues of the Little Rock Nine—Black students who desegregated Little Rock Central High School in 1957—commemorate the sacrifices and struggles made along the road to equality.

embrace the image of the "Thug Life" or "gangsta." Statistics show Black Americans account for 37 percent of violent crime, as well as for 54 percent of robberies and 51 percent of murders. At the start of the 21st century, it was estimated that any black boy born in 2001 had a 33 percent chance of going to jail in his lifetime.

The most alarming statistic for Black America has to do with the family, long the cornerstone of Black life through the great civil rights movement. In 1940, before the start of the civil rights movement, 75 percent of Black youth lived with both of their parents. By 1990, the U.S. Census Bureau reported that only a third of black children could go home and find both their mother and father. In fact, about 70 percent of black children are now born to single mothers.

IMPORTANT TRUTHS

The civil rights movement of the mid-20th century emphasized pride in Black intellectual and moral strength as equal to that of any race. Black people had overcome the horror of slavery, social exclusion, and legal segregation, and those strong souls insisted, as a matter of justice, on equal rights.

Today, the great truth of the civil rights movement—black people as champions, not victims, willing to see the truth and deal with it—is as important as it was when Mary McLeod Bethune, Jackie Robinson, Thurgood Marshall, Martin Luther King, Jr., and Rosa Parks led their revolutions. The truth is that, given the successes of the civil rights movement, black and white Americans know that strategies and coalitions have to be put in place to deal with inferior schools and to support children coming from broken families.

The civil rights movement revealed the truth about the need to struggle, to sacrifice for the next generation, to believe in ourselves, and keep our eyes on the prize of America's ideals of liberty and justice for all. Today, all of America needs to reflect on that truth as we go forward with a continuing civil rights movement. ■

Previous pages: A mural in Los Angeles's Union Station—"City of Dreams/River of History" by Richard Wyatt—captures California's ethnic heritage and multiculturalist future. Populations throughout the U.S. continue to diversify, with more and more Americans claiming multiethnic identities.

ACCEPTANCE: TOWARD A MORE PERFECT UNION

The roots of slavery in America run deep. The country was a slave nation longer than it was free. Yet the gradual expansion of civil rights during the 1960s enhanced educational opportunities since the landmark U.S. Supreme Court ruling in *Brown* v. *Board of Education* in 1954, and the participation of Blacks at the highest levels of the nation's corporate, academic, and public institutions have gradually created a more equitable system.

As the Civil War loomed in March 1861, President Lincoln called on all Americans to draw upon "the better angels of our nature." Evidence of these angels appeared one hundred years later, when the U.S. Congress passed the Civil Rights Act of 1964, which required states to apply the 14th and 15th Amendments regardless of race, and the Voting Rights Act of 1965, which expressly forbade poll taxes and other discriminatory practices at the voting booth. Thus, one hundred years after they were first approved, supporting legislation shored up the 13th, 14th, and 15th Amendments.

A similar time span passed between the emergence of Jim Crow laws and the end of legally sanctioned segregation in public facilities. In 1892, Homer Plessy, a light-skinned black man—in whom that infamous "one drop" was scarcely visible—boarded a white-only train car in New Orleans. He refused to disembark when asked to do so by the conductor, and "with the aid of a police officer," according to court records, was "forcibly ejected from said coach, and hurried off to, and imprisoned in, the parish jail of New Orleans." Plessy lost his legal challenge. The Supreme Court upheld the "separate but equal" ruling, and the court's majority opinion included a startling claim: "If one race be inferior to the other socially, the constitution of the United States cannot put them upon the same plane."

In 1925, the same year that Homer Plessy passed away, a young man living in Baltimore graduated from high school, and set his eyes on college, then law school. During the 1930s, Thurgood Marshall studied law at Howard University and pursued the inspired quest of its dean, Charles Hamilton Houston, to banish "separate but equal" to the past. As chief counsel for the National Association for the Advancement of Colored People (NAACP), Marshall accomplished just that. In 1954, he argued and won the landmark *Brown* v. *Board* case before the Supreme Court, in which Chief Justice Earl Warren delivered the court's unanimous decision:

> *To separate them [children in grade and high schools] from others of similar age and qualifications solely because of their race generates a feeling of inferiority as to their status in the community that may affect their hearts and minds in a way unlikely to ever be undone. . . .*
>
> *We conclude that in the field of public education the doctrine of "separate but equal" has no place. Separate educational facilities are inherently unequal.*

Later appointed to the U.S. Supreme Court by President Lyndon Baines Johnson in 1965, Thurgood Marshall continued to use the legal system to address the injustices that Homer Plessy's brief train trip showcased. Although Marshall's legacy cast a long shadow, and few have topped his record number of victories before the Supreme Court, he paved the way for others to follow. Since the 1960s, greater numbers of Blacks have been selected to lead and serve by primarily white electorates. They have worked at the highest levels of city, state, and federal governments, universities, and major corporations, gradually fulfilling the promise of America.

Believed to have been made by a slave, this solid oak daybed is among many artifacts collected by the U.S. National Slavery Museum to showcase the forgotten contributions of Africans in the U.S.

The "Second Founder": Father Patrick Healy

Although born into slavery in the pre–Civil War South, Patrick Healy rose to positions of prominence in both the worlds of the church and of academia.

Healy started life on a plantation in Macon, Georgia, in 1834. His father, Michael Morris Healy, was a white Irish immigrant who acquired a 1,000-acre plantation after the War of 1812. He owned many slaves, including a mixed-race teenager named Mary Eliza Smith. Beginning around 1820, they had ten children together, including Patrick.

Michael Healy publicly recognized all of his children, but he was not allowed to marry his common-law wife or to free her under Georgia law. In addition, his children were considered slaves by law. To assure their freedom if he should die, and to provide for their education, which as slaves they were denied in the South, he sent his children and their mother north to live.

It was here that most of the Healy children were introduced to the vocations in which they later became accomplished. All of Michael Healy's sons first attended Quaker schools in New York and New Jersey, where they experienced some discrimination not because of their race, but because of their father's status as a slave owner.

As a result, they next attended a new Jesuit school in Worcester, Massachusetts, called the College of the Holy Cross. Since the brothers were light-skinned, most people assumed that they were white. The oldest son, James Augustine Healy, became the first black Roman Catholic priest in the United States. He would later go on to become the bishop of Portland, Maine.

Patrick Francis Healy, Michael's younger brother, became the first African American to earn a doctoral degree, the first black Jesuit, and the first black president of a predominantly white college. He took his vows of poverty, chastity, and obedience in the early 1850s, and was ordained a priest in 1864. He earned his doctorate degree the following year from the University of Louvain in Belgium.

The son of a white father and a mixed-race mother, Father Patrick Healy is remembered as one of Georgetown University's most dynamic presidents.

Upon returning to the United States, he became a professor of philosophy at Georgetown College in Washington, D.C. He later became vice president in 1869, vice rector by 1873, and president on July 31, 1874, a position he held until 1882. During his tenure, Healy expanded the school's curriculum in science and law, built a new library, added more classrooms, and founded an alumni association

According to a university publication, "Georgetown College gradually moved towards university status in the nineteenth century, due mainly to the efforts of Patrick F. Healy, S.J. . . . Father Healy was one of the University's most dynamic presidents and is often referred to as its second founder." One building that was constructed under his authority, Healy Hall, was named in his honor after his death.

Despite all of the advances that Father Healy brought to the university, though, he did not press for the admission of Blacks to Georgetown; African Americans would not gain that right until after World War II. Father Healy was forced to retire in 1882, due to ill health, and he died in 1910. He is buried in the Jesuit cemetery on the school's campus.

Other Healy siblings went on to gain prominence as well. Michael Augustine Healy became an officer in the precursor to the U.S. Coast Guard, the Revenue Cutter Service; Eliza Dunmore Healy became a teacher and a convent superior and later was made mother superior of a community of white nuns at Villa Barlow, a prestigious convent in Vermont; and Amanda Healy worked at a boarding school and convent in Saint Johns, Quebec. *C. J. C.*

"The founders of our liberation movement drew deep inspiration at the turn of the century from black Americans striving under difficult circumstances to fulfill our common aspiration for the restoration of human dignity. It is small wonder that the struggle to end apartheid drew such strength from here, or that we now look to you to work with us as we seek to banish poverty, hunger, illiteracy and ignorance from our land."

— Former President Nelson Mandela, South African freedom fighter

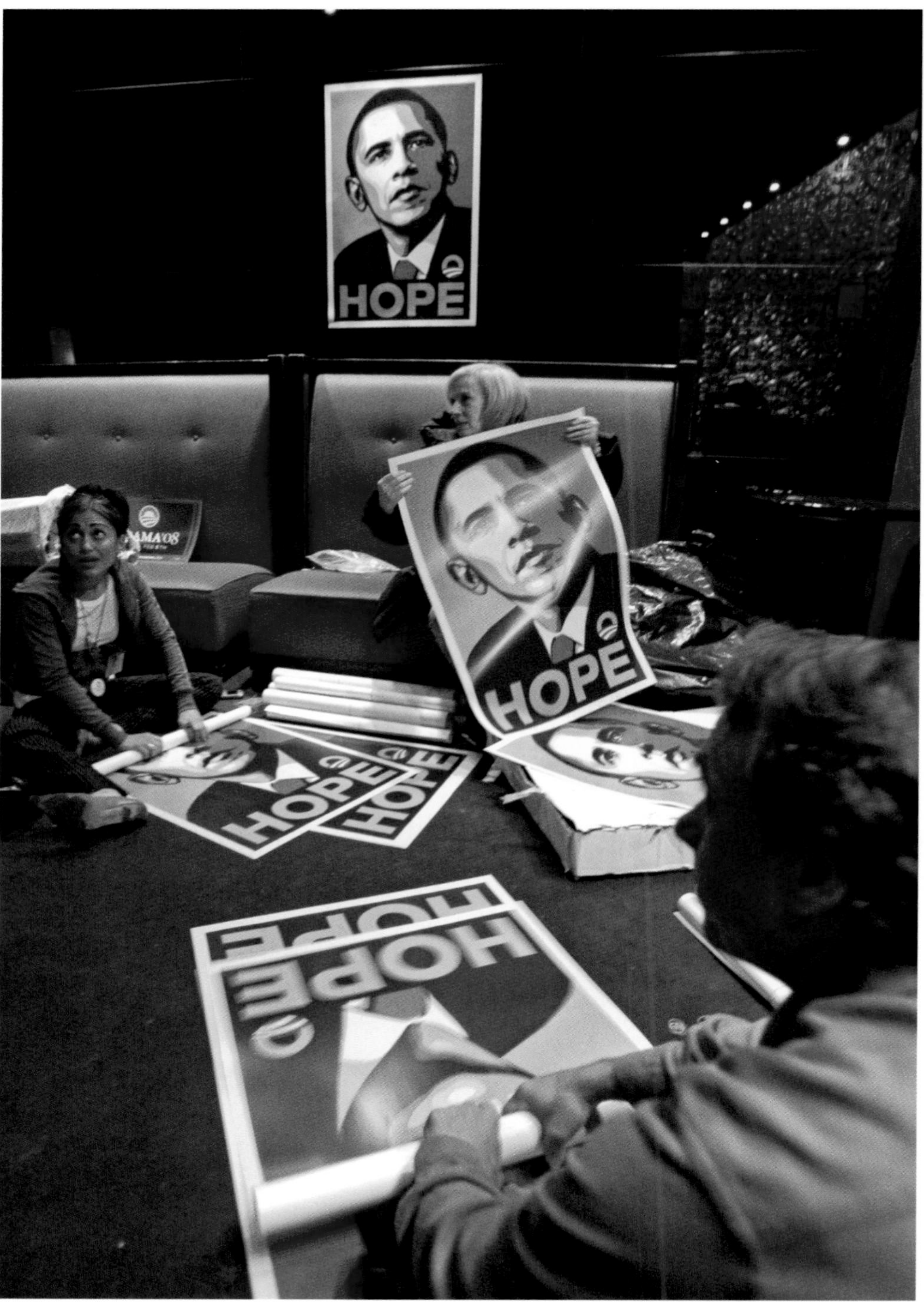

Senator Barack Obama's message of hope has ignited a presidential campaign unlike any other in recent history. The popular Illinois senator is the first African-American presidential nominee of a major party.

The United States may still be "the last best hope of earth," not because it has avoided social and racial conflict, but precisely because it has weathered unrest and rebellion, discord and dissent. The rights enumerated in the Constitution and Bill of Rights have gradually extended past the narrow sphere of free, white, literate, and propertied males, as originally conceived by the Founding Founders. Gradually, men without vast property voted alongside gentry, women next to men, Blacks alongside whites. This process of expanding the definition of who is fully American—and which rights each American actually enjoys—is continually unfolding. America is a more equitable place because the

Climbing the Ivy: Ruth J. Simmons, Ph.D.

The former president of Smith College, Ruth J. Simmons, was sworn in as the 18th president of Brown University on July 3, 2001. According to a university publication, "as an academic leader, Simmons believes in the power of education to transform lives. She champions the university as a haven of reasoned debate with the responsibility to challenge students intellectually and prepare them to become informed, conscientious citizens. She has spent her career advocating for a leadership role for higher education in the arena of national and global affairs."

Simmons was born in in 1945 in Grapeland, Texas, the youngest of 12 children. Although the product of segrated schools, she did well academically and received a scholarsip to Dillard University, a historically black college in New Orleans, Louisiana. Simmons spent a year at Wellesley College in New England while she was still an undergraduate, and because she loved the Northeast, she went on to Harvard University. In 1973, she earned her doctorate degree in Romance languages and literature. Fluent in French, she has written on the works of poets David Diop and Aimé Césaire.

Simmons held several positions in California and Louisiana in teaching and administration for ten years. In 1983, after serving as associate dean of the graduate school at the University of Southern California, Simmons joined Princeton University as acting director of the Afro-American studies. While there, she overhauled the program, hired renowned experts such as Toni Morrison and Cornel West, and redirected its focus from political expression to intellectual query.

Simmons was soon appointed to the position of associate dean. After that, she took an appointment as provost at Spelman College, a prestigious women's college in Atlanta, Georgia, that was founded for African Americans. After two years, she returned to Princeton as vice-provost. While in that position, she wrote a celebrated report on campus racism that became known as the *Simmons Report*.

Her report led the university to create an ombudsman's office to handle complaints and to effect changes in its hiring practices and student recruitment. Like her Afro-American studies program, the ombudsman program became a model for many universities nationwide. She would then move on to become the president of Smith College from 1995 to 2001. While there, she inaugurated the first engineering program at a U.S. women's college.

Simmons serves on numerous boards including Texas Instruments, Goldman Sachs, and Howard University board of trustees. She holds more than 27 honorary degrees from colleges and universities, and she is a member of many professional societies. In 2001 *Time* magazine named her America's best college president. In 2007, she was named one of *U.S. News & World Report*'s top U.S. leaders and—for the second time—a *Glamour* magazine Woman of the Year.

The first Black president of an Ivy League college, Brown University President Ruth Simmons, shown here in 2004, has encouraged the institution to explore the legacy of slavery in its own foundations.

In 2004, Simmons appointed a Committee on Slavery and Justice to investigate Brown's historic ties to slavery and, among other things, to recommend whether and how the university should take responsibility for its connection to slavery. As it turns out, even though Nicholas Brown, Jr., who was an ardent abolitionist, is the university's namesake, his uncle John Brown, a slave trader, put up half the money for Brown's first library. On July 1, 2007, Brown created a ten-member Commission to Commemorate the History of Slavery in Rhode Island. In cooperation with the city of Providence and state of Rhode Island, the commission is charged with developing ideas for how best to acknowledge the university and community's historical relationship to slavery and the transatlantic slave trade.

While her charge to the committee that looked into Brown University's involvement in slavery drew various conclusions and made several recommendations, President Simmons has continued to represent the best of the university. *C. J. C.*

"To engage in a serious discussion of race in America, we must begin not with the problems of black people but with the flaws of American society—flaws rooted in historic inequalities and longstanding cultural stereotypes."

—Cornel West, Ph.D., professor

Teaching aids published by the U.S. National Slavery Museum help students understand the full story of slavery and the racism left in its wake.

Africans it once enslaved overcame adversity and injustice, in steps both large and small, to become Americans.

WE ARE ONE PEOPLE

Slavery acted upon and transformed the individuals it touched. As it left its mark on the nation's financial and political landscape, it also left indelible traces in a realm more difficult to describe or quantify: the psyches of both slaves and slave owners, victims and victimizers. Arguably, the attitudes that made slavery possible became embedded in America's collective unconscious ("the inherited part of the unconscious that . . . is shared by all the members of a people or race," as defined in *Merriam-Webster's Collegiate Dictionary*).

Four hundred years after slavery began in Virginia, self-hate and anger on the part of some Blacks is matched by a sense of entitlement and shame on the part of many whites. To break through this impasse requires personal reflection, a process that is neither painless nor swift. Novelist Ralph Ellison described his experience on this quest as a "struggle to stare down the deadly and hypnotic temptation to interpret the world and all its devices in terms of race." Only through this form of individual reflection is collective change possible. To create a future no longer defined by the past requires nothing less, and a nation founded on the truth that "all men are created equal" deserves nothing less.

Despite the emphasis on race that ran throughout slavery and its long aftermath, it was first and foremost an economic institution. In the words of Garrison Frazier, a former slave who met with General William Tecumseh Sherman and Secretary of War Edwin M. Stanton in Savannah in January 1865, "Slavery is receiving by the irresistible power the work of another man, and not by his consent." Historian Ira Berlin summarized as follows: "Slavery's moral stench cannot mask the design of American captivity: to commandeer the labor of the many to make the few rich and powerful. Slavery thus made class as it made race, and in entwining the two processes it mystified both."

The powerful economic engine made possible by generations of unpaid labor acted upon individuals with disastrous consequences: It corrupted slave owners as it crushed slaves' psyches. As Thomas Jefferson mused in *Notes on the State of Virginia* in 1781, "the whole commerce between master and slave is a perpetual exercise of the most boisterous passions, the most unremitting despotism on the one part, and degrading submissions on the other."

This cycle of despotism and degradation passed from one generation to the next, a pattern of learned behavior that nonetheless became unconscious and automatic: "The parent storms, the child looks on, catches the lineaments of wrath, puts on the same airs in the circle of smaller slaves, gives a loose to his worst of passions, and thus nursed, educated, and daily exercised in tyranny, cannot but be stamped by it with odious peculiarities. The man must be a prodigy who can retain his manners and morals undepraved by such circumstances."

As Frederick Douglass witnessed, his mistress, "a woman of the kindest heart and finest feelings," became a "demon" as a slave owner:

> *But, alas! this kind heart had but a short time to remain such. The fatal poison of irresponsible power was already in her hands, and soon commenced its infernal work. That cheerful eye, under the influence of slavery, soon became red with rage; that voice, made all of sweet accord, changed to one of harsh and horrid discord; and that angelic face gave place to that of a demon.*

continues to suffer from crippling social problems that stem from the artificial concept of race.

America's failure to address and eradicate the issue of race is unacceptable. The Center of Learning is providing the tools to eliminate racism in each of its increasingly insidious forms—in our media and in our minds, in our schools and in our spirits. We can only imagine the potential of our fellow Americans, once they are unencumbered by this burden.

Nurturing Mind, Body, and Spirit

The new Center of Learning facility will be a dynamic, interactive institution designed to support the learning and wellbeing of our visiting audience. The 40,000 square foot facility will include:

- Classrooms and conference rooms
- Senior citizen's wing
- Children's wing (with playground area)
- Young adult's wing (with arcade room)
- K-12 teacher's wing (with theatre and waiting area)
- Gymnasium
- Lecture hall (with terrace for outdoor events)
- Theatre/auditorium (450 seats)
- 2 Libraries
- Outdoor learning opportunities

Delivering Success

The Center of Learning is implementing its goals through a comprehensive master plan for success. In-depth training, staff development, and cultural sensitivity workshops and seminars will be conducted on site and off, under the auspices of the Center of Learning. Our client/audience and constituency is targeted to include corporations, civil service departments, human service workers, policy makers, as well as educators (K-12) and college teacher preparatory programs. Current programs include:

- **USNSM Slavery Research Consortium**
  University consortium generating and consolidating original faculty and student research from Howard University, University of Richmond, Brown University, University of Mary Washington, Virginia Commonwealth University, and Chicago State University
- **Traveling USNSM exhibits**
  Exhibit development and management, as well as acquisition and study of visitor feedback
- **University of Richmond/USNSM Study**
  Research and analysis of student reactions to USNSM Slave Video
- **Virginia State Department of Education Collaboration**
- **USNSM Lesson Plans**
  Workbooks, activities, resources and online information
- **Standards of Learning/No Child Left Behind**
  Adapted lesson plans to meet these new standards
- **National Geographic Partnership**
  Map project, book publication project, slave ship project
- **Slavery and Racism Awareness Programs**
  Workshops and classes, now in development with world-renowned experts on recovery and reconciliation, will be tailored to the needs of individuals, educational institutions, and corporations
- **USNSM History Competition**
  National High School research and writing competition on the subject of slavery
- **Slavery Resource Center**
  Definitive resource for slavery research (including the source for update and development of all permanent and temporary USNSM exhibitions)

U.S. NATIONAL SLAVERY MUSEUM

1320 Central Park Boulevard; Suite 251
Fredericksburg, Virginia 22401
540-548-8818
www.usnsm.org.

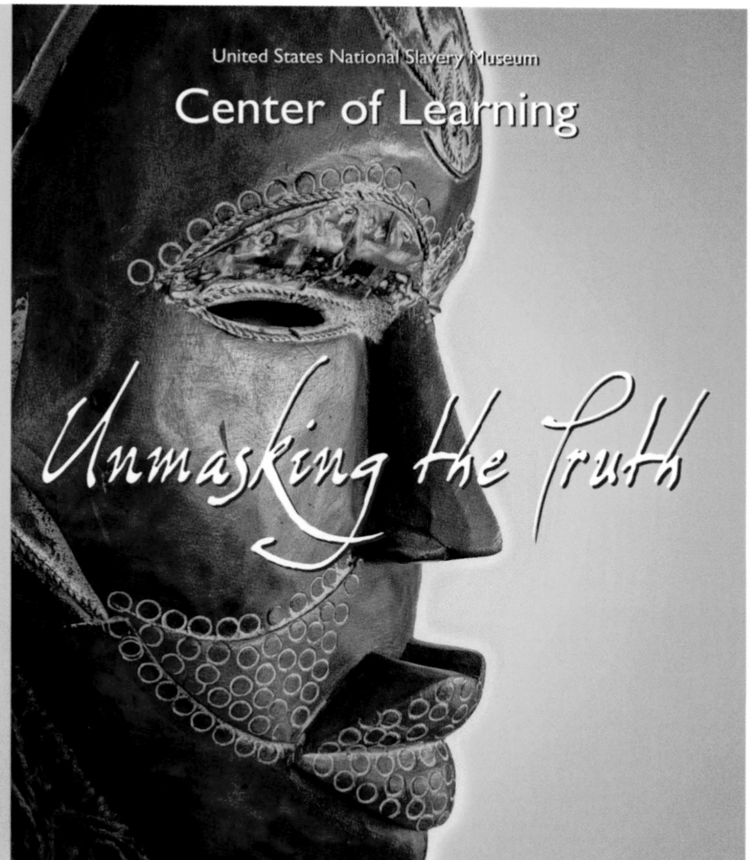

Other publications by the museum's Center of Learning seek to dispel myths about slavery and in their place establish a deeper understanding of this institution and its place in American history.

From a contemporary perspective, this demonic transformation corresponded to a "disease of the soul" for all concerned. In his best-selling book *Race Matters*, Dr. Cornel West, professor of religion at Princeton University, described an individual remedy for this collective predicament: "Any disease of the soul must be conquered by a turning of one's soul. The turning is done through one's own affirmation of one's worth—an affirmation fueled by the concern of others. A love ethic must be at the center of a politics of conversion."

To foster this "turning of one's soul," the museum first envisioned by Douglas L. Wilder in the slave castle at Gorée will provide a common ground for a new understanding of the past and future of America. The mission of the United States National Slavery Museum is to tell the complete story of slavery in America. In so doing, it will inspire visitors to accept and acknowledge the centrality of slavery in American history in order to apply a new understanding of human relations in the 21st century. In the heart of the Old Dominion, where slavery first began in America, visitors will find an environment that seeks not to assign blame, but to spark the confidence to speak knowledgably about the nation's most difficult subject: slavery and its legacy of racism.

Without the enslaved Africans and their descendants who built America, our nation would be a lesser place. In order to become a "more perfect union," it is time to acknowledge the millions of anonymous slaves whose forced labor built the country. The United States National Slavery Museum will guide visitors on a personal odyssey through America's wilderness of slavery to emerge with a new understanding.

We are truly one people: In origin, we are all African, and in opportunity, equality, and nationality, we are all American.

On Hallowed Ground

A GALLERY

Being named as architect of the United States National Slavery Museum is one of the greatest honors I have received. When I learned of the project, I asked to meet Governor Wilder to see if I could help. What started out as an offer to share my knowledge of the design and construction of museums turned into a unique experience, during which I became convinced of his vision for the museum. The architect's job is to make form out of his client's vision. In this case, it was much easier because I was convinced.

The truth about slavery in America is something that is largely unknown by most Americans. If African Americans knew the history and the contributions of their enslaved ancestors, they would be proud. Of course, part of the story is hardship and suffering. In spite of all that they had to endure, slaves and their descendants have made tremendous strides economically, culturally, and in many other ways. Everything that we think of as uniquely "American" has been influenced and molded by the African heritage brought by the slaves. What would American music, art, dance, writing, and so on be without this influence? White Americans also need to understand that Africans and their descendants helped to build this country. We all need to know more about those facts. This museum will tell that story.

An exhibit hall in the USNSM explores conditions of the perilous Middle Passage and includes a replica slave ship.

I know Governor Wilder feels that this museum, by telling the truth, will be a place for reconciliation, not for recrimination. It will be a place for all Americans, no matter what race. It will be a museum whose purpose is to help Americans learn from the past, but also to look forward. And so the architecture had to be equally forward-looking. The time is ripe for Americans to accept their past and join together—black and white.

When I met Doug Wilder, developer Larry Silver had just made his generous donation of the marvelous site in Fredericksburg. It is bordered on the north by the Rappahannock River and rises to a high bluff overlooking I-95, the most heavily trafficked highway in the nation. The visibility was an asset too good to be neglected, and we located the museum near that bluff. We made decisions about the features of the museum with the thought in mind that we wanted everyone to enjoy both the building and the extensive grounds. We want them to enjoy the beauty of the site. Part of the exhibits, perhaps cotton fields, will be outdoors. There will be places for reflection and recreation.

Governor Wilder told the story of his seminal visit to Gorée Island (now part of Senegal), one of the places from which slave ships departed for the Middle Passage trip to the Americas. This was the middle leg of a triangular voyage that started in Europe, went to the Americas, and then returned to Europe. Every leg contained a full cargo, making this extremely lucrative. Traders from Europe and from what became the United States made enormous fortunes. Governor Wilder felt that the museum's centerpiece should be a full-scale slave ship replica. So, I designed the building with that in mind. The ship will become a haunting presence seen by all travelers going southbound on I-95. At the very next exit, visitors will come to the road leading to the museum.

I think this museum is something that has been a long time coming. I know that it will have a great impact on everyone who visits it. I hope everyone will recognize and appreciate the great vision of Governor Wilder and his contribution in realizing such a worthy mission.

Upon entering the hallowed grounds of the United States National Slavery Museum, a gate holding a striking logo, comprised of one child and eight adult silhouettes, greets visitors. The figures begin at the point of slavery and end with freedom. The first exhibition on the grounds of the United States National Slavery Museum is the Spirit

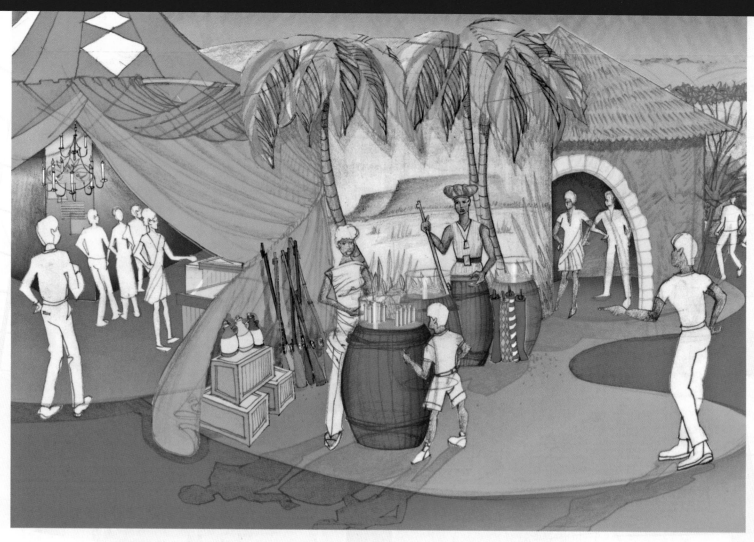

An African village exhibit highlights the continent's vibrant cultural heritage, much of which was abandoned or lost when slaves were uprooted from its shores.

of Freedom Exhibit Garden: "In Honor of Those Who Risked Everything to Be Free." The exhibit opened in 2007, as part of America's 400th celebration in Virginia.

Some of the main attractions include the Hallelujah sculpture created by Ken Smith of Staunton, Virginia. This exhibit anchor depicts an African-American male slave with powerful arms outstretched, as if he is reaching for freedom. The 4,700-pound sculpture is eight feet tall.

Educational displays and West African wooden carvings capture the attention of visitors as they reflect on the importance of freedom. Sandra Taylor of Richmond, Virginia, donated wooden carvings created by artists from Ghana, West Africa. The garden has nine educational displays that inform visitors about abolitionists, runaways, acts of bravery, and the need for endurance on the road to freedom.

Johnny Johnson and his colleagues of Fredericksburg, Virginia, created intriguing artwork in the garden that provides a view of the importance of freedom through the perspective of the slave in the United States of America.

—*C. C. Pei, AIA, Partner, Pei Partnership Architects*

The museum's grand interior space, designed by C. C. Pei, is anchored by a reconstructed slave ship at its far end.

Epilogue

JOHN HOPE FRANKLIN

The history of slavery in the United States is the history of its economic development, its social relations, and even its foreign relations. Nothing in the nation's history has been so deeply decisive, so divisive, or so permeating as the subjugation of Africans by Europeans in the New World. Despite its reality and the inescapable truth of its existence, and even its brutality, the reluctance to discuss it—even to confront it—bears testimony to the shame that is inherent in dealing with the institution as a persistent force in the history of the New World, and particularly of the United States.

This attitude of evasion or avoidance may be due to the contradiction of slavery with almost everything else that was a part of this country's history: the traditional claim for individual rights and respect, the need to be independent and resourceful in describing the rich American experience, and the nexus of natural resources and individual initiative. These claims could not flourish or even appear to be valid in a culture in which the exploitation of one group of human beings by another constitutes the basic foundation on which a civilization is built.

Even today many whites are comfortable only by denying or belittling slavery's importance as part of our collective history. They readily see the incompatibility inherent in the subjugation and exploitation of one group of human beings by another. It is a sign of inconsistency, they insist, between a national commitment to equality and the oppression of a group of human beings because of their race or for any other consideration. Even many African Americans avoid the study of the history of slavery or even acknowledge its existence because of the fear that somehow the very knowledge of the role of their ancestors in such a bizarre experience could have a debilitating effect on them and their progeny. Thus, both groups conspire silently not to give credence to such a despicable relationship.

Whether one is white or black or whether one is a Northerner or a Southerner, though, there is no escape from the influence of slavery on all who are a part of history of the United States. The study of that history reveals how it is such an integral part, whether one views the nation's economy, its wars, or even its music. Try to study economic development leaving out the cotton kingdom, or World War II without seeing the impact of Jim Crow in the fight against Hitler, or American folk music without giving attention to American Negro spirituals. Indeed, much of the richness of the American experience comes from the interaction of the races.

The U.S. National Slavery Museum represents a valiant effort to confront slavery not only as it was but also how its influence persisted in the years since slavery ended.

In 1912, to commemorate the 50th anniversary of the Emancipation Proclamation, African-American author James Weldon Johnson penned these stirring words:

> This land is ours by right of birth,
> This land is ours by right of toil
> We helped to turn its virgin earth,
> Our sweat is in its fruitful soil.
>
> Then should we speak but servile words,
> Or shall we hang our heads in shame?
> Stand back of new-come foreign hordes,
> And fear our heritage to claim?
>
> No! stand erect and without fear,
> And for our foes let this suffice—
> We've bought a rightful sonship here,
> And we have more than paid the price. . . .

Yet the end of the institution in 1864 did not eliminate its ongoing influence. Indeed, through segregation, the careful definition of race, the legalization of racial differences, and the persistence of violent means to legalize racial differences have worked to sanctify racial distinction on American society. These efforts over several generations have resulted in the postponement of racial equality in America. The challenge of the 21st century is to eliminate every vestige of racial distinctions or differences.

Afterword

GOVERNOR TIM KAINE (D-VA)

The first Africans who came to America were indentured servants who were brought to Jamestown Island in 1619. The forcible transport of Africans to Virginia began nearly 400 years of deep, painful, and ultimately transcendent history in this nation. No single issue has so shaped our lives and institutions as the presence of slaves, the moral contradiction between slavery and the nation's religious and governing principles, the efforts to overthrow slavery, and the ongoing work to build a society of true equality where none are considered inferior citizens.

The history of Virginia has been a daily lived record of this struggle. Generations of Virginians fought to preserve slavery; legions of other Virginians died to defeat it. We were the Capital of the Confederacy and the state that first elected an African American, L. Douglas Wilder, to serve as governor. And, for the past 30 years, as the laws compelling inequality have been abandoned, intense and intentional work for racial reconciliation has been carried out in numerous formal and informal ways.

Recently, we have grappled with the notion of an official apology for slavery. In 1998, as mayor of Richmond, I apologized for the myriad of official ways in which my city had supported and defended the institution that sold hundreds of thousands of human beings into bondage within blocks of the state capitol. And in 2007, the General Assembly of Virginia, which was born at Jamestown in the same year that the first Africans arrived, joined international efforts to heal our difficult racial past through the process of a formal apology. Just as England's famous city of Liverpool led the way through an official apology for its role as the center of the slave shipping business, so Virginia has led a struggle in America to transform the hearts of its citizens by bravely tackling the sensitive wording of a formal apology.

Though shackles were loosed from the feet and hands of slaves by the Emancipation Proclamation, the invisible shackles of hatred, superiority, and inferiority remained locked around the hearts of too many of our citizens for too long. A revolution without guns—a revolution utilizing civil, moral, and spiritual weaponry—had to be engaged in order to break those shackles. An apology was necessary to clear the path toward real community, true commonwealth, among our citizens.

Apologies can help us turn the page in our collective histories—acknowledging the real tragedy of what has happened but also stating plainly that we are now moving to a day in which all citizens can write into our history greater achievements not previously possible. Apologies—personal and social—acknowledge a transformation of attitudes and a resolution to turn from the past into a different and better future.

The debate in Virginia about the slavery apology was not easy. Some questioned the need for such a step with hostility, condescension, or insensitivity. But the process of legislation—vigorous debate and a willingness to listen to others—worked. And, by winning this important battle, we also cleared a path through the emotional minefield of blame. It is our collective future that matters. In the words of Dr. Martin Luther King, Jr., "We may have come over on different ships, but we're in the same boat now."

But while we move forward, focused on the future America we will build together—one worthy of Dr. King's vision—we must not lose sight of the past. We cannot move forward without a true understanding of our past. Keeping our full, true history, even its most shameful and painful parts, in clear view is the best insurance against repeating our mistakes or sliding backward. The United States National Slavery Museum offers us a way to stay in touch with our past, even as we are aspiring toward better days. By telling the honest and complete story of slavery, the museum offers us the chance to keep the light of truth shining on our past, to help light the way to our future. And I can't think of a more fitting place for the museum to stand than in Virginia, where American slavery began.

America's best days are yet in front of us. Having applied the political balm of an official apology over enslavement of our citizens, Virginia has sought to clear the way to progress by engaging the power and abilities of our citizens of all races. Having done so, we can afford our citizens greater opportunities to make their best contributions to America, truly making it the land of the free.

Bibliography

Adams, Francis D., and Barry Sanders Adams. *Alienable Rights: The Exclusion of African American in a White Man's Land.* HarperCollins, 2003.

Asante, Molefi K., and Mark T. Mattson. *Historical and Cultural Atlas of African Americans.* Macmillan Publishing Company, 1991.

Badger, Tony. "Southerners Who Refused to Sign the Southern Manifesto." *The Historical Journal* (June 1999), 517-34.

Bell, Janet Cheatham. *Famous Black Quotations: From Ancient Egypt to America Today, the Portable Wit and Wisdom of a Great People.* Warner Books, 1995.

Berlin, Ira. *Generations of Captivity: A History of African-American Slaves.* Harvard University Press, 2003.

Many Thousands Gone: The First Two Centuries of Slavery in North America. Harvard University Press, 1998.

Slaves without Masters: The Free Negro in the Antebellum South. Oxford University Press, 1981.

Berlin, Ira, Marc Favreau, and Steven F. Miller, eds. *Remembering Slavery: African Americans Talk about Their Personal Experiences of Slavery and Freedom.* The New Press, 1998.

Bial, Raymond. *The Strength of These Arms: Life in the Slave Quarters.* Houghton Mifflin, 1997.

Blassingame, John W. *Slave Testimony: Two Centuries of Letters, Speeches, Interviews, and Autobiographies.* Louisiana State University Press, 1977.

Blumrosen, Alfred, and Ruth G. Blumrosen. *Slave Nation: How Slavery United the Colonies And Sparked the American Revolution.* Sourcebooks, 2005.

Breen, T. H., and Stephen Innes. *Myne Owne Ground: Race and Freedom on Virginia's Eastern Shore, 1640-1676.* Oxford University Press, 1980.

Byfield, Judith A. *The Bluest Hands: A Social and Economic History of Women Dyers in Abeokuta (Nigeria), 1890-1940.* James Currey, 2002.

Carter, Cynthia Jacobs. *Africana Woman: Her Story Through Time.* National Geographic Society, 2003.

Clarke, John Henrik. *Christopher Columbus and the Afrikan Holocaust: Slavery and the Rise of European Capitalism.* A and B Publishers Group, 1993.

Darwin, Charles R. *The Descent of Man, and Selection in Relation to Sex.* J. Murray, 1901.

Davidson, Basil. *The Lost Cities of Africa.* Little, Brown and Company, 1959.

Dillon, Merton L. *Benjamin Lundy and the Struggle of Negro Freedom.* University of Illinois Press, 1966.

Dodson, Howard, and Sylviane A. Diouf. *In Motion: The African-American Migration Experience.* Schomburg Center for Research in Black Culture and National Geographic Society, 2004.

Dray, Philip. *At the Hands of Persons Unknown: The Lynching of Black America.* Modern Library, 2003.

Ellis, Joseph J. *Founding Brothers: The Revolutionary Generation.* Vintage Books, 2000.

Estabrooks, Henry L. *Adrift in Dixie Or A Yankee Officer Among The Rebels.* Thomas Gale, 1866.

Fleischner, Jennifer. *Mastering Slavery: Memory, Family, and Identity in Women's Slave Narratives.* New York University Press, 1996.

Foner, Eric. *Reconstruction: America's Unfinished Revolution, 1863-1877.* Harper and Row, 1988.

Foster, Vonita White. *Black Hanoverians: An Enlightened Past.* ITS, 1999.

Franklin, John Hope, and Alfred Moss, Jr. *From Slavery to Freedom: A History of African Americans,* 8th ed., Alfred A. Knopf, 2002.

Franklin, John Hope, and Loren Schweninger. *Runaway Slaves: Rebels on the Plantation.* Oxford University Press, 2000.

Goodwine, Marquetta L., ed., *The Legacy of Ibo Landing: Gullah Roots of African American Culture.* Clarity Press, 1998.

Guelzo, Allen C. *Lincoln's Emancipation Proclamation: The End of Slavery in America.* Simon and Schuster, 2006.

Guinn, Jeff. *Our Land Before We Die: The Proud Story of the Seminole Negro.* Tarcher, 2002.

Hale, Grace E. *Making Whiteness: The Culture of Segregation in the South, 1890-1940.* Vintage Books, 1998.

Hall, Gwendolyn Midlo. *Slavery and African Ethnicities in the Americas: Restoring the Links.* University of North Carolina Press, 2005.

Harding, Vincent. *There Is a River: The Black Struggle for Freedom in America.* Vintage Books, 1983.

Hendrick, John D. *Harriet Beecher Stowe: A Life.* Oxford University Press, 1994.

Herskovits, Melville J. *The Human Factor in Changing Africa.* Alfred A. Knopf, 1962.

The Myth of the Negro Past. Beacon Press, 1958.

Horton, James Oliver, and Lois E. Horton. *Slavery and the Making of America.* Oxford University Press, 2005.

Howell, Donna Wyant. *I Was a Slave: True Life Stories Dictated by Former Slaves.* American Legacy Books, 1995.

Inikori, Joseph E. "Guns for Slaves." In *The Atlantic Slave Trade*, ed. David Northrup. Houghton Mifflin Company, 2002.

Jackson, John G. *Introduction to African Civilizations.* Citadel Press, 1970.

James, George G. M. *Stolen Legacy: Greek Philosophy is Stolen Egyptian Philosophy.* Africa World Press, 1992.

Johnson, Charles, Patricia Smith, and the WGBH Series Research Team. *Africans in America: America's Journey through Slavery.* Harcourt

Brace, 1998.

Karenga, Maulana. *Introduction to Black Studies,* 2nd ed. University of Sankore Press, 1993.

Koger, Larry. *Black Slave Owners: Free Black Slave Masters in South Carolina, 1790-1860.* University of South Carolina Press, 1995.

Levy, Andrew. *The First Emancipator: the Forgotten Story of Robert Carter, the Founding Father Who Freed His Slaves.* Random House, 2005.

Mariners' Museum, The. *Captive Passage: The Transatlantic Slave Trade and the Making of the Americas.* Smithsonian Books, 2002.

Mayer, Brantz. *Captain Canot, An African Slaver.* Arno Press, 1968.

McCarthy, Timothy, and John Stauffer, eds. *Prophets of Protest: Reconsidering the History of American Abolitionism.* The New Press, 2006.

Melish, Joanne Pope. *Disowning Slavery: Gradual Emancipation and "Race" in New England, 1780-1860.* Cornell University Press, 2000.

Moorland-Spingarn Research Center. Battle, Thomas C., and Donna M. Wells, eds. *Legacy: Treasures of Black History.* National Geographic Society, 2006.

Morrison, Michael A. *Slavery and the American West: The Eclipse of Manifest Destiny and the Coming of the Civil War.* University of North Carolina Press, 1997.

Mullane, Deirdre, ed. *Crossing the Danger Water: Three Hundred Years of African-American Writing.* Anchor Books, 1993.

Nash, Gary B. *The Forgotten Fifth: African Americans in the Age of Revolution.* Harvard University Press, 2006

The Unknown American Revolution: The Unruly Birth of Democracy and the Struggle to Create America. Viking, 2005.

Newman, Richard S. *The Transformation of American Abolitionism: Fighting Slavery in the Early Republic.* University of North Carolina Press. 2001.

Nieman, Donald G. *Promises to Keep: African-Americans and the Constitutional Order, 1776 to the Present.* Oxford University Press, 1991.

Painter, Nell Irvin. *Creating Black Americans: African-American History and Its Meanings, 1619 to the Present.* Oxford University Press, 2007.

Phillips, Ulrich B. *American Negro Slavery: A Survey of the Supply, Employment and Control of Negro Labor as Determined by the Plantation Regime.* Louisiana State University Press, 1966.

Quarles, Benjamin. *The Negro in the American Revolution.* Norton, 1973.

The Negro in the Making of America. Touchstone, 1987.

Rediker, Marcus, *The Slave Ship.* Viking, 2001.

Robertson, Natalie S. *The Slave Ship Clotilda and the Making of AfricaTown, U.S.A.: Spirit of Our Ancestors.* Praeger, 2008.

Robertson, Natalie S., ed. *African-American History in Trans-Atlantic Perspective.* Tapestry Press, 2000.

Rothman, Adam. *Slave Country: American Expansion and the Origins of the Deep South.* Harvard University Press, 2007.

Savage, William Sherman. *The Controversy Over the Distribution of Abolition Literature, 1830-1860.* The Association for the Study of Negro Life and History, 1938.

Schneider, Dorothy, and Carl J. Schneider. *Slavery in America: From Colonial Times to the Civil War.* Facts on File, 2000.

Schomburg Center for Research, Howard Dodson, and Sylviane A. Diouf. *In Motion: The African American Migration Experience.* National Geographic Society, 2005.

Sluby, Patricia Carter. *The Inventive Spirit of African-Americans: Patented Ingenuity.* Praeger, 2004.

Stringer, Chris. "Human Evolution: Out of Ethiopia." *Nature* (June 2003), 692-95.

Sudarkasa, Niara. "African and Afro-American Family Structure: A Comparison." *The Black Scholar* (November-December 1980), 43-47.

Van Sertima, Ivan. *African Presence in Early America.* Transaction Publishers, 1992.

They Came Before Columbus. Random House, 1976.

Van Sertima, Ivan, and Larry Williams, eds. *Great African Thinkers: Cheikh Anta Diop,* Transaction Books, 1986.

Varon, Elizabeth R. *Southern Lady, Yankee Spy: The True Story of Elizabeth Van Lew, A Union Agent in the Heart of the Confederacy.* Oxford University Press, 2003.

Virginia Writers' Project, comp. *The Negro in Virginia.* John F. Blair, 1994.

Wax, Darold D. "Preferences for Slaves in Colonial America." *Journal of Negro History* (October 1973), 376, 379.

Weiner, Mark Stuart. *Black Trials: Citizenship from the Beginnings of Slavery to the End of Caste.* Alfred A. Knopf, 2004.

White, Deborah Gray. *Ar'nt I a Woman?: Female Slaves in the Plantation South.* W. W. Norton and Company, 1987.

Williams, John A., and Charles F. Harris. *Amistad 1: Writings on Black History and Culture.* Vintage Books, 1970.

Wong, Kate "Sourcing Sapiens." *Scientific American* (August 2003), 23-24.

Woodson, Carter Godwin. *Mind of the Negro as Reflected in Letters Written During the Crisis, 1800-1860.* Negro Universities Press, 1969.

The Negro in Our History. Associated Publishers, 1931.

Zinn, Howard. *A People's History of the United States,* 2 vols. The New Press, 2003.

About the Contributors

AUTHORS

Governor (Former) L. Douglas Wilder was born in Richmond, Virginia, the grandson of slaves, and was named after abolitionist-orator Frederick Douglass and poet Paul Lawrence Dunbar.

Wilder graduated from Howard University Law School and Virginia Union University before embarking on a career that is is highlighted with many precedents. As state senator representing Richmond from 1969 to 1985, Wilder became the first African American in Virginia to hold the position since Reconstruction. he served as lieutenant governor from 1986 to 1990, when he became the first African American to be elected governor in the U.S., leading the Commonwealth of Virginia from 1990 to 1994, when Virginia was ranked as the best managed state in the U.S. for two consecutive years. He became Richmond's mayor on January 2, 2005.

Vonita White Foster, Ph.D., was one of the 1,700 black students denied a public school education between 1959 and 1964 due to massive resistance to desegregation on the part of state and local elected officials in Prince Edward County, Virginia. In spite of this, she has gone on to distinguish herself as an educator, administrator, researcher, and civic leader. She initiated the resolution: Regret over Prince Edward County School Closures, which passed in the Virginia General Assembly, January 2003. The patron was Delegate Viola Baskerville.

Foster has held professional appointments at the Library of Virginia, Virginia State University, Virginia Commonwealth University, Virginia Union University, and Virginia Power. She serves as Executive Director of the U.S. National Slavery Museum.

Other distinguished accomplishments of Foster's include being appointed the first black woman to serve on the Hanover County School Board for more than nine years; the first Black elected president of the Virginia Independent College and University Library Association; the first Black librarian hired by the Library of Virginia, among other state appointments.

Tim Kaine became the 70th governor of Virginia on January 14, 2006. Governor Kaine practiced law in Richmond for 17 years, representing people who had been denied housing opportunities because of their race or disability. He won many precedent-setting cases in this area and was recognized by local, state, and national organizations for his fair-housing advocacy. Kaine also taught legal ethics for six years at the University of Richmond Law School. Governor Kaine entered political life in 1994 and was elected to four terms on the City Council, including two terms as Richmond's mayor. Governor Kaine was elected Virginia's lieutenant governor in 2001. He worked for four years with Governor Mark Warner to reform the state's budget and invest new resources in education. He became chairman of the Southern Governors Association in the summer of 2008.

John Hope Franklin, Ph.D., is the James B. Duke Professor Emeritus of History and former professor of legal history in the law school at Duke University. He is a recipient of the Presidential Medal of Freedom. His books include the award-winning *From Slavery to Freedom: A History of African Americans*.

Gerald A. Foster, Ph.D., is the Scholar-in-Residence for the U.S. National Slavery Museum. In this capacity, he developed the Content Master Plan that provided the guidance and focus for the exhibits and their historical relevance to the heretofore untold stories about slavery in America. Foster formerly served as dean of the Hampton University School of Arts and Letters as well as director of the University's Center for Social Research. He also was vice president for academic affairs at Virginia Union University and has held faculty appointments at City University of New York, Fordham University, and the University of Richmond.

Heather Lindquist has worked in interpretive exhibit design for over 20 years. With a background in American history, she approaches each project with an eye toward its ability to connect to diverse audiences and inspire life-long learning. Recent exhibit planning projects include the United States National Slavery Museum, the National Prisoner of War Museum, the Lincoln Home National Historic Site, Manzanar National Historic Site, the Thaddeus Kosciuszko National Memorial, and the Naval Live Oaks Visitor Center. Ms. Lindquist received a B.A. in American studies and a B.A. in French studies from Stanford University in 1982.

Natalie S. Robertson, Ph.D., is an award-winning scholar who has held prestigious research and teaching appointments on national and international levels, including the Smithsonian Institution's National Museum of African Art and the Advanced Studies in England Program, affiliated with University College, Oxford. Currently, she is a senior scholar at the U.S. National Slavery Museum, and she is an associate Professor at hampton University. She is the author of *The Slave Ship Clotilda and the Making of AfricaTown, U.S.A.: Spirit of Our Ancestors*.

Donna M. Wells is Prints and Photographs librarian at Howard University's Moorland-Spingarn Research Center. She has a bachelor of arts degree from Hampton University and a master's degree in library science from the

University of Maryland at College Park. She lectures and writes on photographic history; Washington, D.C., history; and African-American culture. She was research scholar for the National Geographic book *Africana Woman: Her Story Through Time*. She is co-author with Dr. Thomas C. Battle of National Geographic's *Legacy: Treasures of Black History*.

EDITOR

Cynthia Jacobs Carter, Ed.D., is a development director at Africare in Washington, D.C., and most recently was appointed Research Scholar in Women's and Gender Studies at Georgetown University. An author and lecturer, Carter wrote *Higher Education and the Talented Tenth* and National Geographic book *Africana Woman: Her Story Through Time*. She has designed and taught courses in women's studies and African-American culture including Black Women in the African Diaspora and The Gullah Culture. She has taught women's studies courses at George Washington University and at Georgetown University. Carter has also curated several exhibitions about women of African descent, including Africana Women at the Dawn of the New Millennium, which was sponsored by the White House Millennium Council and George Washington University. She earned a bachelor's degree from Virginia State University and master's and doctorate degrees from George Washington University in Washington, D.C.

ESSAYISTS

Ira Berlin, Ph.D., is Distinguished University Professor at the University of Maryland at College Park. He has written extensively on American history and the larger Atlantic world in the 18th and 19th centuries, particularly the history of slavery. His first book, *Slaves Without Masters: The Free Negro in the Antebellum South* (1975), won the Best First Book Prize, awarded by the National Historical Society. Berlin is the founding editor of the Freedmen and Southern Society Project, which he directed until 1991. The project's multi-volume *Freedom: A Documentary history of Emancipation* (1982, 1985, 1990, 1993) has twice been awarded the Thomas Jefferson Prize of the Society for History in the Federal Government, among others. His 1999 study of African-American life between 1619 and 1819, entitled *Many Thousands Gone: The First Two Centuries of Slavery in Mainland North America,* received numerous honors, as did *Generations of Captivity: A History of Slaves in the United States,* published in 2002.

Charles L. Blockson is the founding curator, now retired, of the Charles L. Blockson Afro-American Collection of rare texts, slave narratives, art, and a host of other artifacts significant in African-American history at Temple University. Born in Norristown, Pennsylvania, he graduated from Pennsylvania State University and holds an honorary doctorate from Villanova University. He has written several essays and books centered on African-American history, especially in Pennsylvania, including *The Underground Railroad* and *Liberty Bell Era: The African American Story.* He has written articles on the Underground Railroad and the Gullah culture for the National Geographic Society. He travels extensively and continues to add to one of our nation's largest collections of African-American and African culture.

Ambassador Pamela Bridgewater is the U.S. Ambassador to Ghana and holds the rank of Career Minister. She is the former Ambassador to South Africa and has worked extensively with President Nelson Mandela. Ambassador Bridgewater holds honorary doctorate degrees from Virginia State University, the University of Cincinnati, and Morgan State University.

Bill Cosby's interest in education led him to earn M.A. and Ed.D. degrees at the University of Massachusetts. He became the first African-American actor to star in a weekly television dramatic series, *I Spy* in the mid -1960s, winning two Emmys. His other successful TV shows include *The Cosby Show,* which projected a new image of the middle-class African-American family. He continues to have a successful career in public speaking, TV commercials, comedy shows and records, and books. In later years, Cosby and his wife, Camille, have become generous contributors to various causes and institutions, including Atlanta's Spelman College. In 2003 he was honored with the Bob Hope Humanitarian Award.

Dorothy Height, Ph.D., is the chair and president emerita of the National Council of Negro Women in Washington, D.C. Before joining the staff of NCNW, Height was on the national staff of the YWCA. She also served as national president of the Delta Sigma Theta Sorority, Inc. She has marched at major civil right rallies, sat through White House meetings, and witnessed every significant victory in the struggle for racial equality. Height has been given several prestigious awards, including the Presidential Medal of Freedom, the Franklin Delano Roosevelt Freedom Medal, the Citizens Medal Award, and in 2004 the Congressional Gold Medal, which was presented to her by President George W. Bush. She has been awarded more than 30 honorary degrees.

Chien Chung (C.C.) Pei earned a bachelor of arts degree cum laude in physics from Harvard College in 1968 and graduated in 1972 from the Graduate School of Design with a master's degree in architecture. As the middle son of celebrated architect I. M. Pei, he learned during his formative years the vision, commitment, and professional standards essential to the creation of significant and lasting architecture.

Before founding Pei Partnership Architects in 1992 with his brother, Li Chung (Sandi), C. C. Pei spent the first 20 years of his professional career contributing to many of I. M. Pei's most celebrated projects, including the Grand Louvre in Paris and the National Gallery of Art in Washington, D.C. There, he developed nationally recognized expertise in museum architecture. C. C. Pei designed the U.S. National Slavery Museum.

Ellen Johnson-Sirleaf is the 23rd president of Liberia. After an early education in Liberia, she earned undergraduate and graduate degrees in the United States, including a master's degree in public administration from Harvard University in 1971.

Before becoming president in 2006, Sirleaf spent nearly four decades in local and international public life. She served as the first female minister of Finance of Liberia, and after a military coup in 1980 was appointed president of the Liberian Bank for Development and Investment. She also worked as assistant administrator and director of the Regional Bureau of Africa for the United Nations Development Program with the rank of assistant secretary general of the United Nations. Sirleaf has also served in the private sector in a number of capacities.

Ben Vereen, in addition to playing the role of Chicken George in the landmark TV production of *Roots,* has appeared in numerous plays on Broadway. He travels widely, performing in the United States, Europe, Asia, and the Caribbean. His cabaret-style show won him Entertainer of the Year, Rising Star, and Song and Dance Star from the American Guild of Variety Artists (AGVA). He is the first simultaneous winner of these awards.

Juan Williams is a news analyst, appearing regularly on radio shows including *Morning Edition* and *Day to Day.* Williams hosted National Public Radio's *Talk of the Nation* and aired pieces on *Morning Edition* and *All Things Considered.* He is the author of the critically acclaimed biography *Thurgood Marshall: American Revolutionary* and author of the nonfiction bestseller *Eyes on the Prize: America's Civil Rights Years, 1954-1965,* the companion volume to the TV series. During his 21-year career at the *Washington Post,* Williams served as an editorial writer, op-ed columnist, and White House reporter. He has won an Emmy award for TV documentary writing and won widespread critical acclaim for a series of documentaries including *Politics—The New Black Power.*

Acknowledgments

Special appreciation goes to Barbara Brownell Grogan—editor extraordinaire and dear friend—and to all of the other great folks at National Geographic, including Nina Hoffman, Kevin Mulroy, Ruth Chamblee, Amy Briggs, Judith Klein, Peggy Archambault, Kristin Hanneman, and everyone who gave their all from the beginning to make this idea a reality. Thanks also to everyone else at Geographic who made this project a joy to work on as we strove to shed light on a history far too long in the shadows.

Sincere appreciation to Governor Wilder, whose dream sparked this work and special thanks to Vonita Foster, Debra Daniels, and all of the writers from the Museum who worked tirelessly to fill in the pages that history conveniently forgot. Without the scholarship and great dedication of each essayist, this book would not have been possible, so thanks to each and every one of you. A very special debt of gratitude is owed to Donna Wells, who helped in countless ways, day and night, to make this book the best that it could possibly be.

—*Cynthia Jacobs Carter, Ed.D.*

Dedication

To the untold millions of slaves and "free" Blacks who endured more than 200 years of atrocious inhumanities, yet who, through their ingenuity, courage, perseverance, and spirituality, left a legacy not just for their progeny but for all fair and open-minded people of the world.

Freedom In My Heart is a modest attempt to ensure that this story of American slavery will not remain one of the most important underreported chapter in American history.

— *Vonita W. Foster, Ph.D.*

For our ancestors who gave everything so we could be free, and for my loved ones who continue to give the treasure of their love and support. In particular, I dedicate this work to my husband, Karl Carter; my mother, Flossie Purnell; and my father, Charles Purnell. And last, but not least, may this book serve as a beacon for a bright future for my children and my grandchildren Mohammad, Zoë, Kulthum, and Fatima Carter. *Nam Myoho Renge Kyo*—everlasting joy

— *Cynthia Jacobs Carter, Ed.D.*

Quotation Credits

Chapter One

page 18: From *African Presence in Early America*
page 28: From *How Came Civilization*
page 32: From *The African Origin of Civilisation*

Chapter Two

page 52: From *The Description of Africa*
page 54: From *Africana Woman*

Chapter Three

page 62: From *Before the Mayflower*
page 64: From *Narrative of Two Voyages to the River Sierra Leone during the Years 1791-1792-1793*
page 76: From "Black Woman"
page 78: From "Education for a New Reality in the African World," prepared for the Phelps-Stokes Fund and delivered on November 14, 1994

Chapter Four

page 86: From *L'Esclavage aux Antilles Françaises avant 1789*
p. 88: From *A Narrative of the Life and Adventures of Venture, a Native of Africa, but Resident Above Sixty Years in the United States of America. Related by Himself,* available online at *http://docsouth.unc.edu/neh/venture2/venture2.html*
page 98: From *Notes on Political Economy, As Applicable to the United States, by a Southern Planter*
page 100: From *Twelve Years a Slave,* available online at *http://docsouth.unc.edu/fpn/northup/northup.html*

Chapter Five

page 108: From *Emile: Or, on Education*
page 110: *From Narrative of the Life and Adventures of Henry Bibb, an American Slave, Written by Himself,* available online at *http://docsouth.unc.edu/neh/bibb/bibb.html*
page 112: From *A Quiet Abiding Place,* manuscript by Paul Hughes, available at the Weeks Public Library, Greenland, New Hampshire
page 116: From Williams, Heather Andrea. *Self-Taught: African American Education in Slavery and Freedom.* University of North Carolina Press, 2005.
page 122: From *The Life, Experience, and Gospel Labours of the Rt. Rev. Richard Allen,* available online at *http://docsouth.unc.edu/neh/allen/allen.html*

Chapter Six

page 130: From Rediker, Marcus. *The Slave Ship.* Viking, 2001.
page 132: From Aptheker, Herbert. *Essays in the History of the American Negro.* International Publisher, 1945.
page 134: From *The Confessions of Nat Turner*
page 138: From "An Address to the Slaves of the United States of America, 1843"
page 144: From *Uncle Tom's Story of His Life. An Autobiography of the Rev. Josiah Henson,* available online at *http://docsouth.unc.edu/neh/henson/henson.html*

Chapter Seven

page 160: From "What to the Slave Is the Fourth of July?" available online at *http://www.teachingamericanhistory.org/library/index.asp?document=162*
page 164: From *Men of Color, to Arms!*

Chapter Eight

page 174: From *My Larger Education,* available online at *http://celebratebookert.com/library/books/My_Larger_Education/01.php*
page 176: From *The Souls of Black Folk*
page 186: From "African American Perspectives: Pamphlets from the Daniel A.P.Murray Collection, 1818-1907," Library of Congress
page 188: From "African American Perspectives: Pamphlets from the Daniel A.P.Murray Collection, 1818-1907," Library of Congress

Chapter Nine

page 206: "I,Too"
page 208: "Harlem"
page 210: From a speech delivered to the National Negro Business League Convention, July 1912
page 218: From *Notes on the State of Virginia, 1781*
page 220: From Cruz, Bárbara C., and Michael J. Berson. "The American Melting Pot? Miscegenation Laws in the United States," *OAH Magazine of History* (Summer 2001).
page 222: From *12 Million Black Voices: A Folk History of the Negro in the United States*
page 230: From a speech at the White House, September 22, 1998

Illustration Credits

Front Jacket artwork (detail):
Elizabeth Catlett (American, b. 1915)
Singing Their Songs, 1992
Lithograph on paper (a.p.VI)
15 3/4 x 13 3/4 in.
National Museum of Women in the Arts, Washington, D. C.
Purchased with funds donated in memory of Florence Davis by her family, friends, and the Women's Committee of the National Museum of Women in the Arts © Elizabeth Catlett/Licensed by VAGA, New York, NY

Back Jacket (left to right): Kenneth Garrett, Brooklyn Musuem/CORBIS, AP Photo/Brian K. Diggs.

INTRODUCTION: 1, United States National Slavery Museum (USNSM), photographed by Kenneth Garrett; 2-3, Library of Congress, #LC-USF351-91; 4-5, Library of Congress, #LC-USZC4-3327; 7, USNSM, photographed by Kenneth Garrett; 8, Courtesy the Honorable L. Douglas Wilder; 11, Tyrone Turner/The New York Times; 12-13, Library of Congress, #LC-USZ62-38150.

CHAPTER ONE: WE ARE ONE PEOPLE 14-15, Daniel R. Westergren, NGS; 16, Kenneth Garrett; 18, Photograph by Kenneth Garrett, ©2006 ARCCH; 19, NGS Maps; 20, Walter Meayers Edwards; 21, David L. Brill; 22 (LE), USNSM; 22 (RT), The Granger Collection, NY; 23, Marc Brasz/CORBIS; 24, General Research and Reference Division, Schomburg Center for Research in Black Culture, The New York Public Library; 25, Justin Sutcliffe/Polaris; 26, Réunion des Musées Nationaux/Art Resource, NY; 27, Kenneth Garrett; 28, The Granger Collection, NY; 29, Kenneth Garrett; 31, Courtesy Dr. Rick Kittles; 32, AP Photo/Michel Lipchitz; 33, Topkapi Palace Museum, Istanbul, Turkey, photographed by James L. Stanfield; 34, Science Museum/Science & Society Picture Library; 34-35 (BACK), Kenneth Garrett; 35 (UP), Jim Henderson/Alamy; 35 (LO), The Art Archive/Egyptian Museum, Cairo/Dagli Orti.

CHAPTER TWO: HOMELAND 36-37, The Art Archive/Eileen Tweedy; 38, Art Resource, NY; 40 (LE), USNSM, photographed by Kenneth Garrett; 40 (RT), Bildarchiv Preussischer Kulturbesitz/Art Resource, NY; 41, USNSM, photographed by Kenneth Garrett; 42 (LE, BOTH), USNSM, photographed by Kenneth Garrett; 42 (RT), René Geoffroy de Villeneuve, L'Afrique, ou Histoire, moeurs, usages et coutumes des africains : le Sénégal, courtesy University of Virginia Library; 43, Marc Garanger/CORBIS; 44 (UP), René Geoffroy de Villeneuve, L'Afrique, ou Histoire, moeurs, usages et coutumes des africains : le Sénégal, courtesy University of Virginia Library; 44 (LO), USNSM, photographed by Kenneth Garrett; 45, Smithsonian American Art Museum, Washington, DC/Art Resource, NY; 46, Courtesy Ambassador Pamela Bridgewater; 47, Ian Berry/Magnum Photos; 48, Werner Forman/Art Resource, NY; 49, The Art Archive; 50, Werner Forman/Art Resource, NY; 51, Art Resource, NY; 53, AP Photo/John McConnico; 54, South Carolina State Museum, photographed by Susan Dugan; 54-55, AP Photo/Charlotte Observer, Layne Bailey; 55 (LO), Photograph by Judith Wragg Chase, courtesy the Acacia Collection; 56, Mamma Haidara Commemorative Library, Timbuktu, Mali; 56-57 (BACK), Stapleton Collection/CORBIS; 57 (UP), Candace Feit for The New York Times; 57 (LO), Alyssa Banta.

CHAPTER THREE: STOLEN AWAY 58-59, The Art Archive; 60, David Cleaves/Alamy; 63, NGS Maps; 64, The Art Archive; 65, Photo from Prince Among Slaves PBS Documentary - Unity Productions Foundation Photo taken by Wanakhavi Wakhisi; 66 (LE), USNSM; 66 (RT), USNSM, photographed by Kenneth Garrett; 67, AP Photo/The Natchez Democrat, Anne McDaniel; 68, Courtesy Dr. Natalie Robertson; 69, Royal Naval Museum; 70, The National Archives of the UK, ref. FO84-1310; 71 (LE), USNSM, photographed by Kenneth Garrett; 71 (RT), North Wind Picture Archives/Alamy; 72, The Mariners' Museum, Newport News, VA; 73 (UP), New York Public Library, Wallach Division; 73 (LO), Gerald French/CORBIS; 74 (LE), USNSM, photographed by Kenneth Garrett; 74 (RT), Mary Evans Picture Library/MARY EVANS ILN PICTURES; 75, Richard Bickel/CORBIS; 76-77, James Estrin/The New York Times/Redux; 79, North Wind Picture Archives/Alamy; 80-81 (ALL), Victorio Loubriel, courtesy Moorland-Spingarn Research Center, Howard University.

CHAPTER FOUR: LIFE IN A NEW WORLD 82-83, The Art Archive/Private collection Washington/Laurie Platt Winfrey; 84, New York Historical Society; 86, USNSM, photographed by Kenneth Garrett; 87, Mary Evans/Photo Researchers, Inc.; 89, AP Photo/Linda Spillers; 90 (BOTH), USNSM, photographed by Kenneth Garrett; 91, Alpha Kappa Alpha Archives; 92, College of the Holy Cross Archives; 93, NBC-TV/The Kobal Collection; 94 (LE), Science Museum/Science & Society Picture Library; 94 (RT), CORBIS; 95, Library of Congress, #LC-USZC4-2524; 96 (UP), Francis G. Mayer/CORBIS; 96 (LO), Wm. B. Becker Collection/American Museum of Photography; 97, ABC-TV/THE KOBAL COLLECTION; 98, Library of Congress, #LC-B8171-152-A; 99, AP Photo/John Gillis; 100, Sample Noel Pittman Collection, Schomburg Center for Research in Black Culture; 101 (UP), CORBIS; 101 (LO), North Wind Picture Archives; 102, Cameron Davidson/Photographer's Choice/Getty Images; 102-103 (BACK), NASA; 103 (UP), Library of Congress, Geography and Map Division; 103 (LO), Library of Congress, Manuscript Division, Papers of Thomas Jefferson.

CHAPTER FIVE: BUILDING A CULTURE 104-105, Library of Congress, #LC-USZC4-4575; 106, Monticello/Thomas Jefferson Foundation, Inc.; 108, University of Virginia Special Collections Library; 109, Winfield I. Parks, Jr.; 110, Library of Congress; 111, Courtesy of the Moorland-Spingarn Research Center, Howard University; 113, Stephen Berend/For The Times; 114, John T. Consoli, courtesy University of Maryland; 115, Library of Congress, #LC-USZ62-2573; 116, USNSM, photographed by Kenneth Garrett; 117, CORBIS; 118, Ring shout image Record Group III box 6 folder 40, MS 997, Margaret Davis Cate papers, Georgia Historical Society,

Savannah, Georgia, and the Fort Frederica National Monument; 119, Creole Heritage Center, Northwestern State University in Natchitoches; 120, British Museum, London; 121, Susie Post Rust; 122-123, The Granger Collection, NY; 124, Phillip Simmons Foundation, photographed by Mark McKinney; 124-125 (BACK), Phillip Simmons Foundation, photographed by Steve Lepre; 125 (UP), South Carolina State Museum, photographed by Susan Dugan; 125 (LO), Phillip Simmons Foundation.

CHAPTER SIX: RESISTANCE TO SLAVERY 126-127, North Carolina Museum of Art/CORBIS; 128, Courtesy of the Moorland-Spingarn Research Center, Howard University; 130-131 (BOTH), New Haven Colony Historical Society and Adams National Historic Site; 132, The Granger Collection, NY; 133, The Granger Collection, NY; 134, USNSM, photographed by Kenneth Garrett; 135, Roland L. Freeman; 136, Charles L. Blockson Afro-American Collection/Temple University; 137, Tony Jones/ Cincinnati Enquirer; 138, USNSM, photographed by Kenneth Garrett; 139, The Granger Collection, NY; 140, NGS Maps; 141 (UP), Brooklyn Museum/ CORBIS; 141 (LO), USNSM, photographed by Kenneth Garrett; 143, STR/ AFP/Getty Images; 144 (LE), USNSM, photographed by Kenneth Garrett; 144 (RT), From "Reverend Josiah Henson: 'Uncle Tom' in Scotland," courtesy Toronto Public Library; 145 (UP), Historical Picture Archive/ CORBIS; 145 (LO), Bettmann/CORBIS; 146, Used with Permission of Documenting the American South, The University of North Carolina at Chapel Hill Libraries.; 146-147 (BACK), The New York Public Library/Art Resource, NY; 147 (BOTH), Carl Elmore/Savannah Morning News.

CHAPTER SEVEN: QUEST FOR FREEDOM 148-149, Library of Congress, #LC-B8171-7890; 150, From the Collection of Madison County Historical Society, Oneida, New York; 153 (BOTH), Massachusetts Historical Society; 154, CORBIS; 155, Courtesy of the Moorland-Spingarn Research Center, Howard University; 156 (UP), CORBIS; 156 (CTR), SCHOMBURG CENTER/Art Resource, NY; 156 (LO), National Portrait Gallery, Smithsonian Institution/ Art Resource; 157, SIMON MAINA/AFP/Getty Images; 158, AP Photo/ Manuel Balce Ceneta; 159, Bettmann/CORBIS; 161 (UP), Wilberforce House, Hull City Museums and Art Galleries, UK/The Bridgeman Art Library/Getty Images; 161 (LO), The Art Archive; 162, The Granger Collection, NY; 163, Bob Adelman/Magnum Photos; 165, AP Photo/Al Behrman; 167, Military History, Smithsonian Institution; 168, Library of Congress; 168-169 (BACK), Library of Congress, #LC-USZ62-64712; 169 (UP), Courtesy Mrs. Gladys Bryant, photographed by Jim Gensheimer; 169 (LO), The Granger Collection, NY.

CHAPTER EIGHT: LEGACY OF SLAVERY 170-171, Library of Congress, #LC-USZ62-89776; 172, Manuscripts, Archives and Rare Books Division, Schomburg Center for Research in Black Culture, The New York Public Library; 174-175, Courtesy of the Moorland-Spingarn Research Center, Howard University; 176, The Granger Collection, NY; 177 (UP), The Granger Collection, NY; 177 (LO), David J. & Janice L. Frent Collection/ CORBIS; 179, Jessica Rinaldi/Reuters/CORBIS; 180, Courtesy Dr. Gerald A. Foster; 181, Library of Congress, #LC-USZ62-33790; 182, USNSM, photographed by Kenneth Garrett; 182-183, Hulton-Deutsch Collection/ CORBIS; 184, Library of Congress, #LC-D401-16155; 185, National Portrait Gallery, Smithsonian Institution/Art Resource, NY; 186, Kansas State Historical Society; 187, AP Photo/Gary Knight/VII; 189, Smithsonian American Art Museum, Washington, DC/Art Resource, NY; 190, Library of Congress, #LC-F9-02-4503-320-02; 190-191 (BACK), Geoffrey Clements/ CORBIS; 191 (UP), Library of Congress, #LC-USZC4-6161; 191 (LO), Library of Congress, #LC-F9-02-4503-321-11.

CHAPTER NINE: I, TOO, AM AMERICA 192-193, James Karales Collection, Rare Book, Manuscript, and Special Collections Library, Duke University courtesy Mrs. Monica Karales; 194, Danny Lyon/Magnum Photos; 196, USNSM, photographed by Kenneth Garrett; 197, USNSM, photographed by Kenneth Garrett; 198, Library of Congress, #LC-USF33-030577-M2; 199 (UP), Bettmann/CORBIS; 199 (LO), David J. & Janice L. Frent Collection/CORBIS; 200, Library of Congress, #LC-USF34-040828-D; 201, Library of Congress, #LC-USZ62-84496; 203, AP Photo/Brian K. Diggs; 204-205, Library of Congress, #LC-USF34-038814-D; 206, George Karger/Pix Inc./Time Life Pictures/Getty Images; 207, AP Photo/William J. Smith; 208, Howard University Gallery of Art; 209, AP Photo/Ed Bailey; 211 (UP), Bruce Davidson/Magnum Photos; 211 (LO), Steve Schapiro/ CORBIS; 212, Library of Congress, #LC-USZ62-137048; 212-213 (BACK), Bettmann/CORBIS; 213 (UP), AP Photo/The News Tribune, Peter Haley; 213 (LO), National Archives, #208-NP-3AA-1.

CHAPTER TEN: TRUTH AND REFLECTION 214-215, Chris Johns, NGS; 216, Vincent Laforet/The New York Times/Redux; 219, Gordon Gahan; 220, Library of Congress, #LC-USZ62-23602; 221, Library of Congress, #LC-USZ62-77086; 222, USNSM, photographed by Kenneth Garrett; 223, Ludovic/REA/Redux; 224, AP Photo/The Rosen Group, Stuart Ramson; 225, AP Photo/Danny Johnston; 226-227, AP Photo/Damian Dovarganes; 228, USNSM, photographed by Kenneth Garrett; 229, Library of Congress, #LC-USZ62-48174; 230, AP Photo/Kevork Djansezian; 231, AP Photo/ Victoria Arocho; 232, USNSM; 233, USNSM; 234, Courtesy of the Henley Company and USNSM; 234-235 (BACK), Courtesy Pei Partnership Architects LLP; 235 (UP), Courtesy of the Henley Company and USNSM; 235 (LO), Courtesy Pei Partnership Architects LLP.

Index

Freedom in My Heart

VOICES FROM THE UNITED STATES NATIONAL SLAVERY MUSEUM

PUBLISHED BY THE NATIONAL GEOGRAPHIC SOCIETY
John M. Fahey, Jr., *President and Chief Executive Officer*
Gilbert M. Grosvenor, *Chairman of the Board*
Tim T. Kelly, *President, Global Media Group*
John Q.Griffin, *President, Publishing*
Nina D. Hoffman, *Executive Vice President; President, Book Publishing Group*

PREPARED BY THE BOOK DIVISION
Kevin Mulroy, *Senior Vice President and Publisher*
Leah Bendavid-Val, *Director of Photography Publishing and Illustrations*
Marianne R. Koszorus, *Director of Design*
Barbara Brownell Grogan, *Executive Editor*
Elizabeth Newhouse, *Director of Travel Publishing*
Carl Mehler, *Director of Maps*

STAFF FOR THIS BOOK
Amy Briggs, Judith Klein, *Editors*
Peggy Archambault, *Art Director*
Kristin Hanneman, *Illustrations Editor*
Lauren Pruneski, *Contributing Writer*
Richard Wain, *Production Project Manager*
Rob Waymouth, *Illustrations Specialist*
Al Morrow, *Design Assistant*

Jennifer A. Thornton, *Managing Editor*
R. Gary Colbert, *Production Director*
Meredith C. Wilcox, *Administrative Director, Illustrations*

MANUFACTURING AND QUALITY MANAGEMENT
Christopher A. Liedel, *Chief Financial Officer*
Phillip L. Schlosser, *Vice President*
Chris Brown, *Technical Director*
Nicole Elliott, *Manager*
Monika D. Lynde, *Manager*
Rachel Faulise, *Manager*

Founded in 1888, the National Geographic Society is one of the largest nonprofit scientific and educational organizations in the world. It reaches more than 285 million people worldwide each month through its official journal, *National Geographic,* and its four other magazines; the National Geographic Channel; television documentaries; radio programs; films; books; videos and DVDs; maps; and interactive media. National Geographic has funded more than 8,000 scientific research projects and supports an education program combating geographic illiteracy.

For more information, please call
1-800-NGS LINE (647-5463)
or write to the following address:

National Geographic Society
1145 17th Street N.W.
Washington, D.C. 20036-4688 U.S.A.

Visit us online at www.nationalgeographic.com/books

For information about special discounts
for bulk purchases, please contact
National Geographic Books Special Sales:
ngspecsales@ngs.org

For rights or permissions inquiries,
please contact National Geographic Books
Subsidiary Rights: ngbookrights@ngs.org

Library of Congress Cataloging-in-Publication Data
Freedom in my heart : voices from the United States National Slavery Museum / Cynthia Jacobs Carter, editor ; foreword by L. Douglas Wilder.
p. cm.
Includes bibliographical references and index.
ISBN 978-1-4262-0127-1
1. Slavery--United States--History. 2. Slaves--United States--History. 3. African Americans--History. 4. National Slavery Museum (U.S.) I. Carter, Cynthia Jacobs. II. National Slavery Museum (U.S.)
E441.F775 2008
306.3'62074-- dc22 2008025930

Printed in U.S.A.